What Went Wrong?
The Nicaraguan Revolution

Historical Materialism Book Series

The Historical Materialism Book Series is a major publishing initiative of the radical left. The capitalist crisis of the twenty-first century has been met by a resurgence of interest in critical Marxist theory. At the same time, the publishing institutions committed to Marxism have contracted markedly since the high point of the 1970s. The Historical Materialism Book Series is dedicated to addressing this situation by making available important works of Marxist theory. The aim of the series is to publish important theoretical contributions as the basis for vigorous intellectual debate and exchange on the left.

The peer-reviewed series publishes original monographs, translated texts, and reprints of classics across the bounds of academic disciplinary agendas and across the divisions of the left. The series is particularly concerned to encourage the internationalization of Marxist debate and aims to translate significant studies from beyond the English-speaking world.

For a full list of titles in the Historical Materialism Book Series
available in paperback from Haymarket Books, visit:
https://www.haymarketbooks.org/series_collections/1-historical-materialism

What Went Wrong?
The Nicaraguan Revolution

A Marxist Analysis

Dan La Botz

Haymarket Books
Chicago, IL

First published in 2016 by Brill Academic Publishers, The Netherlands
© 2016 Koninklijke Brill NV, Leiden, The Netherlands

Published in paperback in 2018 by
Haymarket Books
P.O. Box 180165
Chicago, IL 60618
773-583-7884
www.haymarketbooks.org

ISBN: 978-1-60846-823-2

Trade distribution:
In the US, Consortium Book Sales, www.cbsd.com
In Canada, Publishers Group Canada, www.pgcbooks.ca
In the UK, Turnaround Publisher Services, www.turnaround-uk.com
All other countries, Ingram Publisher Services International, ips_intlsales@
ingramcontent.com

Cover design by Jamie Kerry of Belle Étoile Studios and Ragina Johnson.

This book was published with the generous support of Lannan Foundation
and the Wallace Action Fund.

Printed in Canada by union labor.

10 9 8 7 6 5 4 3 2 1

Library of Congress Cataloging-in-Publication data is available.

Contents

A Marxist Analysis

With the victorious revolution of 1979 – 'The Triumph' as it was called – that overthrew the Somozas' dynastic dictatorship, Nicaragua became the hope of socialist revolutionaries and a focus for solidarity from a wide spectrum of religious, labour, and left activists around the world. It also became a symbol in the eyes of many of the struggle of the small nations of Central America and of small nations everywhere for self-determination and social justice. Most importantly, Nicaragua raised the possibility of an anti-capitalist revolution that rather than giving rise to a one-party-state regime such as those in the Soviet Union, China, Vietnam or Cuba, might lead to a democratic socialist society. Nicaragua, not quite as big as the State of Wisconsin and then with a population of only three million, seemed to many to be the hope not only of Latin America – much of which was then living under dictators – but also the hope for humanity.

There was a sudden surge of interest in Nicaragua and in the rest of Central America. Activists in countries around the globe rushed to the university libraries to study the history of Nicaragua and to learn about the Sandinista Front for National Liberation (FSLN), the organisation that had led the revolutionary movement. Who were these Sandinistas? Who were the leaders? What was the party's social base? What was its ideology and what was its programme?

The hope for something new on the left was palpable. By the late 1970s, what was often then called 'really existing socialism', that is, bureaucratic Communism, had a bad name, and rightly so. The Soviet Union had long since become a new sort of class society ruled by a privileged bureaucracy and dominating Eastern Europe, an imperial great power much like the others. Mao Tse-Tung, the Communist leader of the People's Republic of China, who oversaw a similar state and social system, had embraced president Richard M. Nixon in 1972, initiating a geopolitical alliance with the United States. Then in 1978, the country's new leader, Teng Hsiaop'ing, embraced a series of market reforms that set China on the road to capitalism. Vietnam, another bureaucratic collectivist society, would follow China on the capitalist road within a couple of decades. Even Cuba, whose revolution was then only twenty years old, had structurally assimilated to the Soviet state politically and economically, and if it was not a Stalinist state in the most horrifying sense of that word, it could not by any means be called a democratic socialist society.

So when the Nicaraguan Revolution began and in the first days there emerged a group known as Los Doce (The Twelve), a leadership that included

Catholic priests committed to the Theology of Liberation, democratic socialist intellectuals, and even businessmen who had opposed the Somoza dictatorship – all of these groups prepared to work with the Sandinista revolutionaries – it appeared that this might be a revolution led by a coalition of forces committed to democracy. Here, it seemed to many, was a revolution that not only the left but many others as well might embrace.

Though US President Jimmy Carter had let Anastasio Somoza fall (even as he attempted to save the existing regime), and though his successor President Ronald Reagan worked to crush the Sandinista government, still there were reasons to remain optimistic. Support among political parties and governments in various parts of the world represented a significant counterweight to US power. The support in Latin American nations for Nicaragua's revolution was remarkable, reaching from the Institutional Revolutionary Party of Mexico to Democratic Action in Venezuela, from leftist military *caudillo* Omar Torrijos of Panama to the National Liberation Party of Costa Rica, and, of course, the revolution had the support of Fidel Castro's Communist Cuba. Most of the Socialist Parties of Western Europe, as well as the Communist Parties of Eastern Europe – both groups interested in shaping the future course of the revolution – offered material and diplomatic support to the new government. So it seemed that the fledgling revolutionary government might have a chance in a hemisphere where for decades the United States had used its economic power and military might to determine the fate of nations, crushing its opponents and installing trusted, often authoritarian governments.

Perhaps something even grander was on the horizon, many of us thought at the time. The existence of revolutionary movements in other Central American countries – the Farabundo Martí National Liberation Front (FMLN) in El Salvador and the National Revolutionary Unity (UNRG) in Guatemala – seemed to raise the possibility of a broader anti-imperialist, democratic, and socialist movement that might converge in a perfect anti-capitalist storm, so that one could envisage developments bringing about a United Socialist States of Central America. A series of events, it could be imagined, that might also have a salutary effect on the sclerotic Cuban Communist government. A socialist revolution in Central America might encourage South Americans still living under the dictatorships in the southern cone and perhaps other leftist movements around the world as well. To say the least, after the great let-down that had followed the decline of the radical movements in America, Europe, and other parts of the world by the mid-1970s, hope – and perhaps illusion – was in the air again.

Leftist organisations around the world – Communist, Trotskyist, Maoist and independent revolutionary socialist groups – rushed to show solidarity with

Nicaragua. Every party, big and small alike, sent its emissaries to learn what was happening, to offer support, as well as to proffer their criticisms and their advice. Inspired by the revolution, Catholic religious and lay activists, Protestant ministers, and secular humanist idealists, dreamers and do-gooders, radical tourists and young revolutionaries-in-the-making – the *sandalistas* as they were collectively called because of their footwear – made their way to Nicaragua to help in hospitals, to work in agriculture, to teach, or to do whatever they might to help insure the survival of the Nicaraguan experiment and to see it prosper. Among the pilgrims, for example, was the 26-year-old Bill DeBlasio, today the mayor of New York, but then a radical youth who in 1988 visited Nicaragua and subsequently spent several years working to support the fledgling revolutionary government there.[1] Another was the author of this book who with his future wife and another friend visited Nicaragua in 1985 taking medical supplies to a hospital in Estelí. There were thousands of us who, in part because of the inspiration of the Nicaraguan revolution, returned home to continue our work or to take up work as labour union activists, community organisers, public health physicians, civil rights lawyers, and in general as part of the American progressive community. Such was the Nicaraguan Revolution's impact on us in America and on others from Europe and Latin America.

Both the commercial press and the little leftist weeklies reported every new development in the Nicaraguan revolutionary process: The Triumph, The Twelve, then The Junta, followed by its crack up, and finally the Sandinista government. The Sandinistas became the ruling party and carried out a spectacularly successful literacy campaign, began the construction of a national healthcare system for all, nationalised banks, much of the land, and many factories, encouraged the organisation of labour unions, and created a national women's organisation. There were also clear signs of problems: the Sandinistas' disturbing conflict with the Miskito Indians, and then the Contra War and the Sandinistas' adoption of a military draft hated by the population at large. The Sandinista National Directorate took all political power into its hands as it struggled to fight the war and defend its socialist project. As events rapidly developed, so did questions about the entire process: Where was Nicaragua headed? Would Nicaragua recapitulate in some tropical way the history of the French or Russian Revolutions? Or would Nicaragua go the way of Mexico or Cuba? Or was something else, a more democratic, humane and more profoundly revolutionary and democratic socialism, imaginable? All three alternatives seemed possible at the time.

---

1   González 2013.

Then, after a decade of impressive social programmes, economic crisis, widespread social conflict, and war, in 1990, in an unprecedented experience – a free election held by a revolutionary government in the midst of a civil war – the Sandinistas were, to their own and to their supporters' great shock, voted out of power. Violeta Chamorro was elected president at the head of a broad, unwieldy, and fractious coalition that stretched from the right-wing Liberals to the Communists. Almost immediately, however, her coalition collapsed and in order to govern she quickly formed an alliance with the Sandinistas that lasted through the six years of her administration, years in which land was returned to the landlords, businesses to the capitalists, foreign corporations were invited to invest, and the working class, peasantry and the poor sunk into the most abject conditions. Her administration was followed by the even more disturbing return to power of politicians of the Somoza era, as first Arnoldo Alemán and then Enrique Bolaños served as president during years of neoliberal austerity and of the most sordid corruption and impunity.

With the end of the Sandinista government and the coming to power of Chamorro, the left around the world lost interest in Nicaragua. The democratic left turned its attention to Polish Solidarity's struggle for democracy against the Communist government there or to the Korean unions' strikes against South Korea's authoritarian capitalist state. Those particularly concerned with the Latin American left turned from Nicaragua to an interest in the Workers' Party of Brazil. By the 1990s, Nicaragua was completely off the radicals' radar.

Then, in the 2006 election, Daniel Ortega and the Sandinistas won the national elections by a plurality of just over a third of the vote and again took power, but it was a very different Ortega and it was not the same FSLN. Allied with the Liberal Party, the Catholic Church, and the country's wealthiest capitalists, the Sandinistas no longer had the radical agenda of the 1970s and 1980s. Ortega constructed a powerful political machine within the context of a liberal state and a capitalist market. The FSLN controlled the presidency, the parliament, and the Supreme Court. The Sandinistas dominated the labour unions and the community organisations, while many Sandinistas themselves had become successful businessmen. Ortega formed an alliance with the Nicaraguan business class and invited foreign capital to become more deeply invested in the country. Under Ortega and the FSLN, a neoliberal economic order was established in Nicaragua very like those that had been established in the period from 1980 to 2000 in most countries.

The FSLN created a massive public relations campaign and a cult of personality around 'Daniel', and in 2012 Ortega was re-elected as president by an even larger majority, though in what was widely believed to be a fraudulent election. The enormous election billboards in Managua that stayed up long after the campaign pictured Daniel Ortega and his wife Rosario Murillo proclaiming 'Nicaragua: The Joy of Living in Peace: Christian, Socialist, and in Solidarity'. By the second decade of the 2000s, however, there was no socialism, little solidarity, and, for many Nicaraguans, not a lot of joy either. The Ortega administration continued the neoliberal policies first introduced by its predecessors with some attention to the social needs of the poor; yet unemployment, poverty, and malnutrition remained serious problems.

The general public and even those on the left outside of Nicaragua knew little about all of this, of course. Few intellectuals followed these events, and even those on the left who were once so enthusiastic about the revolution were often ignorant of what had transpired over the last few decades. While progressives may have some sense of the nation's trajectory, few knew much of the story after 1990. Ortega and Murillo put themselves forward as champions of the people and issued vaguely progressive statements for foreign consumption. The Sandinista government's alliance with Hugo Chávez of Venezuela and with Raúl Castro's Communist government in Cuba, governments that to the world represented the socialist project in Latin America, tended to obscure and to silence criticism of the Sandinistas from the left. Still, socialists abroad who learned what was going on in Nicaragua asked, 'What had gone wrong?'

I have to say that a couple of years ago I was not much better informed than most. I had been in Nicaragua in the 1980s, but even though I had taught Latin American History, because I specialised in the study of Mexico, I had not followed developments in Nicaragua very closely. When, in November 2012, my colleague Dr. Irene Hodgson of Xavier University in Cincinnati, Ohio, invited me to lead a student delegation there for a service learning semester abroad, I seized upon the opportunity, leaving for Nicaragua in January 2013. Here would be a chance to catch up on things, to see what had happened to the revolution.

The Xavier programme, originally inspired by the Theology of Liberation and working with Christian base communities in Nicaragua, over a period of 25 years had established a national network of partner organisations. Based in Managua where the students lived with local families, studied Spanish, history and other subjects, and worked for hospitals and children's nutrition programmes, for three days each weekend, and sometimes for a whole week at a time, we travelled throughout Nicaragua, including to the Caribbean coast, meeting with dozens of groups and individuals from every social class and political perspective. Our guides were people who had lived and worked in Nicaragua for decades, such as Lillian Hall, a Cornell-trained agronomist who had gone to Nicaragua in 1985 and stayed until 2013, working with ranchers to improve their livestock. I and the students had opportunities to meet and speak with men and women who had been national figures in the revolutionary and post-revolutionary period, such as leftist Jesuit priest Fernando Cardenal and right-wing banker Eduardo Montealgre, as well as with grassroots activists in today's social movements, such as Azahalea Solís, an attorney and a leading figure in the Autonomous Women's Movement (MAM).

While staying in *Ideas de Mamá*, the small guest house where I lived for almost four months, I read many histories, novels, and, of most interest to me, personal memoirs by participants in the revolutionary and counter-revolutionary movements. Fascinated by the experience, I soon sketched out the idea of a book organised around the question: 'The Nicaraguan Revolution: What went wrong?'

I brought to this question my own convictions as a Marxist socialist of the 'third camp' or 'socialism from below' tradition. The term 'third camp' was coined in the late 1930s by revolutionary socialists who opposed both bureaucratic Communism and capitalism. During the 1960s, when I first encountered this political tradition, it was embodied in the slogan, 'Neither Washington nor Moscow but International Socialism'. The idea of socialism from below, as opposed to top-down socialism, was first elaborated by Hal Draper in his important essay 'The Two Souls of Socialism'.[2] Draper and his co-thinkers were equally hostile to both the Social Democratic Parties of Western Europe and the Communist Parties of Eastern Europe, advocating the organisation of socialist, working-class movement at the grassroots. Today this tradition, which rejects not only capitalism but also the 'anti-imperialism' of such dictators as Bashar-al Assad of Syria, is represented by American socialist journals such as *Against the Current, International Socialist Review*, and *New Politics*. This outlook is, in my view, essential to understanding the experience of a country like Nicaragua.

What Went Wrong?

I am not the first person to ask the question, 'What went wrong?'[3] Some liberals, leftists, and religious activists who were supporters of the Revolution in the 1980s hold the view that the Nicaraguan revolution's failure was almost entirely because of external pressures and the betrayal of Daniel Ortega. They believe

---

2 Draper 1966.

3 I am not even the first person to use that title. Only later did I discover that there were already an article and a book with this title, though written about 25 years earlier: González 1985 and Vilas 1990.

the revolution was initially a healthy one that became sick principally because of exogenous factors. Roger Burbach is one of the strongest and most eloquent advocates for this position:

> The core of this legacy was the revolution's commitment to popular democracy. Seizing power in 1979 from the dictator Anastasio Somoza, the Sandinista movement comprised Nicaragua's urban masses, peasants, artisans, workers, Christian base communities, intellectuals, and the *muchachos* – the youth who spearheaded the armed uprisings. The revolution transformed social relations and values, holding up a new vision of society based on social and economic justice that included the poor and dispossessed. The revolution was multi-class, multi-ethnic, multi-doctrinal, and politically pluralistic.[4]

The Sandinista government, he argued, was committed to popular democracy as seen in the mass participation of people in the insurrections and their involvement in the revolution that followed. He believes that it was the Sandinistas' commitment to democracy that led them to hold elections in 1984 and again in 1990, elections that put them out of office.

Burbach goes on to give an excellent account of the historical events that gradually beat down the Sandinistas: the US-sponsored Contra War, the economic embargo, the failure of the guerrillas in El Salvador to seize power, and the US backing for the right-wing governments that came to power after 1990. Yet there is no explanation of how or why this process affected the Sandinistas and their leadership in the way that it did. For Burbach, everything seems to turn on Daniel Ortega: 'Ortega ran in every election, drifting increasingly to the right, while exerting an iron hand to stifle all challengers and dissenters in the Sandinista party'.

The combination of tremendous external pressures and the ambition of one man is not a very intellectually or politically satisfying explanation of what went wrong. What he and others who take this approach fail to ask is: What was *already present* in Nicaragua's history, as well as in the FSLN's experience, its politics, and its ethos, that under the impact of these events led to the betrayal of the revolution by its leaders in the specific way that it occurred? What was the interaction between the external events, national developments, and the predispositions of the Sandinistas based on their long and firmly held political ideas and actions? That is the question that I focus on in this book.

---

4 Burbach 2009.

This book is a synthetic history based principally on the work of other historians though also incorporating primary sources in order to offer a new interpretation of Nicaragua's recent history in the light of its past. My own view of the matter is that the failure – and some would say betrayal – of the revolution was largely due to the fact that the FSLN, with politics principally shaped by Soviet and Cuban Communism, never had a commitment to genuine democracy either within the revolutionary movement or within society at large, and therefore the FSLN, even had its leaders wished, could never have led Nicaragua in the creation of a democratic socialist society. The Sandinistas' 'popular democracy', meaning mass participation and mobilisation, had little to do with democracy in the real sense, that is, a democracy where the working class and peasant majority have a voice, vote, and real decision-making power.

While it is true that the Contra War, the attending economic collapse, and the failure of the Central American revolutions in El Salvador and Guatemala may have ultimately doomed the Nicaraguan Revolution, the FSLN's lack of commitment to democracy contributed significantly to the revolution's failure. Betrayal of the revolution in one form or another – either Communist dictatorship or capitalist restoration – was inevitable unless a democratic socialist current with a mass following among labouring people, workers and peasants, developed within the revolution. It was this problem – the lack of democracy – that led to the specific sort of betrayal of the revolution, and to the unique way in which the FSLN was transformed into an authoritarian party led by the *caudillo* Daniel Ortega who took command over the FSLN, the mass social organisation, and eventually the nation. It was the authoritarian politics and ethos of the FSLN that created Daniel Ortega, not the other way around.

The FSLN leaders – from the founder Carlos Fonseca to Daniel Ortega – believed that a vanguard revolutionary party would lead the masses to the creation of a society modelled on the Soviet Union and Cuba. Virtually no Sandinista believed that power over the party, the mass organisations, the society at large, or the state should be exercised from below by working people and peasants. The dominant concept from beginning to end was the idea of the vanguard party that transmits its ideology, its strategy and its organisational directives from above to the masses below. Working people were encouraged, even required, to participate in organisations, meetings and political demonstrations – that was the meaning of 'popular democracy' – but participation is not democratic control and it is not power. At almost no time – except for very brief local outbursts – did working people exercise any control over the workplace, labour unions, the party, the economy, or the state institutions. The Sandinistas' Marxism-Leninism had made them opponents of the self-activity and self-organisation of the working class which can be the only basis for democratic socialism.

Some may say, 'Your criticism of the FSLN as being Communists is the same as that of the Republican Party, the capitalist press, and the US State Department'. But that would be a mistake. The Republicans, and the Democrats as well, the commercial media, and the State Department hated the Sandinistas because, as Communists, they were hostile to capitalism. I am critical of the Sandinistas because, as Communists, they were also hostile to working-class power and democratic socialism. We can only understand what was happening in the Nicaraguan Revolution (and in many other Third World countries in the postwar period) if we recognise that for about 70 years there was a three-cornered struggle for power between three social and political systems: capitalism, bureaucratic Communism, and working-class movements struggling to establish democratic socialism. Each of these systems was hostile to the other two, and so workers had to fight both the capitalism they knew and the bureaucratic Communism which in some countries strove to impose itself on them.

One should be clear that while bureaucratic Communism was hostile to socialism and independent workers' movements, so was Social Democracy. After World War II, first in Great Britain and then in Scandinavia and other Western European countries, the Social Democratic and Socialist Parties came to political power. These parties, which had their origins in the nineteenth century labour and socialist movement, rejected Marxism, repudiated revolution, and took on the role of managing capitalism, alternating with their more conservative Christian Democratic competitors. In Latin America, only in Venezuela did a Social Democratic Party, Democratic Action, come to power, later reaching a power-sharing arrangement with the Christian Democrats. Much like the Communists, the Social Democrats and their trade-union bureaucracies were hostile to independent workers' movements and were appalled by the idea of revolutionary socialism.

By the 1980s, as Soviet Communism declined, a Euro-Communist current developed and the Communist Parties began to evolve in the direction of Social Democracy, a process that culminated in the total transformation of most of the Communist Parties into social democratic parties in the 2000s. From then on, when the Social Democratic and former Communist Parties became governing parties, just like their Conservative and Liberal competitors, they imposed neoliberalism and administered austerity. In Nicaragua, the Sandinistas may be said to have eventually broken with their Communist and Castroite origins and to have evolved into a kind of *sui generis* social democratic party, carrying out similar neoliberal policies of austerity. In any case, in both its original Communist-inspired and its later corrupt and authoritarian social democratic avatar of the 2000s, the Sandinistas were also a party hostile to independent worker organisation and activity.

It is my argument that the FSLN's lack of commitment to democracy was a key factor in the way that revolution was betrayed and in the way that the FSLN was transformed from a revolutionary organisation on the left in the 1970s and 80s to a counter-revolutionary party on the right since the 1990s. The lack of democratic mechanisms by means of which the rank-and-file might have controlled the FSLN left all decision-making in the hands of the National Directorate that ultimately placed that power in the hands of Daniel Ortega. Consequently, it was possible for Ortega, beginning in 1990, to make alliances with the capitalist parties, as well as for him and other Sandinistas to enrich themselves and become junior partners in the capitalist class. While the Sandinistas had begun by trying to create a state and society like that in Communist Cuba, they ended up constructing one much more like that in capitalist Mexico. In any case, the failure to construct a democratic socialist society made it easier to re-establish a capitalist state and economy. Yet today in Nicaragua there remain critical independent thinkers and social struggles; and over time the struggle for democratic socialism may once again emerge.

Dan La Botz
2013–16
Managua, Nicaragua;
Cincinnati, Ohio;
Erlanger, Kentucky;
Brooklyn, New York

Acknowledgements

My first experience in Nicaragua was in 1985, hitch-hiking through the war-torn country with Dr. Bruce Bernard and Dr. Sherry Baron, friends whom I had met while working as the organiser for the House Staff Association at Cook County Hospital. We travelled hitching rides in private pick-up trucks and sometimes in huge dump trucks conveying Sandinista soldiers to the front during the Contra War. Our mission was to take some equipment and medicine to a hospital in Estelí. As we went along in our utterly unofficial delegation, we visited cigar manufactories, coffee plantations, and labour unions, and talked with Nicaraguans from many walks of life. I would never have made that trip had I not been with the two of them who combined a commitment to social justice and international solidarity with a spirit of adventure. One could say that they started me on the writing of this book.

I want to thank my colleague Prof. Irene Hodgson of Xavier University, who brought me on to her team for the spring semester of 2013 as co-teacher and trip leader for a student service-learning, study-abroad programme. Prof. Hodgson had spent 15 years constructing the programme which provided both instructors and students with a remarkable experience of work, study, reflection, and travel. Prof. Hodgson's lectures, talks with the students, and conversations with me taught me a great deal about Nicaraguan society and culture.

I also learned much from other members of the team, such as Prof. Julia O'Hara, Professor of History at Xavier, whose excellent reader and discussions with me and her students helped to educate me about Nicaragua's complicated social and political history. In Nicaragua, Martín Castro, mechanic, driver and indispensable guide for the Xavier team, spent hours with me discussing his own experience as a Sandinista Youth organiser, as a member of a coffee brigade in the early 1980s, and as a soldier in the Sandinista revolution, as well as sharing his views on contemporary Nicaragua. Lillian Hall, a Cornell-trained agronomist who had gone to Nicaragua in 1985 and stayed until 2013 working with ranchers to improve their livestock, was also part of the team. Her discussions of her experience living and working in the countryside during the Nicaraguan Revolution gave me another view of life during those years. Father Joseph Mulligan, s.j., who spent over thirty years as a priest in Nicaragua and authored a book on the Catholic Church in the Nicaraguan Revolution, shared his views in group discussions with the students and me, and later kindly read and commented on my manuscript. Taylor Fulkerson, one of the Xavier undergraduate students also read and commented on a chapter of the manuscript.

While in Managua in 2013, to escape the heat and to enjoy iced coffee and good books, I spent hours in El Literato Café not far from the guest house where I lived. It was there that I first discovered the many of the recent memoirs by former Sandinistas and other figures from the era of the Nicaraguan Revolution. It was also there that I discovered the books of Andrés Pérez-Baltodano, a Nicaraguan political scientist who teaches at the University of Western Ontario in Canada. Impressed with his analysis, I wrote to him and we began a correspondence. He kindly sent me articles he had written and read; he also commented on my manuscript, and made some very important suggestions.

A number of long-time friends and collaborators, none of them Nicaragua experts, but also knowledgeable about Latin America and committed to democratic socialism, also read and commented on my manuscript. Robin Alexander, the former International Affairs Director of the United Electrical Workers (UE), with whom for almost twenty years I collaborated in the production of *Mexican Labor News and Analysis*, offered her comments. Sam Farber, author of several important books on Cuba and for many years a friend and colleague, also kindly commented on this manuscript, as did Kent Worchester, a former editor of *New Politics: A Journal of Socialist Thought*; Dianne Feeley, an editor of *Against the Current*; and Todd Chretien of the International Socialist Organization and contributor to the *International Socialist Review*. Finally, other socialists from various parts of the left also offered me their views and insights: Ken Blum, Rust Gilbert, Charlie Post, and Kit Wainer.

Brill's Historical Materialism series editor Sébastien Budgen and his colleagues Danny Hayward and Cas Van den Hof helped to move this book along and keep it on track. Their anonymous peer reviewer made many useful suggestions, including recommending secondary sources that provided a broader context, particularly in the area of foreign relations.

While appreciating my friends' and colleagues' help, I alone am responsible for any mistakes and for the interpretation offered here.

When my wife and I had moved out of our home in Cincinnati, Ohio, but had not yet moved on to our new place in Brooklyn, our friend John Morawetz took us into his beautiful home in Erlanger, Kentucky, where I wrote the first full draft of the manuscript of this book. Thanks to John for his hospitality.

Finally, thanks to my wife Sherry, with whom I began the Nicaraguan adventure in 1985 and with whom I have been travelling ever since on a much longer journey.

Acronyms

AC	Alternative for Change
ALBA	Bolivarian Alternative for the Americas
ALBANIISA	Alba of Nicaragua, Incorporated
ALPROMISU	Somoza era indigenous organization
AMNLAE	'Luisa Amanda Espinoza' Association of Nicaraguan Women
ANDEN	National Association of Nicaraguan Educators
ANS	Sandinista Children's Association
APRA	American Popular Revolutionary Alliance
APRE	Alliance for the Republic
ATC	Association of Rural Workers
BCIE	Central American Bank for Economic Integration
CA	Christian Alternative
CAFTA or CAFTA-DR	Central American Free Trade Agreement
CAUS	Confederation for Action and Labour Union Unification
CEI	Centre for International Studies
CELADEC	Latin American Commission of Christian Education.
CGTi	General Labour Confederation-Independent
CIA	Central Intelligence Agency
CIERA	Centre for Research and Studies on Agrarian Reform
CIPRES	Centre for Research and Promotion of Rural and Social Development
CISPES	Committee in Solidarity with the People of El Salvador
COFARMA	Pharmaceutical Corporation
COIP	Industrial Corporation of the People
CORNAP	National Corporations of the Public Sector
COSEP	High Council of Private Enterprise
CPC	Citizens' Power Councils
CROC	Revolutionary Front of Workers and Peasants
CSE	Supreme Electoral Council
CSN	Nicaraguan Labour Union Coordination
CST	Sandinista Confederation of Workers
CTN	Nicaraguan Workers' Confederation
CUS	Confederation of Labour Union Unity
ECLA	Economic Commission for Latin America of the United Nations
EDSN	Army in Defence of the National Sovereignty of Nicaragua, Sandino's Army
EMECU	Magnetic-Spiritual School of the Universal Commune

ENACAL	National Water and Sewage Company
ENAL	Nicaragua Cotton Enterprise
ENCAFÉ	Nicaraguan Coffee Enterprise
ENIA	Nicaraguan Enterprise of Agricultural Inputs
ENAZUCAR	Nicaraguan Sugar Enterprise
EPA	The Peoples' Literacy Army
FAO	Broad Opposition Front
FEDETRASEP	Democratic Federation of Public Sector Workers
FETSALUD	Federation of Health Workers
FLN	National Liberation Front
FMLN	Farabundo Martí National Liberation Front of El Salvador
FNP	National Patriotic Front
FNT	National Federation of Labour
FO	Workers' Front
FRS	Sandino Revolutionary Front
FSLN	Sandinista National Liberation Front, also 'Sandinistas', also 'the Front'
FTAA	Free Trade Area of the Americas
GATT	General Agreement on Trade and Tariffs
GPP	Prolonged Peoples War (a tendency within the FSLN)
HIPC	Highly-Indebted Poor Countries
IDB	Inter-American Development Bank
IMF	International Monetary Fund
INE	state electrical company
INNA	state water company
INSS	Nicaraguan Institute of Social Security
INVIERNO	Institute of Peasant Welfare of Nicaragua
IPADE	Institute for Development and Democracy
IRI	International Republican Institute
JOC	Young Christian Workers (Belgium)
LRM	Revolutionary Marxist League
MAM	Women's Autonomous Movement
MAP-ML	Popular Action Movement (Marxist-Leninist)
MCR	Christian Revolutionary Movement
MDN	Nicaraguan Democratic Movement
MEC	Working and Unemployed Women's Movement 'María Elena Cuadra'
MERCOMUN	Central American Common Market
MILPA	Popular Anti-Sandinista Militia
MIR	Movement of the Revolutionary Left (Chile)

MISURASATA	Sandinista-era indigenous organization
MNN	New Nicaragua Movement
MPRS	Movement for the Rescue of Sandinismo
MPS	Sandinista Peoples Militias
MPU	United Peoples' Movement
MRS	Sandinista Renovation Movement
NED	National Endowment for Democracy
OAS	Organisation of American States
OECS	Organisation of Eastern Caribbean States
ONU	National Opposition Union
OSN	National Security Office of Nicaragua
PAC	Citizens Action Party
PALI	Neoliberal Party
PAM	Multi-ethnic Indigenous Party
PCD	Democratic Conservative Party
PC de N	Communist Party of Nicaragua
PLI	Independent Liberal Party
PLC	Constitutionalist Liberal Party
PLO	Palestine Liberation Organisation
PPSC	Popular Social Christian Party
PPSCA	Authentic Popular Social Christian Party
PROAGRO	Nicaraguan state's agricultural distribution company
PSC	Social Christian Party
PSD	Social Democratic Party
PSN	Nicaraguan Socialist Party
PT	Proletarian Tendency
PTN	Nicaraguan Workers Party
PUCA	Central American Unity Party
SI	Socialist International
SIM	Military Intelligence Service of Nicaragua
TELCOR	the state telephone company
UCA	University of Central America
UDEL	Democratic Union of Liberation
UN	United Nations
UNAG	National Farmers Union
UNE	National Union of Public Employees
UNICA	Catholic University 'Redemptoris Mater'
UNRG	National Revolutionary Unity of Guatemala
UPA	Agricultural Production Units
UPN	Nicaraguan Journalists Union

USAID	United States Agency for International Development
Vatican II	Second Vatican Council
VCE	We're Going with Eduardo [Montealegre]
WTO	World Trade Organisation
YATAMA	Sounds of Mother Earth Indigenous Party

What Happened to the Nicaraguan Revolution?

Why write about Nicaragua? It is such a small country in territory and population, and so apparently irrelevant to most of the world. Yet, while only the size of Wisconsin, and with a population of just three million at the time (and less than six million today), in 1979 Nicaragua suddenly became a laboratory of revolutionary experience, thought, and practice. The Sandinista government declared that it was struggling for socialism, but argued that it would be different from other socialist experiences. The Nicaraguan Revolution preoccupied the American government, won the support of other governments, and inspired millions around the world. What happened in Nicaragua was a microcosm – but also a unique variant – of the experience of the left in many countries in the post-World War II period. The lessons of the Nicaraguan Revolution, that is, the answers to the question *'What went wrong?'*, therefore have valuable broader implications, not only for understanding the past, but also for contemporary politics and for the struggle for socialism in the future.

Throughout what in the postwar period was called 'the Third World', peoples in Asia and Africa, Latin America and the Caribbean often succeeded in winning their political independence – or if already nominally independent, as was the case in Central America, they struggled to assert their political independence – only to find within a decade or two that because they had not achieved economic independence, they had no independence at all. They also often found that one system of political oppression and economic exploitation was overthrown only to be replaced by another. The fight for socialism became transformed into the imposition of some variant of bureaucratic Communism or of savage capitalism. Those of us on the left who continue to support fights for national liberation *and* socialism have a responsibility to try to understand what went wrong in all of these countries, of which Nicaragua is one quite important example.

Each of these postwar revolutionary experiences was unique, and yet they also had much in common. Revolutionary movements led by 'Marxist-Leninists' claimed to represent 'the proletariat' and to have organised it in 'vanguard parties' that practiced 'democratic centralism'. They were inspired by the Soviet Union, Cuba or China, which served as models both of revolution and of modernisation. Upon taking power, these parties frequently nationalised industry and agriculture, claiming to have 'socialised' the country's economy and to have created a 'people's republic' or a 'democratic socialist state'. Supported by the

Soviet Union, Eastern Bloc nations, and Cuba (or in some cases by China, which had suddenly changed sides in the 1970s and allied with the United States), these parties generally worked to create Communist societies like their patron states. But upon taking power, the new leaders found that the Communist countries could not provide all that they had promised; and by 1989 the entire Communist system had gone into a final paroxysm and collapsed in 1991 leaving many states without their former benefactor. Capitalism, which had been in crisis from the late 1960s and through the 1970s, suddenly globalised, liberalised, and expanded in the 1990s, giving rise to a new form of economic imperialism called globalisation, as well as to supposedly humanitarian interventions and so-called anti-terrorist wars.

The countries of the Third World, today called 'the developing nations', suddenly discovered that their future depended upon adhering to structural adjustment programmes pressed upon them by the International Monetary Fund (IMF) and the World Bank. These programmes insisted upon the dismantlement through privatisation of the developing nations' nationalist and would-be socialist economies, as well as dramatic reductions in their social programmes, while at the same time encouraging the creation of export platforms, free trade zones, and maquiladoras. These neoliberal programmes usually ended up being imposed upon the nation by the very parties that had led the national revolution twenty, thirty, or forty years earlier, though sometimes other parties – religious conservatives and neoliberals – displaced the old revolutionary parties and came to power.

Often, however, it was the former revolutionaries who ushered in the counter-revolution. The revolutionary nationalist political parties – never democratic to begin with – had typically within a few years of the revolution fused with the state, leading to a state-party usually led by a big man, a *caudillo*, or a dictator. In many countries, the formerly revolutionary leadership acquired property for itself while at the same time forming a partnership with remnants of the former ruling class and with international capital. The degree of authoritarianism, repression, and violence in these societies varied greatly, though as a rule it was impossible to make a transition from the heroic era of the struggle for national liberation and socialism first to a nationalist dictatorship, and then to a capitalist state and a neoliberal economy based on high unemployment, low wages, and endemic poverty, without a good deal of force and brutality. What happened in Nicaragua is a very particular version of what happened in so many Third World or developing nations in the late twentieth century.

How are we to study and understand what happened in these countries? How do we discover what went wrong? In my view, Marxism is the method to be used in attempting to understand the successes and the failures of previous revolutionary experiences, though it is important to be clear that Marxism has nothing to do with the 'Marxism-Leninism' of the Sandinista Front for National Liberation (FSLN) and of other guerrilla groups and revolutionary states. 'Marxism-Leninism' is the term originally coined by Joseph Stalin and other Communist leaders in the Soviet Union in the 1930s to describe the set of theories, political strategies, and organisational forms that guided the Communist Parties and the Communist States, ideas that became a quasi-religious dogma. That doctrine combined economic reductionism, political voluntarism, strategic opportunism, authoritarian party discipline, and a conviction of the inevitability of socialism that bestowed a great sense of historical mission on its true believers.

Marxism-Leninism remained the dogma of Communists even when they left the orbit of the Soviet Union. When Mao Tse-tung broke with the Soviet Union, he did so in the name of 'Marxism-Leninism-Mao Tse-tung Thought', not even much of a variation on the original. When Fidel Castro and Ernesto 'Che' Guevara led the Cuban Revolution of 1959, and then went on to inspire guerrilla movements throughout Latin America, though they rejected the Communists' postwar strategy of a peaceful and parliamentary road to socialism, they continued to adhere to virtually all the rest of Marxist-Leninist creed.

Marxism-Leninism – the ideology of the Communist bureaucracy that justified the Communist bureaucracy's rule and privileges – is of no use to us whatsoever in attempting to understand what went wrong. From the point of view of contemporary neo-Stalinists and some orthodox Trotsksyists who hold some variant of the Marxist-Leninist theory, the fundamental problem in Nicaragua was that the FSLN failed to sweep aside capitalism entirely and to replace it with a one-party state and nationalised property. Such an 'analysis' does not really allow us to understand the intricacies of the social processes and transformations that took place, nor does it grapple with the key problem of the relationship between socialism and democracy.

Marxism is a method of social analysis which examines any society from the point of view of the working class and of society's underdogs, with the long-term objective of creating an egalitarian, democratic, and just world. We might call this outlook revolutionary humanism. A Marxist analysis must therefore ask a number of embarrassing but critical questions of Marxist-Leninist regimes. Did the party actually represent the proletariat, that is, the working class? Was it the tribune of other exploited sectors of society? Was its centralism really democratic? What were the rights of political minorities? Was the party really the vanguard, that is, did it really become and did it remain the leadership of the working class and the oppressed? That is to say, was it really a revolutionary working class party? Did the nationalisation of the nation's factories and its fields really constitute their socialisation? Was what was called the democratic socialist state genuinely democratic? How did the people participate in making decisions and in the elaboration of the economic plan? To these we must add other fundamental questions. What was the role of women in the leadership, in the revolutionary process, and in the new government? What was the role of ethnic and other minorities in the society? How did the new state confront the environmental questions that arose under both capitalism and Communism?

It is impossible to figure out what went wrong unless one takes an independent and critical position vis-à-vis the political and economic leadership of *any* society. The apologists for authoritarian Communist and Third World regimes almost always argue a logic of extenuating circumstances, claiming that capitalism and imperialism *forced* the leaders of these societies to adopt undemocratic political systems in self-defence. That is, identifying with the leaders of these parties and states, these apologists argue that the defence of the revolution required at each step another retreat from the revolution's supposed goals of democracy, equality, justice and genuine socialisation, until, in the end, in order to keep the revolution afloat, the very ideals for which the revolution fought had to be thrown overboard. It is a method in which to understand is to forgive.

To try to answer the question 'What went wrong?', I use the Marxist method, that is, a critical analysis from the point of view of the working class and all of society's oppressed with the long-term goal of human liberation, social well-being, and individual fulfilment. At the centre of such an analysis are the following questions: What is the political economy of the society? Who owns and controls property and profits from it? What is the role of the market? Or, what is the role of the state plan? Who makes the decisions about the state's investments and about the investment of private capital? Who is employed and who is unemployed? What sorts of salaries and wages do people receive? How equal and fair is the distribution of wealth in society? Who must migrate to find work? What sorts of social programmes – health, education, and social welfare – exist in the society? What are the democratic rights of all people in the society? What are their human rights? And it still remains the case that the condition, treatment, and rights of women are the key indicator of the health of any society.[1] We might better say women and their children, since

---

1   As Charles Fourier wrote in 1806: 'As a general thesis: Social progress and historic change occur
    by virtue of the progress of women toward liberty, and decadence of the social order occurs
    as the result of a decrease in the liberty of women'; Bell and Offen (eds) 1983, pp. 40–1.

women remain the principal guardians and caretakers of their children in most societies. What kind of power do working people and the poor have in the society? And finally, what is the character of the class struggle in the society?

Those same questions must be posed whether one is talking about Nicaragua in the era of Spanish colonialism, of British or American imperialism, whether examining the country as it was under the Somozas or under the Sandinistas' revolutionary government, or looking at Nicaragua as it is today. The answer to the question 'What went wrong?' has to be found in the history of the country's political economy, that is, in the series of political-economic institutions, laws, and the related social structures that determined the country's development and its destiny. All of these institutions and the ideologies that surrounded them created the political and social structures of each period in which various groups fought for power.

To answer more completely the question 'What went wrong?' in the era of the Sandinistas and their successors, one has to also understand the burden of Nicaraguan history. This is why I dedicate the first two chapters to the period before the Somoza dynasty began, followed by the Sandinista seizure of power. From the very beginning, Nicaraguan history has often been even more difficult than that of its Central American neighbours and other Latin American countries. Many different factors – Nicaragua's small size and population, its strategic location, the failure over two centuries to unite with its neighbours and create a United States of Central America, its experience of political authoritarianism, the lack of virtually any democratic traditions in the country, the history of politics by rebellion, its proximity to the United States, and the long history of foreign military intervention; all these factors contributed to the conditions that made it difficult to make a revolution and even more difficult to defend it.

In each chapter, I have attempted to show how historical developments led to the creation of a particular political economy, that is, not only to a certain set of economic structures, but also to the dynamic interaction between economics and politics, between the existing ideology and everyday life, which resulted in the particular character of the struggles of social classes. The Social Democratic theorists of the late nineteenth century and the Communist ideologues of the twentieth century tended in their analyses toward an economic reductionism or determinism that argued that changes in the economic 'base' of society were reflected in its 'superstructure' of law, politics, and culture. The Marxist method, however, while recognising the centrality of economic relations, sees them as interacting with social relations more broadly, as well as with ideological controversies and political struggles for power. The state may at times become relatively autonomous from social classes, though in the long-run class interests and class power always tend to reassert themselves. Yet ideas can also become a material force. The ideas of the Marxist-Leninist vanguard party or the *guerrilla foco* become historical practices, and as practices they cease to be mere ideas and become part of the material reality. The truth is the whole.

For Marxists, society is not a political cupola erected upon a pyramidal social base, but rather a complicated web of interacting relationships at the centre of which sits the spider of private property, class political power, and social privilege. Our job is to analyse the webs of power in each period. While this sounds pretty neat and tidy when I write it here in the Introduction, it proves to be very complicated and messy in the execution, amid a narrative of complicated struggles for power in a society riven by all sorts of social conflicts and competing ideologies. But that is also what gives the Nicaraguan Revolution and its aftermath its intriguing particularity. In any case, it is well worth sorting out, for what we learn from the particularities of the Nicaraguan Revolution can help us to generalise about other revolutionary experiences and to draw conclusions that may help to guide those of us who today continue to work for revolutionary, international, and democratic socialism.

Nicaragua: A Nation but Not a State (from the Beginning to 1893)

Nicaragua, a tropical land of lakes and volcanoes located in Central America between the Caribbean Sea and Pacific Oceans, has had the misfortune almost from the beginning of being a small country in a strategic location. It has been from early on a sardine among the sharks, a minnow among Mayan, Aztec, Spanish, British and American predators.[1] The sharks almost swallowed the minnow in the middle of the nineteenth century, when American businessmen and politicians began to take an interest in Nicaragua. Cornelius Vanderbilt, one of the wealthiest men in the United States, had developed important shipping interests and he saw Nicaragua as offering his passengers a faster route to the gold rush in California. William Walker, a pro-slavery adventurer, had a political project; he saw Nicaragua as a potential American-controlled state in an empire built on plantation slavery, linked to and led by the American South. These two men, representative of two different American approaches to Latin America and to the question of empire, anticipated later and more important American military interventions at the end of the nineteenth century that would bring Nicaragua into the US sphere of influence and put it effectively under American control. To understand how these two individuals – neither of them operating with the full backing of the US government – could have such an important impact, one must know something about the origins of Nicaragua as a nation and its weakness as a state.

The first inhabitants of Nicaragua, like all other early Americans, were descendants of migrants who came across the Bering land bridge between 40,000 and 14,000 years ago. Over thousands of years these hunting and gathering peoples migrated down the Pacific Coast by land and sea and eventually reached Nicaragua, while others went on to South America, though some of them later turned around, migrated back north, and also settled in Nicaragua. We know from petrified footprints found in Nicaragua that there were people living there 6,000 years ago. Later explorers from the Mayan and Toltec king-

---

1 Arévalo 1961, *passim*. Juan José Arévalo, who was president of Guatemala from 1945 to 1951 and an ardent reformer, knows something about sharks. He was succeeded by another reformer, President Jacobo Árbenz, who served from 1951 until 1954 when he was overthrown by a US military coup.

doms of what are today Guatemala and Mexico arrived in Nicaragua, bringing their advanced agriculture, religion, and Mayan and Nahuatl languages. The Aztecs who had established a beachhead in Nicaragua in the late 1400s seemed, with their more advanced social organisation and military might, destined to conquer Nicaragua, and so it might have been. But then the Spanish arrived.[2]

Columbus's initial 'discovery' of the New World, beginning in the Caribbean islands in 1492 – including the taking of Indian slaves – was followed by the takeover of Cuba and then within a generation by Hernán Cortez's conquest of Mexico in 1521, laying Central America open to Spanish subjugation. The division of Central America into rival indigenous kingdoms and tribes made the region particularly vulnerable; no coalition or federation of the indigenous opposed the Spanish. On the contrary, some Indians fought, others surrendered, and yet others joined the Spanish in the conquest of their indigenous rivals. The political fragmentation of Central America and the Caribbean Islands is a *Leitmotiv* of the region's history from ancient times until today. The Spanish, British, and the Americans would all strive through the succeeding centuries to divide and rule, and they would generally succeed.

When the Spanish explorer Gil González Dávila arrived in Nicaragua in 1552, as many as one million indigenous people were living in the region.[3] González Dávila encountered three major indigenous groups, the Nicaindios, Choroteganos, and Chontales, though there were also many others. This was no tropical paradise. These were sedentary agricultural societies with a class structure and private property. The upper classes oppressed, exploited, and lived off the labour of the lower classes. These indigenous societies were generally organised in theocratic or military chiefdoms with a nobility of headmen and their subordinate *principales* ruling over the labouring classes who paid tribute and were liable to be conscripted for military service. Among the Nicaindios, both noblemen and some commoners owned slaves.[4] Civilisation – with all its benefits and liabilities – had arrived before the Spanish.

The *cacique* Nicarao, chief of the Nicaindios who ruled the area between Lake Nicaragua and the Pacific Ocean, welcomed the Spanish conquerors, gave them gold, and accepted conversion to Christianity, as did several thousand members of his tribe, though exactly what they understood about Christianity or Spanish rule is a matter of conjecture. The Spanish, now having a base on the coast, moved on to conquer the interior of Nicaragua but encountered stiff res-

2   MacLeod 2008, pp. 31–8.
3   Newson 1982, pp. 253–86.
4   Newson 1987, pp. 56–60.

istance from Chief Diriangén of the Niquirianos – today a national hero – who fought the Spanish and in 1523 briefly drove them away. The Indians, however, were no match for the Spaniards with their ships, horses, steel armour, firearms, war dogs, and above all the diseases that they unknowingly communicated to the Indians who – geographically isolated for thousands of years from Europe, Africa, and Asia – had no immunity and succumbed in enormous numbers. In 1524, Francisco Hernández de Córdoba returned to Nicaragua, defeated Diriangén, and completed the conquest of the largest indigenous groups. When Hernández de Córdoba was later accused of mismanagement, Pedro Arias Dávila (Pedrarias), the governor of Panama, took over the governorship, sentenced his predecessor to death, and ruled the country until July 1531.[5] By then the Spanish were firmly in control of the Pacific coastal region.

Perhaps no other Latin American region suffered as much from the Spanish conquest as did Nicaragua. While the encounter with the Spanish was initially a disaster for all of Latin America, triggering as it did the demographic catastrophe that in the next 100 years would reduce the indigenous population by 90 percent, none fared worse than Nicaragua. This was because the Spanish built Nicaragua's first economy principally on the export of the native Nicaraguans. The Spanish captured and enslaved the indigenous people and shipped them off by the tens of thousands to work in the mines of Panama and Peru. It is estimated that in the sixteenth century, half a million Nicaraguans were exported to work, and often to die from overwork, in other Spanish colonies. A large percentage never even made it to the mines, but died on the slave ships before reaching their destinations.

The combination of the slave trade, warfare, forced labour, and above all disease devastated the Nicaraguan indigenous population which by the end of the sixteenth century fell from an estimated one million to a mere 30,000.[6] The original sin of the Spaniards' Indian slave trade meant that the region's population collapsed leaving few inhabitants to develop and defend its vast spaces. With the exception of the Pacific Coast, the rest of the country, largely made up of mountains and jungles, had few patches of cultivated land. For centuries Nicaragua would remain extraordinarily underdeveloped, always poorer than its Central American neighbours.

The Spanish called their new territory Nicaragua, after the first rulers and tribes they had met, and imposed upon it the same regime they established throughout the Americas. The Spanish Crown's imperial system existed to

---

5 Library of Congress Studies n.d.
6 Newson 1982, pp. 253–86; Macleod 2008, pp. 51–5; Newson 1987, pp. 104–6.

extract gold, silver, and later agricultural products from the colonies. Spain was an absolute monarchy and its political system authoritarian, hierarchical, and bureaucratic, extending across the Atlantic a long chain of command capable of exerting considerable authority over its subjects, if seldom full compliance with its wishes. The King ruled the American empire through the Council of the Indies in Spain, and the Council in turn governed through Viceroys, Audiences, Captains, and local government officials sent to the New World.

To oversee the Central American region, the Spanish established the Kingdom (or Captaincy) of Guatemala, made up of the territory that today makes up the Mexican state of Chiapas and the nations of Guatemala, Costa Rica, Honduras, El Salvador, and Nicaragua. The rulers of the region, Spanish appointees from Iberia, *peninsulares* as they were called, were sent to America to govern, to extract wealth, and to send it on to the motherland. Spain's great problems at the time came not from the Indians, but from Spanish conquerors who wished to establish themselves as feudal lords in the New World. The Crown crushed them and with a relatively small military force, the Spanish were able to exert control over all of their far-flung American colonies.

The Spanish Catholic Church, also controlled by the crown, established a similar hierarchical and bureaucratic system of Archbishops, Bishops, Cardinals and priests, together with the various monastic orders such as Dominicans and Franciscans. Catholicism was at first forced upon the natives, their sacred places demolished and transformed into Catholic churches, their idols destroyed or hidden by the natives, their rituals prohibited. Later, significantly modified by the admixture of native traditions and beliefs, Catholicism became deeply rooted in the society, one of the most religious in Latin America. Yet the Church's influence was principally in the Pacific Coast region, since it did not have the resources and personnel to cover the immense territory. The indigenous people of mountains, jungles, and Caribbean coast remained pagan, though over centuries, they too would gradually succumb to Christianity.

The Spanish settled in cities, while the Indian survivors of the plagues – after being regrouped during the demographic catastrophe of the sixteenth century into new communities called *congregaciones* – lived in villages on their own collectively owned land. Nicaragua's indigenous population declined precipitously, but small numbers of Spanish immigrants, mostly male, arrived and settled, as well as a few Africans brought as slaves. By the end of the eighteenth century, the importation of enslaved Africans from a variety of West African tribes increased significantly. Sexual relations between Spaniards and Indians or Africans gave rise to respectively the mestizos and mulattoes – as well as to a dozen other kinds of new racial groups given derogatory names (such as *salto atrás*, 'a jump backwards') that arose from relations between and among the indigenous, the mestizos, mulattoes, and the Spanish. *Las castas*, as these mixed-race people were called, came to form the urban labouring class of artisans and servants, served as rural foremen, and later as soldiers. The result was that Nicaragua's population became mostly mestizo and mulatto, though the important African genetic and cultural contribution to Nicaragua was often ignored or denied.[7]

In Nicaragua's Pacific lowlands, Hernández de Córdoba established the cities of León and Granada. The urban-dwelling Spaniards imposed on the indigenous groups the *encomienda*, a system of tribute and forced labour that in practice was often little better than slavery. The Spanish rulers of Nicaragua had the chiefs of the various indigenous communities collect tribute and help organise the labour force. In northern Nicaragua where the Spanish found gold, they forced pacified Indians and imported black slaves to work the mines.[8] In the port of Realejo, the Spanish established a lumber and shipbuilding industry, the heavy labour done by the Indians.[9] The Nicaraguan *criollos*, that is, the Spanish descendants of the conquerors and colonisers, created haciendas and plantations where they raised cattle, grew cacao and indigo, and produced cochineal (a red dye made from an insect that lives on cactus plants), which became the principal exports.[10] The wealth and power of Nicaragua's elite class was based on their landed estates, some owning cattle grazing lands comprising hundreds of thousands of acres, yet they never created a society (such as Mexico) totally dominated by haciendas or the large estates known as *latifundios*. It was simply impossible at that time for the tiny Spanish elite and the reduced numbers of indigenous people, together with the mestizos and mulattoes to occupy the vast spaces of Nicaragua. The Caribbean coast in particular remained sparsely populated.

By the end of the eighteenth century, Nicaragua's indigenous population, now with greater immunity to European diseases, had begun to recuperate. At about the same time, the Hapsburg dynasty ended and the Bourbons came to the throne in Spain in 1700, introducing a series of reforms based on French governmental structures and economic policies. King Charles III issued a so-

---

7   Ramírez 2008. Sergio Ramírez has made the case both for the important African contributions to Nicaraguan history as well as criticising the neglect and rejection of that African contribution by both scholars and the Nicaraguan public. A genetic study of modern Nicaraguans suggests that most Nicaraguans today are descendants of Spanish men and Indian women with some admixture of African DNA. See Núñez et al. 2010.

8   MacLeod 2008, p. 57.

9   Medal Mendieta 2010, pp. 34–8.

10   MacLeod 2008, pp. 62–3, 170–3, 176–8; Medal Mendieta 2010, pp. 57–87.

called 'Free Trade Decree' that permitted greater trade among Spain's Latin American possessions and ended the control of trade by four colonial ports (Veracruz, Cartagena, Callao, and Panama). Yet because free trade was not permitted between the Spanish colonies and other nations or their colonies, some merchants were disappointed. These Bourbon Reforms of the mid-eighteenth century generally stimulated the colonial economies of most of Latin America – but not in Nicaragua, which saw virtually no economic improvement.

Even worse, the administrative reorganisation of Nicaragua led to conflict between León, which became a separate intendancy under the new system, and its rival Granada, a contention that ultimately erupted in violence and established a historic antagonism between the two cities that would last into the twentieth century. Meanwhile the Spanish administrators of Nicaragua found themselves forced to devote their energies and resources to organising political and military resistance to the British presence on Nicaragua's Caribbean coast. Britain had established colonies and trading posts and had entered into an alliance with the Miskito Indians, eventually turning the region into a British protectorate in 1739. The Miskitos, having seen what had happened to the other indigenous troops under the Spanish, welcomed the British presence and protection. Mosquitia, as the region was called, would not be incorporated into Nicaragua until the dawn of the twentieth century.[11] By the end of the eighteenth century then, Nicaragua was divided into three regions – the Pacific Coast, the Segovias in the Northwest, and the Miskito Coast – with little connecting them beyond a name.

The Bourbon Reforms had a contradictory impact on Latin America as a whole. On the one hand, the Spanish imposition of a new administrative system staffed by *peninsulares* created antagonism between them and the *criollo* landlords and merchants born in the New World. At the same time, except for Nicaragua, the Latin American regional economies improved. The limited 'free trade' with other Spanish colonies, rather than being appreciated, led the *criollo*'s to resent that they could not also trade with other European nations. When Napoleon Bonaparte invaded Spain in 1808, deposed the King Fernando VII, and placed his brother Joseph Bonaparte on the throne, the Spanish colonies in Latin America suddenly found themselves in a situation of de facto independence.

The French Revolution and the Napoleonic wars in Europe led to a divide throughout all of Latin America's elite groups between conservatives and liberals. While some Latin American cities and regions supported the King and the

---

11   Newson 1987, pp. 255–71.

status quo ante, others supported the *Cortes* or parliament in the city of Cádiz. The Cádiz *Cortes* – inspired by the American Revolution of 1776 and the French Revolution of 1789 – adopted the liberal Spanish Constitution of 1812, creating a constitutional monarchy and passing laws theoretically granting universal suffrage, land reform, free enterprise, and a free press. The events of the period of the Latin American nations' struggle for independence between 1810 and 1821 thus established the fundamental political division between the Conservatives who admired the Spanish Catholic monarchy, and the Liberals who admired the secular republics of France and the United States. Nicaragua, small and insignificant, had no role in the independence revolutions that were fought out in Mexico and South America; yet it nevertheless also experienced, on a small scale, the great struggle taking place between different political and economic models throughout Spanish America.

Nicaragua's Post-Independence Period (1821–49)

While the post-independence period was difficult for almost all of the Latin American nations, it may have been most difficult for Nicaragua. With a territory of over 130,000 square kilometres (about 50,000 square miles), that is, about the size of Wisconsin or New York State, Nicaragua's population at independence was only about 180,000, more than 75 percent of which lived along the Pacific coastal plain. As happened throughout the rest of Spanish America, the elite divided into two political parties, the Liberals and the Conservatives. León became the centre of Liberalism while Granada became the headquarters of Conservatism, two rival groups that in reality had more in common socially than they had differences politically.

Throughout Latin America the period from 1821 to 1870, often referred to as the 'lost half century', war took place between the Liberals and Conservatives, both of which were made up of landowners, merchants, and church leaders; there was no role in politics for those without property and wealth. This was also the case in Nicaragua. In this contest, there was no concept of democracy, there were no democratic institutions, and there were virtually no orderly and peaceful changes of government. The constant warfare meant that a stable political order could not be established and consequently that there was no economic development.

It is important to note that from the beginning in Nicaragua and throughout the nineteenth and twentieth centuries, politics was always a matter of armed struggle, of *coups d'état* and little 'revolutions' in which elite groups mobilised small numbers of plebeians to seize power. When attempting to understand

the developments in the twentieth century such as Somoza's violent coup of
1936 and the Sandinista revolution of 1979, it is important to recall, on the
one hand, the centuries of elite domination, the constant violent warfare,
and, on the other hand, the utter lack of any democratic ideas or political
institutions.

Most Latin American nations went through a period of territorial definition
between 1821 and 1850. So too did Nicaragua. Guatemala, which at the time
included Nicaragua, declared Central America's independence from Spain in
1821. León, however, declared its independence from Spain and Guatemala,
and joined Agustín de Iturbide's short-lived Mexican Empire. With the fall
of Iturbide in 1823, Nicaragua became independent, but a civil war between
the Liberals of León and the Conservatives of Granada prevented Nicaragua
from organising even the semblance of a state. Centrifugal forces began to
pull Nicaragua apart. It lost the province of Guanacaste to Costa Rica in 1824.
The Miskito Coast, which had never been effectively held by the Spanish or
by Nicaragua, became a British Flag Protectorate in 1834 and remained so
until it was finally reincorporated into Nicaragua in 1894. The mountainous
Segovias remained a frontier region uncontrolled by either of the two rival
capital cities.

Not only was the newly independent country politically crumbling, but
there were also no roads or highways to help hold it together. It was a collection of a few small cities and even smaller towns, of scattered haciendas and
plantations, and of various indigenous communities in the hinterlands. What
transportation there was took place on the seas, the lakes and the rivers, or on
horses, burros, and oxcarts travelling over dirt paths. In 1840, the first date for
which we have any reliable population figures in the modern era, the country
had 260,000 inhabitants. Nicaragua's small size, its lack of social cohesion, and
its political divisions made it particularly vulnerable to foreign intervention.

A Decade of American Intervention (1849–59)

The founding fathers of the United States of America had in mind from the
beginning that their nation would absorb parts of Latin America. Referring
to Cuba and Puerto Rico, US Secretary of State John Quincy Adams wrote in
1823: 'These islands are natural appendages of the North American continent ...
There are laws of political as well as of physical gravitation. If an apple, severed
by the tempest from its native tree, cannot choose but fall to the ground, Cuba,
forcibly disjoined from its unnatural connection with Spain, and incapable of
self-support, can only gravitate towards the North American Union, which, by

the same law of nature, cannot cast her off from its bosom'. Similarly, Thomas Jefferson had written, 'the annexation of Cuba to our Confederation is precisely what is needed to complete our national power and maximise its interests'. Not only Cuba, but all of the Spanish possessions in Mexico, Central America, and the Caribbean seemed to many of America's political elite as if they should belong to the United States.[12]

The growth and expansion of the United States in the nineteenth century brought it quickly into commercial, diplomatic, and military involvement in the Caribbean and Central America. At the same time, the political struggle in the United States between the North and the South over the newly acquired Mexican territories led some southerners to see Mexico, Central and South America as potential slave territories. Thus two kinds of American interlopers in Central American politics arose: the commercial tycoon on the one hand, namely Cornelius Vanderbilt, and the filibuster or political pirate on the other, William Walker. Both economic and political interests brought Nicaragua into what American politicians were coming to see as the US sphere of influence, a vision that would bring the United States into conflict with Great Britain, which since the independence of the Spanish colonies in 1821 had been the dominant power in the region.

Cornelius Vanderbilt's Canal Venture

Cornelius Vanderbilt, the richest and most powerful tycoon of his era, was the first American to become deeply involved in Nicaragua. Vanderbilt was born on 27 May 1794 on Staten Island, New York, the son of a ferryboat operator. At the age of 11, Vanderbilt went to work with his father in his ferry business and later as a young man bought a schooner and began to ship goods in the New York and New Jersey region. Thomas Gibbon, the owner of a shipping company, offered Vanderbilt a job with his company as a ship captain, leading to the honorific title 'Commodore' by which Vanderbilt came to be known. Later, as manager of Gibbon's company, Vanderbilt led a successful commercial and legal fight against the heirs of Robert Fulton, inventor of the steamboat, and Robert Livingston, Fulton's wealthy partner, who had a monopoly of steamboat traffic on the New York waterways. The struggle culminated successfully for Vanderbilt in the Supreme Court case *Gibbons v. Ogden*. Continuing to work

---

12   For Adams's complete quotation, see Cuba History, n.d. For an account of the US role in Latin America, see Peter H. Smith 2000US.

with Gibbon and later with his son, Vanderbilt also became a secret partner with the entrepreneur Daniel Drew, and gradually one of the moguls of the era. During the 1830s and 1840s, Vanderbilt, engaging in ruthless competition with his rivals, continued to expand his steamboat companies while at the same time acquiring real estate in Staten Island and Manhattan. He became very, very rich.

Much broader horizons, far beyond New Jersey, were opening up for Americans, including Vanderbilt. In the Mexican-American War of 1846 to 1848, the United States defeated Mexico and took half its territory, including the future states of California, Nevada, Arizona, New Mexico, and Utah. Even before the treaty was signed, gold was discovered in California and there was a rush of Americans to the West hoping to get rich quick. Most travellers to the California Gold Fields left from New York City, travelling either to Panama or around the horn of South America. Vanderbilt immediately shifted his emphasis from steamboats operating in the New York–New Jersey region to steamships travelling from New York to Panama.

The Commodore's ships carried passengers to the Atlantic coast of Panama where they then crossed the isthmus on carriages travelling on the newly constructed Panama highway before being transferred to other ships that then picked them up on the Pacific coast and took them on to San Francisco by ship. Looking for a way to beat the competition engaged in that same trade, Vanderbilt proposed to take passengers across Nicaragua first by coach and boat, and later via a canal he would build. Vanderbilt used his influence and Secretary of State John M. Clayton instructed Ephraim George Squier, archaeologist and US *chargé d'affaires* in Central America, to support Vanderbilt's efforts and to attempt to weaken Great Britain's hold on the Miskito Coast of Nicaragua.

In 1849, Vanderbilt visited Nicaragua and obtained exclusive rights to the construction of an interoceanic canal and, pending its construction, right-of-way in Nicaragua between the Caribbean and the Pacific for his boats and carriages. His ocean-going steamship company was already carrying passengers from New York to Nicaragua. To complete the voyage to the Pacific, his American Atlantic & Pacific Canal Company signed a contract with the Nicaraguan government to build a 12-mile canal from Lake Nicaragua to San Juan del Sur, that is, an interoceanic canal linking Atlantic and Caribbean with the Pacific.[13] Meanwhile, he created the Accessory Transit Company to take passengers from the Caribbean, up the San Juan River 120 miles, across Lake Nicaragua another

---

13   Stiles 2009, p. 181.

110 miles, and then over the 12-mile stage coach route that deposited them at the Pacific Port of San Juan del Sur.[14] Vanderbilt's Nicaragua route was eight days shorter and therefore cheaper than his rivals'. At $300 for first class and $180 for steerage, Vanderbilt's fares were half those of his competitors. By 1852, it was possible to travel from New York to California in just 25 days on Vanderbilt's Nicaraguan coach-and-boat route.

Vanderbilt's plans to build a canal in Nicaragua alarmed Great Britain, the hegemonic capitalist power in the world at the time, the dominant sea power on the globe, and a country with interests in British Honduras, Belize and the Bay Islands, as well as on Nicaragua's Miskito Coast. Britain feared that an American-owned canal across Nicaragua would immediately threaten its Central American and Caribbean interests, as well as its domination of the world's seas. The British claimed the port of San Juan del Norte, where the Commodore planned to build his terminal, as part of the British protectorate on the Miskito Coast, but the American government protested. Vanderbilt ignored the British claims and went ahead with his plans. When Great Britain then attempted to stop the Accessory Transit Company, a violent confrontation broke out between the British naval forces and the Commodore's men.

To resolve the matter, the British envoy Sir Henry Bulwer met with US Secretary of State Clayton to discuss the American and British concerns about Nicaragua. The result was the Clayton-Bulwer Treaty of 1850, which represented a compromise between the two countries. Under the terms of the treaty, neither nation would dominate the canal, which would remain neutral; nor would either nation attempt to 'occupy, or fortify or colonise' Nicaragua, Costa Rica, the Miskito Coast, or any other part of Central America.[15] Vanderbilt then could have his canal, but only so long as the canal was open to the traffic of the United States *and* Great Britain, and the US did not attempt to acquire Nicaraguan territory.

For Vanderbilt, everything had fallen into place. The Accessory Transit Company, which operated the boats on Lake Nicaragua was by 1856 – after a struggle among the owners – completely under the control of the Commodore, who had also signed the contract for the construction of the canal. The United States and Great Britain had also reached an agreement removing obstacles to the canal's construction. Vanderbilt was at the time one of the wealthiest and most politically influential men in the United States with strong ties to both the economic elite in New York City and to politicians in Washington DC. It seemed that his

---

14   Stiles 2009, pp. 176–7.
15   Clayton-Bulwer Treaty of 1850.

ventures in Nicaragua would proceed apace, giving him the dominant position in transportation between New York and California – but at that very moment the American freebooter William Walker seized control of Nicaragua.

William Walker – The Filibuster

William Walker was a prodigy who grew to become an adventurer and a mega-lomaniac. Born in 1824 in Nashville, Tennessee, to a Scottish immigrant and the daughter of an American Revolutionary War officer, Walker graduated *summa cum laude* from the University of Nashville at the age of 14. He then went off, supposedly to study medicine at Edinburgh, Heidelberg, Göttingen, and Paris. At the age of 19, he received his medical degree from the University of Pennsylvania, but then moved to New Orleans to practice law as well as becoming editor of the liberal, anti-slavery *New Orleans Crescent* newspaper. Still restless, in 1849 he moved to California where, after surviving three duels, he dreamed up his scheme to conquer territories in Latin America. He became a filibuster or freebooter, that is, the leader of a private military force aimed at conquering foreign territory, usually with the goal of annexing it to some other foreign country, often an American with the goal of bringing that territory into the United States.[16]

Many Americans had by that time come to believe, in the famous phrase of John L. O'Sullivan writing in the *United States Magazine and Democratic Review* in July of 1845, that it was the 'manifest destiny' of the United States to conquer the entire continent of North America. Some thought that ruling over all of North America meant conquering all of Mexico, Central America and the islands of the Caribbean as well. Often this idea was linked to the notion of Anglo-Saxon racial superiority over the Indians, peoples of African descent, and mixed-race peoples who inhabited the rest of North America. The notion that Protestantism was the real Christianity, while Catholicism was a superstition foisted upon the natives, a faith that only fostered ignorance, also formed part of the American sense of superiority. The aggressive expansionism of the era had already led, of course, to the detachment of Texas from Mexico in 1836 and its later incorporation into the United States in 1845, followed by the

---

16   There are several popular biographies of Walker, among them: Greene 1937; Gerson 1976; Rosengarten 1976; Bolaños Geyer 1976 is intended to identify and clarify the role of Clinton Rollins who provided much of the journalistic information about the life of Walker. I have relied on Rosengarten for much of the narrative in this chapter.

Mexican-American War of 1846–7, which ended with the United States taking half of Mexico's territory and at least 100,000 of its citizens. Why not take Central America too?

Filibusters thought they would.[17] Filibustering had begun shortly after the founding of the United States and continued until the Civil War, usually aimed at taking some Spanish possession, though at times also attempting to take a piece of Canada.[18] The filibuster was a man of action, an adventurer who delighted in military exploits. He typically believed in the superiority of the Anglo-Saxon Protestant peoples or more generally the European peoples and their fight to rule over the darker and benighted races and more specifically he believed in the doctrine of Manifest Destiny. Many of the filibusters were Southerners who believed that it was necessary to conquer more territory both for the expansion of the plantation slavery system and possibly to acquire more states and therefore more southern Senators in the US Congress in order to maintain a majority.[19] For example, Narciso López, a Venezuelan by birth, led two unsuccessful attempts, sponsored by wealthy Americans from New York and from the South, to invade and conquer Cuba in 1850 and again in 1851. While his invasions of Cuba were a failure, still they encouraged other such efforts.[20]

The United States was concerned to control the Filibusters whose piracy threatened to jeopardise relations not only with Latin American countries, but also more importantly with Great Britain. The US Constitution empowered Congress to penalise 'offenses against the Law of Nations', on the basis of which Congress passed a series of neutrality laws in 1794, 1797, 1800, 1807, 1817, 1818, and 1838 which imposed serious criminal penalties on filibusters.[21] Yet, at various times, government officials, from presidents like Andrew Jackson and Franklin Pierce to military officers and government attorneys, sympathised with and sometimes winked at the filibusters' activities. Still, by and large the neutrality acts were enforced and, even if they did not deter the pirates,

---

17   Academic treatments of Filibustering include: Stout 1973; May 1973; Brown 1980; Chaffin 1996; and May 2002.

18   May 2002, pp. 1–7.

19   Brown 1980, p. 355. Brown explains, 'Much of the enthusiasm in the South for the filibusterism in Cuba and Nicaragua had its basis in the hope of annexation – the bringing of new slaves states into the Union to maintain control of Congress. The strength of the free-soil movement had made it clear that extension of slavery into the new states to be formed of the territories, dramatised in the war going on in Kansas, was a losing proposition'.

20   Chaffin 1996 is the most complete account of Narciso López's filibustering against Cuba. See also the brief account in May 2002, pp. 20–35.

21   May 2002, pp. 1–7.

they were on several occasions used to indict them, though juries were often sympathetic to the filibusters and sometimes found them innocent despite the best evidence.[22]

While Americans filibusters were most active in Mexico, Central America and the Caribbean, there were also filibusters from other nations who wished to re-establish a European presence on the continent, or simply to take control of some particularly valuable resource. Count Raousset-Boulbon, a French citizen, attempted an invasion of Sonora, Mexico, in 1852 with the goal of both acquiring its mineral resources and blocking the expansion of the United States. Raousset-Boulbon, who fancied himself the 'sultan of Sonora', combined political intrigue with military intervention, but the Mexicans defeated him and then executed him on the beach at Guaymas on 12 August 1854. His experience would serve as a model for William Walker.

As a child in Tennessee, Walker's family had not owned slaves nor had his parents been advocates of slavery, and in his early days as a journalist he had been an abolitionist, but somehow his experience of the growing conflict between North and South in the United States transformed him into a true believer in slavery as the ideal social system. It may have been his friend Edmund Randolph, a Virginia lawyer who was the grandson of George Washington's attorney, who turned Walker from an abolitionist into an advocate of slavery. In any case, Walker underwent a complete ideological conversion. Walker's filibustering campaigns first in Mexico and later in Nicaragua were based on the idea – one common among southern intellectuals and politicians at the time – that the plantation slave system and the institution of slavery must be spread into Latin America in order to protect the American South. Southerners and their filibusters saw slavery as a higher form of civilisation than northern capitalism, a society and culture derived from ancient Greece and Rome. This southern cause, that is the defence of the slave system, provided the vehicle for Walker's own personal ambitions, his megalomaniacal desire to make himself the head of a slave state, the hubris that would lead him to proclaim himself president of the Republic of Sonora and Baja California and later of Nicaragua.

Walker first conceived his filibustering plans in the heart of the Gold Rush country in the town of Auburn in Placer County, California, in 1852. After Raousset-Boulbon turned down Walker's offer to join the French campaign, Walker decided to launch his own. Walker's idea, modelled on that of Raousset-Boulbon, was to create a separate state between the United States and Mexico,

---

22   May 2002, pp. 127–43.

ostensibly to protect both nations from the Apaches. To finance his operation he sold bonds in the name of the *Republic of Sonora*, backed by land there that he did not yet possess. Walker and his small army of 45 soldiers of fortune crossed from the United States into Mexico at the tiny town of Tijuana, and sailed south along the coast of Baja California, eventually landing at the tip of the peninsula at the town of La Paz, which they intended to use as a base of operations to take Sonora. Walker landed. He imprisoned the governor, lowered the Mexican flag, and ran up his own flag with red and white bars and two stars for Baja California and Sonora. After moving their capital to Ensenada where they survived on stolen sheep and cattle, on 30 November 1853 Walker declared the independence of Baja California and proclaimed himself to be the president, with his partner Henry P. Watkins as vice-president.[23]

In June of 1853, Walker and Watkins sailed to Guaymas to meet with the governor of Sonora, from whom they requested a grant to establish a base to defend the Mexicans from the Apaches. The governor was not fooled and the Mexican authorities refused to permit Walker to leave the port and move on into the interior of Sonora. The locals in Guaymas stoned the American invaders, hollering, 'Death to the Yankees'.[24] Walker was not to be stopped so easily. On 18 January 1854, he issued a proclamation declaring Sonora to be independent of Mexico and himself its president. To his original force of just under 50, some 250 new recruits had been added as Walker prepared to launch his invasion of Sonora. However, with the United States and Mexico engaged in negotiating the Gadsden Purchase, the last step in settling the Mexican-American War, both countries were hostile to Walker's military intervention and both posted war ships at Ensenada harbour to restrain his little army. Walker therefore decided that he and his men would march north and east through the desert. Walking north around the end of the Sea of Cortez, they crossed into Sonora where they were quickly confronted, defeated and routed by the Mexican Army and volunteers.

Walker's bedraggled band, hungry, exhausted, and decimated by desertions, walked back across the border into the United States. Despite his ignominious defeat, Walker still claimed for a while to be the president of the Republic of Sonora and Baja California, though he had never succeeded in gaining control of an inch of territory in either region. He justified his military intervention by arguing that Mexico had failed to bring civilisation to Sonora which was practically controlled by the Apaches. As Walker later wrote about these events,

---

23   Stout 1973, pp. 81–102; May 2002, pp. 40–2.
24   Stout 1973, p. 94.

'On none more immediately than on the American people, did the duty devolve of relieving the frontier from the cruelties of savage war'.[25] The idea of American paternalism – of white Americans' responsibility for the custody and care of the inferior Indian, African, and mestizo people of Latin America – became a central part of Walker's ideology.

When he returned to California, Walker was indicted for violation of the Neutrality Acts of 1794 and 1818 which made it illegal for any American as a private individual to engage in a military enterprise or expedition against a country with which the United States was at peace. But filibustering had widespread popular support in the West, and, defended by his friend Edmund Randolph, Walker was acquitted in a matter of minutes. His indictment and trial would, however, make him more cautious in the future and lead him to seek invitations from foreign powers and some sort of US government support for his future activities.[26]

In California, where he edited a daily newspaper, Walker became part of a network of men who were engaged in dreaming up and planning filibustering expeditions in Central America. One was the proprietor of the newspaper for which Walker worked, Byron Cole, who was focused on Nicaragua. American freebooters like Cole were interested in seizing Central American territory for the United States and in particular for the slave South and naturally saw themselves as enemies of the British who had ended slavery in 1833 and began to suppress the international slave trade in the 1840s. Politically the Americans and British stood on opposite sides in the great political conflicts of Latin America in the nineteenth century. Throughout the nations of Central America, the British generally supported the Conservative Party while the Americans tended to support the Liberals. Since the beginning of the 1850s, Nicaraguans had recruited Americans to fight for them in Nicaragua, and American opportunists saw an opportunity to stake a claim. Filibuster, Henry L. Kinney had urged Americans, as the title to a pamphlet publicising his plan proclaimed, to find *A Home in Nicaragua!* He was attempting an invasion of Nicaragua at virtually the same time as Walker would. And there were several other British and American filibusters probing Nicaragua in the same period as well.[27]

---

25 Walker 1860, p. 26. Walker's first-hand account of his exploits in Nicaragua provides the most detailed and valuable account we have. All of the biographies and academic histories reply to Walker's narrative, even if they disagree with his interpretation of motives. See Brown 1980, pp. 442–4, for his discussion of Walker's memoir.

26 May 2002, pp. 140–3.

27 Brown 1980, pp. 257–64.

Cole urged Walker to take an interest in Nicaragua, a politically unstable country where between 1847 and 1855 there had been thirteen different presidents and where at the time the Conservatives (also known as the Legitimists) and the Liberals (also called the Democrats) were engaged in civil war. Cole had been in contact with Francisco Castellón, head of the Provisional Liberal Government of Nicaragua based in León, who had risen up in rebellion against the government of Fruto Chamorro of the Conservative Party based in the city of Granada. Cole promised to bring American aid to the Liberal cause. Nicaragua, Cole told Walker, was the place and now was the time. Former US Senator John C. Fremont, a key figure in the US acquisition of California who had recently been in Nicaragua, encouraged Walker as well.[28]

In 1854, Cole sailed to Nicaragua, met with Castellón, and signed a contract with him to provide 300 men for military duty who would receive a monthly salary and a certain number of acres of land at the end of the war with the Conservatives. When Cole returned to California, he urged Walker to undertake leadership of the force, but Walker, burned by his earlier experience with the Neutrality Act, refused to enter the country as head of a military force, insisting that Cole secure a colonisation grant instead. Cole then returned to Nicaragua and procured a colonisation grant for 300 men who would be permitted to bear arms. Walker, who wanted the support of the US government for his coming expedition, took his colonisation grant to the US District Attorney for the Northern District of California and to US General Wool, and only when he was convinced that he had not only 'the sanction of the proper Federal authorities' but even their blessing, did he finally embark.[29]

Though warned by Secretary of State Marcy that the US government would invoke the neutrality laws if his expedition were a military one, Walker set sail for Nicaragua on 4 May 1855 with 58 armed men in what he saw as an event of enormous historic significance for both Nicaragua and the United States. As he later wrote, 'From the day the Americans landed at Realejo dates a new epoch, not only for Nicaragua, but for all Central America. Thenceforth it was impossible for the worn-out society of these countries to evade or escape the changes the new elements were to work in their domestic as well as their political organisation'.[30] Setting aside his rhetoric of racial and cultural superiority, Walker was right – Nicaragua would never be the same after Walker had brought it to the broader attention of the United States. Walker's was the open-

---

28   Brown 1980, p. 268.
29   Walker 1860, pp. 24–8.
30   Walker 1860, p. 34.

ing wedge of what would become decades of US military intervention and occupation in Nicaragua. The US would eventually – and it would not be long – bring Nicaragua within its sphere of influence.

Upon Walker's arrival in Nicaragua in June of 1855, Castellón, the director of the Liberal Party government, made the American adventurer a colonel in the Nicaraguan Army, with the other Americans being either commissioned as officers or incorporated as enlisted men. At the same time, the American Phalanax or *Falange*, as Walker called his troops, became naturalised Nicaraguan citizens. Walker also incorporated into his little army scores of other Americans then living in or passing through Nicaragua as well as signing up over 150 native-born Nicaraguans. His force of two- to three-hundred armed men, known in the American press at the time as 'The Immortals', would prove sufficient to take control of Nicaragua and gain a foothold in Central America.

Walker immediately proposed an attack on Rivas that would give him control of the transit route and thereby of the entire country.[31] Almost immediately the war began and despite an initial defeat in July, when his men were routed, Walker's forces remained intact, reorganised, and continued their campaign over the next several months. Walker's *Falange* subsequently defeated the Conservatives first at the town of La Virgen on Virgin Bay and then in their capital city of Granada on 15 October 1855, winning the war for the Liberals. During the course of the war, Walker, who headed the strongest military force in Nicaragua and perhaps in all of Central America at the time, had in effect become the country's dominant figure.

A shrewd politician, Walker went to mass at the Cathedral and spoke with Padre Augstín Vigil in order to win him over to his programme. The US Ambassador to Nicaragua, John H. Wheeler, acted as an intermediary to carry the Liberal peace proposal to the Conservatives.[32] The treaty of 23 October dictated by the Conservative leader Ponciano Corral and signed by the Liberals and the Conservative Parties made Patricio Rivas, a Liberal, the president and Walker commander of the Nicaraguan Army. In reality, with his command over the army, Walker was the power behind the throne, Rivas merely a puppet. Soon after the treaty was signed, Walker had Corral, who had headed the Conservative Party government, tried by a court made up exclusively of Americans and executed by a firing squad.[33] Walker also had both the Conservative and most of the Liberal forces demobilised, leaving him with the only army in the coun-

---

31   Brown 1980, pp. 276–7; May 2002, p. 47.
32   Brown 1980, pp. 298–9.
33   Brown 1980, pp. 305–7.

try. John Wheeler, the US representative in Nicaragua and a friend of Walker's immediately recognised the new government, though under the terms of the Clayton-Bulwer Treaty, US recognition would soon be withdrawn by the US State Department, which judged that the time for such a move was not ripe. President Franklin Pierce also issued a proclamation discouraging travel to Nicaragua and instructing US authorities to prevent criminal activities, i.e. filibustering.

By an earlier agreement with the Nicaraguan Liberals made during the war, Walker had been given authority to 'settle all differences and outstanding accounts between the Government and the Accessory Transit Company' owned by Cornelius Vanderbilt.[34] Urged on by his friend Edmund Randolph in San Francisco, who was involved with a rival shipping company, Walker had president Rivas revoke the charter of Vanderbilt's Accessory Transit Company on 18 February 1856, arguing that ATC had failed to build either the railroad or the ship canal which it agreed to construct as well as failing to pay the royalties on its profits as stipulated in the charter. It was also alleged that the ATC had carried Conservative troops hostile to Walker during the recent war. Not only did Walker revoke the charter but he also seized the company's assets, including its ships, boats and carriages.[35] As Walker wrote explaining his actions, 'The control of the Transit is, to Americans, the control of Nicaragua: for the lake, not the river as many think, furnishes the key to the occupation of the whole state. Therefore, whoever desires to hold Nicaragua securely must be careful that the navigation of the lake is controlled by those who are his staunchest and most reliable friends'.[36] Walker then turned the ATC and its assets over to his friend Randolph, who was a front man for Charles Morgan and C.K. Garrison, two business rivals of Cornelius Vanderbilt. With the ATC's steamboats in the hands of his friend Randolph, Walker felt sure that he could be supplied with new American colonists, that is, with fresh troops, from either San Francisco or New York. However, by seizing the ATC and turning it over to Vanderbilt's competitors, Walker had in effect declared war on Vanderbilt.[37] That was a strategic error that proved to have disastrous consequences.

To defend his little kingdom, Walker continued to bring Americans into the country with promises of high salaries for serving in the military and gifts of hundreds of acres of land when their terms of service ended. Several new contingents of American fighters arrived in groups of between 50 and 150 after

---

34   Walker 1860, p. 75.
35   Walker 1860, pp. 153–4.
36   Walker 1860, p. 157.
37   May 2002, p. 175.

Walker's defeat of the Conservatives.[38] By March 1856, he estimated that there were 1,200 Americans capable of bearing arms present in Nicaragua.[39] Walker now sought and expected to receive recognition of the Rivas government by the government of President Franklin Pierce in the United States. But when Walker sent Parker H. French, a notorious soldier of fortune and swindler, as his ambassador to Washington, Pierce's Secretary of State William L. Marcy refused to recognise the Nicaraguan government or to accept French as its ambassador. The US denial of diplomatic recognition to Nicaragua was a terrible blow for Walker. Later, however, Pierce, then the Democratic Party incumbent candidate for the presidency desirous of southern political support for his campaign, reversed himself and recognised Nicaragua's government.

In June of 1856, Walker removed Rivas from the presidency, accusing him of being a traitor in league with other Central American governments planning to overthrow Walker's government. Walker named one of his associates, Fermín Ferrer, to be interim president until an election could be held. That fraudulent election held on 29 June made Walker president with 16,000 of 23,000 votes cast by the voting upper classes in a country with a population of over 250,000. Angry at having been betrayed by Walker and realising that not only Nicaragua but all of Central America might fall to the American filibuster, Rivas and some other former Nicaraguan officials and Nicaraguan Army officers went off to the other Central American capitals to convince their governments to raise armies and drive Walker out.[40]

Walker's filibustering campaign in Nicaragua made him a hero to much of the South and to many in the North of the United States. He was lauded in southern newspapers, poems and plays were written about him, and southern politicians praised him while some northern politicians excoriated him. Walker had no greater or more influential booster than Pierre Soulé, the former US Senator and slavery advocate whom he had met during his time as editor of the New Orleans *Crescent*. Soulé was notorious at the time for his role as Minister to Spain and the principal author of the Ostend Manifesto, a document published by the US House of Representatives, which argued that the United States should offer to buy Cuba, but if refused should take the island through force. Since both England and France supported Spain in keeping possession of Cuba, the manifesto was provocative and dangerous.[41] Reaction

---

38   Brown 1980, pp. 308–10.

39   Walker 1860, p. 159.

40   May 2002, p. 48.

41   Soulé feared that the 'Africanisation' of Cuba would lead either to another slave revolution

to the Manifesto was so hostile in the North and in Europe that it was quickly dropped and no resolution ever passed.

With the hopes of acquiring Cuba dashed, Soulé turned to Nicaragua. Soulé raised funds for Walker by selling Nicaraguan land – as much as $500,000 – to New Orleans merchants with the promise that Nicaragua would become part of the United States as a slave state.[42] As head of the Louisiana delegation to the Democratic Party Convention taking place in Cincinnati, Ohio, in June of 1856 and as a member of the platform committee, Soulé also drafted a plank in the party platform alluding to Walker and expressing support for US expansion in Central America. Then, in August of 1856, Soulé went to Nicaragua to support and to advise Walker who had by then become president.[43]

Walker in Power: Programme for a Society Based on Slavery

Walker was now the dictator of Nicaragua, his power dependent upon his small army – much like other prior and future rulers of Nicaragua. Once he was inaugurated as president on 12 July, Walker proceeded to carry out his political programme. First, Walker reintroduced slavery, an institution that had been abolished in Nicaragua in 1838.[44] While Soulé may have advised him, this was Walker's decision, and, as he saw it, his most important one. As Walker later wrote in his memoir *War in Nicaragua*, 'By this act must the Walker administration be judged; for it is the key to his whole policy ... for on the establishment of African slavery depended the permanent presence of the white race in that region'.[45] That is, Walker's goal was the establishment

---

such as that which had taken place in Haiti, or to the freeing of the slaves which would make the acquisition of the island impossible for the American South, both undesirable developments threatening to the United States. The Manifesto reads: 'After we shall offer Spain a price for Cuba far beyond its present value, and this shall have been refused, it will then be time to consider the question: Does Cuba, in the possession of Spain, seriously endanger the internal peace of our whole nation? Should this question be answered in the affirmative, then by every law, human and divine, we shall be justified in wresting it from Spain, if we possess the power; and this upon the very same principle that would justify an individual in tearing down the burning house of his neighbor, if there were no other means of preventing the flames from destroying his own home'; Cited in Webster 1893, pp. 1–32.

42   Brown 1980, p. 351.

43   May 1973, pp. 106–7; Moore 1955, pp. 203–23.

44   The other Central American republics abolished slavery in 1824.

45   Walker 1860, pp. 252–3.

of a white colonial settler state in Nicaragua based on the exploitation of African labour, a regime modelled on the slave states of the American South. Walker's reinstitution of slavery in Nicaragua was also intended to win material assistance from the Southern states which could now look with hope to the expansion of the South's peculiar institution of slavery to Central America.

While Walker had the immediate objective of southern support in mind, he also had a broader vision, the creation of a higher form of civilisation, as he saw it, organised along racial-caste and class lines and dominated by a white ruling class:

> The introduction of negro-slavery into Nicaragua would furnish a supply of constant and reliable labour requisite for the cultivation of tropical products. With the negro-slave as his companion, the white man would become fixed to the soil; and they together would destroy the power of the mixed race which is the bane of the country. The pure Indian would readily fall into the new social organisation; for he does not aim at political power, and only asks to be protected in the fruits of his industry. The Indian of Nicaragua, in his fidelity and docility, as well as in his capacity for labour, approaches nearly the negroes of the United States; and he would readily assume the manners and habits of the latter. In fact the manners of the Indian toward the ruling race are now more submissive than those of the American negro toward his master.[46]

Meanwhile, until there were enough African slaves, Walker's government decreed that persons without visible means of support would be charged with vagrancy and sentenced to forced labour on public workers. And any worker who had entered into a contract with another person and failed to fulfil it would be sentenced to forced labour.[47] The chief goal of Walker's policy was clearly to provide labour for landowners and to make Nicaragua attractive to white investors in agriculture.

As part of his national project, Walker also made English, in addition to Spanish, an official language of Nicaragua; in truth, English became in effect the primary official language. As Brown writes, the very purpose of the English language decree was 'to facilitate the domination of the country by the Anglo-Saxon race'. Walker himself explained the reason for introducing the English language: 'The decree concerning the use of the two languages tended to

---

46   Walker 1860, p. 261.
47   Brown 1980, p. 352.

make the ownership of the lands of the State fall into the hands of those speaking English'.[48] This was part of a broader programme of land reform. He declared that the Nicaraguan state would confiscate and sell all the lands belonging to enemies of the state and that the American soldiers who had fought in Nicaragua could purchase those lands with the military scrip with which they had been paid. In addition, all of Nicaragua's land titles had to be recorded within six months, a policy that was intended to sweep away preexisting Spanish or Nicaraguan land grants which had indeterminate time limits. In general, Spanish land law was to be replaced by English-American land law. As Walker makes clear, 'The general tendency of these several decrees was the same; they were intended to place a large proportion of the land of the country in the hands of the white race'.[49]

Beyond Nicaragua, Walker had other imperial ambitions. He saw Nicaragua as providing a base for the conquest of all of Central America, Cuba and the other islands of the Caribbean as well. Walker wanted to extend slavery to Nicaragua and other Central American countries, hoping that this would strengthen the US South in its struggle with the North. But, interestingly, in his memoir *War in Nicaragua* and in proclamations at the time, Walker denied that he wanted to join Nicaragua to the United States. In fact, Walker urged his southern compatriots and the United States to forestall annexing both Nicaragua and Cuba.[50] He argued that the South was already too compromised by its relations to the northern Free States. At the same time, the former Spanish territories with their debased mixed-race populations, their slaveless societies, and their decadent civilisations were already too problematic to be incorporated into the United States. Walker wanted to make Nicaragua an object lesson for the South, showing that the only alternative for the South was to expand slavery to other subject nations.[51] Walker saw that slavery had to become imperialist, though his own megalomaniac ambition of becoming emperor of Central America and the Caribbean came to be more important than his American or Southern patriotism.

---

48   Walker 1860, p. 252.
49   Walker 1860, pp. 253–4; May 2002, p. 196.
50   Stiles 2009, p. 290.
51   Walker 1860, pp. 260–70.

Vanderbilt vs. Walker

Furious that Walker's conquest of Nicaragua and his seizure of the ATC steam-boats were threatening his economic empire, Cornelius Vanderbilt began to act on several fronts: political lobbying, economic pressure, and the organisation of his own agents with their own small forces to attempt to defeat Walker militarily. Vanderbilt travelled to Washington to meet with Secretary of State Marcy and urged him to take action to 'sustain the rights of American citizens in Nicaragua', – namely his right to run his shipping line on the rivers and lakes there. He also got in contact with Senator John M. Clayton, a former secretary of state, whom he convinced to denounce Walker on the Senate floor. Still neither the administration nor Congress was willing to take action.[52]

On the business side, the ATC board voted to give Vanderbilt 'full powers to conduct all such negotiations and do such acts as in his judgment might be necessary'.[53] Vanderbilt then immediately announced that the ATC was shutting down its Nicaragua line because he no longer considered travel through that country to be safe, though his ships would continue to travel to Panama. Stopping at least some of the steamship traffic to Nicaragua would help to isolate Walker and prevent him from receiving men and munitions via Vanderbilt's own shipping line.

In the diplomatic arena, Vanderbilt began discussions with the emissaries of the Central American governments, all of which were alarmed at Walker's depredations in Nicaragua and feared that they would be next on his list. Juan Rafael Mora, president of Costa Rica, a nation allied with Great Britain, was already planning war against Nicaragua and agreed to cooperate with Vanderbilt. Since President Pierce had recognised Walker's government, this agreement placed Vanderbilt on the side of Great Britain at a time when the United States and Great Britain were engaged in a low level yet quite serious struggle over control of Central America. With Vanderbilt urging him on, Mora raised an army of 3,000 men and on 1 March 1856 declared war on Nicaragua, the beginning of what Nicaraguans call the National War of 1856–7. Mora led his troops into Nicaragua, but was defeated, in part by Walker's Nicaraguan Army and in part by a cholera epidemic that swept through his army. A few months later, Costa Rica once again invaded Nicaragua, soon followed by Honduras and El Salvador, with Vanderbilt's encouragement and Great Britain providing arms and surreptitious support for the Central Americans.

---

52   Stiles 2009, p. 281.
53   Stiles 2009, p. 283.

Vanderbilt meanwhile sent his own agent to Nicaragua to retake control of the ATC's boats so that they could not be used to control the lake and to supply Walker with reinforcements. Vanderbilt chose Sylvanus Spencer, an experienced seaman once accused and acquitted of murder, to go to Costa Rica to meet with President Mora and lay out Vanderbilt's plan to retake his fleet. Mora, convinced by Spencer's arguments, by the $40,000 sent to cover expenses, and by the cases of modern rifles and ammunition, made Spencer a captain and put him at the head of 250 Costa Rican troops. Spencer proceeded through a series of clever manoeuvres to take command of the ATC boats on Lake Nicaragua with the tacit support of the British commander of a squadron of warships. Spencer then turned over the ATC fleet to President Mora who used the boats to cross Lake Nicaragua and attack Walker's 900 Nicaraguan Army troops at the city of Rivas in January 1857, defeating the filibuster. Walker recovered and the Costa Rican forces were driven back, but they launched a second attack and Mora and his army then marched on to Walker's capital at Granada. As Walker's troops fled without a fight, one of his mercenary officers, General Charles Frederick Henningsen, ordered the city of Granada to be blown up and burned, leaving a sign on a spear reading, 'Here was Granada'.

Fleeing the victorious Central American armies, Walker surrendered to the United States Navy on 1 May 1857 and was repatriated. In New Orleans, he received a hero's welcome, speaking for two hours to an enthusiastic crowd of 20,000 people and calling upon them to join with him 'to Americanise Nicaragua'.[54] In Washington, President Buchanan, a Democrat, invited Walker to the White House, while in New York City Walker received a standing ovation from the crowd at Wallack's Theater. No doubt encouraged by the widespread public support, Walker returned to Central America on another filibustering mission in 1857, but was arrested by the US Navy and again tried for violation of the Neutrality Act and again acquitted. Once again, a few months later, Walker was back in Central America, but this time he was arrested by the British Navy which turned him over to the Honduran government, which executed him by firing squad on 12 September 1860.[55]

Walker was defeated by the soldiers of the allied Central American nations, by those mixed-race peoples whom he looked down upon as racial inferiors. A British diplomat estimated that the Central American war against Walker had taken the lives of 40,000 Nicaraguans, Costa Ricans, Guatemalans, Hondurans and Salvadorans. The Nicaraguans paid the heaviest price in terms of both the

---

54   Rosegarten 1978, p. 178.
55   May 2002, pp. 50–1.

loss of human life and the destruction of property. Granada, one of the country's two important cities, was left little more than ruins.[56]

What sort of conclusions can we draw from the history of Vanderbilt's and Walker's involvement in Nicaragua? The most obvious is that Central America and the Caribbean were a region of diplomatic, economic, and sometimes military struggle between Great Britain and the United States, both struggling to control it. America had grown in the half century since it was founded to become an economically and politically powerful country with expanding economic interests – and consequently geopolitical interests – in Central America and the Caribbean. In the 1850s, the conflict over slavery in the United States tended to shape its international interventions as well as to inhibit them, and divided at home the United States was not always effective when it acted abroad. The filibusters like Walker, mostly allied with the slave South, refused to be constrained by American politics or the State Department. As long as Nicaragua remained a small, sparsely populated and economically backward nation whose divided ruling class had failed to forge a state capable of resisting them, the British and the Americans would continue to attempt to control the country, and filibusters like Walker might return, though with the American victory in the Spanish-American War of 1898, the British ceased to be a significant factor in the Caribbean, which became 'the American lake'. The United States would become the dominant imperial power and Nicaragua's nemesis.

We see in the interventions of Vanderbilt and Walker the two classic strategies of American imperialism in the nineteenth century. Walker represents the older strategy of conquest and acquisition used throughout the westward movement of the United States against native peoples and most spectacularly in the defeat of Mexico and the acquisition of half of its territory, though it would also continue in Hawaii as well as in Cuba, Puerto Rico and the Philippines.[57] Vanderbilt's economic intervention, on the other hand, was more typical of modern US imperialism, where territory was never formally conquered and acquired, but economic interests, backed by the American state, came to influence and even control governments. During the period of 1900 to 1930, the United States would become the hegemonic power in Central America and the Caribbean, though – with the exception of Cuba and Puerto Rico – it would primarily dominate through economic investment accompanied by military interventions of varying lengths, without the formal acquisition of colonies.

---

56   Stile 2009, pp. 292–9.
57   While Cuba never became an actual colony of the United States, the Platt Amendment made it a virtual colony.

Walker's defence of slavery was, of course, reactionary in the purest sense of the word, an attempt to create a society on forms of property and labour – the plantation slavery system – being made obsolescent by the growth of capitalism and the uneven spread of representative and increasingly democratic forms of government. Yet the assumption of white racial and cultural superiority that informed Walker's mission would continue to be found in future American involvement in Nicaragua. So too would his notion that Americans knew best what was good for the Nicaraguan people and other Central Americans. Throughout the twentieth century, American leaders continued to think of the United States as the centre and the nations of Central America as its satellites.

One of the lessons of the Walker mission in Nicaragua, one that would be grasped in the future by both Anastasio Somoza García and by the *comandantes* of the Sandanista Front for National Liberation (FSLN), was that a relatively small body of highly disciplined armed men under a centralised leadership, if they acted decisively and had the support of some significant faction of the country's elites and at least the passive support of a sizable proportion of the population at large, could take control of a small country like Nicaragua. Walker's use of land reform, the seizing of the land of disloyal Nicaraguans (that is, opponents of Walker) and its redistribution to his supporters, followed the example of the Spanish conquest and the post-colonial Liberal reformers, but it also anticipated the land reform of the FSLN and later of Violeta Chamorro. Land reform – either concentrating it or distributing it – would be central to the programme of any group taking power because Nicaragua was an agricultural country and land was the central means of production.

The Thirty Year Regime (1858–93)

Nicaragua's historically weak state was at its weakest in the period immediately after Walker's brief period of rule. After the defeat of Walker in the National War, Nicaragua, still deeply divided between the Liberals in Leon and the Conservatives in Granada, might well have become two rival states or might have been absorbed in part or whole by other Central American nations or perhaps by Mexico. Such a development was prevented when the Liberal Máximo Jerez and the Conservative Tomás Martínez joined together to create a bipartisan Provisional National Government.[58]

---

58   Pérez-Baltodano 2008, pp. 249–52.

The Constituent Assembly was convened and wrote a new Constitution of 1858 which embodied the terms of the Pact of the Oligarchy – an agreement between Nicaragua's wealthiest families – on which the new Nicaraguan government was to be based. The Pact, which formed the basis for the Thirty Year Regime (1858–93), was predicated on, on the one hand, collaboration among the elites and, on the other, the exclusion of the majority of Nicaraguans from politics by imposing literacy and property qualifications that made them ineligible to vote. The Republic was not intended for the mestizos, the mulattoes, and the Indians. During these thirty years, the Conservatives held the presidency while the Liberals generally had a large presence in the legislature. The judicial power was divided into two branches, one for Liberal Leon and one for Conservative Granada. Much power was invested in local prefects beholden to the local landlords. With the exception of two brief Liberal rebellions in 1867 and 1869, the Pact of the Oligarchy provided the basis for stable government for thirty years.[59]

Yet neither the Conservatives nor the Liberals had a vision for the future of a genuinely unified Nicaragua, their goal being fundamentally the preservation of the existing order and their respective roles in it. Unlike other Central American states which had begun to produce coffee and other export products for the world capitalist market, Nicaragua remained an isolated region, with little insertion into the global economy. The Conservatives, reacting to changes taking place in the Central American region and in the international market, implemented a moderately liberal economic programme, beginning with the first steps in the construction of a modern infrastructure: stagecoach routes, railways and telegraph lines. As historians have argued, railroad construction was due more to the ready availability of foreign capital and technology than it was to the Nicaraguan elite, many of whose members were not convinced of the need to build the railways. Progress was slow. The Conservatives spent years debating and laying plans for the construction of railroads, though construction only began during the last years of President Pedro Joaquín Chamorro Alfaro (1875–9) and by 1890 built only 130 kilometres of track (by 1940 it would have 378 kilometres). The telegraph was introduced in 1879 and the telephone in 1890, though few owned one.[60]

The Conservatives' other principal project, however, was not liberal in character; it was fundamentally conservative, even reactionary. They imposed a system of state and employer control over the labour force. The principal problem

---

59   Pérez-Baltodano 2008, pp. 253–5.
60   Pérez-Baltodano 2008, p. 325.

was that Nicaragua was a large territory with a sparse population. In agricultural societies where there is much more land than labour, there is an almost permanent condition of labour scarcity and of labour indiscipline, since peasants can acquire their own land either at no cost or at low prices and can then leave the labour market to engage in subsistence agriculture.

Unlike Mexico and some other Latin American nations, Nicaragua was not dominated by large haciendas employing a significant part of the labour force. The Nicaraguan economy's most important product in the early nineteenth century had been hides and tallow from cattle driven to pasture by a small workforce of cowboys. Most Nicaraguans had small plots of land, *milpas*, where they produced corn, beans, and greens for subsistence. Indigo and cacao remained important plantation crops in that period as well, though they did not encompass a large part of the land and labour force. In Nicaragua, most farmers were smallholders; the minifundia not the latafundia prevailed. Even as late as 1880, 90 percent of all landholders owned less than 50 *manzanas*, with the average being 8.5 *manzanas*[61] (1 manzana = 1.68 acres). Owning their own land and being able to feed their families, they did not feel obligated to work for landlords with large plantations. But with coffee growing in importance from the 1840s on, and becoming the principal export crop by the 1870s, the labour problem took on greater urgency for plantation owners, leading to the new authoritarian land and labour laws.

During colonial times, the government – a government of Spanish officials, landlords and merchants – had created systems of forced labour and tribute to insure landlords a reliable workforce. Forced labour was theoretically abolished in the early nineteenth century, though peasants still often paid rent in labour services or in kind. By the mid-nineteenth century, Liberals and some Conservatives had become committed in theory to attempting to create a free labour market, though in practice they created a system of debt peonage that would last into the twentieth century. Employers advanced money to peasant families who remained indebted, sometimes for generations, tying them to the employer's plantation. Debt peonage was complemented by forced labour laws. Nicaragua's Conservative government of the Thirty Year Regime passed laws against vagrancy, which in effect created a system of mandatory labour. To enforce the labour laws, in 1859 the Nicaraguan government created agricultural magistrates with broad powers to compel peasants to report for work on the landlords' plantations. The Agricultural Law of 1862 forced peasants, who the authorities had determined had no job or means of subsistence, to work for

---

61   Wolfe 2004, p. 61.

the planters. In 1867, the legislature created a special police force to assist the rural magistrates in enforcing these agricultural labour laws.

As coffee boomed in the 1880s, new laws were passed giving the authorities the power 'to pursue, capture, and remit fugitive workers'. The state created a blacklist of runaway workers, provided by the hacienda and coffee plantation workers, which it distributed to the local authorities. The telegraph system was made available to landowners for free so that they could report on fugitive workers. When nothing else worked, local planters and officials organised extra-legal labour drafts to provide a workforce for the plantations. If the authorities failed to deal with fugitive or delinquent workers, plantation foremen frequently detained, whipped, and locked up the recalcitrant labourers. Of course, workers resisted all of these measures through individual escape or flight in small groups as well as occasionally through armed resistance with their machetes.[62]

One other response to the labour problem would be to bring the indigenous population into the labour market. The Conservatives, however, made little headway on that front. Nicaragua had a population of about 275,000 in the 1860s; the indigenous people represented a significant proportion of the population, about ten to twenty percent. Bringing them onto the labour market would help relieve labour shortages if it could be achieved. Since colonial times, Spanish and later Nicaraguan *criollo* landlords had encroached on the Indians' lands through a combination of legal action, intimidation, and force. Nevertheless the Indian communities remained in control of hundreds of thousands of acres of land of their own. When Indians were forced to work on the plantations, they also resisted through flight, through legal cases, and occasionally through armed rebellions. While landlords did continue to encroach on indigenous community lands, there was no concerted Conservative push to create a legal or concerted extra-legal mechanism for taking the Indian lands.

The Conservative's infrastructure projects built with Indian labour and the planters' expanding demands for indigenous labour for the coffee plantations led to a major Indian rebellion in the town of Matagalpa in 1881. The Indians complained that they were being forced to work on the construction of the telegraph lines for low wages, that they feared that their women would be sent to Managua to pick coffee for nothing, and that their children would be 'sold to the Yankees'. They also objected to the census, which was used for taxing them and for military conscription purposes, and they opposed the prohibition against making *chichi*, their corn liquor.

---

62   Pérez-Baltodano 2008, pp. 288–9; Wolfe 2004, pp. 57–83; Dore 2003, pp. 521–59.

After an initial rebellion in March, in July some 5,000 Indians launched a guerrilla war against the government. In August, they rose up and attacked the city of Matagalpa shocking the *criollo* elite. The Conservative government, declaring a struggle of 'civilisation against barbarism', convinced some Indians to support and join the government troops, and with the Indians divided, the rebellion was crushed. The government's victory over Matagalpa's indigenous communities left the natives defeated and divided; yet, only three years later, some of the Indians joined another anti-government movement.[63] The Conservative government failed to take advantage of the Indian defeat to dismantle the community and take its land, while the Indians were too divided and isolated to lead a general rebellion, and as a small minority of the population they could not hope to overthrow the government.

Under the Conservative presidents, Nicaragua at the end of the nineteenth century remained a backward, stagnant society not much different from what it had been in colonial times. Failing to recognise and adapt to the changes taking place in Central America and the rest of the world, the Conservatives had become a barrier to the future development of the Nicaraguan economy. But change could not be stopped. In the late nineteenth and twentieth century, three different forces would change Nicaragua and, for better or worse, bring it into the modern world: the Liberals, the United States, and the Nicaraguan people.

---

63   Gould 1973, pp. 400–1.

The Struggle to Construct a Sovereign State: Zelaya and Sandino (1893–1932)

The Conservatives had done little to change Nicaragua, but the country was changing anyway. The reason was coffee. The rise of coffee, which by the 1880s had become a boom crop, transformed Nicaragua's economic and political system. Coffee drew Nicaragua into the modern global economy as never before and for a simple reason: there was money to be made. The coffee planter class, many of whom lived in Managua, grew in importance, competing with the old elite groups based in Granada and León. Around the large coffee planters there developed a constellation of medium and small coffee planters, merchants, professionals and new immigrants who were also taking advantage of the opportunities in the world market.

The coffee planters and their social entourage had new interests and needs that could not be met by the traditional elites and certainly not by the Conservative government. They had new demands for capital investment that would require more modern financial institutions. They had a desire for better education that could not be fulfilled by the Catholic schools. And they had a somewhat different and more liberal view of the role of women in society. They wished to see a more dynamic development of the railroad and telegraph system and improvements in the shipping ports. In most of Nicaragua, about the size of the State of New York but with a population of only 321,000 in 1890, there was a constant labour shortage. And then there was also the 'Indian problem' as it was called. The coffee planters wanted to get hold of the Indians' land and wanted to be able to employ the Indians' and other peasants' labour. The coffee planter class based in Managua became a new axis of power within the society, one that implicitly challenged the Pact of the Oligarchy, the Constitution of 1858, and the ruling Conservative party.[1]

The older order, unable to respond to changing conditions, began to disintegrate and then to collapse. In May of 1893, Robert Sacasa, the last president of the Thirty Year Regime and the first victim of the rising coffee planters, was pressured to resign in favour of a bipartisan provisional government. Then, just a month later, there was a coup. In León, home of the Liberals, the military

---

1 Pérez-Baltodano 2008, p. 286.

rebelled against the first provisional government and established a rival provisional government, this one headed by José Santos Zelaya. Zelaya soon became head of the Nicaraguan state and the dominant figure in Central America for the next sixteen years. His regime, characterised by economic development and the assertion of Nicaragua's sovereignty, represented the attempt to create a modern, sovereign republic, though it was doomed to failure by the Colossus of the North, for just as Zelaya came to power, America was tightening its grip on Central America and the Caribbean.

Like so many of the important figures in Nicaraguan history (and for that matter in all of Latin American history), Zelaya was a *hijo natural*, a bastard, the son of a wealthy man and his lower class mistress. He was born on 1 November 1853, the son of José María Zelaya and his mistress Juana López Ramírez. Sent as a young man by his father to study in France and Belgium, he was exposed to modern, liberal ideas. After graduating from the Lycée Hoche in Versailles, he returned to Nicaragua in 1875 and became involved in the Liberal Party. In 1883, he was elected mayor of Managua, the capital of the rising coffee planter class, and soon became the undisputed leader of the Liberal Party nationally. A conspirator and a rebel, he became involved in a coup and in 1884 was expelled from Nicaragua by Conservative President Adán Cárdenas. Zelaya's banishment only hardened his Liberal politics while it also gave him a chance to put them into effect, albeit in another country.

Zelaya went into exile in Guatemala where he collaborated in the Liberal government of Justo Rufino Barrios, the figure most responsible for the liberal transformation of that country and at the time the dominant figure in Central America.[2] Zelaya participated in 1885 in Barrios's attempt to unify all of Central America into one nation again, as it had been united ever so briefly after independence. Zelaya's experience in Barrios's militantly liberal government had an enormous influence on the young Nicaraguan's political outlook. Consequently, when back in Nicaragua both Liberals and Conservatives turned against Sacasa, it was to be expected that Zelaya would be involved in the provisional government of which he quickly became the head. The civilian transfer of power, however, quickly became a military conflict. At the *Batalla de la Cuesta*, fought in late July 1893, Zelaya defeated the provisional government forces, clearing his way to power. Zelaya, the Liberal Party, and the rising coffee planter class had become the new rulers of Nicaragua.

---

2 Luján Muñoz 2002, pp. 175–202. In imposing a Liberal regime on Guatemala, Barrios was ruthless in his dealings with the indigenous people and labourers.

In September, a Constituent Assembly elected Zelaya provisional president as well as president for the first new constitutional term. In his inaugural address, Zelaya called upon the Assembly to break with the 'absolutism' and 'theocracy' of the conservatives and to begin the process of developing and perfecting Nicaragua.[3] On 10 December 1893, the Assembly adopted the new constitution called La Libérrima (The Freest) that went into effect on 4 July 1894, the date chosen in honour of the United States, the first republic of the New World. La Libérrima was a remarkable document representing the dismantling of the Thirty Years Regime and the construction of a new, liberal, national state. The original version of La Libérrima represented one of the most progressive constitutions of the time with advanced civil rights and human rights principles.

Under La Libérrima, all Nicaraguans became citizens with the right to vote at the age of eighteen if they were literate or married; the property requirements found in the Conservative Constitution of 1858 were ended. The new constitution abolished the death penalty, established the writ of habeas corpus, granted the right of prisoners to communicate with those outside of the prison, and called upon authorities to exhibit prisoners whose lives might be in danger in custody (to prevent beating or torture), as well as establishing the right of prisoners to a legal defence. Imprisonment for debt was abolished as well. The new constitution annulled the Concordat of 1861 which had made Catholicism the state religion and had given the church responsibility for education. Under the Libérrima, a secular regime was created, with free, lay, public education, accompanied by the secularisation of cemeteries and the establishment of civil marriage. It was a revolution in law. Yet only a few years later – because of repeated challenges from both the Conservatives and from the society's underdogs that might have led to the overthrow of his government – the reforms of October 1896 eliminated virtually all of the Constitution's civil and human rights provisions.

Zelaya, having set aside the liberal Constitution, became an authoritarian president who used repressive legislation and police action to maintain his regime. He caused himself to be repeatedly re-elected by the National Assembly and he frequently declared a 'state of siege' to keep order, and he kept the press in check. He even considered making himself the formal and legal dictator of Nicaragua, though he ultimately rejected that idea, content to simply centralise power in the presidency. It did not matter what he called himself; the people's opinion prevailed. He has gone down in history as the 'dictator Zelaya'. To

---

3   Stanisfer 1974, p. 51.

insure his power, he revamped the army, establishing universal military service, created a new organisational structure, and provided the soldiers with modern equipment.[4] Conservative rebellions in 1896, 1899, and 1903 failed to unseat him and all were put down violently, though Zelaya did not (as the Somozas later did) arbitrarily imprison, torture, or murder his political opponents.[5] Zelaya's goal was neither the creation of a democratic republic nor the establishment of some sort of police state. He was interested exclusively in transforming Nicaragua into a fully modern capitalist society, one in which the capitalist class – principally landowners producing products for sale on the international market – would rule.

As a Liberal and leader of the coffee planter class, one of Zelaya's primary and immediate objectives was insuring adequate labour to tend and to harvest the coffee crop. In 1894, despite the Libérrima Constitution then in effect, his government reinstituted imprisonment for debt as a measure to keep the agricultural day labourers in place and at work. In the period from 1897–8, General William Reuling, Zelaya's political boss of Matagalpa, used coercion to force Indians to work on the plantations and collected tribute in the form of food contributions.[6] Such exploitation and oppression of the Indians, together with the crushing of any resistance, had gone on for 300 years, from colonial times through the Conservative regimes. What distinguished Zelaya's Liberal government was its attempt to finally eliminate the Indian problem altogether by abolishing the Indians' collective land ownership.

In 1906, the Nicaraguan Congress passed the Decree on Indigenous Communities and Ejidal Lands which declared: 'All common lands and Indian communities are extinguished for evermore'.[7] While this law was later overturned and Indian communities re-established, the 1906 legislation had an enormously destructive impact on native communities at the time, tending to dissolve the unity of the indigenous community, to undermine the religious and cultural practices that held it together, and to encourage Indians to sell their land to private investors. Sometimes the land that Indians and other non-indigenous peasants had used for grazing, for the collection of firewood, or to gain access to rivers and streams was declared to be vacant as a pretext for its seizure and sale. During Zelaya's regime, the government measured and titled half a million hectares (hectare = 2.47 acres) of 'vacant

---

4 Millett 1977, p. 21.
5 Stanisfer 1974, p. 52; Millet 1977, p. 22.
6 Gould 1973, p. 405.
7 Dore 2003, p. 528.

land', principally for coffee plantations.[8] Many Indians thus lost their land and many were thrown on the labour market as agricultural labourers. As a result of these and other measures, coffee production doubled after 1899. The reforms brought about an increase in the proletarianisation of the peasantry, though many Indians and peasants remained subsistence farmers or debt peons.[9]

Zelaya thus went far in achieving liberal objectives. The goals of the Liberals in Latin America throughout the nineteenth and early twentieth centuries were to found a liberal democratic state, to establish an economy where private property and free markets determined social relations, and to create a society of modern social classes, capitalists and wage earners, the former, of course, holding power. The objective everywhere then was to eliminate the corporative property of the Church and the Indians or peasant communities, to place the Church and Indian land on the real estate market, and to get the Indians and peasants on the labour market. At the same time, capitalists would take control of that land, creating plantations and agricultural processing industries (sugar refineries, coffee patios, lumber mills) and employing the former peasants who had been reduced to wage labourers. Zelaya was well on his way to fulfilling this agenda.

While capital and labour relations were at the centre of his concerns, Zelaya had other objectives as well. He aspired to make Nicaragua a modern state, which meant reforming nearly all aspects of the government, the economy, and society. He encouraged the continued development of the railroad and telegraph systems, of steamship lines, and of port facilities. He invited foreign investment and made sweeping concessions to American companies that invested in transportation, gold, lumber, and bananas mostly in eastern Nicaragua. He not only ended state patronage of the Catholic Church, but he also expelled the most vociferous of his clerical opponents, nationalised the property of the *cofradías* (the religious societies), banned the wearing of clerical garb on the streets, suppressed religious demonstrations, and, in general, worked to bring about a secularisation of Nicaraguan society, though it would remain a deeply religious society.[10]

Though many of his reforms were more aspirational than effective, some had a significant impact. Zelaya's government – in a country where there were, in 1893, virtually no public schools – made primary education free, lay, and

---

8   Stanisfer 1974, p. 55.
9   Biderman 1983, pp. 7–32.
10   Stanisfer 1974, p. 53.

obligatory. It also created high schools and trade schools in the country's most important cities. By the end of his administration, the government was spending ten percent of its budget on education and there were 20,000 students in school. A small number of students from both private and public schools were selected for study in Chile, Europe, or the United States. The university was reformed, creating modern academic departments for professional education on the French model. The army was also modernised. A military academy was founded, the army reorganised internally, a new machine gun unit created, and a small navy established with ships on the Caribbean and Pacific coasts as well as on Lake Nicaragua.[11]

One of Zelaya's most significant accomplishments was the reincorporation of the Mosquitia, the Caribbean coast of Nicaragua with its population of indigenous and English-speaking descendants of African slaves. La Mosquitia had never really been a part of Nicaragua under the Spanish or Nicaraguan governments, though the country had claimed the region since independence. The British, through a series of treaties with the Miskito Indians, had controlled it; politically, linguistically, and culturally it was part of the British Caribbean. But Zelaya was determined to change all that. First, he expelled the British Consul. Then in February of 1894, Zelaya sent general Rigoberto Cabezas at the head of Nicaraguan troops to take control of the city of Bluefields. Taking advantage of the shifting balance of power in Central America between the United States and Great Britain, Zelaya then negotiated the Harrison-Altamirano Treaty in 1905 in which Great Britain recognised Nicaragua's right to the Miskito Coast. Cabezas then became the inspector general for the region. While Zelaya looked down upon the Afro-Nicaraguan population of the region as racially inferior, his reassertion of Nicaragua's control of the region brought them under the Constitution of 1893 and made them citizens.[12]

Finally, as part of his modernisation programme, Zelaya continued to encourage the European immigration that had already begun during the Thirty Year Regime. A small number of British and German immigrants settled in Nicaragua, most of them establishing themselves as coffee planters in Matagalpa. European immigration was seen by both Conservatives and Liberals as a way of whitening and thereby civilising and uplifting Nicaragua's mestizo population. European immigrants brought capital and skills, as well as social and cultural expectations that helped to quicken the pace of development.

---

11 Pérez-Baltodano 2008, pp. 354–5.
12 Pérez-Baltodano 2008, pp. 355–8.

They also brought Protestant faiths that began in a small way to break the Catholic Church's religious monopoly.[13]

Zelaya's foreign policy and his regional ambitions would lead to his downfall. Like his mentor Barrios, Zelaya wished to create a United States of Central America, a federal government that could develop the region more efficiently and could more effectively resist the Great Powers and especially the United States. In 1886, he succeeded in bringing Honduras and El Salvador into a union known as the Greater Republic, though a change in the government in El Salvador led to its downfall only two years later. During the 1890s, he attempted through a series of conferences and pacts to bring about Central American unity, but when those failed he made war on Honduras in 1907 and invaded El Salvador twice in 1908. His army, using new machine guns, easily defeated the Honduran and Salvadoran forces. Mexico and the United States were both alarmed at his attempt to unify Central America and called conferences of the five small republics in an attempt to bring peace and to block Nicaragua.[14] Zelaya's failure through peaceful or belligerent methods to create a regional government in Central America left him weaker in the face of the United States.[15]

During the period of Zelaya's government, the role of the United States in the Caribbean and Central America changed dramatically. The United States had already under President James Monroe promulgated the Monroe Doctrine in 1823, claiming the right of the United States to act militarily to prevent European intervention in the Americas, though in fact, until after the US Civil War, Great Britain remained dominant in the Caribbean, Central and South America. The victory of the United States over Spain in the Spanish-American War of 1898 led to the American government taking effective control of Cuba while reducing Puerto Rico to a colony. Suddenly the United States had become the most important power in the Caribbean. Then, in 1903, the United States, through the ruse of fomenting a rebellion in Panama, succeeded in taking that territory from Colombia. The following year, the United States began work on the canal which was finished in August 1914, just in time for the First World War. The American control of Cuba, Puerto Rico, and Panama made it the hegemonic power in the Caribbean and Central America, while the building of the canal in Panama also changed Nicaragua's prospects and possibilities.

---

13   Pérez-Baltodano 2008, p. 358.
14   Millet 1977, p. 23.
15   Stanisfer 1974, p. 58.

In 1904, President Theodore Roosevelt, in what became known as the Roosevelt Corollary to the Monroe Doctrine, declared that the United States had the right to intervene in Latin American affairs any time that a country became so economically or politically vulnerable that it might invite European intervention. The Roosevelt Corollary was used, however, far more broadly to justify US intervention to protect American interests in Latin America, for example, by removing unfriendly or insufficiently deferential governments. By the late nineteenth century, Secretary of State James G. Blaine was arguing that, in addition to those policies, the United States should take a leading role in Latin America in order to open the region's markets to US exports. The first Pan-American Conference was held in 1889–90 in Washington, DC, and a series of them every few years thereafter. The Pan-American Conferences and the agreements reached at them during the early twentieth century provided for the arbitration of disputes, while at the same time the United States was prepared to engage in military intervention when such arbitration failed. Finally, in the era of William Howard Taft, the United States adopted the policy known as 'dollar diplomacy', the idea of using loans to, and investments in, other nations to strengthen ties to the United States; these economic investments then became American interests that might have to be protected by military intervention.[16]

Zelaya clearly recognised the growing danger that the United States represented to Nicaragua's sovereignty, so, to keep the US government at arm's length, he declined Wall Street loans, preferring instead to negotiate loans with the British government. He hoped that by balancing the British against the Americans, he could maintain Nicaragua's economic and political independence. Juan José Arévalo, the former president of Guatemala (1945–51), argues in his book *The Shark and the Sardines* that it was Zelaya's refusal to accept American loans that ultimately led to his overthrow and to the US intervention in Nicaragua.[17] Zelaya also cancelled or threatened to cancel concessions granted to foreign companies and it was alleged that he was considering granting rights to Germany or Japan to construct a transoceanic canal in Nicaragua. A foreign-owned canal in Nicaragua, which would have challenged America's domination of Central America and the Caribbean, was absolutely unacceptable. All of these measures antagonised the US government, including some cabinet members who had economic interests there, like Secretary of State Philander C. Knox who was an advisor to the US mining companies in Nicaragua.

---

16   Pérez-Baltodano 2008, pp. 360–6.
17   Arévalo 1961, p. 60.

As Zelaya wrote, 'The United States, whose imperialism is already too well known, had for some time been trying to exercise a protectorate over [Nicaragua] and endeavour[ed] to appropriate part of the isthmus for a Canal on the territory of Nicaragua ...'.[18] When Zelaya refused to accept American loans and to grant exclusive political and territorial concessions, the US government fomented a 'revolution'. In 1909, Adolfo Díaz, an accountant employed by the American mining companies in Nicaragua, working with the US State Department, organised a Conservative rebellion against Zelaya led by Governor Juan José Estrada who was based in Bluefields. Through Díaz, US corporations provided $600,000 to finance the Estrada rebellion and the United Fruit Company's ships carried the troops.[19]

When two Americans involved in the rebellion, Lee Roy Cannon and Leonard Gross, attempted to blow up a Nicaraguan troop ship, they were captured and executed. The execution of the two American mercenaries provided the occasion for the United States to break off diplomatic relations with Zelaya and to openly offer its political support to his opponents. Secretary of State Knox wrote his famous Note of 1 December 1910 declaring Zelaya's government 'a blot upon the history of Nicaragua and a discouragement to a group of republics whose aspirations need only the opportunity of free and honest government'.

Knox declared: 'The Government of the United States is convinced that the revolution represents the ideas and the will of a majority of the Nicaraguan people more faithfully than does the government of President Zelaya ...'.[20] Knox argued that Zelaya's government had violated the Pan-American conventions and international law, providing the justification for support for the Nicaraguan armed opposition and later for US intervention.[21] Threatened with American military intervention, Zelaya was forced to resign in favour of José Madriz. Madriz, however, continued to prosecute the war against the Estrada rebels, leading the US Navy to declare the city of Bluefields 'a neutral zone' so that US Marines could be landed there in order to prevent a Liberal victory. After a year of civil war, Madriz resigned and Estrada entered Managua on 23 August 1910. The Zelaya era was over. The United States was now in charge.

Zelaya, like Walker before him and Anastasio Somoza García and Daniel Ortega after him, was the *caudillo* whose power had originated in a military uprising and who dictated to his party and to the nation. More than any Nicaraguan leader before him, he laid the foundations for a modern nation state, the

---

18   Zelaya 1910, no page.
19   Arévalo 1961 p. 60.
20   Knox 1910, pp. 249–52.
21   Knox 1909, no page.

final construction of which would be carried out by the US government and Somoza. Working on the very limited basis of his Conservative forerunners, Zelaya took important steps not only to construct a modern state but also to create a capitalist economy. His overriding goal was the creation of a political-economic regime that would permit planters to make higher profits and accumulate capital more rapidly, a goal in which he was partially successful.[22] Lamentably, representative government, democracy, and social justice had no place in his programme. Zelaya's broader ambition, following his mentor the Guatemalan president Justo Rufino Barrios, that is, his desire to make himself the dominant figure in the region and to finally succeed in reuniting the Central American nations into a Central American federation, combined with his unwillingness to accept the demands and dictates of the United States, led to his overthrow by the American government.

The US Occupation of Nicaragua (1909–27)

With the overthrow of Zelaya, and 3,000 US troops in the country, the United States effectively took control of Nicaragua. The American-organised and American-financed rebellion ended with Estrada assuming the presidency, while Díaz, the bookkeeper of the American mining companies, served as vice-president. Estrada requested that the United States send a special commission to Nicaragua to resolve outstanding issues. US President William Howard Taft and Secretary Knox sent Thomas C. Dawson, a member of Knox's law firm and a career diplomat in Latin America, to negotiate with Estrada and Díaz. The Dawson Pact that they negotiated in 1910 provided for a Constituent Assembly to create a new Nicaraguan government, a mixed commission to deal with the claims, contracts and concessions, the pledge of a US loan to Nicaragua, and an election for a new president. The Dawson pact made the United States decisive in Nicaragua's political and economic development for the next 25 years. The US Marines, who had landed in 1909, occupied Nicaragua almost continuously from 1909 to 1933.

American capitalists owned much of the Nicaraguan economy and controlled important arms of the government as well. American Charles Butters and his Canadian partner Thayer Lindsley controlled the San Albino gold mine, the Bragman's Bluff Lumber Company controlled the Miskito Coast lumber industry, and other Americans found new opportunities in agriculture. Brown

---

22   Stanisfer 1974, pp. 47–59.

Brothers Bank and W. & J. Seligman took control of the country's finances, rail-roads, and the Bank of Nicaragua. They immediately arranged a $1.5 million loan to Nicaragua, part of a larger $15 million loan guaranteed by the country's customs revenues, with the customs houses now run by the Americans. An American veteran of the Teddy Roosevelt's Rough Riders, Greg Scull, took charge of reorganising the Managua police force, while the US ambassador in Managua advised the Conservative government.[23] As Sergio Ramírez summed up the situation, 'There did not remain a single strategic sector of that wholly backward economy that was not under American power, so that the oligarchic Conservative faction that returned to government in (1910) was nothing more than a bureaucratic intermediary of the American occupation'.[24]

To keep the Conservatives securely in power, the United States – even while it maintained a small Marine presence in Nicaragua – was forced repeatedly to intervene on a larger scale. General Luis Mena, who had earlier revolted against Zelaya, rebelled in 1912 against the Conservative government and the Liberal forces led by General Benjamín Zeledón and laid siege to Managua. Díaz once again called for a US intervention. The US Marines landed in August of 1912 and by the end of the summer their numbers had grown to over 2,700. Major General Smedley D. Butler landed at Corinto and another detachment occupied Bluefields.[25] General Zeledón was killed by the Marines as he defended Coyotepe Fortress and the City of Masaya, and his forces were defeated. Zeledón, the Liberal martyr, became, like the native warrior Diriangén of the colonial period, a national hero. The US forced the opposing Nicaraguan factions to reconcile. Díaz was elected president and General Emiliano Chamorro became Nicaraguan ambassador to the United States. Once again firmly in control, the United States government took the next step in its conquest of Nicaragua, obtaining the right to the canal, a canal it did not want to be built.

In August of 1914, Chamorro and US Secretary of State William Jennings Bryan negotiated the Bryan-Chamorro Treaty, a remarkable document that granted 'in perpetuity to the Government of the United States, forever free from all taxation or other public charge, the exclusive proprietary rights necessary and convenient for the construction, operation and maintenance of an interoceanic canal by way of the San Juan River and the great Lake of Nicaragua or by way of any other route over Nicaraguan territory'. The United States was also given a 99-year lease to the Corn Islands in the Caribbean and the right

---

23   Millet 1977, p. 30. Scull did not last long as Inspector General of the Managua Police
      because of conflicts with Díaz and Mena.
24   Sandino 1990, pp. 425–6.
25   Millet 1977, pp. 32–3.

to establish a base in the Gulf of Fonseca. In exchange, the US government agreed to pay Nicaragua three million dollars, though that was held in US banks and paid out to Nicaragua only as the United States pleased.[26] While the US government, which owned the Panama Canal, had no plan to fulfil Cornelius Vanderbilt's dream of a Nicaraguan canal, its possession of exclusive rights to build a Nicaraguan canal blocked rival powers from injecting themselves into the American sphere of influence.

The Conservatives governed occupied Nicaragua from 1910 until the elections of 1924 when a US-inspired electoral reform led to what has been called the freest and fairest election ever held in Nicaragua. The moderate Conservative Carlos Solórzano and the Liberal Dr. Juan Bautista Sacasa were elected president and vice-president, respectively, by a two-to-one majority, but because of a lack of a reliable military organisation, their government was vulnerable to yet another coup. Throughout the early 1920s, the United States was concerned about instability in the Caribbean and Central America – stability being important US corporate investments – and came to the conclusion that the highly politicised and corrupt military organisations of the nations in that region needed to be replaced by non-partisan constabularies, disciplined forces trained by the United States. In 1923, the US government began to pressure Central American governments to sign treaties in which they pledged to create such National Guard forces.[27]

The US had trained such forces in the Philippines, Haiti and the Dominican Republic, though Nicaragua resisted pressures to create such a police force until the election of Solórzano, who took office in January of 1925. In February of that year, the US State Department submitted to Solórzano a plan to create a force of 23 officers and 392 men which would replace the existing police, army, and navy of Nicaragua. Because of Nicaraguan popular and congressional opposition to the creation of a force that might oppose a popular revolution, the plan was changed, establishing a new police force that would not replace the army. That plan was accepted, and retired US Army Major Calvin B. Carter became the Chief of the Constabulary and head of the School of Instruction of the National Guard. The creation of the guard allowed for the US withdrawal of the Marines in August of 1925.[28]

With the election of Solórzano and the withdrawal of the US Marines from Nicaragua, it appeared that the country might be returning to at least the

---

26 Sandino 1990, p. 9.

27 Millet 1977, pp. 41–2.

28 Millet 1977, pp. 42–3.

appearance of independence and normalcy. Within weeks, however, Díaz and Chamorro revolted, forcing Solórzano to resign. The Nicaraguan Congress named Chamorro president, but the US government refused to recognise either Vice-President Sacasa or the usurper Chamorro. The newly created National Guard, underfunded and made up of raw recruits, disintegrated under the impact of these events.[29] When the Liberals seized the port Bluefields, the US Marines landed and once again established 'neutral zones' that prevented a Liberal military victory. With the Marines having re-established order on American terms, the Nicaraguan Congress then elected Aldofo Díaz president once again, and US President Calvin Coolidge quickly recognised his government.

Nevertheless, the Liberal Juan Sacasa's so-called Constitutionalist Government continued to wage a civil war against the Conservative Chamorro and Díaz factions. Fearing Sacasa might lead the Liberals to victory, Adolfo Díaz called once again for US intervention. Six thousand Marines landed and, in what was this time a full-scale occupation of the country, took control of the nation's ports, railroads, and major cities. World public opinion, especially Latin American opinion, was shocked and outraged by the American military invasion and reoccupation of Nicaragua in 1926. But US Undersecretary of State Robert Olds justified the extensive intervention, arguing that Central America and Panama constitute 'a legitimate sphere of influence of the United States'. The United States, after all, he said, had to protect its considerable economic interests in Nicaragua. 'Central America has always understood that governments which we recognize and support stay in power, while those which we do not recognize and support fall. Nicaragua has become a test case. It is difficult to see how we can afford to be defeated'.[30]

US President Calvin Coolidge sent Major Henry L. Stimson, former secretary of war, to Nicaragua to 'straighten things out'.[31] Stimson and Díaz offered the Liberals the following proposal: there would be an immediate end to hostilities; both armies would hand over their weapons to the United States; there would be a general amnesty and return of exiles; Díaz would agree to include some Liberals in his cabinet; the government would create a constabulary or National Guard to be commanded by US officers; the United States would supervise the 1928 election and future elections; and the U.S. Marines would remain to enforce the agreement. Stimson presented these terms to General Moncada and the Liberal representatives, perhaps having threatened them with the use

---

29   Millet 1977, p. 47.

30   Sandino 1990, p. 9.

31   Morrison 1966, p. 223.

of force if they did not accept. In the end, they did accept, and at the town of Tipitapa the Peace of Espino Negro was signed.[32] Sacasa protested against the agreement and he and a small group of supporters left for exile in Costa Rica. All of Moncada's generals, however, accepted the agreement – except one, an obscure and insignificant figure named Augusto C. Sandino. President Coolidge told the 6,000 Marines in Nicaragua: 'Get Sandino dead or alive'.[33]

Not all Americans agreed with the Marine intervention in Nicaragua or Stimson's role in negotiating the treaty. Progressive Republicans were particularly outspoken. US Senator Burton K. Wheeler told the Senate: 'The State Department has literally gutted Nicaragua ... Its sovereignty is a ghastly mockery ... The country in its every aspect is absolutely under the merciless heel of the State Department and the New York bankers. Every strategic post, fiscal and military, is in the hands of appointees of the State Department'.[34] Other US Senators, such as Lynn J. Frazier of North Dakota and William E. Borah of Idaho, also sharply criticised the Coolidge administration for its actions in Nicaragua, as did a small but vocal progressive, anti-imperialist minority of the American people; but the majority of Congress supported the president's imperial policies, as did the press and therefore most Americans. As the Senators understood, between 1910 and 1927, the United States had dictated to the Nicaraguan Conservative governments the policies they would pursue, and they in turn created an economy organised around the interest of American banks and corporations. Nicaragua was transformed into a virtual colony of the United States.

Most Nicaraguans came to loathe the United States. As one American coffee planter in Nicaragua wrote in 1931: 'Today we are hated and despised. This feeling has been created by employing the US Marines to hunt down and kill Nicaraguans in their own country'.[35]

Sandino the Rebel

The one Liberal general who had refused to sign the Peace of Espino Negro, Augusto C. Sandino, decided that he would continue the struggle against the Conservative government and against the United States which had imposed Conservative government and the treaty on the Nicaraguan people, even if

32   On the question of Stimson's possible threat of force, see Morrison 1966, p. 229, fn. 14.
33   Diederich 2007, p. 16.
34   Sandino 1990, p. 10.
35   LeoGrande 1998, p. 13.

he had to do so alone. He and what came to be called his 'crazy little army' would spend seven years fighting both the Nicaraguan National Guard and the US Marines, only agreeing to sign a peace when the Marines finally left the country.

Sandino was born on 18 May 1893 in the town of Niquinohomo, about fifteen miles from Granada. His father Don Gregorio Sandino, a descendant of Spanish immigrants, was a moderately wealthy landowner; his mother Margarita Calderón was an Indian peasant who worked on the Sandino plantations. The couple never lived together; both parents were still under 18 when their illegitimate child was born. Since he had no legal father, Sandino was named Augusto Calderón. His father later married another woman, Doña América, and they had several other children who grew up in their comfortable home, while Sandino spent his first several years living with his impoverished mother. She worked picking coffee on the plantations, gave birth to several children by different fathers, and often could not clothe or feed her family. Finally she left for Granada, but the nine-year-old Sandino did not accompany her, and instead stayed with his equally impoverished maternal grandmother.

Sandino himself grew up labouring in the coffee fields with his mother, later working odd jobs, and, when necessary, stealing from the plantations to get food. He later told a reporter that at the age of 11, he confronted his father on the street and asked why he was not treated like his brother Socrates, whom he had met. Moved by Sandino's words, so the story goes, his father took Sandino to live with his wife and legitimate children. By the age of 14, and now called Augusto Calderón Sandino, he was living with his father and attending the local school where he proved a mediocre student, more interested in playing war with the other boys than studying. In his father's home, he read the classics and history, and through reading and conversation he absorbed his father's Liberal political philosophy. Impressed by the Roman general and statesman Julius Caesar, Sandino changed his middle name to César, the first indication that he believed himself to be destined for greatness. After attending the commercial high school in Granada, Sandino returned home to work for his father as an administrator and then began his own business as a grain broker.[36]

Sometime between 1913 and 1916, because of disagreements with his stepmother, Sandino left Nicaragua for Costa Rica where he worked for a while as a mechanic, first on a hacienda and then on sea ships. During this period he may

---

36   Somoza 1936, pp. 5–6; Román 1983, pp. 43–9. Sandino told reporter José Román that he had confronted his father at age 11. Somoza writes that Sandino went to live with his father at 14.

have visited New Orleans and possibly other US ports.[37] He claimed to have travelled widely in Central America, Mexico and the United States, and he was reputed to have learned some English.[38] In 1919, he returned to Niquinohomo and his grain business, but then in 1922 Sandino became involved in a gunfight over either some personal issue or a business matter in which he shot and wounded a neighbour who happened to be a leading Conservative in the area. To escape the law, Sandino fled to Honduras where he worked in gold mines and on a plantation owned by the American Vaccaro Brothers and Company, the future Standard Fruit Company. While working there, Sandino became involved either in another gunfight or, as another version has it, in some romantic affair, but in any case once again he fled, this time to Guatemala where he found a job with an American company working in his trade as a mechanic. Still restless, he moved on to Tampico, Mexico, where in 1923 he found work first at the South Penn Oil Company and then at the Huasteca Oil Company, both American-owned businesses.[39]

Tampico at the time was a booming oil industry port with a population of 100,000. The oil industry was owned by American and British companies and there was conflict between the Mexican nationalist government and the foreign petroleum companies as well as between the companies and the industrial working class. The most violent stage of the Mexican Revolution had ended in 1920, but it was followed by the rise of a militant agrarian reform movement with peasants seizing hacienda lands, a tenant housing movement accompanied by rent strikes in Veracruz, and a radical labour movement engaged in constant strikes in industry. In Tampico, Spanish anarchists, revolutionary syndicalists of the Industrial Workers of the World, as well as the small and newly founded Mexican Communist Party were all active in oil fields and on the shipping docks.[40] Though there is no record that he ever participated in any leftist organisation or movement at that time, Sandino was exposed to Mexico's new nationalism and to these militant movements and they influenced him.[41]

Sandino, according to his employment records, settled down in Tampico, reportedly took a wife, and had a daughter, though we know nothing about this family. Men in Mexico and Nicaragua in that era married easily and some-

---

37   Somoza 1936, p. 143, quotes an AP news story saying he had lived in New Orleans. Ships sailed regularly between the Mosquito Coast and New Orleans, so this is very possible.

38   Somoza 1936, p. 2.

39   Román 1983, pp. 53–5; Macaulay 1985, pp. 48–51.

40   La Botz 2006, pp. 563–90.

41   Macaulay 1985, p. 53.

times often, and she was only one of Sandino's various wives and mistresses. Sandino became an autodidact, reading history and sociology, the biographies of famous figures, pamphlets about labour unions, and books dealing with philosophy, religion, phrenology and astrology. He could not help but be influenced by the recent Mexican Revolution which had created a new Constitution in 1917 giving the nation the right to the subsoil and its minerals and petroleum, allowing the distribution of land to peasants and indigenous communities, establishing free, lay, public education, as well as recognising labour unions and providing for protective legislation for workers. At the same time, both in Mexico and throughout Latin America, the idea of an Indo-Hispanic or mestizo Latin American identity was in the air and being articulated by thinkers like the Argentine Manuel Ugarte and José Ingenieros as well as by the Mexican José Vasconcelos, who in 1925 published his influential book *The Cosmic Race*. Sandino absorbed this new consciousness of the importance of the indigenous people and their culture and began to think of himself as not only a Nicaraguan, but also as partly indigenous and thoroughly Latin American.

Sandino studied Yoga, practiced vegetarianism, and developed his own exercise regime. For a while he took an interest in Seventh Day Adventist Church, but also joined the Masons, and became interested in theosophy and spiritualism. He eventually became a member of the Magnetic-Spiritual School of the Universal Commune (EMECU), a spiritualist sect founded by the Argentine Joaquín Trincado. Trincado amalgamated spiritualism, the idea of pan-Hispanic identity, and communalism into a mystical religious and social doctrine. Trincado believed not only in the spirit world, but also in the unity of the Spanish-speaking people, and in the project of establishing a universal commune which would bring about a new society of peace and justice. Such an eclectic and swirling mixture of spiritualism, pseudo-science, and socialism was common in the 1910 and 1920s around the world, but it was especially strong in Latin America. Sandino synthesised his experiences and his eclectic reading in Mexico in a unique personal philosophy, a combination of Trincado's spiritualism and the Mexican Revolution's ideals of social justice. He was a mystic and a millenarian who later came to believe that he was chosen to conduct a holy war against the United States and against those Conservatives and Liberals who had betrayed Nicaragua and sold out to the Americans.[42] It was his

---

42   Navarro-Génie 2002 makes the strongest case for Sandino's mystical, millenarian and messianic beliefs. Hodges 1992 provides useful information, but I find unconvincing his argument that 'What is distinctive about Sandino's communism ... is a synthesis of anarchism

religious faith, his spiritualism, that made Sandino ready to lead his army for
seven years against overwhelming odds and, should it be necessary, to martyr
himself for the cause.

Sandino's Liberal Revolution

While in Mexico, Sandino had followed developments in Nicaragua and supported the Liberal revolution against the Conservatives, but despite the legend,
it is not clear that that was why he returned to his homeland. Ultimately,
Sandino left Mexico in 1926 at the urging of his father, but also because he
was homesick and eager to return to Nicaragua to make his fortune and claim
his bride. But his desire to return to his fiancée proved impossible because of
his outstanding problems with the law dating back to the shooting in Niquinohomo. At the same time, his plan to re-establish his grain business could not be
carried out because a grasshopper plague had ravaged crops and raised grain
prices.[43] While biding his time in the city of León and pondering his future,
Sandino met a group of miners from the San Albino gold mine and left with
them when they returned to work in the mine. This impetuous act set Sandino
on a new course.

San Albino was a company town where workers were paid in scrip that
could only be spent at the company store, an arrangement meant to keep
them in debt and at work in the mine. Fresh from the Mexican Revolution and
its Constitution of 1917, which had banned the company store, Sandino was
outraged at the San Albino Mine's 'unjust and illegal' practice. In an interview
that illuminates the connection between Sandino's nationalism and his views
on social issues, he told reporter José Ramón in 1933:

> I for my part began to work on the souls of those workers, explaining
> to them the cooperative system of other countries and how sadly we
> were exploited and that we should obtain for ourselves a government
> that would really be concerned about the people, so that they would
> not be so vilely exploited by the capitalists and the great foreign firms,

---

and communism on communist terms'. Sandino was not a systematic thinker and not a
communist of any sort. The argument that Sandino is a libertarian communist represents
Hodges's imposition of his own ideals on Sandino, just as he has done in his study of Mexican leftists. See my review of Hodges's *Mexican Anarchism* in La Botz 1997.

43   Navarro-Génie 2002. I am convinced of his interpretation of Sandino's return to Nicaragua
and adopt it here.

since the people are the nation and we should demand, as in all civilized countries of the world, that all of the companies that operate in Nicaragua should provide their workers with medical attention, schools, laws and organisations, such as workers' unions and that we had none of those. I explained to them that I was not a communist, but rather a socialist. That each man has the right to enjoy his labour, but never to exploit another's ignorance. In short, I explained to them the rights that are basic in the civilized countries. Little by little I went along gaining popularity and control of the men of the mine, among whom there were some who would follow me through all of my vicissitudes, risk their lives every moment, and who are still loyally at my side.[44]

Sandino's words make clear just how much he had fallen under the influence of the Mexican Revolution, its nationalist ideology, its progressive Constitution, and its labour union upsurge. Sandino describes himself here as a 'socialist', but it should be remembered that in the 1920s in Mexico and Central America, socialism might mean anything from agrarian reform to the creation of cooperatives and the organisation of labour unions, from a regulatory state to one that nationalised industry, from liberalism to populism. To be a socialist often simply meant to be on the side of the underdogs.

Sandino and his fellow mine workers pooled their money, bought arms, and joined the Liberal Revolution of President Sacasa and his Minister of War Moncada. On 2 November 1926, Sandino led his little band in an attack on the small military garrison at Jícaro, but the four or five defenders succeeded in routing Sandino's forces. Realising that he needed more arms, he and his few remaining men went down the Coco River to Puerto Cabezas where Sacasa and Moncada had set up the Liberal Constitutionalist headquarters. Sandino told the two Liberal leaders that he wanted to be made the commander of an independent force and that he needed arms. They understandably declined to commission and arm the unknown Sandino. Moncada would later write that he immediately distrusted Sandino because he talked about 'the necessity of workers to struggle against the rich and other things that are principles of communism'.[45] Sacasa and Moncada suggested that Sandino and his friends join an existing Liberal force.

On 13 December, US naval forces landed at Puerto Cabezas, declared it a 'neutral zone', and gave Sacasa, Moncada, and their troops 24 hours to get out

---

44   Román 1983, p. 57, my translation – DL.
45   Macaulay 1985, p. 55, citing Moncada 1942, pp. 23–4.

of the city, forcing them to leave their arms behind. With the help of local women, including the town's prostitutes, Sandino and his men gathered up and took away with them all the arms and ammunition they could carry, 30 rifles and 7,000 cartridges. Sandino then went on to the town of Prinzapolka where he caught up with Sacasa and Moncada and persuaded them to allow him to keep the arms. Sandino, now commanding his own force, joined up with Liberal General López Irías in Yucapuca, participated in the fight to take the town of San Rafael, and then in the Liberal capture of the important city of Jinotega, a provincial capital. General Sandino, as he now called himself, rejoined Moncada's forces in the area of Boaco, south of Matagalpa, just as the latter went off to meet with the US Envoy Henry Stimson at Tipitapa. Disgusted with Moncada for having agreed to Stimson's terms in the Treaty of Espino Negro, Sandino was the only Liberal general who refused to sign the pact.

Sandino initially thought of himself as a real Liberal, standing firm when the others caved in to the Americans. He was in fact a Liberal, like former president José Santos Zelaya, who was standing up to the Conservatives and to US imperialism. Liberalism, however, was a big tent that included both bourgeois Liberals such as Zelaya and Sacasa and populist Liberals on the side of the people, of whom Sandino was one. Similarly in Mexico, Ricardo and Enrique Flores Magón had begun as Liberals and ended up as anarchists. Sandino's trajectory would be somewhat different, but he too would take Liberalism in a more radical – and a more spiritual – direction.

Meanwhile, the United States government paid the poor peasant soldiers, both Conservative and Liberal, ten US dollars for each weapon they turned in, and both armies melted away. Under the direction of the US Marines, the Moncada government established the Nicaraguan National Guard trained by the US Marines, first as a police force and then as the country's first real national army. At the same time, withdrawing toward the north, Sandino began his seven-year struggle against the American occupation of Nicaragua with an attack on the town of Ocotal on 16 July 1927. Defeated by the US Marine troops and aircraft, he withdrew to Mt. Chipote where he established a base camp while laying plans for future campaigns.

On 1 July 1927, Sandino issued his first Manifesto 'To the Nicaraguans, to the Central Americans, to the Indo-Hispano Race'.

> I am Nicaraguan and I am proud because in my veins flows above all the blood of the Indian race, which by some atavism encompasses the mystery of being patriotic, loyal, and sincere.
>
> ...

I am a mechanic, but my idealism is based upon a broad horizon of *internationalism*, which represents the right to be *free* and to establish *justice*, even though to achieve this it may be necessary to establish it upon a foundation of blood ... My greatest honour is that I come from the lap of the oppressed, the soul and spirit of our race, who have lived ignored and forgotten, at the mercy of the shameless hired assassins who have committed the crime of high treason, forgetful of the pain and misery of the Liberal cause that they pitilessly persecuted, as if we did not belong to the same nation.

...

For myself and for my companions in arms who have not betrayed the Liberal revolution, who have not faltered and who have not sold our weapons to satisfy our own ambition, the revolution continues, and today more than ever before it is powerful because only those who have displayed the valour and self-denial that every Liberal should possess remain involved in it.[46]

Sandino went on to argue that Nicaragua should not be the victim of the United States, which had been invited into the country by traitors, and that the nation should not give to the United States rights over the construction of a canal.

In a second Manifesto released on 14 July 1927, Sandino distinguished his political and social programme from that of General Moncada, writing:

General Moncada does not know about and disregards the needs and suffering of the working class because he does not belong to that community of people who are forced to earn their living by their physical labour, with their bare hands, in order to eat and dress themselves badly ... I want nothing for myself; I am a mechanic, *the sound of my hammer on its anvil echoes at a great distance, and it speaks every language in matters of labour.* I aspire to nothing. I desire only the redemption of the working class.[47]

On the basis of this nationalist, populist, and one can say quasi-socialist programme, Sandino founded his Army in Defense of the National Sovereignty of Nicaragua (EDSN). He adopted the slogan *'Patria Libre o Morir'* (Free Fatherland or Death) and a red-and-black flag with a skull-and-cross-bones in the middle.

---

46   Sandino 1990, pp. 74–6, original emphasis.
47   Sandino 1990, pp. 80–1.

Sandino had no doubt come across the red-and-black flag in Mexico where it was the labour unions' symbol of a strike, red for socialism or communism and black for anarchism, some say. Sandino said that in his flag the red represented resurrection and the black symbolised death.[48]

Sandino was in many respects an unlikely redeemer. He had little more than a high-school education, a checkered career in a variety of working-class jobs in Mexico and Central America, and just a handful of followers, only 29 men when he first established his revolutionary army. He was physically unimpressive: less than five feet tall and quite thin, almost always described wearing his khaki shirt and trousers, tall boots, his oversized Stetson hat, and a holster holding a long-barrelled revolver. But he was an extremely charismatic figure whose mystical manifestos and binding oratory inspired his men, while his populist politics held out the hope that one day a good government would do something for them, their families and their communities. The American radical journalist Carleton Beals, who visited Sandino's camp, wrote that Sandino '... had lighted fierce affection, blind loyalty; had instilled in every man his own burning hatred for the "invader"'. In another passage Beals wrote, 'I myself sensed an uncanny power of domination in Sandino, something subtle, devious, not at all obvious'.[49] Sandino was a *caudillo*, a charismatic military and political leader whose magnetic personality was capable of imposing a strong discipline on his band of poor, illiterate, untrained and angry rebels.

Throughout the period of his struggle against the Liberal government of Moncada – a government of traitors, as he saw it – and the US Marines, Sandino operated in the mountainous northern region of Nicaragua known as Las Segovias, made up of the five departments of Matagalpa, Jinotega, Estelí, Madriz and Nueva Segovia, as well as in the area between the Honduran border and the Coco River on the Miskito Coast. These were remote areas where, outside of the major cities, there were no railways, highways or even roads, a region of mountains and jungles accessible only by foot trails or by canoe. With the exception of the coffee plantations in Matagalpa, these were sparsely populated areas of cattle ranches, subsistence farmers and Indian villages where the Nicaraguan government had little presence and exerted virtually no control outside of the few cities and towns. As in most of Nicaragua there were no post offices, health clinics or schools, but in these areas neither were there any government offices or police departments.

---

48   Román 1983, p. 70.
49   Beals 1932, pp. 265 and 272.

Historically these were zones of discontent and rebellion. Matagalpa had been the scene of Indian uprisings throughout the late nineteenth and early twentieth centuries. Indians and mestizo peasants both had withdrawn into the northern mountains to escape the owners of haciendas and coffee *fincas* and of government tax collectors. The Miskito Coast, with its indigenous and Afro-Caribbean population, speaking native languages or English more than Spanish, more Moravian Protestant than Catholic, had only come under the nominal control of Nicaragua in 1894 and had never been integrated into Nicaraguan society or controlled by the Nicaraguan state. The Miskito Coast was more closely connected by ship to New Orleans than it was by land to Nicaragua. The most important institutions in these areas were the American mining and lumber companies and the shipping companies in the ports. Among these isolated and largely alienated populations, Sandino built his social base, his network of supporters and spies.

Sandino's War

In the Segovias, Sandino organised the Army in Defense of the National Sovereignty of Nicaragua or EDSN, his unpaid, completely volunteer guerrilla army which at its height numbered about 2,000 men and another 1,800 reservists, among them some women. The army included a Latin American Legion of officers and soldiers principally from other Central American, but also from some South American countries. He refused to permit Europeans or US Marine deserters to join his army, though he claimed that he helped the American deserters to escape to Costa Rica.[50]

In 1933, Sandino asserted that he had absolute control over 30,000 square kilometres of territory and was the dominant force in another 80,000 square kilometres, out of the country's 130,000 square kilometres. While he claimed to control more than half of the country, most historians believe he controlled a third to a half, but none of the cities. Sandino claimed to be supported by 180,000 Nicaraguans, as well as by another 100,000 members of various Indian tribes, mostly in the Miskito Coast. The civilian population, he said, provided his intelligence service with constant reports on the US Marines and the Nicaraguan National Guard and their movements. While he did appear to have significant popular support, he also experienced betrayal by his own military officers and soldiers, as well as from some civilians. We can never be sure of exactly how

---

50   Román 1983, pp. 115–19 and 134–9.

much support Sandino actually had, since like any group of armed men, his army intimidated the civilian population in the regions where they operated.

As commander-in-chief of the army, Sandino created a traditional hierarchical military structure with the usual ranks and chain of command. The army was well disciplined and the officers were strict. Those who violated orders were court martialled and for serious charges could, if convicted, be executed, as some were. He had a number of soldiers, several officers, and two generals shot for treason, looting, or rape. Sandino also appointed the governors, mayors, councillors, and other civilian officials in the regions that he controlled. While Sandino called for free national elections under the existing system of representative democracy, and while he believed in the organisation of cooperatives, there is no evidence that he ever called for a democratic election in any territory that he controlled. Though he wished to improve the lives of workers and peasants, there is no evidence that he did anything to empower them politically.[51]

Within the territories he controlled, Sandino's military regulations forbade his soldiers from 'bothering peaceful civilians', but he did force national and foreign capitalists to contribute money to the maintenance of his army. There were also some large landlords of Liberal persuasion who supported his army, and, though he called himself a socialist, Sandino did not expropriate the large haciendas of either his allies or his enemies. Sandino's socialism apparently did not entail the workers' and peasants' expropriation and socialisation of the means of production owned by the capitalist. We see here why it is difficult to simply accept his claim that he was a socialist. As he told the journalist Román Belausteguigoitia in the early 1930s, 'Without a doubt capital can do its work and develop itself, as long as the worker is not humiliated and exploited'.[52] Sandino said:

> At various times there have been attempts to twist this national defence movement into a struggle of a more social character. I have opposed this with all my power. This is a national and anti-imperialist movement. We hold up the banner of freedom for Nicaragua and all of Hispanic America. With regard to the rest in the social realm, this is a popular movement and we advocate an idea of an advance in social aspirations. The International Labour Federation, the Anti-Imperialist League, and the Quakers

---

51 Sandino's document laying out military organisation and rules, together with his explanation of them, can be found in Román 1983, pp. 115–57.

52 Sandino 2010, pp. 151–2.

have come here trying to influence us. We have always opposed [other organisations], our decisive criteria being that this is essentially a national struggle. [Farabundo] Martí, the Communist propagandist, saw that he could not win with his programme and he withdrew.[53]

Sandino fought for Nicaragua's sovereignty, and he wanted to see improvements in the lives of ordinary workers and peasants, and, in particular, he advocated the establishment of cooperatives. Yet he accepted the idea that there would be a return to the sort of representative government that had existed before, and believed capitalists would continue to own their businesses and haciendas. He sometimes called himself a 'socialist', though he did not give this word a programmatic character, and he strongly rejected the 'Communist' label and evaded any association with Communists and their organisations. He sometimes talked about 'communising the earth', but for him the word 'communise' meant the establishment of the mystical brotherhood called the universal commune, not the establishment of a socialist or Communist political regime.[54]

Moncada's Liberal government and the US Marines fought Sandino for seven years, denying that he was a patriot fighting a revolutionary war and declaring him to be a traitor, a brutal bandit, interested only in his own power, wealth, and glory, though sometimes calling him a Communist. The Nicaraguan and American commercial press and particularly the Associated Press described Sandino in similar misleading and derogatory terms. Only the left press reported favourably on Sandino and his activities.

Froylán Turcios, the Honduran writer who became Sandino's official spokesman, used his magazine *Ariel* to publish Sandino's manifestos and to give accounts of the campaigns of the EDSN. Turcios's accounts presented Sandino as an anti-imperialist and progressive revolutionary fighting against the United States not only for the people of Nicaragua, but also on behalf of all Latin Americans. Turcios's articles in *Ariel* were reprinted in the Peruvian journal *Amauta* edited by the Marxist revolutionary José Carlos Mariátegui. Turcios also collected funds and channelled support for Sandino from his followers throughout Latin America. No doubt the articles in *Ariel* and *Amauta* helped to recruit the student activists who joined Sandino's army in Nicaragua.[55] In the United

---

53   Sandino 2010, p. 150.

54   On several occasions Sandino dissociated himself from the Communist Party. Macaulay 1985, p. 226.

55   Funes 2010, pp. 181–208. The university student volunteers from several Latin American countries who joined Sandino's army are mentioned in Román 1983, pp. 136–8.

States, Carleton Beals wrote sympathetically about Sandino for *The Nation* as did the writers for the Communist *Daily Worker*.[56] Sandino also had many supporters among Latin American intellectuals on the left and among radicals in Europe, such as the French author Henri Barbusse. But, under the influence of the Associated Press and the Hearst papers, in the minds of many Americans, Sandino was the Nicaraguan bandit.

We cannot recount Sandino's campaigns here, but we can discuss the balance of forces and the nature of the struggle.[57] Throughout the war, the US Marines numbered as many as 5,000, the National Guard grew to almost 2,000,

---

56 Carleton Beals's articles provided the material for his book *Banana Gold*. Cartoons from the press of the period can be found at: http://www.sandinorebellion.com/HomePages/airtoons.html.

57 Sandino's military campaigns are too complicated to be narrated or described here, but the war can be divided into several short, distinct periods. First, the period of his alliance with Moncada and other Liberal forces who attacked and took Jinotega as well as his failed attack on the town of Jícaro. A second period began immediately after his break with Moncada, when Sandino acquired arms and began to fight the Liberal government and the US Marines, but was defeated at the large Battle of Ocotal on 16 July 1927, at which point he and his troops found themselves for the first time under attack by US Marine aircraft. The third period, the latter half of 1927, involved Sandino's retreat to Mt. Chipote where he established his headquarters and base camp and conducted guerrilla operations until the US Marines drove him out on 26 January 1928. During the fourth period in 1928, the US Marines reorganised and became more effective in fighting Sandino and his army; as a result, hundreds of ESDN troops deserted. Nevertheless, from February to November 1928, Sandino and his troops continued to attack small towns, haciendas, the Standard Fruit Company, Bragman's Bluff Lumber Company, and the American-owned mines. These attacks undermined the US claim that it was protecting American property in Nicaragua. Sandino also conducted a campaign of terror and propaganda against the Nicaraguan election of 1928. The fifth period, during 1929, saw the Conservative government recruit a force of 'volunteers' under the command of the former Mexican revolutionary General Juan Escamilla, a particularly brutal man who routinely executed those suspected of helping Sandino. Also in 1929, Sandino went to Mexico where he spent several months in a failed attempt to win further support from President Emilio Portes Gil. During his absence, he left the notoriously cruel Pedro 'Pedrón' Altamirano in charge of operations in Nicaragua. Throughout the sixth period, encompassing 1930 and 1931, Sandino came under attack from a major National Guard offensive, but with the announcement of a reduction in the US Marine forces, Sandino responded with a guerrilla offensive in west and central Nicaragua. In the final seventh period in 1932, Sandino's army returned to the fight in the east of Nicaragua, while continuing to make forays in the west. The US Marines and National Guard suffered 'shocking reverses' in this final period as Sandino's army became more aggressive. Macaulay 1985 is the best source for the military history of the war. The quotation comes from p. 222.

and Sandino's forces counted as many as 2,000. Most battles, however, involved only small groups numbering scores, dozens, or just a handful of men. Only on a few occasions did hundreds of fighters confront each other. From 1927 to 1932, there were hundreds of encounters, from small skirmishes to larger battles, between the US Marines and the National Guard on the one hand and Sandino's army on the other.[58]

The fighting on the ground was particularly brutal and often accompanied by horrifying mutilation and torture. Sandino's troops engaged in a practice known as the '*corte de chaleco*' or the 'vest cut' in which they decapitated and cut off the arms of their enemies, disembowelled the body and placed the head in the abdominal cavity. Others were castrated and the victim's genitals placed in his mouth, a time-honoured practice of armies everywhere. The US Marines were also accused of beheading and castrating Sandino's soldiers – a group of Marines was photographed holding the guerrillas' severed heads – and of torturing peasants suspected of aiding the guerrillas. The US Marines had a small air force of about twenty planes in Nicaragua as well as an autogiro, an early helicopter. US Marine aircraft bombed and strafed the guerrillas, and were also accused of doing the same to peasant villages and to labourers in the fields.[59] All accounts suggest that both sides engaged in atrocities not only against soldiers but also against peasant men, women and children who were killed or physically and psychologically injured.

Early on, Sandino adopted a guerrilla war strategy, stationing his forces in remote mountains and jungles, and then venturing forth to attacks towns, haciendas, and the US-owned banana plantations and mining companies. From the beginning, the Conservative government demonstrated that it could not be dislodged from the cities, and by the late 1920s, the US Marines and the National Guard gained control of the rivers as well. Still, Sandino recognised that, though he could not take cities or hold large regions, he might succeed if he could simply continue to make forays and to mount attacks that demonstrated the powerlessness of both the Conservative government and the United States Marines to stop him.

---

58   The National Guard reported 510 contacts between 16 July 1927 and 31 December 1932, though one authority estimates there were actually as many as 735. Schroeder n.d. – a.

59   Ramón 1983, pp. 165–6; Somoza 1936, *passim*; much of Somoza's book is dedicated to documenting the atrocities of Sandino's troops. Macaulay 1985, pp. 228–9.

   Sandino admitted that his men practiced the *corte de chaleco* and engaged in other horrifying practices. The US Marine bombings of Sandino troops and of villages was widely reported at the time.

Sandino believed that the struggle of the EDSN against the US Marines was part of a broader struggle of all Latin Americans against the United States and its imperial ambitions and an element of an even broader struggle of all oppressed nations and peoples against Great Power imperialism. Sandino entertained the possibility of alliances with political organisations that shared that outlook, particularly the All American Anti-Imperialist League, the Communist International and its affiliated Communist Parties, and the American Popular Revolutionary Alliance (APRA). Farabundo Martí, the Salvadoran Communist, and Esteban Pavletich of the APRA, were both close to Sandino in the late 1920s – Martí became a colonel in his army and his personal secretary – and through them he gained a deeper understanding of their organisations and their political programmes. Sandino, who never joined any of those organisations, eventually found his entanglements with them to be too problematic, and by 1929 he had broken off all relations with them. While he wanted international support, he valued his own political independence too much to subordinate himself and the EDSN to a larger international organisation such as the Communist International or the APRA. At the same time, association with the Communists, who were viewed by all governments and by many other parties, labour unions, and social movements as pariahs, only tended to contribute to isolating him politically.

Sandino also tried another strategy, namely, to try to align the majority of Latin American governments and peoples behind his struggle. He published manifestos calling for international cooperation and support for Nicaragua and attempted to form international alliances of Latin American nations. In August of 1928, Sandino wrote to the presidents of the Latin American nations, asking them to support the struggle against the Liberal government – as well as calling for a fight against the dictatorships of Juan Vicente Gómez of Venezuela, Augusto Leguía of Peru, and Gerardo Machado of Cuba and against the United States.[60] Many of the other Caribbean and Latin American governments were, like Nicaragua, run by authoritarian governments subservient to the United States or Britain, so not much came of his appeal.

Less than a year later, in March of 1929, he wrote to the Latin American nations and to the United States, calling for a hemispheric American Congress organised around the principle that the Latin American peoples must have the right to chart their own destiny and control their own resources.[61] That same month, he presented to the 22 Latin American states an 'original project'

---

60 Sandino 1998, pp. 204–6.
61 Sandino 1998, pp. 248–50.

to realise Simón Bolívar's dream of continental unity. Sandino was proposing an international political programme calling for the abolition of the Monroe Doctrine, asserting the right of the Latin American states to associate with each other as they wished, calling for periodic meetings of the Latin American nations, establishing a Latin American Court of Justice with its own Latin American international army to enforce its decisions, and creating a Latin American Congress of Representatives. It was in reality a call to found a United States of Latin America to resist the United States of North America. All of these appeals had the immediate goal of uniting Latin America behind his struggle in Nicaragua but also a broader objective of promoting Latin American unity against the United States. While these initiatives elevated Sandino's image, projecting him as an international statesman, and received some publicity, they were ignored by the other Latin American nations and had no impact on the Nicaraguan situation.[62] With or without support from Latin America, Sandino struggled on.

Sandino's army not only continued to fight, but also became more aggressive and more successful in 1932. It was not, however, Sandino's successes that finally led to the withdrawal of the US Marines in 1933 – it was the American economic and political situation. The Great Depression in the United States and the beginning of America's turn to the left in the 1930s with the election of Democrat Franklin D. Roosevelt made the US intervention in Nicaragua to protect American businesses less popular. The American people were becoming less willing to protect u.s.-owned mines and banana companies from the righteous anger of the working class and poor people exploited by them. The United States government made it clear that it was going to withdraw the US Marines after the 1932 elections as originally scheduled, leaving the defence and policing of the country in the hands of the National Guard.

As the elections approached, the Conservatives and Liberals met together in October 1932 to come up with a plan to share political power amongst themselves and to deal with Sandino through 'peaceful and conciliatory' means. They were joined by the anti-interventionist Patriotic Group led by Sofonías Salvatierra, a man sympathetic to Sandino and his cause, who had in the past attempted to mediate between the government and Sandino.[63] Sandino had already announced his peace terms in the summer of 1932, calling for the withdrawal of US Marines *before* the election and proposing his own candidate for president, Horacio Portocarrero, an old Liberal who had been living in exile

---

62   Sandino 1990, pp. 251–62.
63   Macaulay 1985, pp. 230–1.

in El Salvador. Sandino called upon all Nicaraguans to support Portocarrero as the candidate of national unity, and declared that in any case he would put him in power through force of arms if necessary. Sandino had also considered establishing his own provisional government of Nicaragua in the Segovias, but dropped the idea when it became clear that no Latin American government would recognise it. In mid-1932, he apparently had no intention of laying down his arms and making peace. He believed that with his allies, Portocarrero in El Salvador and Pedro José Zepeda in Mexico, he would be able to acquire arms so that he could renew fighting in the coming year if his candidate for president was not accepted.[64]

Henry L. Stimson, who had promised that the US would supervise the 1932 elections, now found that the US Congress was unwilling to pay to send 500 more US servicemen to Nicaragua to do the job. Consequently, the United States supervised the elections through Nicaragua National Guard units commanded by American officers, though there were too few to oversee all of the polls. US servicemen were not sent to polls in rural areas for fear that they would be attacked by Sandino's army. As the election approached, the Conservatives nominated America's loyal servant Adolfo Díaz for president, while the Liberals put forward Dr. Juan B. Sacasa. In a victory for the Liberals and for Nicaraguan sovereignty, Sacasa won the November election by a considerable majority, though he was not sworn in as president until 1 January 1933. Meanwhile, out-going president Moncada made what would prove to be an all-important decision: that Anastasio Somoza García would, also on 1 January 1933, become head of the National Guard. Until then, Somoza would continue to serve as the assistant to the Guard's current commander US General Mathews. When he became commander, Somoza would choose his own staff, while the top officers of the Guard would be chosen from 50 names, half proposed by the Conservative and half by the Liberals.

As the sun rose then in Nicaragua on 2 January 1933, everything had changed. The Liberal Sacasa was president, Somoza García was head of the National Guard, and the last of the US Marines left Nicaragua. Sacasa immediately proposed a peace conference and just as quickly Sandino responded, sending his wife Blanca Aráuz de Sandino as his envoy. With the Sacasa government's permission, on 6 January in the city of Managua she informed Nicaragua of Sandino's willingness to negotiate a peace. His demands were remarkably modest: (1) his army to have military and political control of a new department in the Río Coco valley from El Chipote to the Caribbean coast; (2) the removal

---

64   Macaulay 1985, p. 236.

from government archives of all references to the Sandinistas as 'bandits'; and (3) the promise of the new Nicaraguan government that it would work to convene an inter-American conference to discuss the proposed Nicaraguan canal.[65]

With the support of both Conservatives and Liberals, Sacasa announced a truce on 29 January. Sandino responded in kind, and by 2 February Sandino and his advisors – Protocarrero, Zepeda, and the Liberal Salvador Calderón Ramírez – were in Managua to negotiate. Sandino was greeted by both President Sacasa and National Guard Commander Somoza, and as the party drove through Managua they were cheered by onlookers who had lined the streets. Sandino now changed his negotiating position, telling the press that he was prepared to make peace *without any conditions whatsoever*. The peace was signed just ten minutes before midnight that same day.

The treaty provided that Sandino would end his war and that his troops would be disarmed; that the Conservative and Liberal parties would pay 'homage to the noble and patriotic attitude of General Sandino'; that there would be a general amnesty for acts committed between 1927 and 1933; and that the government would set aside land for an agricultural colony in the Río Coco Valley. The rebel leader was also allowed to keep a force of 100 men under arms for at least one year. At about the same time, Sandino sent to the *New York Herald Tribune* a letter of condolences to the families of Americans killed in Nicaragua and told the press he had nothing against the Americans and that they were welcome to come to Nicaragua, so long as they came not 'as bosses' but rather to work.[66] Sandino's army was disarmed on 22 February 1933. Now there was no other military force in the country except the National Guard. The war was over. The fighting, however, was not.

One has to wonder what Sandino was thinking when he negotiated this agreement which would prove so disastrous for his country and for himself. No doubt after seven years of guerrilla warfare, he and his soldiers were exhausted. Sandino's wife was pregnant and he was looking forward to becoming a father and hoped to raise his child in peace. He had also had a premonition that if he did not quickly negotiate peace, he would be killed. While those psychological elements may all have been involved in his thinking, the most important political factor was that the United States had changed its policy, helping to install a Liberal president, extracting the Marines, and installing Somoza as head of the National Guard. With the Marines having left, Sandino no longer

---

65   Macaulay 1985, p. 242.
66   Macaulay 1985, pp. 246–7.

had what had been the justification for his revolution. With a Liberal president in power, he had no alternative political programme to offer.[67]

Sandino could see no way to respond to this new situation except to acquiesce. So, he accepted the election of Sacasa, and with it the appointment of Somoza, and allowed his troops to be disarmed. In a sense, he was giving up everything he had fought for. Though things had changed profoundly, they had also remained remarkably the same. The United States still dominated Nicaragua, which was its economic colony, and the Nicaraguan Liberal and Conservative elite remained in power, while the country's working people remained powerless and poor. If the war had been a heroic struggle, the peace was a pathetic defeat. Sandino went off to pursue the illusion of his cooperative and the universal commune.

The Sacasa government proved to be unstable because Somoza, who had his own ambitions, controlled the National Guard and the Guard itself was riddled with conspiracies. Sacasa told the American embassy in November 1933 that he feared that Somoza was planning a coup. In an attempt to calm the public's fears and to solidify the peace, Sandino met with Somoza in Managua in December 1933 and together they issued declarations of peace and conciliation, but Sandino could see the writing on the wall. In January, he wrote to President Sacasa pledging to support him against the 'unconstitutional' National Guard, but Sacasa feared that Sandino himself might be planning to take military action and summoned him to Managua in the hope of avoiding further conflict.

Sandino arrived on 16 February 1934, announcing to the press that he would never surrender his arms to the 'unconstitutional' National Guard. (While the body of his army had been disarmed, he still had his guard of 100 armed men). Sandino, his father and brother, two of his generals, and his advisors dined with president Sacasa on 21 February 1934. When the Sandino party left the house, Major Lisandro Delgadillo and a group of heavily armed National Guardsmen took them prisoner, loaded them on a truck, and took them to the Managua airfield. A machine gun was set up, and Sandino, his brother Socrates, and Generals Estrada and Umanzor were marched in front of it and executed. The next morning, the National Guard attacked the Wiwilí Cooperative that Sandino had established. Within a few weeks the Guard had crushed what remained of Sandino's movement.[68] Somoza admitted that he had ordered Sandino's

---

67   One thinks of the remark of the Russian-German revolutionary Eugen Leviné, 'We Communists are all dead men on leave'. Leviné-Meyer 1973.

68   Macaulay, pp. 250–6. The town is sometimes spelled 'Guiguilí'.

murder, but only after he had consulted the US Ambassador. The Ambassador and the US State Department denied any role in the assassination.[69]

What had been the cost of the war? Sandino claimed that between 4 May 1927 when he began his independent revolutionary war and 2 February 1933 when it ended, his army suffered 2,800 fatal casualties of men and boys. The number of civilians killed by the US Marines and the Nicaraguan National Guard, he said, 'no one knows and no one can calculate'.[70] Sandino also claimed that his army had killed 'thousands' of Marines, though the US Marine Corps reported that from 1 January 1927 to 2 January 1933 there were 136 US Marines killed – 32 died in action, 15 from their wounds, 24 from disease, 41 accidentally and 24 from other causes (homicide, suicide, and resisting arrest).[71] The National Guard reported that between 16 July 1927 and 31 December 1932 it had 197 casualties, 75 killed and 122 wounded. They estimated Sandino's forces' casualties as 1,115 killed and 526 wounded.[72] There is no reason to doubt the reports of the Marines or the Guard. Though there are no reliable statistics, it seems likely that hundreds, perhaps even as many as 2,000 Nicaraguan civilians were killed. Altogether one could estimate that the war took as many as 5,000 lives, and perhaps more, out of a total population of 681,000 in 1930. Since the war was fought mostly in rural areas, many of those uncultivated areas, property damage was not great, though the buildings on some Nicaragua haciendas and *fincas* were affected and some American-owned businesses on the Atlantic coast were damaged or destroyed.

Sandino's Legacy

Sandino took credit for having driven the US Marines from Nicaragua with his seven-year guerrilla war. His guerrilla war had an impact in several ways: he publicised and discredited the United States, the US Marines, and their role in Latin America by revealing the brutally violent character of American intervention in Nicaragua; he forced the United States to spend millions to transport, arm, equip, and pay the Marines, and he caused the deaths of enough US Marines that it disturbed US politicians and the American public. There is no doubt that he caused members of the US Congress to reconsider their nation's foreign policy. But there were other factors in the US decision to withdraw from

---

69   Diederich 2007, p. 19.

70   Román 1983, p. 131.

71   Schroeder n.d. – b.

72   Schroeder n.d. – a.

Nicaragua. The Crash of 1929 and the Great Depression of the 1930s put additional economic pressure on the United States. The rise of Fascism and Nazism in these years raised the spectre of class conflict and war in Europe and the possibility of the US being drawn into conflict there. Already under President Herbert Hoover, the US government had begun to rethink its role as policeman of Central America and the Caribbean. With President Franklin D. Roosevelt's ascendance to power, the United States abandoned that role, adopting instead the Good Neighbour Policy in March of 1933. Roosevelt's Secretary of State Cordell Hull declared: 'No country has the right to intervene in the internal or external affairs of another'.[73] Roosevelt himself said in December: 'The definite policy of the United States from now on is one opposed to armed intervention'.[74] What this meant in practice was that the United States would withdraw the Marines from Central American countries and the Caribbean islands, leaving in their place governments – often dictators – loyal to the US government and friendly to American banks and corporations.

What was Sandino's importance as an individual for the history of Nicaragua? Sandino is certainly one of those figures who determine the history of a country for an entire period. If Sandino had not declared that he was going to fight the Conservatives and the US government that had put them in power, it is doubtful that anyone else would have declared a revolutionary war to protect the sovereignty of Nicaragua. Sandino deserves much credit for his patriotic struggle and his fight for social justice for the poor. At the same time, Sandino also bears much responsibility for the seven-year war and for the politically worthless treaty that ended it, leading within two years to his own assassination, the dispersal of the military movement he had led, and Somoza's rise to power.

Sandino's principal legacies were his own personal example of heroism, his willingness to fight and to die for his country, and his army's long and persistent struggle for the independence of Nicaragua. As Andrés Pérez Baltodano says, 'He was a man of principles, but not of ideas'.[75] While he held a nationalist and populist worldview – expressed in the unique form of his spiritualist and communalist philosophy – Sandino never developed his own ideas of politics or government in a systematic way. Though at times he called himself a socialist, it was never clear what he meant by this term. He did, however, have a political practice. Sandino was a *caudillo* who led his men and ruled his territory

---

73   La Feber 1994, p. 376.

74   Nixon 1969, pp. 559–60.

75   Andrés Pérez-Baltodano, personal communication, 21 January 2014.

through his charisma and the force of his personality. A part of that personal power was exercised through his spiritualist-social justice ideology and his populist politics. He attracted and held his men in part because he envisioned the creation of a spiritual brotherhood and an egalitarian community. He often talked of how brotherhood and the universal commune would unite all. That community was in the future; in the present he ruled as a benevolent dictator.

Eventually, calling himself the Supreme Commander of the Autonomist Army and Ruler of Central America, he came to exert intermittent control over about one-third of the territory of Nicaragua. In that region, he appointed all military officers and civilian authorities as well as all other officials, all structured in a hierarchical system that he commanded. Nowhere did Sandino create democratic forms of organisation. This authoritarian rule can of course be explained, and perhaps even justified, by the fact that he was engaged in an ongoing war that did not permit him the luxury of democratic government; yet the fact remains that he governed as a military dictator in the areas he controlled. He demanded taxes, principally from those most able to pay them, and commandeered whatever his army needed, giving both landowners and peasants receipts payable by the US government which he held responsible for the war. These could not have been much comfort to a peasant who had lost a chicken or a head of cattle. While he opposed US domination of Nicaragua and rejected the Conservative and Liberal parties, Sandino accepted the traditional form of representative government that had existed in the past, provided only that there were free and fair elections. He never developed a critique of representative government, nor did he offer a more democratic political model that would have empowered the peasant and worker majority whose lives he fought to improve.

Similarly with political parties and programmes: Sandino never developed a programme beyond his demand for the withdrawal of the United States from Nicaragua and new national elections. Beyond his demand for Nicaragua's national sovereignty, he also believed that the conditions of workers and peasants should be improved. Yet he never organised peasant leagues or workers unions, never developed a programme of workers' and peasants' demands, and never, either during the war or after, did he found a labour, socialist or communist party. Sandino believed that workers should have labour unions, but he also argued that capital should be allowed to do its work and make a profit. After he and his army laid down their arms, he laid out no strategy for the struggle for political power in post-civil war Nicaragua. In the course of his struggle and through the members of his Latin American Legion, he came into contact with the most important revolutionary currents in Latin America at the time, the Communists and the APRA, but he never joined them, both because they would have limited his independence and because he hesitated to be associated with them, associations which he feared would only lead to his greater isolation. His greatest personal commitment, perhaps growing out of his belief in the spiritualism of the Magnetic-Spiritual School of the Universal Commune, was to the creation of cooperatives through which he hoped to develop the poor rural areas of the Rio Coco region after the war ended, though he never explained how such cooperatives would be organised and governed.

Sandino believed that peasants were entitled – individually or collectively – to own a piece of land which would allow them to support themselves and their families through subsistence farming and the production of a small surplus for the market, either as individuals or in his preferred form of the cooperative. That is, he held a view similar to the traditional folk outlook of the majority of Nicaraguan peasants and indigenous people who, when left to their own devices, led just such a life or tried to. While Sandino wished to improve the lives of peasants, farmers and workers, he never discussed how they might have a greater voice in the society; that is, he never developed a theory of democratic working-class government, and apparently did not see such a government as central to the struggle for social justice. Sandino's legacy provided the Sandinista Front for the Liberation of Nicaragua of the 1970s with a model of revolutionary leadership and struggle, but it did not provide a vision of socialism nor did it offer a model of democracy. Sandino also provided the FSLN with the example of the *caudillo* who rules through his personality and creates authoritarian institutions to govern the territory he controls. It was not Sandino, however, who provided the essential political model for the Sandinistas: it was Cuba.

The Somoza Dynastic Dictatorship (1936–75)

Anastasio Somoza García became president of Nicaragua through a coup carried out on 9 June 1936, leading to the creation of a dynastic dictatorship that lasted for over forty years. The Somoza dictatorship established the state and transformed the society that ultimately incubated the Sandinista Front for National Liberation (FSLN). One could say that it was the Somoza dictatorship, supported by the United States, with its modernisation programme, its political support from the Nicaraguan capitalist class, and its selective and brutal repression that created the Sandinistas. Consequently, an understanding of the Somoza regime is essential to comprehending the origins and growth of the FSLN.

Anastasio Somoza García, known as Tacho, the commander of the National Guard who would rule Nicaragua for twenty years and establish a dynasty that lasted four decades, was a child of upper class privilege who married into aristocratic wealth and power. Born on 1 February 1896 in San Marcos, Department of Carazo, Tacho was the son of Senator Anastasio Somoza Reyes and Julia García, a wealthy, coffee planter family. His father had served as Conservative Party senator from the department of Carazo for eight years and in 1914 was elected vice-secretary of the senate.[1] He was also a signer of the Bryan-Chamorro treaty in 1916. One could say that politics was in Tacho's blood.

After Tacho finished high school, when he was 19 years old he seduced a maid in the family's home and when she became pregnant his parents, to remove him from that relationship and the scandal that might come to surround it, sent him to live with relatives in Philadelphia. He studied at the Pierce School of Business Administration (later Pierce College) and became fluent in English.[2] While living in Philadelphia he met and courted Salvadora Debayle Sacasa, the daughter of Dr. Luis Henri Debayle Pallais, known as *El Sabio* (the Wiseman), and wife Casimira Sacasa Sacasa, daughter of an extremely wealthy and politically well-connected family. Salvadora DeBayle's wife's maternal grandfather had served twice as president of Nicaragua. When *El Sabio* learned of his daughter's plan to wed Somoza he forbade her from marrying because her suitor, who was not from the elite *criollo* circles, was socially unacceptable. Salvadora, however,

---

1 Diederich 2007, pp. 1–7.
2 Diederich 2007, p. 10.

defied her father and married Somoza in a civil ceremony in Philadelphia. After they returned to Nicaragua, her parents reluctantly accepted the fait accompli and saw the couple married again in grand style in a Catholic ceremony in the León Cathedral. While his business school education proved to be of negligible significance, his marriage to Salvador Debayle and his fluency in the English language acquired during his stay in Philadelphia would be all-important for Somoza's future career.

Returning to Nicaragua, Somoza went into business, but proved to be not very good at it, failing at a succession of careers. He opened an agency selling Lexington automobiles, but the business folded, perhaps because Nicaragua had so few drivable roads at the time. He introduced boxing into Nicaragua and became a promoter of the sport, serving as a referee, but this never provided him a significant income. He was forced to take a job at the electric company in León as a meter reader and later worked for the Rockefeller Foundation's Sanitary Mission to Nicaragua as an inspector of latrines. Desperate to make more money, he became a counterfeiter working with a printer producing false *córdobas*, the country's currency. Only the intervention of a politically connected relative kept him from going to prison.[3]

When rebellion against the Conservatives broke out in 1926, Somoza joined the Liberal rebellion that aimed to put in the presidency his wife's uncle Juan Bautista Sacasa. Somoza, taking the title of 'General', led an unsuccessful armed attack on the San Marcos barracks and then fled to Costa Rica to represent the Liberals from there. When the shooting had stopped, Somoza returned to Nicaragua and attached himself to Liberal General José María Moncada's staff and served as an interpreter during the negotiations between the Americans and the rival Nicaraguan factions. His position as interpreter put him in a position to talk with everyone. He had finally found his métier: politics. When Moncada assumed the presidency in 1929, Somoza served first as governor of León, then as Consul to Costa Rica, and finally as Minister of Foreign Affairs and as the president's personal aide.[4] When an earthquake destroyed much of Managua on 31 March 1931, Somoza worked as a liaison with the US Marines and also as a negotiator with the taxi drivers' and truck drivers' unions, settling strikes that, it has been suggested, he himself had instigated.[5]

3 Diederich 2007, p. 11.
4 Diederich 2007, pp. 12–13.
5 Diederich 2007, p. 14.

Somoza was a charming man who established a warm relationship with US Ambassador Matthew Hanna, and he may have had an affair with his wife.[6] When the US Marines organised the National Guard in 1927, Somoza succeeded in becoming an officer and then being named assistant to the commander.[7] When the Marines left in 1933, he became head of the National Guard and by virtue of that the most powerful person in the country.[8] All of this was a result of his wife's family's political connections, his ability to speak English, and his own charm, shrewdness, and ambition.

Somoza to Power: A Coup and an Election

On 14 May 1936, Liberals and Conservatives, both leery of Somoza's power as head of the Guard and hoping to isolate him, came to an agreement in the presence of President Sacasa that two representatives from each party should choose the future president from the Liberal Party and divide up seats in the Cabinet, the Congress and the Supreme Court. Somoza instead proposed to them that, as the most popular figure in the country, he should choose the presidential candidate. He also demanded the power to appoint all officers in the National Guard, the creation of a military academy and a military aviation school, and raises in the Guard's pay. Somoza's proposal was rejected and representatives of the two parties meeting with Sacasa chose instead Leonardo Argüello as the sole candidate for president.

Seeing that the leaders of the two parties intended to exclude him from power, Somoza – urged on by his wife – organised and carried out a military coup on 9 June 1936. With relatively little violence, he easily ousted president Sacasa.[9] He then replaced him with his own candidate for acting president, Carlos Brenes Jarquín. The Nicaraguan Congress both accepted Sacasa's resignation and Jarquín's nomination with little dissent, while the US State Department also recognised Somoza's puppet president as legitimate, paving the way for Somoza's own election to the presidency.[10] Somoza was nominated for president at the Liberal Party convention held in León on 16 June, just a week after the coup.

---

6   Diederich 2007, p. 13.

7   Millet 1977, pp. 61–3.

8   Millet 1977, pp. 134–5.

9   Historian López Maltez avers that it was Salvador Debayle Somoza who urged Anastasio Somoza García to carry out the coup. See López Maltez n.d.

10   Walter 1993, pp. 50–2.

With Sacasa out of the way, Somoza proceeded to eliminate virtually the entire old guard of the Liberal Party, filling party posts with supporters from his coalition linked to the major agricultural, commercial, and financial interests in Nicaragua.[11] He also brought into his coalition the Blue Shirts (*Camisas Azules*), a small fascist movement made up of youth from middle-class families and from upper-class families-in-decline, a group also linked to the National Guard which provided their military training. They were useful for demonstrations, street fighting, and harassing political enemies.[12] The Blue Shirts' role was negligible organisationally and ideologically, and after the election they were disbanded and disappeared from the country's political life.

Somoza also wanted labour support, but on his own terms. With labour, he used the classic carrot and stick. At the time of the coup, he had confined on Corn Island several leaders of the Nicaraguan Workers Party (PTN) which had recently adopted Marxist-Leninist principles. When a strike of taxi drivers and construction workers occurred during his campaign, he intervened in the strike on the side of the workers, but suppressed the PTN which had urged the workers to continue the strike.[13] He later imposed a new tax on liquor, using the revenue to build a Workers House (a union hall) in Managua and other cities as a way of making the unions beholden to him.

Somoza's coup, followed by his presidential candidacy, had divided both the Conservative and Liberal parties. After Emiliano Chamorro went into self-imposed exile, the Conservative Party divided; one faction continued to support Leonardo Argüello's, while the other faction backed Somoza. Somoza supported and financed the rival Nationalist Conservative Party that supported his candidacy unconditionally. He could now claim to be the candidate of both of the country's historic parties running on a common programme. When the opposition withdrew before the election, Somoza was left as the only candidate, but could claim that he was a kind of candidate of national unity. Throughout his presidency, Somoza would depend upon the coalition that he had created between the National Liberals and National Conservatives together with the economic relationships that he fostered among businessmen from those two groups and from his own business interests.

The election held on 8 December had a high rate of abstention by the political opposition, with less than half of all potential voters casting ballots, down from about 85 percent in the two previous elections. Somoza received

11   Millet 1977, pp. 176–8.
12   Millet 1977, p. 177.
13   Millet 1977, p. 175.

64,000 Liberal Nationalist votes and 15,433 Conservative nationalist votes, while Argüello received 1,038 votes from the Historic Conservatives and 162 from the Constitutional Liberals.[14] The overwhelming vote for Somoza meant that the historic Liberals and Conservatives had little recourse but to complain to the US government, which, however, declined to challenge Somoza's election. With the support of National Guard and backed by his Nationalist Liberal-Nationalist Conservative coalition, Somoza began his four-year term on 3 January 1937. He placed in his office photos of his heroes: Nicaraguan Liberal presidents Zelaya and Moncada and the Italian Fascist Benito Mussolini, though later, as World War II approached, he replaced Mussolini's photo with that of US President Franklin D. Roosevelt.[15]

In his book *Guardians of the Dynasty*, Richard Millet argues that responsibility for Somoza's success in becoming the president and dictator of Nicaragua was principally due to the United States. 'In its drive to ensure political and financial stability in Nicaragua the United States insisted upon the creation of the Guardia', writes Millet. 'It was assumed that, by breaking the ties between the political leaders and the military and by giving both officers and men professional training and status, revolution would be discouraged, fiscal responsibility advanced, and democracy made possible'. Millet believes this solution to the problem to be mistaken. 'Nicaragua suffered from economic underdevelopment, concentration of wealth, mass illiteracy, strong regionalism, and weak nationalism'. Only a solution that dealt with those social problems, he argues, could bring about stability and democracy.[16] The US, however, opted for stability through military power.

Anastasio Somoza García, the founder of the dynasty, though he may have been influenced by Nicaragua's reactionary intellectuals and rightwing groups, was not primarily an ideologically driven person.[17] Not only was he motivated by the desire to take and hold power for its own sake, but he was also well aware of the economic benefits that power could bring. His central preoccupation throughout the years of his rule from 1936 to 1956 was to modernise Nicaragua in order to make the investments of the capitalist class more profitable – and to enrich himself along the way. While he was a dictator and could be tyrannical, he tended to be selectively repressive, allowing some political freedom of action for his elite political opponents in the loyal opposition, but never enough to endanger his rule. He reserved serious repression for the disloyal opposition

---

14   Millet 1977, p. 182.
15   Walter 1993, p. 45.
16   Millet 1977, p. 183.
17   Pérez-Boltadano 2008, p. 485.

of the militant Conservatives who plotted coups to overthrow his government, the independent Liberals who refused to participate in his political pacts, and, in its most savage and sadistic form, for the Marxist-Leninist guerrillas who sought to overthrow his regime.

The National Guard which he commanded represented the central pillar of Somoza's political power. The Guard was a body of over 2,000 armed men, a kind of 'mafia in uniform' who not only served as army and national police, but also regularly extorted bribes from Nicaraguan citizens and controlled gambling, prostitution and smuggling.[18] Well paid and provided for, while their criminal activities were overlooked, the Guard, together with their families and friends, represented several thousand loyal, organised, and committed Somoza supporters. The Guard overlapped with the Somoza wing of the Liberal Party, its officers and members also sometimes holding party positions. Then too, in addition to the regular guard, there was also the National Liberal Party Military League, a paramilitary organisation. The Guard provided Somoza's power; the United States put him in a position to use it.

US President Franklin D. Roosevelt's declaration of the Good Neighbour Policy in a speech on 4 March 1933, which had been accompanied by the withdrawal of the US Marines from Nicaragua, provided Somoza with an entirely new political situation. Nicaragua's government would still depend upon the diplomatic recognition of the United States, on its provision of military training and arms, and on its corporate economic investment, but under the new policy the country would no longer be subject to direct military intervention. Somoza would have to keep American investors happy, would have to placate the American Embassy, but he would otherwise have a relatively free hand to run the country as he saw fit. He would quickly learn that he could keep the US Embassy happy by demonstrating his willingness to support US foreign policy, whether in the war with Fascist-Nazi powers in World War II or in the struggle with the Communists during the Cold War. The Embassy in return generally turned a blind eye to the more unpleasant aspects of his government.

Somoza initially put himself forward as a man of the people who would develop and modernise Nicaragua for the benefit of all. His programme of 1935 called for giving land to the peasants, extending protection to the working class, and economic expansion through government support for industry and commerce. At the heart of it was a plan for the state's construction of highways and schools, extending the government's reach into the countryside.[19] He promised

---

18   Walker and Wade 2011, p. 27; Millet 1977, p. 191.
19   Walter 1993, p. 45.

to take care of everyone's problems – but especially to look after his friends and supporters.[20] And though his promises to peasants and workers were not fulfilled, during his presidency, which extended into the mid-1950s, the first Somoza did modernise the state and the economy, while at the same time inserting Nicaragua into the broader economic structures of Central America. The process begun by Somoza Garcia continued under his sons Luis Somoza Debayle and Anastasio Somoza Debayle.

The United States had helped to launch what would become one of Latin America's longest lasting dictatorships, but it was Somoza who took advantage of the opportunity to build the relationships to the political parties and national elites that gave his regime a remarkable stability and longevity. Andrés Pérez-Baltodano, author of an important study of Nicaraguan political history, writes: 'Once in charge, Somoza García would show a great ability to use the state apparatus inherited from the [US] intervention, as well as the domestic political dynamics, *within* a framework established by US foreign policy, by the international Pan-American system, and by the tendencies of the world economic system'.[21] Somoza recognised, having come to power at the moment that Franklin Delano Roosevelt proclaimed the Good Neighbour policy and – for the time being – put an end to US armed intervention in Latin America, that he would have considerable latitude within the parameters established by the United States. When questioned once about his support for the Somoza government, Roosevelt is famously, though perhaps apocryphally, supposed to have quipped: 'He's a son of a bitch, but he's *our* son of a bitch'.[22] Yet, while circumscribed by US interests, Somoza was also his own man.

Whether he looked to Mussolini or later to Roosevelt as his inspiration, Somoza had the notion that the state should play a leading role in economic development and social welfare. Somoza's National Liberal Party triumphed in the 1938 congressional elections, giving him the majority necessary to promulgate a new Constitution, in much of its language a progressive document. Perhaps under the influence of Mexico's magna carta, the Liberals' new Nicaraguan Constitution of 1939 gave no special privileges to the Catholic Church. Also like Mexico it defined property as having a 'social function', allowed the government to tax it, regulate its sale, and even to expropriate it if necessary;

---

20   Walter 1993, p. 46.
21   Perez-Baltodano 2008, p. 484.
22   Diederich 2007, p. 21. FDR is also reported to have said the same thing about Rafael Trujillo, dictator of the Dominican Republic.

it also declared that idle lands of the latifundia could be divided up among middle-sized and small farmers. At the same time, the Constitution gave workers a weekly day of rest, a minimum wage, maximum working hours, severance pay for occupational accidents, and free medical care. There was also the promise to create a national social security system.

Though the 1939 Constitution ostensibly guaranteed freedom of the press without prior censorship, at the same time it was forbidden to make statements that might jeopardise republican government, the established order, public morality or proper behaviour, or cause injury to third parties. The Liberals, just like the revolutionary government in Mexico, hesitated to give women the vote, believing that they were too easily influenced by the Catholic Church which was aligned with the Conservative Party.[23] The new Constitution extended President Somoza's tenure in office to 1 May 1947 – that is, it lengthened his term by six years, meaning that he would hold office for 10 years and six months before a new election was held.[24] Though the Constitution generally adhered to the American model of republican and democratic government, Pérez-Baltodano suggests that its conception of the executive was influenced by the Nazi's totalitarian spirit, giving the example of Article 21, which reads: 'The Executive Power is exercised by a citizen with the title of President of the Republic. He is the Chief of State and Personifies the Nation'.[25]

Firmly in power in Nicaragua, Somoza travelled abroad in 1939, visiting several foreign nations and the United States, where he received 'the full red-carpet treatment'. Somoza met with President Franklin D. Roosevelt and with members of the cabinet. The two presidents discussed continued American support for Nicaragua's Military Academy of the National Guard, plans for the canalisation of the San Juan River, highway building projects, and economic matters. Roosevelt provided Somoza with two million dollars in credit, the money loaned by the Bank of Manhattan Company and guaranteed by the Export-Import Bank. In a further exchange of letters after the meeting, Roosevelt agreed to provide Army Engineers and funding for the canal and highway projects as well as a military officer to serve as director of the Military Academy.[26] His 1939 visit to Washington, DC, represented Somoza's anointment by the head of the American empire as a prince in his own province of Nicaragua. Following his visit, Somoza continued to cultivate Roosevelt, send-

23   Pérez-Baltodano 2008, p. 495.
24   Walter 1993, p. 93; Pérez-Baltodano 2008, p. 490.
25   Pérez-Baltodano 2008, p. 494.
26   Millet 1977, p. 194.

ing him 'an endless stream of flattering messages' and naming Managua's main street Avenida Roosevelt.[27]

His power ratified in the new Constitution and blessed by Roosevelt, Somoza clearly thought of himself as the virtual king of Nicaragua and his family lived like royalty. Throughout his presidencies, his wife Salvadora Debayle, popularly known as Doña Salvadorita, served as a very public First Lady, handing out 25,000 presents to the poor at Christmas in 1938, acting as hostess at state dinners, appearing frequently as the nation's most *grande dame* in the society pages. The Colonia Salvadorita, a neighbourhood in Managua, was named after her, as was May 27 Street, the date of her birth. The pair had three children, Lillian, Luis and Anastasio, all of whom were sent to be educated in the United States. Lillian, who studied at Gunston Hall Academy in Washington, DC, became a good friend of Margaret Truman, the daughter of US President Harry Truman, a relationship with the Trumans that was also quite beneficial to her father.

In 1941, in an extremely controversial event, Somoza had his daughter Lillian crowned Queen of the National Guard by Archbishop José Antonio Lezcano y Ortega in the old Cathedral of Managua. Wearing a designer dress and a twelve inch high gold and silver crown encrusted with sapphires and rubies (said to have been designed by Van Cleef & Arpels and to cost $100,000), she rode through the streets of Managua accompanied by National Guardsmen dressed as Roman soldiers, through the main avenues to the National Palace where she was received by 3,000 guests at the National Palace, where there was music and dancing in her honour. There the high officials of the National Guard presented her with a bracelet decorated with a crown made up of eleven diamonds. While the elite were dancing in the palace, the plebs were served beer on the lawn outside. That same year, Somoza had a portrait of Lillian dressed as an Indian painted and then engraved and printed on the one córdoba bill. Two years later she married Guillermo Sevilla Sacasa, the Ambassador to the United States; he held the post until the 1979 revolution.[28]

Not surprisingly, Somoza used the office of president to enrich himself, accumulating some three to four million dollars in his first three years in office. By the time he had been in office for a decade, Somoza's wealth was estimated at $120 million. How did he do it? Somoza demanded tributes on exports of cattle, minerals, and textiles, funds that he personally controlled. Everyone who did business in Nicaragua could expect to have to fork over to Somoza. He invested

---

27   Millet 1977, pp. 196–7; Diederich 2007, p. 22. The quotation is from Millet.
28   'Lillian Somoza Debayle', n.d.

his money in real estate, often pressuring the owners to sell him the property at below market value prices. Property owners had little choice but to sell at his price or face government harassment. Using these various techniques, 'he soon became the wealthiest man in Nicaragua's history'.[29]

Flamboyant and ostentatious, Somoza 'delighted in cheap and gaudy things'. He had a jukebox with flashing lights in the reception hall at the palace and alongside it a fourteen-foot stuffed alligator. He delighted in cockfights and would sometimes throw a calf into the Tipitapa River to watch the freshwater sharks tear it to pieces. He would invite the cabinet and his hangers-on to his ranch where they would sit on the corral fence cheering as the bulls serviced the cows. He would go out drinking and dancing all night at La Curva and then take his friends to his ranch to continue the party.[30]

World War II

When World War II broke out, there were many throughout Latin America who – had it not been for American pressure – would have supported Hitler's Germany against Great Britain, resenting British control over their economies for over a hundred years.[31] No doubt some in Nicaragua felt the same way, given Britain's long control of the Caribbean coast. But Somoza, ultimately dependent upon the United States for recognition and support, naturally took the side of America and the Allied Powers. Nicaragua, like the United States, declared war on the Axis powers in December 1941. With the excuse of a possible – if highly unlikely – Axis attack on Nicaragua, Somoza declared a state of martial law that limited civil rights. He also expanded the National Liberal Party's paramilitary organisation, the Liberal Military League of Nicaragua, which he himself headed. At the same time, he made himself the head of the National Liberal Party, now buttressed by extensive political patronage and commanding a strong party organisation. With the war as his justification, the Nicaraguan government seized the plantations belonging to Italian and German immigrants in Matagalpa, expropriated them, and turned the property over to the Banco Nacional. Most of that land then passed into the hands

---

29   Millet 1977, p. 197; Diederich 2007, pp. 23–5.
30   Diederich 2007, p. 31.
31   Principally because their nations had been dominated by England and the United States, some Latin American political and military leaders, especially in South America, supported the Axis. Some of them also felt an affinity with Nazi and Fascist systems or with Generalissimo Franco's religious-military Falange.

of Somoza and his cronies.[32] Such mingling of Somoza's role as president and as businessman was common. When the government was considering building a new airport, Somoza first bought the land and then announced the government's plans to build a new airport, sold the land to the Banco Nacional, which in turn sold it to the government, enriching Somoza.[33]

The Crisis of 1944 and the Pacts

The Somoza regime, as it consolidated its power, was not without its critics and opponents. As early as 1937, a group of Liberal Party university graduates organised the Nicaraguan Democratic Group which later became the anti-somocista Independent Liberal Party (PLI). The PLI criticised the lack of democracy and Somoza's use of the government for the benefit of his own businesses. Organisations of middle-class and professional Nicaraguans in exile – such as the moderate Patriotic Abstentionist Nicaraguan Committee in New York and the radical Revolutionary Nicaraguan Committee in Mexico – called for opposition to the Somoza regime, but they had little impact within the country. In February 1940, a group of students printed and distributed the famous photograph of Somoza embracing Sandino not long before the rebel was murdered, together with the headline 'The Embrace of Death' and the caption 'Yesterday he killed Sandino, today he kills the people'. The police called the students 'communist conspirators', arrested them, and eight leaders were confined on Little Corn Island while nine more received thirty days' hard labour. The government's election authorities declared that there were now only two legal political parties, the Nationalist Liberals and the Nationalist Conservatives, because the other parties had not participated in the last election.[34]

Under the impact of rising anti-colonial and democratic movements throughout the Caribbean and Central America, the first significant opposition movement in the country appeared in the spring of 1944 as Somoza began to turn his attention to the coming elections of 1947. The Constitution did not permit presidential re-election, but Congress, dominated by his party, passed a constitutional amendment which would allow a sitting president to run for re-election if his term of office coincided with an international war that had lasted at least two years. To his surprise, Liberals in Managua and León publicly

---

32   Walter 1993, pp. 108–9; Diederich 2007, p. 22.
33   Walter 1993, p. 109.
34   Walter 1993, pp. 111–14.

opposed Somoza's plan for re-election – and were promptly jailed. But when a Liberal congressman proposed a measure calling for their release, which was unanimously approved by the lower house, Somoza yielded, attempting to avoid a split in his own party.

Nevertheless, opposition to Somoza's re-election quickly became a popular cause. At the time, Nicaragua had about 600 university students, half at the Managua campus and the others on campuses in Granada and Leon. At a general assembly of students at the Managua campus, it was decided to march on 27 June in support of the new reform government in Guatemala that had come to power after the overthrow of the dictator Ubico. The march soon became a demonstration for democracy and freedom in both Guatemala and Nicaragua and grew to 2,000 people, only perhaps a quarter of them students. Police and the National Guard suppressed the march and jailed 500 demonstrators.

When, two days later, women dressed in black – mothers and sisters of the jailed protestors – marched to demand the release of those still being held, pro-Somoza demonstrators drove them from the streets. Union officials also demanded the release of workers who had been jailed during the pro-democracy demonstration, while students and professionals in León wrote to Somoza to demand the release of the prisoners. Somoza dealt carefully with the situation, personally supervising the release of the students to their parents, while chastising them for their personal attacks on him. Though the students could have been court-marshalled for protesting in front of military installations, Somoza ordered that they be tried before civilian courts. At the same time, Somoza closed the university to prevent further student organising against him, but that in turn led his own minister of education to resign in protest.[35]

The Liberal Party leadership met on 3 July and one group argued that the time had come for Somoza to give up his re-election plans or even resign, while others were not convinced. The next day, 4 July – coincidentally US Independence Day – became an occasion for both pro- and anti-Somocistas to demonstrate in an attempt to influence the American Embassy. While initially both groups appeared at the US Embassy, soon the anti-Somoza group which had grown to more than 20,000 dominated the space. Opposition leader, businessman Carlos Pasos, addressed the crowd, which cheered him, but when Somoza attempted to speak he was jeered, as were a group of Guard cadets who guarded the embassy. The crowd then marched to the Mexican Embassy, but there the

---

35   Walter 1993, pp. 130–2.

Guard attacked them, leading 500 to seek refuge inside the embassy, though all but twenty were soon allowed to leave.

When shopkeepers called for a strike on 5 July, Somoza threatened to seize their businesses and to expel foreign businesspeople from the country. Cattlemen from Boaco and Chontales, both Conservative Party strongholds, began to hold back meat shipments to the capital. Somoza accused them of subversion and threatened to requisition their beef. Somoza's control of the labour unions was key to preventing the 1944 opposition movement from overthrowing his government. He not only succeeded in keeping the unions from becoming involved in the opposition movement, but also kept most of the unions as active allies of the government. Those led by the pro-Soviet Socialist Party of Nicaragua, following the Communists' Popular Front line of Communist unity with governments supporting the Allied Powers, dissociated themselves from the opposition movement and expressed explicit support for Somoza. The Communist PSN's backing of Somoza discredited it in the eyes of many of the student activists who wanted to act to end the regime.

What had begun as a small student demonstration for democracy had become a national political crisis for the Somoza government. The Liberal party had split, the Conservative Party had begun to raise its head, and society in general was clamouring for Somoza to give up his plans for reelection. On 7 July, he did just that, announcing – under pressure from the US Embassy – that he would not seek re-election for the next term. He promised that he would veto the bill which would have permitted him to seek re-election, and he vowed a free and fair election in 1947. While this ended the immediate crisis, there continued to be repercussions: Leonardo Argüello, the Minister of the Interior, resigned, as did the mayor of León. Carlos Pasos, the dissident Independent Liberal who had become the spokesperson for the movement, left the Mexican Embassy to meet with Somoza, who wanted to bring reconciliation to his party, though no agreement was reached.[36]

Taking advantage of the existing state of martial law which had been declared when Nicaragua entered World War II, Somoza now imposed prior censorship on the newspapers (which lasted two years) and Congress passed a law further restricting freedom of the press. At the same time, as the war was coming to an end, Somoza's government passed a new labour code that on the one hand granted certain trade-union rights, but on the other hand put certain restrictions on the unions. Somoza increased his support for the loyal Organizing Committee of the Confederation of Nicaraguan Workers while clamping

---

36   Walter 1993, p. 133.

down on the leftist trade-union leaders and activists of the Communist PSN, who, despite their recent display of loyalty and their backing of his labour legislation, he still distrusted.

Though he promised not to be a candidate, Somoza actually planned to find a way to run, as became clear from the many Liberal Party meetings – organised by the president himself – calling upon him to be the party standard bearer. The United States had become firmly opposed to the idea that he would run for office again, believing in November of 1945 that if he did, the Nicaraguan government might be overthrown. As Ambassador Fletcher Warren wrote to US Secretary of State James Byrnes, '... Nicaraguan Govt is in tight political situation that may end in revolution'.[37]

The US government, seeing that Somoza was resisting, sent Acting Secretary of State Nelson Rockefeller, Assistant Secretary of State Spruille Braden, and US Ambassador to Nicaragua Fletcher Warren to meet with Somoza, making it clear that his candidacy was unacceptable. When Somoza told Ambassador Warren that he did not really understand what the Americans were saying, Warren replied: 'They are telling you that your government is considered to be that of a dictator'.[38] The United States wanted to see democratic elections in Nicaragua so that it would not be seen as supporting a dictatorship. In what must have been a move even more unnerving for Somoza, US Military Attaché Col. Frederick B. Judson also began to talk to officers of the National Guard about the need for a non-political military, a conversation that threatened to undermine the central pillar of Somoza's government. Somoza must have contemplated the possibility that the US was planning a coup to overthrow him, as it had done to other Nicaraguan and Latin American rulers. Under these pressures, Somoza resigned himself to withdrawing from the election – though he would still make sure that he controlled the outcome.[39]

Somoza prepared to hold the 1947 election, which was meant to create the illusion of a democratic opening. He permitted a large anti-Somoza protest march and demonstration of 100,000 in Manauga and kept the Guard in barracks. The Somoza government declared that while the National Liberals and National Conservatives represented the two major parties, the government would also allow the old Conservative Party to take part in the election, and even the fiercely anti-*somocista* independent Liberal Party would be allowed to participate. Somoza also ended the state of siege that had begun with the

---

37　　Warren 1945, p. 1212.

38　　Ibid.

39　　Walter 1993, pp. 144–9.

war and lifted restrictions on the press. The principal opposition newspaper, *La Prensa*, which had been closed for almost two years, was permitted to reopen.

Another Coup – and More Pacts

Somoza, hoping to placate some of his Liberal opponents, picked as his candidate Leonardo Argüello, the minister of the interior who had earlier resigned to protest against the dictator's handling of the 1944 protests. General Emiliano Chamorro returned from exile to negotiate a pact between the two genuine opposition parties, the historic Conservative Party and the independent Liberal Party. They then chose Dr. Enoc Aguado, an elderly and uninspiring Liberal, as their presidential candidate. Neither Aguado nor his programme made much of an impression on the electorate. Nevertheless, everyone was aware that the principal issue was whether or not Somoza would continue to control the Nicaraguan government. The election was relatively fair and open, with only occasional breaking up of meetings by the Guard, but there was an even lower level of participation than the previous one and massive fraud contributed to the victory of Somoza's preferred candidate Argüello. Yet despite the fraud and the victory of the man who was Somoza's choice, there was little protest.[40]

Argüello, chosen by Somoza to be a front man, proved to be more independent than anyone had expected. Even before his inauguration, Argüello had told the American Ambassador that he intended to remove Somoza from his position as head of the National Guard. In his inauguration speech, Argüello proclaimed: 'I will not be, take this as certain, just another President, carried along passively by the currents of custom and tradition. I will work constantly, and the citizen who loves peace in the honorable exercise of democratic freedoms can be sure that he will enjoy them, as well as of the progress which is their natural product'.[41] The new president did not just announce his intentions; he acted. Once in office, Argüello moved to end illegal gambling businesses run by members of the Guard and by some public employees. He got rid of the corrupt manager of the Ferrocarril del Pacífico, the state railroad, replacing him with an American businessman. He moved to demilitarise the many public services – health, customs, communications, and the railroad – that were

---

40   Walter 1993, pp. 155–9; Millet 1977, pp. 207–8.
41   Cited in Pérez-Baltodano 2008, p. 506.

controlled by the National Guard. All of these measures quickly brought Argüello into sharp conflict with Somoza.[42]

Argüello had promised that he would not touch the officers of the National
Guard or of other security forces, but when Somoza's party in the Congress
designated three *somocistas* as successors to Argüello should he leave office,
that was the last straw. Argüello responded by appointing a new head of the
Managua Police Department, a new head of communications, a new inspector
general of the army, a new head of the general staff, and a new commanding
officer of the presidential guard, all men loyal to him. On 25 May, in a surprisingly courageous and dramatic move, Argüello ordered Somoza to resign as
director of the Guard and leave the country at once.[43]

Asking for time to arrange his affairs, Somoza spent the night organising
the Guard to carry out the coup which took place the next day.[44] The National
Guard seized the National Palace, home of the Congress and most government
ministries, took over the Managua police barracks, and cut off all communications with the Presidential Palace.[45] Argüello refused to resign and took refuge
in the Mexican Embassy. Congress, either loyal to or intimidated by Somoza,
met a week later, fired Argüello, and replaced him with Somoza's puppet president, Benjamín Lacayo.[46] Still neither the United States nor any Latin American
country would recognise his government because it was the result of a coup.
The United States ended all military assistance and training of the Guard and
there were threats not to seat the Nicaraguan delegates at the coming Río Conference for inter-hemispheric defence. All of these events were taking place
at the worst possible moment for Somoza, with a reform president, Jacobo
Arbenz Guzmán, elected in Guatemala and José Figueres leading a democratic
revolution in Costa Rica. Somoza may well have feared that the neighbouring
governments might try to overthrow him.

In an attempt to construct some basis for its legitimacy so that it could
seek US recognition, the government of Lacayo set elections for a Constituent Assembly for 3 August 1947, though the Conservatives refused to participate, meaning that the National Liberals and National Conservatives, both
controlled by Somoza, were the only parties on the ballot. The new Constitu-

---

42   Walter 1993, p. 159.
43   Walter 1993, p. 160; Millet 1977, pp. 209–10.
44   Pérez-Baltodano 2008, p. 506. He calls this a 'golpe de estado técnico', that is, a 'technical
      coup', because while the president was removed from office, all of the state institutions
      remained intact.
45   Millet 1977, pp. 210–11.
46   Walter 1993, p. 160.

ent Assembly was elected, met quickly, and chose Victor Román y Reyes, an uncle of Somoza, to complete the presidential term of Argüello. Still the United States refused to recognise the new government, a situation which encouraged the Conservative Party to attempt a coup d'état. The Conservatives' pathetic effort – small bands of armed men attacking two insignificant locations in Chinandega and Zelaya provinces – was quickly suppressed and the leaders captured. They confessed their ties to General Emiliano Chamorro who immediately requested and received a safe passage to leave the country on 27 September. The government arrested and detained for a month leaders of the Conservative and Independent Liberal parties. By the end of 1947, the entire political crisis that had opened in 1944 had passed and Somoza was firmly in charge once again.[47]

Somoza's contempt for both the institutions of democracy and the people of Nicaragua could be seen in his remarks to *Time* magazine: 'When asked about charges that he had tyrannised Nicaragua, Tacho replied: "These little countries are like children. When a boy's sick, you've got to force castor oil down him whether he likes it or not. After he's been to the toilet a few times he'll be all right"'.[48] For Somoza, the people were a threat who had to be repressed. As he once said: 'My opponents should remember what we, the *gente decente* are only 6 percent; if trouble arises, the 94 percent may crush us all'.[49]

With the all too independent Argüello having been removed and replaced, the question now was to re-establish the regime's legitimacy. Somoza moved to reach an accommodation with the Conservative Party that would restore the social and political basis of his regime. First, Somoza oversaw the writing of a new Constitution. The Constituent Assembly, under Somoza's direction, wrote a new Constitution of 1948 which removed all of the progressive language from the 1939 Constitution. Unlike the secular Constitution of 1939, the 1948 Constitution's preamble referred to God. Under the new constitution, the state no longer had the power to seize land from the latifundia and distribute it to farmers. In line with the Cold War and the new anti-Communism emanating from the US State Department, the Constitution banned Communist and Nazi-Fascist parties with international ties, and it added provisions facilitating the passage of foreign troops across the country and the establishment of foreign military bases on Nicaraguan soil. The new Constitution reaffirmed the legitimacy of the Román y Reyes government and extended its term until May of 1952.

---

47   Walter 1993, 164–8; Millet 1977, pp. 211–12.
48   Diederich 2007, p. 28.
49   Diederich 2007, p. 33.

Second, Somoza reached an agreement with Carlos Cuadra Pasos, a leader of the Conservative Party. They signed an accord that would form the political basis for Somoza's remaining years in power and for the sons who succeeded him. The Somoza-Cuadra Pasos Pact provided: (1) a general amnesty for all of those imprisoned for political offences and permission for exiles to return to Nicaragua; (2) an immediate share of government posts for the Conservative Party through special 'elections' that would give the Conservative's seven deputies and four senators. To make sure that they would win those seats, the National Liberal Party would not participate and other parties would be excluded; (3) one vacancy would be created in the Supreme Court to be filled by the Conservatives; (4) Conservatives would be appointed to positions on the state banks and public service boards and to diplomatic missions and international conferences; (5) Conservatives would be given a majority on the municipal councils where they had had a majority of votes in the 1932 presidential elections. In return, the Conservatives would recognise the Román y Reyes government. Somoza, of course, would remain at the head of the National Guard.

The Somoza-Cuadra Pasos Pact eliminated from the equation the historic leader of the Conservative Party, General Emiliano Chamorro, once again in exile, who rejected the agreement and continued to call for opposition to Somoza. An alliance of the Chamorrista Conservatives and the independent Liberal Party, and the newly created and at best ephemeral National Feminist Association and the Democratic Union of Workers and Peasants, opposed the pact, but their voices had little impact. Unwilling to concede defeat, Chamorro joined with José Figueres of Costa Rica and Juan Rodríguez García of the Dominican Republic to organise the Legion of the Caribbean with the goal of overthrowing the Somoza government, but to no avail. The Pact represented a very low cost means for Somoza to consolidate his power.[50]

Finally in 1950, Somoza and Chamorro reached an agreement for yet another political pact that would bring the recalcitrant Conservative faction into the system. The new Somoza-Chamorro Pact provided: (1) elections on 21 May for both a Constituent Assembly and a new president; (2) Conservatives to receive twenty seats in the Constituent Assembly; (3) the new Constitution would provide for the direct election of municipal governments; (4) Conservatives would hold the portfolios in a new government of ministers of finance and education. The Constituent Assembly then met and chose three National Liberals and two Conservatives for the Supreme Court and similarly for the other courts. The Constitution of 1950 also called for: a non-partisan national army; free elec-

---

50   Pérez-Baltodano 2008, p. 512.

tions; freedom of expression; and women's suffrage (at some indefinite point in the future). It also prohibited presidential re-election.[51]

When Román Reyes died in office on 6 May, that is, two weeks before the coming elections, the Congress chose Anastasio Somoza to serve as interim president; at the same time, he also became the National Liberal Party candidate for president. The Conservative Party, perceived by the public to have surrendered to Somoza, suffered a disastrous defeat at the polls. In an election that the opposition *La Prensa* described as fair and free from intimidation by the Guard, the National Liberals won by overwhelming majorities while the Conservatives received less than a quarter of the vote.[52] Somoza thus returned to the presidency and to legitimacy.

Somoza also moved to restore his relationship to the American government. When the United States promoted the creation of the Organisation of American States (OAS) in 1948 as a way of consolidating its power in Latin America within the context of the Cold War, Somoza rushed to pledge his unconditional support for the new institution. In turn the United States recognised his government and allowed him greater latitude within his own country.[53] Throughout the Cold War, Nicaragua could be relied upon in the OAS and in the United Nations to support the United States and vote accordingly.

While the elections may have legitimised the government in the eyes of the United States and international organisations, and while the pacts may have satisfied the loyal parties and the elite, much of the Nicaraguan public remained dubious, and especially the youth. The Somoza-Cuadra Pasos and the Somoza-Chamorro Pact, as was clear to the Nicaraguan public, had nothing to do with bringing democracy to Nicaragua. The two agreements were simply corrupt bargains between political party leaders that aimed to broaden the regime's base of political support among the elite by divvying up the spoils of office. The pacts were in fact highly undemocratic, since they distributed political posts among the parties before the elections had even taken place. The pacts served to keep political power in the hands of the two parties that represented the country's financial, commercial, and agricultural interests and either excluded or marginalised the middle-class opposition party, the PLI, and the Communist PSN. Somoza's political wheeling and dealing served to discredit the idea of republican government and democracy in the eyes of those who lived under his rule.

---

51   Walter 1993, pp. 176–7.
52   Walter 1993, pp. 178–80.
53   Pérez-Baltodano 2008, p. 513.

Somoza's dictatorship then was re-established on a broader base of support from the business class. While he was a dictator, it is important to remember that Somoza – despite the vicissitudes of protests and attempted coups – was only able to carry out his modernisation programme because he had created a political system supported by the country's landowners and business groups, by those with wealth and property. The support that he had among National Liberals and the Conservatives, a support that grew stronger throughout the 1950s and under his sons in the 1960s, provided the underlying social base for his government without which it could not survive. While US support for Somoza – which wavered in certain periods – was important, and while his control of the National Guard was key, it was broad social support he had among the business classes that gave the regime its long-term stability.

Somoza's Economic Programme of Modernisation

During the first Somoza's rule, not only did he, with US assistance, modernise the army, but he also built significant infrastructure, established a national social security system, and made modest improvements in education, while at the same time developing agriculture and expanding manufacture, all of which resulted in a larger and more prosperous economy and a higher average per capita income. Most of the benefits of that economic expansion went to the capitalists involved in agriculture, industry, commerce and finance, but Nicaraguans of all social classes also benefitted to some degree. As this economic development took place, the old land-owning class came to share power with more modern agricultural producers and factory owners, as well as merchants and bankers; those groups came to constitute a new, more modern capitalist class which was the principal beneficiary of the economic development of the era.

The heart of Somoza's economic programme was the expansion of agricultural exports – bananas, sugar, and coffee, but above all cotton – a programme which, while enriching a few and leading to a slight expansion in the middle class, also led to the loss of land by many peasants who were forced to become agricultural labourers. Agro exports and related industrialisation of agricultural processing based on the concentration of land, investment, financing, infrastructure as well as state support and incentives did not lead to improvements in other sectors of the economy. And agricultural production of food for the internal market, which was always marginal, did not improve. The growth of agricultural export crops tended to drive peasants who produced basic grains and legumes (corn, beans, wheat, and rice) into the agricultural frontier in the mountains. While the capitalist class became more prosperous, many peasants became impoverished, working as seasonal agricultural labours or moving to the cities to join the ranks of the urban poor.[54]

While initially successful, the Somozas' modernisation of the Nicaraguan state and the economy in the 1940s to the 1960s not only led to major changes in class relations and to the social dislocation of many peasants, but also eventually ran up against the general crisis of US and world capitalism in the late 1960s. These developments in the political economy of Nicaragua laid the basis not only for the Somoza political regime, but also for the Sandinista revolution.[55] During the Somoza era, the country's capitalists sent their children for higher education to Europe or the United States, but Nicaragua's economy could not absorb them and their talents, and they tended to become first part of the political opposition and then part of an underground revolutionary movement. As in Russia in the late nineteenth century, Nicaragua created disaffected intellectuals, dislocated peasants, and a new class of workers who wanted improvements in their lives.

Since the late nineteenth century, Nicaragua's economy had been dominated principally by cattle-raising and coffee farming, though in the early twentieth century bananas also became a significant crop. In the pre-war period, both cattle and coffee production took place in rural economy based on large haciendas or fincas as well as on smaller farms, where production methods hardly changed between 1900 and 1950. As agriculture was battered by falling coffee prices beginning in the 1920s, a blight that affected banana production in the 1930s, and then the Great Depression, the Nicaraguan economy declined precipitously.

Anastasio Somoza Garcia determined to use the state to modernise the economy, to improve profits for other capitalists, and to make himself rich in the process. Working with the International Monetary Fund, the World Bank, and the Food and Agriculture Organisation of the United Nations, Nicaragua created a five-year economic development programme in 1952.[56] At the very base of the modernisation programme was the construction of infrastructure. Somoza created a Ministry of the Economy and within it a Department of Highways that undertook the construction of roads and highways to unify the nation, to increase the state's presence throughout the country, and to lay the foundations for increased economic activity. In 1940, Nicaragua had

---

54   Solà i Monserrat 2008, pp. 99–100.

55   This section relies heavily on Biderman 1983, pp. 7–32; Library of Congress, n.d., especially Chapter 3, 'The Economy', by Barbara Annis; and Andrés Pérez-Boltadano 2008.

56   Pérez-Boltadano 2008, p. 526.

52 kilometres of paved roads and highways and 149 unpaved kilometres for a total of a mere 201 kilometres altogether; by 1955, this had increased to 280 paved kilometres, 3,407 unpaved kilometres, for a total of 3,687 kilometres.[57] The development of this highway system for the first time made it possible for the Nicaraguan state to actually exert influence over the entire country, though the East Coast still remained relatively isolated.

The economic stimulus provided by the revival of the US economy in World War II led to an expansion in Nicaragua's traditional agricultural products such as cattle, sugar and bananas. But there was also an increase in the foreign-owned mining, lumbering, and rubber industries. Somoza's National Bank encouraged agricultural diversification, leading to the introduction of new crops such as sesame and cotton. The 1950s hamburger boom in the United States brought prosperity to Nicaraguan cattle ranchers. But the most important of these developments was the introduction of cotton, which, stimulated by the Korean War, grew spectacularly during the period of the 1950s and 1960s. Cotton exports increased from $145,000 in 1946 to $1.8 million in 1950, to $16.7 million in 1954, to $30.9 million in 1955.[58] After the Cuban Revolution of 1959 and the beginning of John F. Kennedy's Alliance for Progress, the United States assigned to Nicaragua some of what had been the Cuban cotton import quota, which also gave another fillip to cotton production.[59] By the mid-1950s cotton was second only to coffee in the national economy.

At the same time, the National Bank encouraged the modernisation of agriculture through the introduction of tractors, beginning the industrialisation of agriculture on the largest farms. While there were many cotton producers, almost 6,000 by the late 1970s, most of the exportation was in the hands of subsidiaries of foreign companies. The agricultural expansion and the opening of the American market led to an expansion of agricultural processing as well: sugar and coffee mills, cotton gins, packing and canning plants, and slaughter houses. The slaughtering of beef also led to the production of leather, to shoe plants, and soap plants. There were machines and pesticide to be sold. Nicaragua's elite families were making a lot of money. The elite economic groups tended to take control of all of the strategic parts of the business – the ginning, the slaughtering, and the exporting – and with oligopoly pricing and tariff protections and financial risk for much of this assumed by the state bank, they prospered. All of these activities of growing, processing, and exportation

57   Pérez-Boltadano 2008, p. 525.
58   Pérez-Boltadano 2008, p. 522.
59   Mayorga 2007, p. 25.

required capital through loans that increased the weight of the major industrial groups – Somoza, Banamérica, and Banic. Cotton, however, was at the centre of it all.[60]

The 1950s represented the turning point in Nicaraguan economic history, with the country for the first time in its modern history achieving significant growth rates. Though affected by periodic downturns, between 1949 and 1955 the Nicaraguan economy grew at a rate of 9.5 percent. Modernisation continued with banks providing loans for more tractors and for airplanes for fumigation with chemical herbicides. Capitalist modernisation meant an expansion of the working class. As cotton production increased, it changed the character of Nicaraguan agriculture and of the society, becoming the largest employer of labour in the country.[61] An economic historian explains:

> ... the cotton harvest remained highly labour intensive, and rapidly increasing production required a growing seasonal labour force, which represented more than 90 percent of the total number of workers and 60 to 70 percent of total annual wages. The number of seasonal cotton workers averaged 150,000 to 200,000 by the 1970s, constituting over half of the estimated economically active population in agriculture.[62]

As acreage dedicated to cotton expanded and labour shortages became a problem, cotton farmers introduced mechanical harvesting machines.

The period between 1940 and the 1970s saw the transformation of many Nicaraguan peasants into a semi-urban, agricultural proletariat. These were landless, agricultural labourers who lived in the cities most of the year, but went to work in cotton during harvest season. Cotton workers' wages were double those of other workers, but most worked only the three months of the harvest, doing odd jobs the rest of the year. Somoza's modernisation programme had created a vast mass of under-employed seasonal labourers who lived in conditions of poverty.

---

60   Mayorga 2007, pp. 25–6.
61   Biderman 1983, pp. 13–16.
62   Biderman 1983, pp. 7–32.

The King is Dead – Long Live the King

While the economic expansion enriched the elite, only a little of the country's growing wealth trickled down to the lower classes. The big planters and industrialists had access to Somoza with whom they could discuss the nation's policies, but the majority were excluded from all real political and economic decision making. The nation's legislature remained a rubber stamp, democracy a myth, and civil rights non-existent. The protest movement of 1944 had been defeated, but discontent still bubbled beneath the surface. When the Liberals, with the collaboration of the Conservatives, passed a new constitution in 1950 that would allow Somoza García to stand for election again in 1957, anger grew among many in the population at his intention to continue in office.

The National Liberal Party held its annual festival in the House of Labour in León on 21 September 1956, an opportunity for the wealthy elite, Liberal Party political operatives, and the labour unions to show their loyalty to the dictator. Rigoberto López Pérez, a young poet and a member of the opposition Independent Liberal Party, managed to gain entrance to the banquet, walked up to Somoza, and shot him. Somoza's guards shot and killed López Pérez, and carried away Somoza who was in grave condition. At first treated in hospitals in Managua, US President Dwight Eisenhower sent a plane to carry Anastasio Somoza to the US-controlled Canal Zone in Panama where the dictator died three days later. As soon as she realised her husband was severely wounded, Salvadora Debayle Somoza ordered her sons Luis and Anastasio to seize control of the government, the National Guard, and the Liberal Party.[63] Luis Somoza, who was president of the congress, immediately became acting president of Nicaragua, and was elected to the presidency a year later. His brother Anastasio Somoza Debayle already headed the National Guard on which the regime relied. By the time word of the senior Somoza's death reached Nicaragua, the sons were securely in power. The Somoza dictatorship thus became a dynasty.

Luis Somoza Debayle had been born on 18 November 1922 and was raised in Nicaragua until his father seized power in 1936. That year he was sent with his younger brother Anastasio to the Saint Leo College Prep School about 30 miles north of Tampa, Florida, then to the La Salle Military Academy on Long Island, New York. Luis later went on to college at Louisiana State University, at the University of California and at the University of Maryland. His American education, where he learned English and became familiar with the United States, was part of the preparation for one day wielding power. At the age of

---

63   López Maltez n.d.

18, his father made him a captain in the National Guard, and by 1950 Luis was serving in the Nicaraguan legislature, first as a congressman and a few years later as a senator. The Nicaraguan presidency had become a virtual monarchy, and Luis was the prince; with his father's death, he assumed the throne.

His brother Anastasio Somoza Debayle became head of the National Guard and immediately rounded up hundreds of persons, holding them for weeks without charge, and subjecting them to beatings. Among those arrested were leading figures of the political opposition: Dr. Enoc Aguado, Pedro Joaquín Chamorro, editor of *La Prensa*, and General Emiliano Chamorro. The latter two were tried by a military court and on the basis of fabricated and circumstantial evidence convicted and sentenced to prison. The three men most closely linked to the assassination, one of whom was a political leader, were held in prison until 1960 and then shot while supposedly trying to escape.[64]

Like his father, President Luis Somoza became the country's dictator, and if he ran the country with less violence, he was only somewhat less authoritarian and his regime was no less corrupt. He did make some gestures toward liberalisation, most notably by restoring the constitutional articles prohibiting immediate re-election or succession to the presidency by any relative of the incumbent.[65] During the period that he ruled the country from 1956 until his death in 1967, Luis Somoza also pulled the strings of the two other men who held the presidency, René Schick Gutiérrez (1963–6) and Lorenzo Guerrero Gutiérrez (1966–7). Other men wore the presidential sash for a few years, but the Somozas' rule never ceased. During the 1960s, Schick attempted to limit the power of the National Guard, but Anastasio Somoza gradually asserted his power not only over the Guard that he headed, but also over the government.[66]

President Luis Somoza had not only inherited the presidency, he had inherited his father's modernisation project. During his presidency he expanded the highway network from 3,687 total kilometres of paved and unpaved roads and highways to 9,952 kilometres. The United States had encouraged the creation of a Central American Common Market (MERCOMUN) and Nicaragua joined Honduras, Guatemala, and El Salvador in establishing it in December 1960 (Costa Rica joined in 1961), which led to even more rapid growth in the Nicaraguan economy. In the period between 1960 and 1965, the GDP grew at a rate of 10 percent in what later came to be seen as the 'golden age' of the Nicaraguan economy. Industrial production as a percentage of GDP increased steadily from

---

64   Millet 1977, p. 224.
65   Ibid.
66   Millet 1977, p. 227.

15.5 percent in 1964 to 17.3 percent in 1967, and then to 21.1 percent in 1971. By 1971, there were 500 more modern factories that employed 21,000 workers, while older and smaller shops employed 59,000 workers. The 80,000 industrial workers represented 10.8 percent of the economically active population.[67]

Under Luis Somoza and under his successor and front man, the reformist somocista René Schick, Nicaragua also increased the state's social services. The Nicaraguan Institute of Social Security (INSS) expanded coverage from 13,469 insured workers in 1957 to 114,692 in 1977. At the same time, the number of students not attending primary school fell from 52.3 percent in 1960 to 28.8 percent in 1966; while those not attending secondary school fell from 93.4 percent in 1960 to 85.5 percent in 1966. While these figures represented significant improvements, Nicaragua still remained the country with the worst such social statistics in Latin America, in virtually every aspect of social wellbeing far behind even the poorer nations of Central America. In the countryside in the early 1960s, for example, only 2.2 percent of the population had potable water.[68]

Another Somoza in the Presidency

On 13 April 1967, Luis Somoza died suddenly of a heart attack while his puppet Lorenzo Guerrero was still holding the office of president. There was little doubt that his younger brother Anastasio Somoza Debayle would attempt to succeed him in office. Anastasio too had been educated in the United States, first with his older brother Luis at the LaSalle Military Academy and then at the United States Military Academy at West Point, New York. It was a brilliant choice. There he became friends with future US Army officers and politicians, such as his lifelong friend John M. Murphy, the Democratic Party representative from Staten Island. Throughout his life, Somoza Debayle would frequently fly to alumni meetings at West Point to maintain those useful political and military connections.

As expected, Somoza Debayle ran for president in the elections of 1967 against Fernando Agüero, a popular Conservative Party candidate who had attempted and failed to entice the National Guard to join a coup against the Somoza regime in January of that year.[69] A large protest in Managua of between 40,000 and 60,000 people calling for the overthrow of Somoza was

---

67   Solà i Monserrat 2008, p. 367.
68   Pérez-Baltodano 2008, pp. 538–9.
69   Pérez-Baltodano 2008, pp. 558–9.

violently put down with 40 demonstrators killed and 100 wounded.[70] Somoza Debayle claimed victory in the election and assumed office despite charges of repression and fraud.[71] As president, Somoza Debayle retained his role as commander of the National Guard. 'The new president re-established the style and orientation of the government of his father, reaffirming its subordination to the United States, the use of force, and the reliance on political pacts', writes Pérez-Baltodano.[72] In 1971, Somoza Debayle reached an agreement on a new pact with Fernando Agüero, guaranteeing the Conservatives positions in the government, and agreeing on a constitutional amendment that would allow the president to run for office again in 1976.

When Richard Nixon became president in January of 1969, he continued America's support for the Nicaraguan dictatorial dynasty. Nixon made his friend Turner B. Shelton, who was also a friend of Nixon's confidant Bebe Rebozo, ambassador.

Somoza Debayle continued the modernisation programme of his father and brother, though now that the capitalist world in general and the United States in particular had entered into a period of economic crisis, not with quite the same dynamism. Still, the overall expansion of the Nicaraguan state and economy under the Somoza governments between 1932 and 1979 was impressive. Exports rose from $4.6 million in 1936 to $566.5 million in 1979. The Gross Domestic Product grew at a rate of 5.3 percent between 1945 and 1950; of 5.4 percent during the 1950s; and of 6.7 percent in the 1960s; and fell to 5.6 percent in the first half of the 1970s. No other Central American country had such high growth rates – though Nicaragua still trailed behind other countries in the region that began the mid-century at a higher level.

With the modernisation of the state, there was also an expansion of government social agencies and public employees. Public employees numbered only 9,000 in 1950; later this grew to 20,000 in 1960, and to 43,200 in 1977. Some of these public employees were professionals and part of Nicaragua's small middle class, but most of these government employees formed part of the expanding working class.[73] Yet, at the same time, hundreds of thousands of Nicaraguans continued to live in poverty and some in extreme poverty, especially in the countryside.

The Somozas had finally succeeded in creating a strong state and the beginnings of a modern capitalist economy, a project that had eluded the Conser-

---

70   Millet 1977, p. 229.
71   Riding 1980, n.p.
72   Pérez-Baltodano 2008, p. 559.
73   Pérez-Boltadano 2008, pp. 580–1.

vative and Liberal elites throughout the nineteenth and early twentieth centuries. The project, however, had not been for the benefit of the country as a whole. As Perez-Baltodano writes: 'The principal beneficiaries of Nicaragua's economic development in the postwar period had remained concentrated in small groups of businessmen and within the circle of economic power controlled by the Somoza family ...'.[74] Under Somoza, Nicaraguan capitalism had produced greater wealth, but also greater social inequality, and new forms of social dislocation and poverty.

Like his father, Somoza Debayle used the state to expand the family business. In his *Somoza*, Bernard Diederich describes the empire that Tacho had amassed:

> By 1977 Somozas were in everything from sugar and coffee to rice and cements, alcohol and Lanica Airlines and the Mamenic steamship line. Tacho owned the Caribe Motors Company and was the agent for Mercedes Benz. The police and traffic cops used Mercedes, as did most Somoza politicians and the National Guard brass. Even the city's garbage disposal trucks were Mercedes Benz. Somoza coffee interests included plantations in the departments of Managua, Jinotega, Matagalpa, Nueva Segovia, Madriz, Estelí, Carazo and Masaya. The amount of choice real estate they owned was vast. They were the proprietors of the Carnica slaughterhouse, and the national cement company, Canal, was founded in 1945 as the family cement monopoly for Nicaragua. All paving blocks were made by a Somoza company. The Somoza farms raised pigs and cattle which went to the export market ... The family held controlling stock in the local cigarette and cigar business, the latter established with the assistance of Cuban exiles. [Somoza's wife] Hope's family owned the construction firm Panelfab, established in 1973 to take advantage of the post-earthquake building boom.[75]

Other Nicaraguan businesspeople accepted Somoza Debayle's dominant role in the economy, just as they accepted the dynastic dictatorship as long as they shared in the wealth. When the economic situation became more difficult in the late 1960s and 1970s, they would come to resent him, laying the basis for a rift in the capitalist class.

---

74   Pérez-Boltadano 2008, p. 556.
75   Diederich 2007, p. 132.

The Somoza Regime and the United States

One could argue that, though the US Marines no longer occupied the country as they had between 1912 and 1933, still the most important factor in Nicaraguan politics remained the US government. Ever since US Ambassador Arthur Bliss Lane had recommended him to head the National Guard, Somoza García had understood that his relationship with American Ambassadors was all-important, a relationship made possible in part by the fact that Somoza had lived in the United States and spoke American English fluently. As we have seen, Anastasio Somoza García sent his sons Luis and Anastasio to be educated in the United States as well, knowing that familiarity with American language and culture would be important to their success. Throughout the dictatorship's 43-year history, the Somozas remained in constant communication with the American Ambassadors, anxious to have their approval for the government's policies and major projects. When in the mid-1940s Somoza García found it necessary to carry out a coup against his opponents and briefly lost US backing, he moved quickly to create a new civilian government so as to restore US diplomatic recognition.

Because their regime depended on remaining in the good graces of the US government, the Somozas strove to align Nicaragua's foreign policy with that of the United States. Nicaragua rallied behind the United States and the Allied Powers in World War II, aligned itself with America and against the Communists in the Cold War, and out of its own self-interest as well as obedience to the State Department, it opposed the nationalist and leftist movements in post-war Central America from the 1950s through the 1970s. Every change in US foreign policy and every new development in Latin America provided opportunities for the Somoza regime to prove once again its loyalty to the United States. So in 1952 Somoza García worked with President Truman to begin to prepare the coup that overthrew the democratically elected government of President Jacobo Arbenz in Guatemala in 1954.[76] The Cuban Revolution provided an opportunity for Luis Somoza Debayle to prove his loyalty to the United States by supporting President John F. Kennedy's organisation through the CIA of the Bay of Pigs invasion of Cuba in April 1961.[77] As *New York Times* reporter Alan Riding wrote of Somoza Debayle: 'Politically, General Somoza served Washington well, acting virtually as an American "proconsul" in Central America, interfering openly in the affairs of his neighbors to keep them

---

76   Doyle and Kornbluh n.d.
77   Kornbluh n.d. Also Pérez-Baltodano 2008, p. 536.

firm against Communism. The United States Ambassador to Nicaragua was invariably a close friend and advisor'.[78]

Since the United States functioned as organiser of security in the Americas, coordinator of Western capitalism, and arbitrator of political differences in the Western Hemisphere, the Somoza government necessarily functioned within the many regional and international organisations created by the United States. Luis Somoza Debayle worked with President Kennedy's hemispheric anti-Communist project, the Alliance for Progress, in the creation of the Central American Market. The Somozas participated in and benefitted from the United States Agency for International Development (USAID) as well as other US programmes. In the Organisation of American States, the United Nations and other lesser international organisations, the United States could count on the Nicaraguan vote. The US government in turn provided military and economic assistance to Nicaragua on which it depended.

The Somozas were well aware that the United States government had the power to pull the plug on them if they failed to support US foreign policy or if domestic issues led to either large-scale violent repression or movements that threatened rebellion. If the US State Department suggested there were problems, if US military assistance were cut off, or if US financial agencies such as Standard and Poor's or Moody's devalued Nicaraguan bonds, the regime could be brought down within a matter of a few months or even weeks. Perhaps most important, if in a moment of stress or crisis the United States shifted its support to another political leader or party, the Somoza dynasty could be replaced. It was therefore a constant concern of the Somozas to remain favoured by the United States. The Somozas were not puppets, but neither were they entirely independent actors, their ability to manoeuvre constantly circumscribed by American foreign policy interests.

The Nature of the Somoza Dictatorship

The state that the Somozas created was a dictatorship, but not all dictatorships are alike. Mussolini's regime was different from Hitler's, Stalin's different from Mao's, Pinochet's different from Videla's, Walker's different from Zelaya's – and Somoza's was different from all of those. What was the nature of the Somoza state that emerged in the 1930s and endured until 1979? What was the character of the Somoza dynastic dictatorship? First, one can argue that the US military

---

78   Riding 1980, n.p.

laid the foundation for the modern Nicaraguan state. The Somoza state had its origin in the US intervention in Nicaragua in the 1920s that created the National Guard and placed Anastasio Somoza García in charge. Yet while the regime was given birth by a military coup, it was not exactly a military dictatorship. And while he may have been a creation of the United States, Somoza was not simply its puppet. Though the United States initially helped to put him in power, it was Somoza who developed the regime and ran it. How did he do so?

The Somoza regime rested upon a set of interlocking institutions. The National Guard, fundamentally an organisation created not to defend the country but to police it, was the fundamental pillar on which the Somoza state was constructed, but it was not by any means its only support. Somoza also took over the Liberal Party and transformed it into an effective political machine, while at the same time he succeeded in dividing the other Conservative Party and winning one faction to support him as well. Somoza managed politics principally through a series of political pacts with the major parties intended to keep himself in power and to subordinate those political parties while placating them with political and governmental positions. Consequently, the major political parties ceased to be rivals and became accomplices. All of this was tacitly accepted by the country's wealthy families. The Nicaraguan people were entirely excluded from the real political life of the country, called upon occasionally to vote in elections where they were expected to endorse the dictator, and, if they failed, their votes were changed anyway.

Somoza as president headed a formally liberal-democratic state under the Constitutions of 1939 and 1948, though those were little more than façades; in reality through his control of the Guard, the Liberal Party, and the political pacts, he concentrated all power in himself. Under the Somozas, the legislature could generally be relied upon to be a rubber stamp. The political system he created gave the Somozas privileges as de facto heads of various financial institutions, positions that made it possible for them to enrich themselves, and the wealth they acquired helped to finance the Somoza political party operations, as well as funding slush funds that could be used to pay off National Guard officers and party politicians. From the time they took power in 1936 until shortly before they fled the country in 1979, Somoza García and his successors, his sons and loyal cronies, were supported by the economic elite of Nicaraguan society, the financiers, the manufacturers, and the powerful agricultural interests. The Somozas enjoyed broad support among the upper class and the professionals and small businessmen of the middle class without whose backing the dictatorship could not have endured. Because it had such broad support, the dictatorship could be relatively liberal in its treatment of its Conservative opponents. The Conservative political candidates and occasional Conservative rebellions never really threatened the regime.

Journalist Bernard Diederich, in his biography of Somoza, described surveillance and repression in Somoza's Nicaragua in the late 1940s.

> Police state? There were no police in Nicaragua, just the army – but army permits were required to go from one city to another. In Managua in 1948, every street corner was under observation and the movements of all important people were charted. Telephone calls were monitored, private mail was opened, and the local press was under strict censorship ... Men disappeared in the streets in Nicaragua. They paused briefly at La Avación prison at the edge of the Taca airfield, just outside Managua, for brutal questioning. Then they were taken to a prison camp on Great Corn Island off the Atlantic coast to nurse their wounds.[79]

Imprisonment was often accompanied by torture, though actual killings were relatively few. Diederich noted: 'Unlike Dominican dictator Trujillo, Somoza killed only as a last resort. A spell in jail usually brought the enemy around. If jail failed, the guard had the little electric device known as *la maquinita* (the little machine). A wire was wrapped around the prisoner's scrotum; if he was stubborn the current was turned on'.[80]

As *New York Times* reporter Shirley Christian wrote: 'As authoritarian regimes go, this one ceded to its political enemies and critics a relatively large amount of space to act in public life'.[81] Somoza Debayle permitted his chief political rival, Pedro Joaquín Chamorro Cardena, a Conservative, to continue publishing *La Prensa* throughout virtually the entire history of the regime. Opponents from the upper classes and the established parties, already compromised by the system of political pacts, were permitted to criticise, organise, and dissent, as long as they understood that they would *never* be permitted to come to power. And as long as they never attempted to organise the sort of mass power that could challenge the dictator. The Conservative Party, even when its members participated occasionally in actual armed rebellion against the Somoza regime, continued to be an accepted political organisation, its insurgent leaders generally jailed briefly and released.

Parties that were genuinely politically independent, especially parties on the left and any independent organisations of working people, on the other hand,

---

79   Diederich 2007, p. 31.
80   Diederich 2007, p. 35.
81   Christian 1986, p. 29.

could expect the most severe repression. The PSN Communists were frequently arrested and sometimes banished to Corn Island. The independent Liberal Party, a genuine opposition party, suffered harassment, its leaders too sometimes arrested. The dictatorship, however, had an altogether different attitude toward the Marxist-Leninist Sandinista Front for National Liberation (FSLN) whose cadres had publicly sworn to the overthrow of the regime through armed rebellion. They faced arrest, imprisonment, torture, and often death, either from combat or starvation and illness in the mountains or at the hands of the National Guard's sadistic jailers. When in the 1970s the society went into crisis, and the FSLN, other guerrilla groups, and youth in general began to revolt, they too felt the full brutal brunt of the dictatorship.

As the regime's crisis grew more acute in the 1970s, the ideology of the national security state took hold, as it did throughout Latin America at the time, and funding was increased for the Military Intelligence Service (SIM) and the National Security Office (OSN), while the National Guard's apparatus was strengthened and the repression became more severe. Guard units took names like the Jackal, the Tiger, and the Rattlesnake, with logos of skull and crossbones, and patrolled the mountains carrying M-16 rifles and Israeli Uzi submachine guns. The Guard was supplemented by the *jueces de mesta*, local magistrates who also functioned as a network of informers. At the same time, the US sponsored Somoza's Institute of Peasant Welfare (INVIERNO) that worked through technical assistance, marketing organisations, and the distribution of transistor radios and other trinkets to create a loyal peasantry.[82]

When the police or the Guard captured FSLN members or others who were considered subversives, they were taken to el Coyotepe prison near Masaya or to the prison cells located on the grounds of the Presidential Palace in Managua where they were threatened, beaten and tortured. In the palace torture chambers, prisoners were caged with the wild cats, panthers and the like, that were Somoza's pets. At the palace or at Coyotepe, prisoners might be waterboarded, electrocuted, or simply bludgeoned into confessing crimes, providing information or repudiating their criticisms of the government. Some of those tortured died, while others were murdered. Many FSLN leaders such as Tomás Borge and Daniel Ortega spent years in prison and were subjected to such tortures. Yet, as the crisis deepened – a crisis that had become economic, social and political – the dictatorship was no longer able to control the growing opposition movement.

---

82   Black 1981, p. 53.

Nicaragua in Crisis and the Growth of the Opposition

While Nicaragua had enjoyed a tremendous economic expansion in the period from 1945 to roughly 1965, by the late 1960s Somoza's programme of modernisation was faltering. The 'Soccer War' of 1969 between El Salvador and Honduras, the result of conflicts arising from Salvadoran migration into Honduras, led to a breakdown of the Central American Common Market that had been established in 1960. That in turn led to a decline in Nicaragua's foreign trade. At about the same time, the beginning of the protracted US economic crisis in the 1960s spelled the end of the Nicaraguan 'golden age'.

In addition to the economic crisis, there were also natural disasters. The Managua earthquake of 23 December 1972 destroyed much of the centre of the capital city, leaving 10,000 dead, 30,000 injured, and many homeless. About 2,500 commercial shops and small manufacturing plants were destroyed. While the work of rebuilding the city – largely financed by foreign loans – provided a fillip to the economy between 1973 and 1975, and particularly to Somoza's businesses, it could not reverse the general trend of the economic crisis. Moreover, the earthquake contributed to the astronomical growth of Nicaragua's foreign debt which expanded rapidly from $165 million in 1970, to $637 million in 1975, to $899 million in 1977, and finally to $1.24 billion in 1978.

Like the United States in the same period, Nicaragua experienced the bane of the era: stagflation – economic stagnation combined with increasing inflation.[83] The United Nations Economic Commission for Latin America (ECLA/CEPAL) found that by 1977 Nicaragua was suffering from 'increasing economic imbalances in its public finances, balance of payments, and inflationary tensions – that punished to a greater extent those strata of society with the lowest incomes – a virtual stagnation of private investment, and problems associated with the country's contraction of an ever greater eternal debt'.[84]

Nicaragua's economic crisis and Somoza's embezzling of the foreign aid and foreign loans intended for the rebuilding of Managua to increase his own economic power and to enrich himself led to increasing competition in the Nicaraguan capitalist class. For example, US President Richard Nixon's government sent Somoza $32 million, though in the end only $16 million could be accounted for.[85] Nicaragua's bourgeoisie divided into three rival groups. (1) The Banamérica, a group rooted in Granada's conservative elite, had interests

83   Pérez-Boltadano 2008, p. 560; Library of Congress, n.d.
84   Cited in Pérez-Boltadano, p. 564.
85   LaFeber 1993, p. 227.

in sugar, rum, cattle, coffee, and retail. (2) The Banic Group, named for the Banco Nicaragüense de Industria y Comercio and tied to León's liberal elite with interests in cotton, coffee, beer, lumber, construction, and fishing. Finally (3), the Somoza group, associated with the Central Bank of Nicaragua, had vast and varied interests, from its ownership of between ten and twenty percent of all arable land, to food-processing industries, to its control of import-export licensing, to its ownership of ports, the maritime fleet, and the airlines. Most important, Somoza was the dictator who could take out loans and forget to then pay them and who used the state to promote his own businesses. By 1979, Somoza was estimated to control 60 percent of the country's economic activity and to be worth between $500 million and $1.5 billion.[86]

During the mid-1970s, the Nicaraguan capitalist class had begun to react to Somoza's growing ambitions. Organised in the High Council of Private Enterprise (COSEP) which had been founded in 1974, the business class 'began to criticise the Somoza administration and to demand the democratisation of the state'.[87] The question was: could the capitalist class unite into one party with a strong leadership and put forward a serious opposition to Somoza? Since the 1960s, Nicaraguan political parties had grown from five to thirteen, most of them splits-off from the historic Conservative and Liberal parties, but there were also various communist, socialist, and labour parties; however, only two of the parties, the National Liberal Party and the Nicaraguan Conservative party, had legal standing. The capitalist class, while organised as a social sector in COSEP, failed to create a strong political party to represent its interests.[88]

With the business class so divided and parliamentary politics fragmented and in any case, as had been proven over the years, with electoral politics having proven to be so futile, the initiative lay with revolutionaries prepared to act outside of the system. The Sandinista Front for National Liberation, which had been active as a guerrilla organisation since the early 1960s, began to carry out a series of spectacular actions that brought it to national attention. We turn now to look at the origins of Nicaragua's revolutionary movement and the Sandinista Front for National Liberation and how it rose to become the principal challenger to the Somoza dynasty.

---

86 Pérez-Boltadano 2008, p. 563; Barbara Annis, 'The Economy', in Library of Congress Country Studies n.d.
87 Pérez-Boltadano 2008, p. 561.
88 Pérez-Boltadano 2008, pp. 561–3.

The Founding of the Sandinista Front for National Liberation (1962–78)

The Sandinista Front for National Liberation (FSLN), founded in 1962, which became the leading force of the Nicaraguan Revolution of 1979, arose out of a complex interaction between national and international events. The Sandinistas have their origin in the Nicaraguan Socialist Party, in reality a pro-Soviet Communist Party that provided the young activists who later founded the FSLN with their initial political education. They became Marxist-Leninists, trained in the Stalinist interpretation of Marx and Lenin and supporters of the Communists' Popular Front strategy of alliances not only with working-class parties, but also with capitalist parties. The PSN activists carried out socialist education, trade-union work, and attempted to work within Somoza's political system.

The Cuban Revolution of 1959 changed everything. The *guerrilla foco* of Ernesto 'Che' Guevara and Fidel Castro provided a new strategy for armed rebellion, leading the FSLN in a completely new direction. The FSLN founders then reached back into Nicaragua's history, finding in Sandino's Army in Defence of the National Sovereignty of Nicaragua (EDSN) of the 1930s an inspiration and a justification for the Guevarist armed struggle and guerrilla warfare. Somoza's dictatorship created the economic and political conditions that prepared a revolutionary situation and gave the Sandinistas their chance. The turn to guerrilla warfare by young leftists was typical of what was happening throughout Latin America between 1959 and the late 1970s, but everywhere else it was a disaster and only in Nicaragua was it successful.

The international and national situation changed significantly from the late 1960s to the mid-1970s in ways that seemed propitious for revolutionary possibilities in Central America. The international economic crisis that began in 1967 would continue into the mid-1970s, leading to greater unemployment, lower wages, and increased poverty in countries around the world and in Nicaragua as well.[1] In the Catholic Church, the Theology of Liberation raised the question of social justice and succeeded in changing the views of both priests and laypeople, leading some of them to become Christian revolutionaries. At the

---

1 Ortega 2010, p. 294. Ortega sees the international financial crisis and the end of the economic bonanza of the postwar period as forming part of the context for the Sandinista revolution.

same time, the election of US President Jimmy Carter in 1976, with his promise to put human rights at the centre of his foreign policy, gave some grounds for hope that the United States might withdraw its support from Somoza, creating a new optimism among Nicaraguans. Finally, it was the genius of a group of Sandinista leaders who saw the opportunities for creating a national movement aimed at armed insurrection which brought about the triumph of the revolution. We look more deeply at all of these developments in this chapter.

Armed struggle was nothing new in Nicaragua. With little chance of changing the country's political leadership through elections, Nicaragua had a remarkable history of rebellions, coups d'état, and assassination attempts on the country's rulers that extends from the early nineteenth well into the twentieth century. There had been rebellions by the indigenous people and by peasants and coups organised by the economic elite's small political parties. The coups were led by the Liberal and Conservative parties, while assassination attempts were generally carried out by small groups of dissidents or disaffected individuals. The goal of all of these armed attempts at taking power was almost always to replace one party or leader with another. Virtually none of the coups d'état or larger rebellions were motivated by a desire to change the fundamental political, economic and social system based on a small political elite that dominated the agricultural economy and the government.

Even Augusto C. Sandino's armed struggle against the US Marine presence in Nicaragua had quite limited political and social objectives beyond the expulsion of the occupiers. Sandino accepted the political system, simply calling for fair elections, and accepted the capitalist system and the haciendas, only asking that workers get a fair deal. He put his hopes in the organisation of cooperatives as a step toward the building of the spiritual brotherhood that was his ultimate goal. And while the Nicaraguan Socialist Party (the PSN, a pro-Soviet Communist Party) aspired to replace capitalism with Soviet-style Communism, that was seen as a very long term objective. The PSN's gradualist and pacifist strategy led it to eschew the armed struggle and to repudiate revolution. It would take decades to create a political party with some sort of collective, revolutionary, and left-wing perspective in Nicaragua.

The Origin of the Nicaraguan Left

The first attempt to create a modern, political labour movement in Nicaragua was the founding of the Nicaragua Workers Party (PTN) in August of 1931. Established by union activists and intellectuals, the PTN was a labour party that, according to its newspaper *Causa Obrera* (the *Workers Cause*) aimed both to challenge 'the bourgeois political system' and to improve the material conditions of workers. Yet, despite its reformist goals, in 1932 the Nicaraguan government expelled some of its leaders from the country because the party had used the word 'socialist' in some article or flyer. Chastened, by 1938 *Causa Obrera* announced that 'guided by national sentiments, it would adopt a position of collaboration with the elected leader [Somoza]'.[2] The PTN's First National Congress was held from 31 August to 1 September 1938 in Managua, but when Somoza declined to give the unions a delegate at the proposed Constituent Assembly, the convention delegates rebelled and elected anti-Somoza leaders. The internal divisions between the pro-Somoza and anti-Somoza leaders led to the organisation's collapse in 1939, followed by repression of the movement including the jailing of some of the opposition union leaders while others went into exile in Costa Rica.[3]

The Nicaraguan Communists of the PSN

Nicaragua's first left party, the Nicaragua Socialist Party (hereafter referred to as the Communist PSN), in reality a pro-Soviet Communist Party, was founded in 1939, during the era of Joseph Stalin's domination of the Soviet Union and the Communist International. Established at the time of the Popular Front and the alliance between the Soviet Union and the western capitalist powers against Hitler and the Axis, the Communist PSN strove to work with the dictator Anastasio Somoza Garcia in what was billed as the great democratic war against Fascism and Nazism, while at the same time attempting to achieve democratic political reforms and to win workers' rights in Nicaragua.

Following the Communist International's position, after 1935 the Central American Communists adopted a two-stage theory of revolution: a bourgeois democratic revolution to be followed later by a proletarian socialist revolution. During the first stage, the revolution would fight against US imperialism, for a republic and civil rights, and for agrarian reform. When those were achieved, the PSN, the vanguard party, would lead the working class in a fight for power to create a society like that in the Soviet Union.[4]

The PSN, most of whose members were either labour union officials or self-employed craftsmen – shoemakers, typographers, carpenters, construc-

---

2   Andrés Pérez-Boltadano 2008, pp. 472–3 and 501.

3   Walter 1993, pp. 103–4.

4   Paszyn 2000, pp. 13–14.

tion workers and day labourers – hoped through trade-union work, political propaganda, and parliamentary action to bring social change and eventually socialism to Nicaragua.[5] The PSN worked principally in the union movement and by the 1940s they had taken control of the labour movement – and backed Somoza as part of the international people's front against Fascism and Nazism. The party played a leading role in the founding of the Bloc of Anti-Fascist Workers which organised a May Day (International Labour Day) parade on 2 May 1943. The Bloc called not only for the defeat of fascism, but also for giving land to peasants and lowering food prices, demands that led to the jailing of its leaders.[6]

The Communist PSN achieved legal recognition in the midst of the protests of June and July 1944 when – turning its back on the mass demonstrations for democracy that were taking place – it pledged to back Somoza's government and its programme of social reforms and vowed to subordinate itself to the national interest.[7] The PSN declared its support for 'the public welfare policies that president Somoza is initiating'.[8] A year later it also supported Somoza's Labour Code of 1945, a code that while ostensibly legalising unions and strikes, actually made labour union recognition and legal strikes extremely difficult.[9] By the end of this period in December 1946, the PSN claimed to have 1,500 members and the support of 25 percent of the electorate.[10]

The Communist PSN refused to take any action against the Somoza government which might have disrupted the war effort. In taking these positions, the PSN followed the lead of the American Communist Earl Browder, head of the Communist movement in the western hemisphere, who looked forward to peace and cooperation between the Soviet Union and the capitalist states and to greater collaboration between the Communists and other political parties.[11] The honeymoon between Somoza and the Communist PSN lasted only as long as the war, and in August of 1945 Somoza expelled several PSN leaders from Nicaragua. With the Cold War Río de Janeiro Pact between the United States and the Latin American governments, the Communist PSN was outlawed and the trade union confederation that it controlled was also made illegal.[12]

---

5   Kurin 2010, n.p. Pérez-Baltodano 2009, p. 151.

6   Walter 1993, p. 105.

7   Walter 1993, p. 138.

8   Pérez-Boltadano 2008, p. 501, citing PSN's first published manifesto.

9   Walter 1993, pp. 139–44. See also Guevara López n.d., *passim*.

10 Paszyn 2000, p. 17.

11 Perez-Baltodano 2008, p. 564.

12 Paszyn 2000, p. 18.

Throughout almost the entire Somoza period, the PSN followed Moscow's direction in pursuing a peaceful, reformist, and parliamentary road to power in Nicaragua. Yet despite its attempt to ingratiate itself with the regime, by December 1945 the party had been declared illegal and was driven underground. When the Cold War broke out and American McCarthyism and anti-communism were extended by the US State Department throughout Latin America, the Communist PSN continued to advocate a peaceful path to socialism. Even after an attempt by groups based in Guatemala and Costa Rica to overthrow the Somoza regime in 1954 and then the assassination of Anastasio Somoza Garcia in 1956 – followed immediately by a period of severe and widespread repression – the PSN continued to eschew violence. Following the dictates of Moscow, for orthodox Communists of the postwar period, revolutionary action in the western hemisphere was simply not on the agenda, no matter what the local conditions.[13]

Despite the democratic veneer of the Popular Front and postwar periods, like other national Communist parties of the era, the PSN remained a Stalinist party whose members were instructed in the Soviet theories of 'Marxism-Leninism' and 'dialectical materialism', quasi-religious, systematic distortions of Marxism that justified bureaucratic Communism, the Soviet state, the Communist Parties and their policies. Even while the Communists' public face was the Popular Front based on alliances with other socialist parties, middle-class radical parties, and even capitalist parties, its leaders envisioned the ultimate creation of one-party states identical to Stalin's Russian and the emerging Eastern Communist Bloc. It was in this Stalinist Communist Party that the future Sandinistas received their leftist education and had their first organising experiences, including several who were sent to the Soviet Union for training.[14] That education and those experiences would leave an indelible mark on the young founders of the Sandinista Front for National Liberation (FSLN).

Carlos Fonseca

In 1954, an eighteen-year-old student named Carlos Fonseca joined the Communist PSN. Like his hero Sandino, Carlos Fonseca, born 23 June 1936, was the illegitimate son of a wealthy landlord and a poor working woman. The tension,

---

13   In 1968, the PSN finally entered the armed struggle, creating the Revolutionary Armed Forces of Nicaragua (FARN), though it never achieved significant military or political presence. Carlos Fonseca Terán 2005, p. 45.

14   Henry Ruiz, 'El faro que alumbró a los combatientes', in Baltodano 2010, Vol. I, pp. 567–609.

between the absent, aristocratic father whom he admired and whose recognition he sought and the working-class mother he loved, marked his life. His father Fausto Amador was a coffee planter, one of the wealthiest men in the Matagalpa region and politically a Conservative until the rise of President Anastasio Somoza, at which point Amador became a supporter of the National Liberal Party. Fonseca's mother, Augustina Fonseca Ubeda, was a washerwoman who would also have three other children by different fathers.

Though he grew up only half a mile from his father, Fausto Amador did not recognise his son Carlos until the boy reached elementary school, and even then he did not support either the mother of his son or her child. Carlos Fonseca began to work as a street vendor while still a child, though he stayed in school to continue his education, entering the Matagalpa region's only secondary school, the National Institute of the North (INN) in 1950. Most of the students were male children of government employees or National Guard soldiers, and parents who were supporters of Somoza's party. Nonetheless, the school had a history of radical political activity, its students having published two anti-Somocista newspapers – the *Vanguardia Juvenil* in 1946 and *Espártaco* in 1947. In 1952, while Fonseca was studying there, the INN was the only high-school student body in the country that supported a university student strike in León demanding that a plaque honouring Somoza be removed from the campus.[15]

Fonseca was politically precocious. Beginning in the early 1950s, he participated in meetings of both the Conservative Party youth group and of the National Union of Popular Action (UNAP) made up of intellectuals who had been involved in anti-Somoza demonstrations in the late 1940s, though he finally found a home in the Communist PSN. Influenced by a radical teacher at the INN, by 1953 or 1954 Fonseca considered himself a Marxist and he appears to have joined the PSN in 1954. As a PSN member he attended local chapter meetings, sold the PSN newspaper *Unidad*, and read and studied the few Communist publications available. Fonseca and two friends began to publish a cultural journal titled *Segovia*, the name of the northern region where Sandino had been active, though his name was never mentioned in a single issue. While it was not anti-Somocista, *Segovia* did take up some political issues, such as women's suffrage, which Fonseca enthusiastically supported. The magazine commented critically on social conditions and advocated education, modernisation, and economic development, a political programme not much different from Somoza's.[16]

---

15   Zimmerman 2000, pp. 12–27.
16   Zimmerman 2000, pp. 28–37.

After graduating from the INN in 1955, Fonseca moved to Managua where he got a job as the librarian of the Instituto Ramírez Goyena, the county's leading secular high school (most high schools were run by the Catholic Church). Under the protection of the school's radical director, Guillermo Rothschuh Tablada, Fonseca became the organiser of student discussion groups that analysed Nicaragua's history and political problems. Fonseca relocated to León in March of 1956, and enrolled in the National Autonomous University of Nicaragua (UNAN) as a law student, one of a thousand students in what was then the only university in the country.

Fonseca quickly became a founder and editor of *El Universitario*, an independent, radical student newspaper, and, as he said, 'threw himself' into student organising. He and his friends also joined a Marxist study group organised by the Mexican Noel Guerrero, a follower of Vicente Lombardo Toledano, Stalin's principal agent in Latin America.[17] Guerrero, who subsequently joined the Communist PSN, became the leader and teacher of Fonseca, Silvio Mayorga, and Tomás Borge, all of whom joined the same PSN cell. It was these young men who became the founders and central leaders of the Sandinista Front for National Liberation.[18] Humberto Ortega later described this as 'the first Marxist student cell' at the University in León.[19] In a certain sense, this was the original seed of the Sandinista movement, though it would take years to reach maturity.

When the poet Rigoberto López Pérez assassinated Anastasio Somoza in 1956, Fonseca did not praise or even condone the act, remaining committed to the Communist PSN's nonviolent approach. Nevertheless, like thousands of others, Fonseca was arrested, and, though he had never known López Pérez, he was jailed from 27 September to 15 November when he was released without being charged. Borge was not so lucky; he was held in prison for two years until student protests won his release. Borge argues that López Pérez's assassination of Somoza was a turning point for Nicaragua's left, an 'extraordinary act [that] marked the end of an era of frigid silence that had commenced on 21 February 1934', when Sandino had been assassinated by Somoza. He writes: 'Rigoberto López Pérez's sacrifice inaugurated a political renaissance'.[20] Anastasio Somoza García's son, Luis Somoza, succeeded his father in the presi-

---

17   While Lombardo Toledano never joined the Mexican Communist Party, he was Stalin's
      man in Latin America, the spokesperson for and organiser of the Communist labour
      movement in Latin America. La Botz 1988, pp. 50–62.

18   Zimmerman 2000, pp. 38–41. Borge 1992, pp. 89 and 138–9, mentions Guerrero's study
      group and his role as PSN leader.

19   Ortega 2010, p. 107.

20   Borge 1992, pp. 90 and 91.

dency, while the other son, Anastasio Somoza Debayle, became head of the National Guard, and the dictatorship became a dynasty.

Fonseca in the Soviet Union

Out of jail, Fonseca was off on a great adventure. One of the Communist PSN's outstanding youth leaders, he was chosen in 1957 to visit the Soviet Union as delegate to the Sixth World Congress of Students and Youth for Peace and Friendship. Flying from Costa Rica where he had supposedly gone on vacation to recuperate from an illness, he arrived in Moscow using the name Pablo Cáceres. While in the Soviet Union he participated in the Congress and in the government's official guided tours. After returning to Nicaragua in 1958, he wrote a book titled *A Nicaraguan in Moscow* describing the Soviet Union 'as a workers' paradise, its five-year plans accomplished in full, social evils like prostitution abolished completely, unemployment and discrimination eliminated for all time'.[21] Even after Nikita Khrushchev's 'secret speech' at the Twentieth Party Congress in 1956 revealing Stalin's crimes against the Russian people, Fonseca continued to admire and to defend Stalin as late as 1958. Finally, he praised the Soviet Union's crushing of the workers' revolution of 1956 in Hungary, arguing that otherwise 'fascist criminals' would have taken over.[22] Unlike many other Communists around the world – who had broken with their former admiration for Stalin either after the Khrushchev revelations of February 1956 or the smashing of the Hungarian Revolution in November 1956 – Fonseca remained a die-hard, rock-solid Stalinist in 1958.[23]

What were the young Fonseca's politics? What did it mean to be a Stalinist in 1958? Stalinism represented a certain interpretation and formulation of working-class and left history into a series of doctrines codified by Stalin and his protégés under the term 'Marxism-Leninism', adopted by the Communist Party of the Soviet Union, and also held by the other Communist Parties around the world.[24] The central ideas of Stalinism, which remained in place even after Khrushchev had discredited Stalin, were these: (1) the Communist Party (of whatever country), governed by democratic centralism, was the vanguard and the one-and-only party of the working class. Its political doctrine and

---

21   Zimmerman 2000, p. 45.

22   Carlos Fonseca 1985, Vol. I, pp. 58–9; Zimmerman 2000, pp. 46 and 61.

23   Nolan 1984, pp. 18–21. He refers to 'Fonesca's uncritical apology of Soviet orthodoxy …'.

24   Particularly important was Stalin 1939.

its political line should be followed by party members and others in the workers' movement and other social movements; (2) the Communist Party, today
working through labour unions and electoral politics, would eventually lead a
revolution – probably peaceful but with force if necessary in particular circumstances – to bring about first socialism and then communism; (3) the Soviet
Union's one-party state represented the model for other socialist societies and,
as it had been reproduced (more or less) in the Communist Eastern Bloc and
then in China and North Korea, so it would be reproduced in other countries.
Fonseca's visit to the Soviet Union convinced him of the notion that a Communist vanguard leadership would hand down through the vertical chain of
command the principles, strategy, and tactics that would lead a revolutionary movement and that same leadership would later direct a Communist state.
While Fonseca would later change his view of the Communists' Popular Front
pacifism, he never wrote or said anything to indicate a break with the elements
of Stalinist theory or politics such as the one-party state.

Fonseca returned from the Soviet Union to law school at the UNAN and
once again threw himself into organising. He helped to put together a successful movement to prevent the university from giving an honorary degree to
Milton Eisenhower, brother of the US President Dwight D. Eisenhower. He then
turned to the organisation of a national student strike demanding the release
of student prisoners, including his comrade Borge. Fonseca was part of a student strike delegation that met with President Luis Somoza, an encounter that
may have led to his brief arrest and imprisonment until his release (probably
through the intervention of his father). During that interview, Somoza is reported to have warned the students that they should be careful, because the Guard
might put a bullet in the head of a student. 'I could care less', he said, 'if a hundred students have their heads broken, or 500 are arrested if they deserve it
for their subversive acts'. Fonseca is reported to have asked Somoza: 'Are you
threatening our freedom?', to which Somoza replied: 'Take it as you like'.[25]

Despite the explicit threats, Fonseca returned to organising and helped put
together a national organisation of high-school students. His activities also
included writing an editorial in support of a dockworkers' strike and very likely
his involvement in an indigenous people's fight for land in nearby Subtiava.
All of this was organising work typical of the strategy of the Communist PSN:
work among students and working-class people for democratic rights, for a
better standard of living, and for the rights of an oppressed minority. There was

---

25   The conversation reported by Vilma Núñez published in various places and cited in Ortega
       2010, p. 114 and fn. 182.

nothing in his activities or those of his comrades to suggest anything different from standard Communist Popular Front work.

The Cuban Revolution and Armed Uprisings in Nicaragua

All of that changed suddenly in January 1959 when Fidel Castro's July 26 Movement succeeded in overthrowing the US-backed dictatorship of Fulgencio Batista. The victory of the Cuban Revolution broke the hold of the pro-Soviet Communist Parties on the left throughout Latin America. The Communist strategy of a combination of trade-union work, participation in social movements, and electoral politics suddenly appeared not only outdated, but also stodgy, reformist, and, above all, a pointless waste of time, since for decades it had proven unsuccessful.[26] With the triumph of the Cuban Revolution, armed revolution became the watchword of political radicals in Latin America throughout the decades of the 1960s and 1970s.

Castro's victory in Cuba suddenly and dramatically changed the political strategy of the Latin American left. In Cuba, Castro and his revolutionary guerrilla band in the mountains, in the *sierra*, had fought Batista's army and had collaborated with the student movement and urban social organisations and labour unions in the cities and towns, who together had succeeded in overthrowing Batista. The strategy of Castro and his comrade Ernesto 'Che' Guevara, termed the *guerrilla foco*, was based on the theory that even a small body of committed revolutionaries could from bases in the mountains carry out a heroic struggle that would eventually spark and lead a popular revolution. The *guerrilla foco* model, hailed and popularised by the French intellectual Régis Debray in his famous book *Revolution in the Revolution*, would during the next two decades inspire tens of thousands of Latin Americans to enter into such guerrilla campaigns.[27] The Cuban Revolution would be the catalyst for the creation of the FSLN.[28]

Castro's success set off almost at once a wave of guerrilla struggles throughout Latin America, including several small guerrilla uprisings in Nicaragua, though in fact there had been some armed uprising of a guerrilla character in Nicaragua shortly *before* the Cuban victory. Ramón Raudales, who had fought

---

26   For discussions of the impact of Castro, Guevara, and the guerrilla foco, see: Debray 1974; Löwy 1982, pp. 11–59; Castañeda 1993, Chapters 3 and 4; Bensaïd 2004, Chapter 10, pp. 175–98.

27   Debray 1967, *passim*.

28   Nolan 1984, p. 22.

with Sandino in the war of 1927–33, organised the Revolutionary Army of Nicaragua in 1958, though Raudales was killed and his band defeated in short order. In 1959, Carlos Fonseca himself joined an armed group led by a former National Guard officer, though it too suffered defeat. Nicaraguan Liberals and Conservatives also engaged in experiments in armed struggle, but without success. Even the cautious PSN Communists experimented briefly with armed struggle by sending some members into the Rigoberto Pérez López Brigade. All these Nicaraguan groups failed in their attempts at armed struggle which in some cases were more like traditional Latin American coups d'état than genuine guerrilla warfare campaigns.[29]

The fighters who participated in those and in other small, unsuccessful armed uprisings in Nicaragua during that first year travelled to Havana, Cuba, which was now a haven for all of the country's opposition tendencies, from the Conservatives and Liberals to the Social Christians and PSN Communists. Various Nicaraguan groups including the Conservative Pedro Joaquín Chamorro's Revolutionary Directorate and a more radical Revolutionary Committee sought support from the Castro government. Che Guevara, however, endorsed and supported a group called the Committee for the Liberation of Nicaragua which in February 1959 published the 'Havana Letter', calling for armed revolution to end the Somoza dictatorship. Guevara chose Rafael Somarriba, a former National Guard member, to be its commander. Though Guevara promised that he himself would join the group, that never happened, and Somarriba led the group into Nicaragua where it was ambushed by the Honduran Army and the Nicaraguan National Guard at El Chaparral, Honduras on 24 June 1959. Six were killed, and fifteen wounded and arrested, and jailed in Honduras, including Fonseca who had been shot through the left lung.

The Break with the PSN

Fonseca, who had been severely wounded in the El Chaparral ambush, left Honduras as soon as he was well enough to travel and returned to Cuba for recuperation. He and other Nicaraguans would spend several months there, harboured by the Cuban government, and taking advantage of the time to rethink their politics. Throughout the experiments in armed struggle in 1958 and 1959, Carlos Fonseca had remained a member of the Communist PSN, though he had become increasingly critical of its approach. While the Cuban

---

29   Zimmerman 2000, pp. 50–6.

Revolution of January 1959 represented a turning point in strategy for Latin America as a whole, the turning point in Nicaragua came in León on 23 July 1959 where the National Guard fired on unarmed protestors demonstrating against the earlier El Chaparral killings. In León on that day, the Guard killed four persons and wounded nearly a hundred others. The León Massacre would lead to a generational break among students and young activists, and brought about the emergence of the radical 'Generation of 1959', breaking with the Conservative, Liberal, and Communist PSN dissidents of the 'Generation of 1944'.[30]

Fonseca became the principal figure of this Generation of 1959, and while for others that meant a break with Conservative and Liberal politics, for him it meant a break with the Communist PSN's strategy. Unlike the Communist Party that believed workers would have to fight first for bourgeois democracy and only later for socialism, the León Massacre led Fonseca to conclude that a revolution was necessary. The Cuban Revolution led him to conclude that 'a socialist revolution was also possible in Nicaragua'.[31] Fonseca and his co-thinkers broke with the notion of a two stage theory of revolution, long held by both Social Democrats and then Stalinist Communists, that is, that there must be first a capitalist and democratic revolution, and then a working-class socialist revolution. Fonseca and the Sandinistas believed that it was possible to make the leap from the Somoza dictatorship to something like Cuban Communism.

This has led some to argue that Fonseca and the Sandinistas had adopted a view like that developed by Leon Trotsky in the early twentieth century, that is, that there could be a 'permanent revolution', combining and passing directly from a bourgeois democratic to a working-class socialist revolution. Nothing could be further from the truth. While Trotsky had argued for a 'permanent revolution', he had held that workers would have to carry out the democratic tasks of the bourgeois revolution, winning civil and political rights for the working class as they fought for working-class power. Fonseca's view had nothing in common with Trotsky, since the working class was not seen as the agent of revolution and neither democracy nor civil rights formed part of the Sandinista worldview. Quite the contrary. Fonseca and his co-thinkers believed that the guerrilla warriors could lead the nation directly to a Cuban-style government where the party ruled and encouraged mass participation, but democracy and workers' power had no place.

---

30   Zimmerman 2000, p. 57.

31   Zimmerman 2000, p. 61.

During the period between 1959 and the founding of the Sandinista Front for National Liberation (FSLN) in 1961, there was a proliferation of small revolutionary groups seeking to overthrow Somoza.[32] A number of the young Nicaraguan radicals from the student movement, including Fonseca, Borge and others – living at different times in Cuba, Costa Rica and Nicaragua – engaged in a debate about revolutionary strategy and revolutionary politics more generally. The discussion revolved principally around a critique of the Communist PSN and its peaceful road to socialism and the question of the guerrilla strategy for armed revolution, though it also touched on the subordination of the Communist parties and the left in general to the Soviet Union. The young radicals eventually came to the conclusion that it was necessary to break with the pro-Soviet Communist Parties, with the Communist PSN, and their peaceful strategy and turn to an armed guerrilla approach. They were also attracting others who shared their outlook. For example, Victor Tirado, who had been expelled from the Mexican Communist Party because of his support for armed struggle, joined the movement; he later became a top FSLN *comandante*.[33]

The Founding of the Sandinista Front for National Liberation

By the early 1960s, Carlos Fonseca had grown to become a revolutionary ascetic who believed strongly in monogamy, drank only on rare occasions, danced only when dragged onto the floor, and dedicated himself entirely to the cause of bringing about a revolution in Nicaragua. He recovered and popularised the figure of Augusto Sandino, wrote the movement's political programmes, and developed its guerrilla strategy. He repeatedly put himself in harm's way in the building of the guerrilla movement in the mountains and in the creation of the clandestine networks in the city; he was repeatedly arrested, sometimes deported, and at other times imprisoned and tortured. His comrades, if they found him somewhat stodgy, respected and admired his honesty, his integrity, his single-mindedness of purpose, his courage, and the role he played as the foremost political-intellectual leader of his generation and his organisation, for Fonseca was the principal leader of every turn taken by the organisation from 1959 until his death in 1976.

During the period from 1959 to 1961, Fonseca and his co-thinkers created a series of small student groups and political organisations as they attemp-

---

32   Ortega 2010, pp. 137–42, writes in some detail about these groups.
33   Ortega 2010, p. 139.

ted to find a vehicle for their new revolutionary politics.[34] While most of those involved were Nicaraguans, there were also other Central Americans and some Mexicans. The participants in these various political organisations held a variety of ideologies, from French liberalism to the PSN's Communism; some came from the Conservative Party, some from the Independent Liberal Party, while some were old veterans of the Sandinista movement of the 1920s and 1930s.[35] Yet the dominant political current was some form of Soviet Marxism-Leninism and the dominant strategy was the Cuban-inspired *foco*.

In July of 1961, Fonseca founded the New Nicaragua Movement (MNN) with the goal of linking the armed struggle with popular movements.[36] Borge writes: 'It was necessary to have a political force with no connection to groups of the Right and which transcended the limitations of the traditional left. To accomplish that, it was proposed to create an organisation with its own political line that used armed struggle as its primary strategic instrument and was able to incorporate other forces as well'.[37] The programme was fundamentally Sandino's: national independence, struggle against exploitation by the oligarchy, national unity and unity of the Latin American peoples. The MNN published on its underground press *The Ideas of Sandino*, the first left group to resurrect his political writings and his reputation. In turn the MMN created the United Sandinista Movements for Revolution, which was the immediate predecessor of the FSLN.

At about the same time, other revolutionaries, working out of Havana, among them Edén Pastora, had created the Sandino Revolutionary Front (FRS). In 1961 or 1962, the MNN and the FRS merged and adopted the name National Liberation Front (FLN), taken from the Algerian organisation fighting the French government in those years.[38] A year or two later, the group would add Sandino's name to their banner, becoming the Sandinista Front for National Liberation (FSLN). Borge makes the important observation that the FSLN was intended to become a genuine 'front', that is, an alliance 'if possible, of all groups opposed to the dictatorship. Such a bloc never came into being, but the original structures gave birth to a political vanguard that responded to the aspirations

---

34   Ortega 2010, pp. 137–43.

35   Ortega 2010, p. 163.

36   Ortega 2010, p. 138. He mentions the organisations that preceded the MNN and lists some members of them.

37   Borge 1992, pp. 128–9.

38   Ortega 2010, pp. 137–42, explains the merger of the two groups.

of broad sectors'.[39] Since it did not become a broad front, the FSLN retained its unitary politics and structure until about the mid-1970s when internal division arose.

Like many other Cuban-inspired revolutionaries of the era, they followed Fidel Castro and Che Guervara, and they took the *guerrilla foco* as their model.[40] But they also remained admirers of the Soviet Union and the Eastern Bloc. To understand the Nicaraguan revolutionaries' sympathy for Soviet Communism, it should be remembered that by the time of the founding of the FSLN, Fidel Castro had already proclaimed his revolution to be 'socialist', had embraced Nikita Khrushchev, and had aligned Cuba with the Soviet Union and the Communist camp. Neill Macaulay, an American who in 1959 had joined the Cuban Revolution and became an officer in Fidel Castro's revolutionary army, gives us some insight into the thinking of many at the time:

> Cuba's turn toward the Soviet Union in 1959–60, however, came about not simply because Castro wanted to spite the United States, but because he became convinced that Marxist-Leninist collectivism was far superior to liberal capitalism as a vehicle for economic and social development. That he was wrong seems obvious today, but in 1960 much of the world was dazzled by Soviet space triumphs, impressed by the USSR's recovery from the ravages of World War II, and captivated by the confident, dynamic personality of Nikita Khrushchev. By contrast, the United States – with its inability to match the Soviet Union in space, its economic recession, the U-2 incident, the humiliation of its president at the Paris summit conference – in 1960 seemed to be a nation in decline. Fidel Castro was hardly alone in believing that communism was the wave of the future. When Castro sponsored the formation of the FSLN in Havana in 1961, it was inevitable that the Nicaraguan revolutionary front would be Marxist-Leninist as well as Sandinista.[41]

The historical record suggests that the claim that the FSLN was founded in Cuba may be mistaken, but that it was founded under the impact of Cuban events, with Cuban support, and that it shared with Castro's Cuba an identification with the Soviet camp, of that there can be no doubt.

---

39   Borge 1992, p. 137.
40   Zimmerman 2000, pp. 61–8, 78.
41   Macaulay 1985, p. 9. Macaulay fought in the Cuban Revolution, briefly owned a farm in Cuba, and then returned to the United States where he became a university professor.

The addition of the word 'Sandinista' in 1963 was the result of Fonseca's desire to identify the FSLN with Sandino's struggle in the 1920s and 1930s. It was a way to justify the Cuban *guerrilla foco* strategy in Nicaragua by finding native roots for armed struggle in the experience of Sandino and fight against the US Marines.[42] Just as Fidel Castro and the Cuban revolutionaries claimed the legacy of José Marti, who had died in the struggle against Spanish imperialism in Cuba, so Fonseca claimed the mantel of Augusto C. Sandino and his anti-imperialist struggle against the United States.

Fonseca dedicated a great deal of time to collecting and reading everything he could find that had been written by or about Sandino and to reinterpreting Sandino's life in such a way as to vindicate a guerrilla strategy of struggle against the Somoza dynasty. To do so, he transformed Sandino from a person who had been seen as a regional leader and described by Somoza García as 'bandit', into a national figure and a hero.[43] For Fonseca, Sandino was a fighter for national sovereignty and a radical social reformer. Finally, Fonseca – ignoring Sandino's rejection of the invitation from Salvadoran Farabundo Martí to join the Communist movement – would suggest that Sandino had been a kind of Communist fellow traveller whose work coincided with that of the International Communist movement of the late 1920s and early 1930s, even if he had declined to join it. At the same time, Fonseca ignored Sandino's spiritualism and mysticism and covered up his complicated romantic and sexual life, neither of which fit into Fonseca's own conception of an ascetic communist militant. Fonseca's appropriation of the history of Sandino's armed struggle against the US intervention in the 1920s and early 1930s was brilliant. It provided a Nicaraguan model and a myth that justified the young former Communists' turn to armed struggle. In the process, Fonseca elevated Sandino into a national hero, the leader of an anti-imperialist, nationalist movement fighting for social justice, and, he sometimes suggested, one that anticipated the contemporary struggles for Communism.[44]

The adoption of Sandino as a model was part of the process of adapting the Cuban guerrilla warfare model to Nicaraguan conditions. Tomás Borge argued that while inspired by Fidel, Che, and the Cuban model, the Sandinistas never adopted the *foco* theory uncritically. Borge writes: 'The fact is that Carlos Fonseca led us to reflect on the nature of guerrilla theory, and we read attentively

---

42   Zimmerman 2000, pp. 72–3.

43   Somoza García 1936, *passim*.

44   Baracco 2005, pp. 61–78; Palmer 1988, pp. 91–109. Both Baracco and Palmer point out how Fonseca used Sandino as a bridge to Castro and Guevara, but they fail to discuss the fact that Fonseca retained the PSN's fundamentally Stalinist politics.

Régis Debray's book *Revolution in the Revolution*. We read Che Guevara and we drew out our own conclusions: first, that before the armed struggle it would be necessary to organise social bases within the country ...'.[45] They would model their strategy after the *guerrilla foco*, but in their own way, attempting to build ties to labour and community groups in their zones of operation.

While Fonseca, Borge and their comrades founded a new organisation – the FSLN – based on the new strategy of the *guerrilla foco*, they never broke with the Stalinist politics and all that implied; Marxism-Leninism, a reductionist economic analysis, an authoritarian and vertical party, and the goal of the one-party Communist state modelled on the Soviet Union all persisted.[46] At the same time, their principal support, at least initially, also came from the Communist world. Several FSLN militants were trained in Communist theory and strategy at the Patrice Lumumba University in Moscow in the 1960s.[47] Others received military training in Cuba, North Korea, and possibly Vietnam.[48] Fonseca made periodic visits to Eastern Europe, North Korea and Communist China to seek support for the Sandinista cause.[49] Revolutionary movements have every right to and will, of course, seek arms and training wherever they can get them, but clearly Fonseca and other FSLN leaders also identified politically with Cuba, China and Vietnam, and still, though to a somewhat lesser extent, with the Soviet Union and Eastern bloc. Their involvement with the Communist countries was not simply opportunistic; they admired and aligned themselves with those states in the Communist bloc and their ruling parties and considered those societies to be socialist.

While Fonseca preferred Castro's strategy to the Russian's, he continued to adhere to Stalin's model of organisation. As Fonseca's son, Carlos Fonseca Terán, has written, the FSLN had 'a typically Stalinist structure'. The Leninist idea of democratic centralism, wrote Fonseca Terán about the FSLN, had been 'deformed by Stalinism', and had a 'militarist vertical command structure'.[50] The FSLN was created as a revolutionary combat organisation, not a political party. It would only become a political party many years after taking

---

45   Mónica Boltodano 2010, Vol. I, pp. 165–81, quotation p. 171.

46   Pérez-Baltodano 2009, pp. 145–59; Kinzer 2007, pp. 57–8.

47   Ruiz, 'El faro que alumbró a los combatientes', in Baltodano 2010, Vol. I, pp. 567–609.; Zimmerman 2000, p. 107.

48   Kinzer 2007, p. 60. Borge talks, for example, of taking mortar courses in Cuba from Cuban and Czech instructors. Ortega 2010, pp. 226–7, describes his six months of training in North Korea.

49   Kinzer 2007, p. 65.

50   Fonseca Terán 2005, cited by Pérez-Baltodano 2009, pp. 149–59.

power.[51] The FSLN's clandestine, vertical leadership structure and its armed, guerrilla organisation would prove to be a useful – if ultimately unsuccessful – military instrument for confronting the Somoza dictatorship. Yet, as time would reveal, it would also prove to be an impediment to building a democratic working-class movement.

The Years of Revolutionary Action

Between 1962 until 1979, the FSLN maintained guerrilla operations in various parts of Nicaragua, though throughout this period the guerrilla operations were extremely small, often only a handful of individuals, sometimes 'shrinking through death and desertion faster than it could be built up by recruits from the city'.[52] Many, including Fonseca himself, suffered arrest and torture; others were murdered in prison or 'while trying to escape' the famous *ley fuga*. The Sandinista guerrillas, however, never succeeded in establishing a permanent base, never had a radio transmitter, and never established any liberated zones until the final push in 1979. While some had guerilla training and actual fighting experience in Cuba or with the Palestine Liberation Organisation (PLO) in Jordan and Lebanon, many had no training whatsoever until they went into the mountains.[53] For a Sandinista militant to accept assignment as a guerrilla fighter in the mountains was often tantamount to accepting a suicide mission.

The Sandinista's first operation in 1962–3 in the area of the Patuca and Coco rivers of the Bocay region, therefore known as the Bocay Campaign, involved about sixty fighters, some armed with hunting rifles, some with military weapons, and others unarmed. They had some contact with indigenous people. They received some assistance from the Sumus but were unable to communicate with the Miskitos, who didn't speak Spanish.[54] The guerrillas suffered from disease and hunger, and lost military weapons when their canoes capsised, while one of the men drowned. They divided their forces, but when one group was ambushed by the National Guard, they were forced to withdraw and end the campaign.[55] Borge says that their experiences led him to briefly doubt

---

51   Fonseca Terán 2005 p. 39. He writes: '... el FSLN era un organización político-militan y no un partido ...'.

52   Zimmerman 2000, p. 79.

53   Kinzer 2007, p. 60.

54   Borge 1992, p. 144 and p. 154.

55   The entire Bocay Campaign is recounted in Borge 1992, pp. 136–69.

the wisdom of the guerrilla strategy, but Fonseca urged them to continue.[56] After the defeat in 1963, the FSLN was reduced to about ten guerrillas in the mountains and perhaps twenty young people in Managua and León.

Victor Tirado wrote: 'As we all know, Bocay was a military defeat. But it was also a great school'.

> We discovered, for example, that we had to plan an end to the old practice of preparing armed movements from outside rather than from within the country.
>
> ... We also learned the elementary lesson that in order to maintain a guerrilla base, links with the masses – in this case with the peasants – must be strong.[57]

Fonseca had returned to Managua where he was arrested in June of 1964, tried, convicted, and sentenced to six months in prison. But just as Fidel Castro had done in his 'History Will Absolve Me' speech in 1953, Fonseca used his trial to make a political statement about the FSLN's political strategy and goals in his defence speech 'From Prison, I Accuse the Dictatorship' (also known as the 'Declaration of July 9, [1964]').[58] Remarkably, Fonseca's speech was published by the Antorcha publishing house in León in 1964 and circulated within Nicaragua.

The Return to Legal, Peaceful Work: 1964–6

Unable to carry out guerrilla actions, from 1964 to 1966 the FSLN once again found itself by default engaged in legal, peaceful actions, working with the Republican Mobilisation Party (PMR), the Communist PSN, and independent leftists.[59] The combination of an economic boom, protests by students and intellectuals, involvement in the 1962–3 upsurge, and a very modest political opening that accompanied it, created more opportunities for just that sort of traditional reform activity. The FSLN concentrated on educational work and community and student organising in León and Managua. Borge edited, and FSLN members and others circulated, the PMR newspaper *Republican Mobilisa-*

---

56   Borge 1992, p. 168.
57   Victor López Tirado, 'El FSLN: un producto y una necesidad históricos', pp. 41–2, cited in Borge 1992, p. 169.
58   Fonseca 1985, Vol. I, 'Declaración, 1964', pp. 256–67; Zimmerman 2000, pp. 83–6.
59   Borge 1992, pp. 182–4; Zimmerman 2000, pp. 90–1.

tion, a joint project of all three groups. The FSLN also engaged in its own organising of labour unions and the first peasant unions in a number of cities and towns. All of this organising was done through the development of conspiratorial techniques and clandestine methods, since even legal peaceful work could expect to be suppressed by the National Guard, especially because the FSLN continued to advocate and to support its tiny *guerrilla foco* in the mountains.[60]

During this period the FSLN also created a small print shop which published Carlos Fonseca's pamphlet 'Social Classes in Nicaragua', and, interestingly, *A History of the Chinese Communist Party*. The publication of a pamphlet on the Chinese Communist Party suggests that while primarily inspired by the Cuban *guerrilla foco* theory, FSLN members were also reading and discussing the Chinese 'peoples war' theory of revolution which involved the creation of mass peasant armies capable of conquering the countryside and then surrounding and subjugating the cities. Later, the Fonseca-Borge tendency within the factionalised FSLN of the mid-1970s would call itself the Prolonged Peoples' War (GPP) Tendency.

At the same time that the FSLN activists were working with the Communist PSN and the PMR, they also organised the Federation of Revolutionary Students (FER) and succeeded in winning the leadership of the student organisations in the two cities with universities, León and Managua. FER members also edited *El Estudiante*, a national newspaper for university and high school students.[61] This was the FSLN's most successful area of work and would continue throughout the organisation's history. Students provided many party cadres and were often recruited to join the *guerrilla foco* in the mountains.

Legal, peaceful organising in Nicaragua nevertheless remained extremely dangerous. When in 1966 students unfurled a banner at the opening game of the baseball season reading 'No More Somoza!', the National Guard attacked and killed several of the young protestors. On another occasion, in January of 1967, Fernando Agüero, leader of the National Opposition Union (UNO) made up of Conservatives, Liberals, Social Christians, and the Communist PSN, organised an anti-Somoza rally of 50,000 who marched down Roosevelt Avenue toward the presidential palace at Loma de Tiscapa. The National Guard fired on the crowd, killing at least 40 people and wounding 100 others.[62]

Later it would be revealed that Agüero had met secretly with Somoza's General Gustavo Montiel in an attempt to organise a *coup d'état* to overthrow

---

60   Borge 1992, pp. 184–6; Ortega 2010, pp. 190–1. Ortega refers to this cooperation between the PMR, the PSN, and the FSLN as the 'triple alliance'.

61   Zimmerman 2000, p. 76 and p. 91.

62   Millet 1977, p. 229.

the dictator. They planned together to have the Guard fire on the crowd in order to provoke a massive, violent attack on Somoza. Informed of the planned coup at the last moment, Pedro Joaquín Chamorro, the Conservative party leader and editor of *La Prensa* condemned it as the most cowardly, criminal and cynical sort of conspiracy. Borge writes: 'It has never been learned how many victims there were. They speak of hundreds, of thousands. What is beyond discussion is that the traditional parties collapsed that day and left nothing behind but ashes'.[63] With the door to legal peaceful change absolutely closed, the FSLN returned to its preferred guerrilla strategy in mid-1966.[64]

The Pancasán Campaign

The 1967 Pancasán operation, personally led by Fonseca at the head of 40 guerrillas, was, like the earlier campaign of 1962–3, based in *la montaña*, that is, the mountains of north-central Nicaragua. The majority of the participants were former student activists with little or no guerrilla training or experience. Just as in the FSLN campaign of 1962–3, the FSLN failed to establish a base among the peasants in the area and the National Guard succeeded in ambushing and destroying guerrilla columns. The campaign was a complete disaster. Borge called it 'the holocaust of Pancasán'.[65] The coincidence of the failure of the Pancasán campaign with the defeat and death of Che Guevara in Bolivia that same year made it seem to some FSLN members as if perhaps the *foco* idea had been a mistake. A debate developed within the FSLN about the wisdom of the guerrilla strategy and the future of the FSLN.[66] Most of the survivors of the Pancasán campaign withdrew to Cuba, leaving only a handful of clandestine FSLN organisers in Nicaragua.[67] The Nicaraguan revolutionaries in Havana undertook a re-evaluation of their strategy that went on for the next two years.[68]

Such a re-evaluation of strategy was not easy given the FSLN's deep emotional commitment to the *guerrilla foco*. Fonseca's organisation, particularly what would later become the Prolonged Popular War (GPP) faction of the FSLN, was imbued with a revolutionary mystique. Nicaraguan revolutionaries often

---

63   Borge 1989, pp. 216–17, quotation from p. 217.
64   Zimmerman 2000, pp. 94–5.
65   Borge 1992, p. 215. He describes the campaign on pp. 220–30 and 242–6.
66   Zimmerman 2000, pp. 96–9.
67   Ortega 2010, p. 222.
68   Ortega 2010, pp. 228, 234–5. He characterises the different groups involved in the discussions. He also lists the documents of their own history that they studied at that time.

use the word *mística* to refer to the profound feeling they experienced that revolved around Che Guevara, the guerrilla organisation, and 'the Mountain'. As David Nolan writes: 'The GPP was the ultimate romanticisation of the guerrilla'. This was especially true after 1967 and the death of Che Guevara which transformed the Argentine-Cuban revolutionary to something like a saint in the eyes of many. The Mountain was seen as the creator of revolutionary consciousness in the individual, the place that created leaders of the class struggle in the country, and the generator of the 'new man' who would produce the socialist society.[69] Even many years later, this romantic and almost mystical conception of revolution would survive in the FSLN's mythology and in its membership's consciousness. Though the organisation evolved and its ideology changed, many members would remain bound by the group's mystique.

Borge would later write of this early period of guerrilla warfare in his memoir *Patient Impatience*:

> In practice, the infant guerrilla struggle was contaminated at birth by the malady of invasion and had no base of support inside the country, except in our imagination and desire, nor even a minimal infrastructure in the zone to be invaded, as had been conceived in the initial projects.
>
> There was, on the other hand, an excessive emotional identification – translated into a mechanical reproduction of the drawing – with the armed experience of Cuba. With a keen olfactory sense we abandoned, both in conception and in practice, the mistaken synthesis attempted by Régis Debray, and this kept our project from dying.[70]

The principal lesson the guerrillas claim to have learned was to build a base of support among the peasants and to establish a logistical structure to support the operation, though they found it extremely difficult to accomplish those goals given the National Guard's effectiveness.

The GPP altered its revolutionary strategy under the impact of study of the Chinese, Vietnamese, Israeli, and Algerian insurgencies. Particularly influential was their reading of Mao Tse-tung's *On Protracted War* written in 1938, which led the FSLN to move away from its earlier *guerrilla foco* theory and to attempt to adopt the Chinese model based on organising in the mountains and the countryside, particularly focusing on building stronger ties to the peasantry with the ultimate goal of creating a genuine army. It was a goal never achieved.

---

69   Nolan 1984, pp. 42–3.
70   Borge 1992, p. 138.

The GPP virtually abandoned the Marxist idea that the urban working class would be the social agent of revolution, finding the city too dangerous and the working classes altogether lacking in revolutionary zeal. Only the *campesinos*, the peasants, they believed, could be counted on. No longer willing to simply react to conditions, the GPP hoped to direct the masses in struggle. The enemy as they saw it was not merely the Somoza regime, but US imperialism, because it was the US that dominated Nicaragua, and Somoza was merely one expression of that power, one dictator who could be replaced with another. One group of FSLN members became so convinced of Mao's theory that they broke away from the FSLN to form the Workers Front (Frente Obrero – FO), at first a Maoist organisation though later becoming followers of Enver Hoxha, the Communist dictator of Albania, an organisation that would remain an opponent of the FSLN and later become a would-be rival for power.[71]

The FSLN's urban organisers were also active in this period, carrying out attacks on symbols of the dictatorship and engaging in bank robberies to finance their work. While dramatic and sometimes successful, the cost of these actions was high. When the FSLN assassinated Gonzalo Lacayo, a known and hated executioner, the National Guard retaliated by killing several FSLN members.[72] The urban actions were no more successful than their rural guerrilla campaigns; they did not build a significantly larger movement and they did not change the balance of power. Fonseca and other leaders and activists associated with these actions were repeatedly jailed, tortured, and some were murdered in prison. Both the FSLN *guerrilla foco* strategy and its urban actions proved to be absolute military failures. Yet the guerrilla movement, while an utter military failure, would ultimately prove to be politically significant, because over a period of more than fifteen years the FSLN would prove its commitment to overthrow Somoza and demonstrate that it represented the only independent organisation with a consistent and unflagging opposition to the Somoza dictatorship.

Zero Hour and The Historic Programme of 1969

After the Pancasán defeat, interpreted by the FSLN, nevertheless, as an important step in their development, Fonseca and other leaders worked on developing their political analysis and programme. Out of the guerrilla experiences

---

71   Nolan 1984, pp. 38–41.
72   Zimmerman 2000, p. 100.

and the discussions of the failures of 1967–9 came two important documents, both written by Carlos Fonseca: 'Zero Hour' and the 'Historic Programme' of the FSLN. 'Zero Hour' presented Fonseca's analysis of the Nicaraguan situation and the need for a revolution of a certain sort. Fonseca argued that the central problem facing Nicaragua was US imperialism which had imposed on the country the Somoza dictatorship and a reactionary clique that had governed since 1932. Supporting the Somoza dictatorship internally were those social classes and political parties, both Conservative and Liberal, that benefitted economically from the status quo. A small handful of wealthy landowners held over half of all property, while the majority lived in poverty. He reminded readers of Nicaragua's long history of resistance and rebellion, and recounted how the Communist PSN, by following Earl Browder's ideas about cooperation between capitalism and communism, had given up on the notion of revolutionary struggle. He also recognised the role of Cuba in helping to inspire the rebirth of revolutionary movements in Nicaragua. He described the FSLN's guerrilla movement and its success and failures, but vowed to continue the revolutionary struggle.[73]

Fonseca's analysis of Nicaragua's situation laid the basis for the programme also written by him and adopted by the FSLN.[74] The programme called for: the overthrow of Somoza and the powers-that-be; an end to representative government and the creation of a revolutionary government with the full participation of the people; and respect for individual liberties and human rights, including freedom of religion. At the same time, the government would hold responsible those who had organised coups, fraudulent elections, and violent repression. The revolutionary government would expropriate the property of Somoza and his cronies, and nationalise banking, foreign trade, and foreign-owned natural resources. It would also expropriate capitalist and feudal latifundia and distribute land to those who worked it. It would guarantee the rights of workers to organise unions in the city and in the countryside. It would protect small- and medium-sized employers, while preventing them from exploiting workers. It would create a planned economy, ending the anarchy characteristic of capitalism, and carry out the industrialisation and electrification of the country. It would create education and health programmes to meet the needs of

---

73   Fonseca 1985, Vol. I, pp. 149–69.

74   The FSLN Programme of 1969, or the Historic Programme as it is often called, appeared in at least two different versions, one issued in 1969 and another issued in 1979. A summary of the programme can be found in Nolan 1984, pp. 36–7. There are versions of the programme online in Spanish and English on various websites, such as FSLN 1999. A shorter summary is also provided in Ortega 2010, p. 236, and also in Zimmerman 2000, pp. 123–4.

the Nicaraguan people. The programme also promised to reincorporate the Caribbean Coast and to emancipate women. It would end US domination of the country's foreign policy, establish an independent foreign policy, and work for the unification of Central America into one nation. It would work with all the peoples of Central America to win their national liberation. It would create a new national people's army and venerate the martyrs who died to bring freedom to Nicaragua.

The 1969 Programme represented a radical, populist and nationalist politics, but it could also be interpreted as laying the basis for a Marxist-Leninist, Communist government and society such as the FSLN hoped to create. It declared to the country and to the world the Sandinista vision of a new Nicaragua.

In his book *The Ideology of the Sandinistas and the Nicaraguan Revolution*, David Nolan observes:

> Reflecting the FSLN's Marxist-Leninist roots, the tone of the 1969 program was strongly anti-capitalist, anti-United States, internationalist, and moralistic. The qualifiers attached to the statements about freedom of expression and religion, the politicisation of education, and the rejection of bourgeois politics of electoral competition (in favour of a single system of state-directed popular participation) all reflected a fundamental antipathy towards pluralism.[75]

The hostility toward political pluralism even on the left would become clearer during the 1980s when the Sandinistas came to power.

During the late 1960s and early 1970s, Fonseca worked to systematise and to inculcate in the FSLN members both the group's Marxist ideology and its political programme. 'The earlier efforts to attract non-Marxists to the revolution were abandoned. Instead, Fonseca called upon revolutionary students to reject hypocritical Social Christian demagoguery about class conciliation and to realise that "Marxism is now the ideology of the most ardent defenders of Latin American man".[76] By Marxism, of course, Fonseca meant the Marxism-Leninism he had first learned in the Communist PSN, except for the strategic change to guerrilla warfare.

---

75   Nolan 1984, p. 37.
76   Ibid.

Silent Accumulation of Forces and Organising in León

The guerrilla group in the mountains remained the Sandinistas' privileged form of organisation and the foundation of its revolutionary strategy, but the guerrilla forces had constantly to be maintained by new recruits. From 1970 to 1974, the Sandinistas engaged in what they called 'the silent accumulation of forces'. Their clandestine operatives in the cities and towns and in the countryside built the FSLN networks and recruited to the organisation, while at the same time they sent select recruits to join the guerrilla forces in the mountains. They worked especially among students at the universities who were involved in legal student organisations, but they also engaged in the decade of the 1970s in organising in communities, with workers, and among the indigenous.

One of the strongest urban organisations was built in León beginning in 1970 by former members of the Revolutionary Student Front (FER), among them the future guerrilla *comandante* Omar Cabezas. In his memoir *The Mountain is More than a Great, Green Steppe*, Cabezas provided an account of how the Sandinistas organised in the cities. He was like many of his contemporaries under the spell of Che Guevara and would eventually find his way to a guerrilla band in the mountains, but he began as a student activist.[77] A handful of young Sandinistas in the FER organised classes in Marxism at National Autonomous University of Nicaragua (UNAN) in León using Marta Harnecker's *The Fundamental Problems of Marxism* as one of the central texts. The Sandinista-led FER organised university reform movements around issues that were meaningful to the students. Among other battles, they fought, for example, to increase the number of students in the department of medicine. They organised mass demonstrations, carried out protests against the university's provost, and in their street theatre even went so far as to ridicule Somoza. They succeeded in gaining a following and being elected to the leadership of the student council University Centre of the National University (CUUN) in various periods.[78]

The student organisation was called upon one day in the early 1970s to find clandestine housing in León for a group of FSLN guerrillas who had returned from training in Cuba as they were being moved to join other combatants in the mountains. The student organisers ended up finding safe houses for them in the nearby indigenous community of Subtiava. The students having met some

---

77   Cabezas 2007, *passim*. Cabezas's book is full of references to Che Guevara as a model for the Nicaraguan revolutionaries. See, for example, p. 57, where he is excited to arrive at the guerrilla camp to meet 'those famous men, the guerrillas, the people like Che'.

78   Cabezas 2007, pp. 27–36.

of the indigenous community activists in Subtiava then went on to organise study groups among indigenous working-class people in the community, beginning with the study of the *Communist Manifesto*. Those indigenous activists in turn helped the FER students to establish other contacts with their relatives in the indigenous working-class communities of León itself. The student activist leaders and their indigenous allies began to establish groups that took up the community's demands and fought for electricity, water and other immediate needs of the poor communities of León. Through these indigenous activists in León's barrios, they also made contacts with workers in the labour unions, 'and began to penetrate the unions of León'.[79]

While Sandinistas in other cities also engaged in building community organisations and labour unions, the FSLN organisation in León was unique in its achievements. The FSLN student organisers in León were particularly successful, much more successful than in other cities, in building up community and labour organisations. León would be a bulwark of the revolutionary movement in the late 1970s, rising up repeatedly in spite of the aerial bombings and massacres. The FSLN work in communities and in labour unions differed from that of the PSN Communists because they were not only building the community and labour organisations, but were also recruiting to a clandestine, revolutionary organisation committed to armed struggle and to the guerrilla strategy. The clandestine organisation recruited students as well as workers and peasants and sent them off to join the guerrilla organisations in the mountains.

While the Sandinistas' guerrilla campaigns, bank robberies and assassinations generally failed miserably, and though its urban organisations remained relatively weak, the FSLN began in the 1970s to carry out brilliantly planned and executed actions of a spectacular character that captured the public imagination, publicised their cause, and gave the group new confidence. The first such action came in October 1970 when five FSLN members, three men and two women, hijacked a Costa Rican airline plane and took hostage two US executives of United Fruit Company. The Costa Rican government agreed to exchange five FSLN prisoners held in its penitentiary, including Carlos Fonseca, for the two United Fruit businessmen. Fonseca and his comrades flew to Mexico City and then on to Havana.

Then in December 1974, the FSLN commandos attacked the home of José María Chema Castillo where an elite dinner party was taking place. The guests included Somoza's son-in-law who was the Nicaraguan ambassador to the United States, as well as the Nicaraguan foreign minister and the mayor of

---

79   Cabezas 2007, pp. 34–9, quotation on p. 39.

Managua. Somoza agreed to the FSLN demands to pay one million dollars in ransom, to publish a Sandinista manifesto in the Nicaraguan newspapers, and to free fourteen FSLN prisoners – including future Nicaraguan president Daniel Ortega. A plane carried the attackers and prisoners to safety in Cuba. Nevertheless, despite these spectacular actions, by 1974 the Sandinistas were in crisis, deeply divided, and unsure about the future direction for their movement.

The Question of the Vanguard Organisation

What did it mean for the FSLN to have adopted the Cuban *guerrilla foco* model? How did that affect the organisation's political work? What was the ethos of the FSLN cadres? Omar Cabezas, who became one of the Sandinista *comandantes* and later a leader of the Sandinista revolutionary government, described the forging of the FSLN vanguard and the emergence of the concept of the vanguard out of the guerrilla experience:

> The solidity of the Vanguard of the FSLN is not just a word. The Sandinista Front for National Liberation was developing – through its practice in the mountain, as well as in the city, and in the countryside – the hardness of iron, of steel, a contingent of men with the solidity of granite amongst themselves, a morally and physically indestructible nucleus of men that was capable of moving an entire society against the dictatorship at different stages of its formation ... Because we, as the Christians say, denied our very selves there.[80]

He goes on:

> A group of men embracing each other, become brothers, we were a group of men with a permanent kiss amongst each other. We loved each other with blood, with anger, but with a love of brothers, a fraternal love.[81]

The guerrillas in the mountain were, writes Cabezas, a group of men who were 'clean, with a clean vision', a group of men 'without egoism', or as one might also translate it 'without selfishness'. And 'therefore we say that the genesis of the

---

80   Cabezas 2007, p. 73. The ellipses are Cabezas's.
81   Cabezas 2007, p. 74.

new man is in the FSLN'.[82] The 'new man', of course, is a term taken from Che Guevara, expressing a vision of the future ideal person of the coming socialist society.[83] Guevara had taken the idea of the 'new man' from the Soviet Union's ideology in the 1930s when Marxism-Leninism was supposed to have overcome individualism and selfishness. Cabezas explains his conception of the 'new man':

> The new man begins to be born who goes forward appropriating a series of values, who goes on discovering them, taking them up, caring for and nursing them, cultivating them in his interior, because one always cultivates that tenderness in the mountain, I cultivated the ability to preserve that beauty. There the new man is born in the mountain, in clandestine activity in the city, in the guerrilla warrior of the countryside ...[84]

He ends the section writing:

> Military training had a lot to do with what we're talking about here; the beginning and the end of things is what most marks the man, the beginning and the end is what most influences the man. The training is the beginning; it is decisive because it is where he begins to receive focused knowledge, systematic information, in order to assimilate it in such a way that his training weighs a great deal on his later conduct, development and way of being a man.[85]

Cabezas describes in these passages the process by which the young men (and some women, whom he does not mention in these passages) were fused into a revolutionary organisation capable of surviving the armed struggle with the dictator Somoza's National Guard. Any encounter could mean death in combat, and capture almost always lead to torture and often resulted in murder. There is no doubt that the FSLN 'Vanguard', inspired by the Cuban model of Fidel Castro and Che Guevara, was made up of incredibly committed and courageous revolutionary guerrilla warriors.

The guerrilla leaders were sometimes linked to mass organisations of students, urban communities, workers and peasants, though the National Guard's

---

82   Ibid.

83   Guevara, 'Socialism and Man in Cuba', in Guevara 2007.

84   Cabezas 2007, p. 74. The ellipses are Cabezas's.

85   Ibid.

terrible repression made it difficult to maintain the links that connected the FSLN leadership to the guerrillas or to the mass organisations. Omar Cabezas gives the example of a National Guard attack on an FSLN training school in Ocotal in 1975 that led to mass arrests. 'All of the structures, the safe houses, the network of collaborators, had been broken, and the people were really terrorised'.[86] This sort of thing happened again and again throughout the FSLN's history up until 1979. The Guard's repression meant that it was impossible to build mass organisations that could interact continuously and regularly with the guerrilla group and its leadership.

The FSLN adopted organisational statutes that gave its militants (the term for its members) the right 'to express themselves freely', 'to elect and be elected' to leadership bodies, and to 'participate in the elaboration of the political-military line of the FSLN through their respective organisms'.[87] In reality, though, with the members dispersed throughout the country, including in remote mountain locations and only able to communicate by messages sent by way of clandestine couriers, communication was very difficult and meetings were only possible among very small groups of people. Consequently, democratic discussion, debate and decision making in the guerrilla and the clandestine movement was impossible. The most durable structure was the political-military chain of command.

The question is: Could such an organisation – an overwhelmingly male, military organisation (there were several women guerrillas and a few female *comandantes*, but it was a masculine milieu), commanded through a hierarchical structure, where both political and military instructions come down the chain of command from above – could such an organisation play a healthy role in creating a democratic socialist mass movement? Certainly the FSLN's *guerrilla foco* experience gave it no understanding or practice of democracy within its own organisation or in dealing with other organisations, of which there was very little. Even more problematic, as we will see in the following chapters, after the Triumph of June 1979 and later the creation of a political party, the FSLN leadership would keep in place the military-style structures, only expanding them in an attempt to control a much larger political organisation and mass organisations which were also organised and run in a top-down manner. The Vanguard created in the mountains with its military structures and chain of command – and its powerful cohesive mystique – would have far-reaching results and implications that affected the Sandinistas in power in the 1980s, in

---

86   Cabezas 2007, p. 133.
87   The statutes can be found in Borge 1992, pp. 247–56.

opposition in the 1990s, and back in power again in the 2000s. The experience of the Cuban *guerrilla foco* strategy and the kind of bureaucratically centralised and authoritarian organisation necessary to carry out such a strategy would mark the FSLN for decades.

The Sandinista Revolution (1975–79)

After a decade of organising, by the mid-1970s the Sandinistas were in crisis. Their guerrilla strategy had proven unsuccessful in creating the sort of organisation and movement needed to overthrow Somoza. At the same time, other political strategies and practices developed within the FSLN that would eventually lead to a three-way split in the organisation. The differences among the rival FSLN tendencies were in the end overcome and the three groups were reunited, though it was under a new leadership, that of Daniel Ortega, that the FSLN finally came to reject the *guerrilla foco* and to adopt a new insurrectional strategy. What remained the same, however, was the Marxist-Leninist ideology, the idea of the vanguard, and the top-down centralised party. But before turning to the crisis of the mid-1970s, we should go back a few years to the mid-1960s and the origins of the other important left current in Nicaragua at the time: Christian socialism.

Vatican II and the Theology of Liberation

The Catholic Church represented an enormous force in Nicaraguan society and within it there were for many years liberal and socialist currents. There was a strong Christian humanist and even Christian socialist current in Nicaragua during the 1940s and 1950s that found expression in the Conservative party and particularly in the Conservative Party Youth organisation (La Juventud Conservadora). Conservative Party leader Carlos José Solózarno wrote the pamphlet *The Ideology that Should Maintain the Conservative Party of Nicaragua* in 1947 in an attempt to reorient the party in the modern world. He argued that the Conservatives should eschew both the far right and the far left, adopting a Christian ethic shared by the Nicaraguan people. While opposing Soviet Communism, he argued, 'we must accept the Christian and humanitarian side of socialism'. He was for a 'spiritual socialism', such as that being advocated by Guatemalan President Juan José Arévalo. Such socialism, while it would not expropriate the capitalists, would restrain capitalist exploitation and improve the lives of workers and peasants. Similarly, Conservative Rafael Paiagua Rivas wrote in 1950 that the country should reject both extreme liberal individualism and the collectivism of the Marxist dictatorship of the proletariat and strive for a 'Social Christian' political order.[1] What these Conservative thinkers called Christian socialism was in reality a call for modest economic and social reform that would still protect traditional class relationships and patriarchal family values. They wanted a society that would improve the lives of the lower classes without threatening the situation of their class.

The Conservative Party Youth that adopted these reformist ideas in the early 1950s found support in *La Prensa*, the national newspaper that had recently come under the editorship of Pedro Joaquín Chamorro. The Youth organisation was led by José Joaquín Cuadra Cardenal, the son of Carlos Cuadra Pasos, the *éminence grise* of the Conservative Party. Under the impact of these humanist and ostensibly socialist ideas, the Great Conservative Convention held in Managua in 1954 called for an end to collaboration with the Somoza regime, the right to free labour union organisation, land reform, and a non-political National Guard. Nevertheless, the continuing control of Emiliano Chamorro over the party and its closed leadership meant that the programme was a dead letter. It would be another decade before Christian socialism would be taken up again.[2]

Just as Fidel Castro and the Cuban Revolution provided the Latin American left with a new strategy, so Pope John XXIII and the Second Vatican Council (Vatican II – October 1962 to December 1965) set a new course for the Catholic Church. Vatican II offered a new direction for Catholicism that would have tremendous importance for the history of Latin America in general and Nicaragua in particular. The Pope promised that Vatican II would 'open the windows and let in fresh air', and indeed it did. Under his leadership, Vatican II adopted a series of positions intended to renew the Church, make it more relevant to the modern world, and to strengthen the sense of solidarity among Christians.

Vatican II adopted resolutions that changed the rituals and practices of the Church, but most importantly it directed the Church to reach out to its followers and bring them closer. The Church gave up the Latin mass for the vernacular, turned the priest from the altar toward the people, found a place for laypeople and women in the mass, while making the Church more attractive, for example, through the inclusion of popular music. The Church encouraged Catholics to read the Bible (as Protestants did) in order to learn for themselves about the life of Christ and to follow his example. Catholics, the Church now argued, should see themselves not as separate from the world, but as part of it, with a responsibility to work in it to bring about justice and peace. The Church

---

1   Walter 1993, pp. 218–20.
2   Walter 1993, pp. 220–1.

and its clergy were encouraged to work more actively not only for spiritual change, but also for human rights, and for social and political solutions to the problem of widespread poverty.[3]

In Latin America, a group of theologians took matters further. Fr. Pedro Arrupe Superior General of the Society of Jesus (Jesuits), in a 1968 letter to the Jesuits of Latin America, suggested that the Church should have an 'option for the poor', or, as it was often put, 'a preferential option for the poor'. The Latin American Bishops Conference held in Medellín and attracting Catholic and some Protestant clergy from throughout Latin America, for the first time discussed not only sinful practices but also the 'integral liberation of the person' from oppressive economic social and political structures. Gustavo Gutiérrez, a young theologian from Peru, brought to the conference the influence of the Cuban Revolution and a clearly socialist orientation. The conference also proposed a new methodology based on active engagement with the communities of working people and the poor.[4] The Medellín conference officially supported the 'theology of liberation' and the promotion of 'Christian base communities'. Not long afterward, in January 1969, Managua celebrated its First Pastoral Encounter calling for the 'courageous denunciation in words and act of the social, economic, political, and religious injustice of the society', with special emphasis on those most in need of help.[5]

Throughout the modern era, the Catholic Church in Nicaragua as throughout Latin America was generally aligned with the economic, political, and military powers-that-be. In Nicaragua, that meant that it did not challenge the Somoza dynasty. On the contrary: for decades the Nicaraguan Church had continuously offered itself as a buttress to the existing economic and political system. The Nicaragua Church generally had no ties with the poor in the city and in many rural areas it was only an occasional presence. After Medellín, however, change was inevitable.[6]

Following the Medellín conference, the Nicaraguan Bishops held the First Pastoral Congress in January and February of 1969, attended by 258 clerics and laypeople and charged with implementing the Medellín conference policies. The Pastoral Congress represented a turning point for Nicaraguan Catholics as the church turned to the examination and criticism of both the religious and the social conditions of the country. The conference emboldened those within

---

3   Sabia 1997, p. 14. For a useful short account, see Dodson and Montgomery, 'The Churches in the Nicaraguan Revolution', in Walker 1982, pp. 161–80.

4   Sabia 1997, pp. 14–20.

5   Perez-Baltodano 2008, pp. 568–9.

6   Sabia 1997, pp. 21–2.

the Church who were critical of the Somoza dictatorship and encouraged the denunciation of social injustices.[7] The appointment of a new and independent-minded Archbishop in March of 1970, Miguel Obando y Bravo, led to a sharp turn from the Church's former course.[8] When Anastasio Somoza Debayle sent the archbishop a new luxury automobile, the prelate promptly and shockingly returned it. Not only was the new Archbishop not to be bought, but he also made it clear that he would not support the Somoza dictatorship, taking it upon himself to bring out a translation of Pope Paul VI's 1967 Papal Encyclical *Populorum Progressio* dealing with social injustices in Latin America. FSLN leaders interpreted this encyclical as justifying revolution.[9]

Under Obando's leadership and with the growing pressure of the developing Theology of Liberation movement, as well as the crisis of the Somoza regime, the Nicaraguan bishops issued a series of remarkable pastoral letters in 1971, 1972, and 1974. The bishops not only spoke of the people's right to dignity and justice, but also criticised the Somoza government explicitly, denouncing 'terror' and 'torture, rape, and extra-judicial executions'.[10] All of these developments at the top of the hierarchy resulted in large measure from grassroots activity taking place at the base of the church inspired by the new Theology of Liberation.

---

7   Sabia 1997, p. 24.

8   Sabia 1997, p. 25.

9   Ortega 2010, p. 280, writes: '... *Populorum Progressio*, legitimated revolutionary insurrection in evident cases of violations of fundamental rights and the common good ...'. But, in fact, it does not seem to do so. Similarly, Fernando Cardenal (cited in Baltodano 2010, Vol. I, p. 351) cites the encyclical as reading: 'War always brings greater dangers, but when it is a question of a situation involving the profound violation of human rights, a significant and prolonged situation, when all peaceful methods have been utilised without providing a solution, an insurrection by the people is justified'. The actual text of the encyclical's section titled 'Reform Not Revolution', actually reads: 'The injustice of certain situations cries out for God's attention. Lacking the bare necessities of life, whole nations are under the thumb of others; they cannot act on their own initiative; they cannot exercise personal responsibility; they cannot work toward a higher degree of cultural refinement or a greater participation in social and public life. They are sorely tempted to redress these insults to their human nature by violent means. Everyone knows, however, that revolutionary uprisings – except where there is manifest, longstanding tyranny which would do great damage to fundamental personal rights and dangerous harm to the common good of the country – engender new injustices, introduce new inequities and bring new disasters. The evil situation that exists, and it surely is evil, may not be dealt with in such a way that an even worse situation results'. Pope Paul VI 1967.

10   Pérez-Baltodano 2008, pp. 568–76.

A popular church began to develop in Nicaragua, led by priests who encouraged Bible study and reflection in small worship groups. These Bible classes
or *cursillos* soon became *cursillos de conscienciación*, that is, consciousness-
raising groups where the participants were encouraged to connect the Bible
stories to their own social and political realities. Women played a particularly
large role in the popular church, if only because there were often so few men
involved. These Christian base communities first established in San Pablo in
1966 gradually spread to many cities, towns and some rural areas. A Jesuit effort
established the first such communities on the long-neglected Caribbean Coast
in 1969. The Christian base communities developed the Nicaraguan popular
mass which included community members playing traditional instruments
and singing songs that expressed the community's experiences.[11] While the
popular church, as the name implies, was really the church of working people
and the poor, the Theology of Liberation also had an impact on Catholics from
the middle and upper classes, many of whom were high-school and college students.

The Sandinistas Approach the Priests

Already in the late 1960s, Carlos Fonseca, Tomás Borge and other FSLN leaders
were holding meetings with the poet and Catholic priest Ernesto Cardenal.
While the FSLN leader Fonseca was a convinced atheist, Cardenal came to
the conclusion that they shared common objectives, or as Borge puts it: 'The
essential thing was the survival of the country, rescuing the people, and saving
their bodies and souls from the Somoza inferno'. Borge continues: 'Besides, we
reassured them that the religious beliefs of the people would be respected and
that – for reasons of political realism and common sense – their survival was
assured and that the Sandinista Revolution would not attack Christianity, but
on the contrary would make efforts to form something closer than an alliance
with the Nicaraguan Church'.[12]

Another FSLN leader, Oscar Turcios, held meetings with Ernesto's brother
Fernando Cardenal. The latter wrote in his memoir: 'We shared our analysis
of the Nicaraguan situation and we found that we agreed on many things.
Finally he told me that they wanted me to enter into the revolution, that
they wanted me to work with the Sandinista Front for National Liberation'.

11   Sabia 1997, pp. 29–40.
12   Borge 1989, p. 266. See also Sabia 1997, pp. 58–80.

When Cardenal asked him about the FSLN position on religion and the church, Turcios told him that it did not matter at all if one believed in life after death while the other believed that one simply returned to the earth; rather, what was more important was 'to see if we could work together to transform the country and create a new Nicaragua that favoured the poorest people, the abandoned and marginal majorities'. Cardenal wrote in his memoir:

> His ideas about religion and believers were totally different from the theory and practice that had been carried out for more than 50 years by the Communist parties of the Soviet Union and Eastern Europe and by Cuba's for decades. It was clear that in those parties one could not be a Christian and be a party militant [i.e. a party member]. In some of those countries there had been real persecution of the Church. The Sandinista Front in this respect began its revolutionary life with a complete originality and in a way that was really appropriate for our profoundly religious people. This position was very satisfying and calmed me tremendously.

Later, after being invited to a left event in Managua and finding himself there with many Sandinistas, Cardenal wrote: 'I knew that we were sharing profound ideas of justice and solidarity with the oppressed, with our people'.[13] Through such conversations and gatherings, the FSLN won over not only the two Cardenal brothers, but also other Catholic priests and laypeople.

A Christian Revolutionary Movement

By the early 1970s, Nicaragua Catholic priests had initiated Christian base communities (*comunidades eclesiales de base*) made up of grassroots people in poor neighbourhoods, served by priests or catechists, Delegates of the Word, as they were called, who offered short courses (*cursillos*) based on what was called 'consciousness raising', that is, using the Bible as a way to interpret contemporary social reality. The Gospels and the Old Testament story of Exodus in particular were used to question and criticise the Somoza regime, the repression, the lack of democracy and the country's backward economic and social situation. The Christian communities adopted the method of the Belgian Young Christian Workers (*Jeunesse ouvrière chrétienne* – JOC) that called upon Catholics 'to

---

13　Cardenal 2008, Vol. I, pp. 61–4.

see, judge, and act'.[14] Many of the communities saw the Somoza dictatorship, judged it to be wrong, and began to take action to change it or to rid themselves of it altogether. Through the Christian base communities, some priests and a number of lay activists and parishioners would come to join the Sandinista organisation or at least to support the FSLN-led movement.[15]

Catholic activists also became involved in the revolution through the Jesuit University and Catholic high schools. Father Fernando Cardenal and other Jesuit priests organised consciousness-raising groups among college and secondary school students. Much like the Christian base communities, these student groups discussed the country's social situation using the Gospels but sometimes also using Karl Marx. Cardenal mentions study groups that read eclectically: Marx, Marta Harnecker, Mao Tse-tung, and liberation theologians such as Leonardo Boff, Gustavo Gutiérrez and Helder Cámara, among others.[16] The students, many of whom came from upper-class and middle-class homes, became radicalised through these discussion groups and some became convinced revolutionaries, leading to the formation in 1972 of the Christian Revolutionary Movement (MCR). Radical, humanitarian, and in a broad sense socialist, the Christian revolutionaries, however, had no distinct revolutionary socialist theory of their own; consequently, they tended over time to fall under the sway of the FSLN.

By the early- to mid-1970s, the Christian base communities and the Christian Revolutionary Movement had turned to activism, joining with working people and the poor to protest against increases in bus fares and in basic food prices, as well as marching with teachers protesting against Somoza's expulsion of the teachers' leaders from their union.[17] Throughout the decade, the Christian activists who participated in protests were photographed, identified, arrested, jailed, tortured, and often murdered, their bodies thrown into the volcanoes or into the lakes. For these reasons, 'Being involved in the urban protest movement was often more dangerous than being involved in the guerrilla', according to Fernando Cardenal.[18] The MCR recruited a number of activists to the Sandinistas, or, when Somoza's repression threatened to kill them, the young Christian revolutionaries ran away to the mountains to join the guerrilla

---

14   Talk by Joseph E. Mulligan, S.J. to Xavier University (Cincinnati) faculty and students in
       Managua, 8 March 2013.
15   Mulligan 1991, pp. 87–98. For a study of one neighbourhood group (Barrio 14 de Junio/Barrio
       la Luz) see Canin 1997, pp. 88–100.
16   Cardenal 2008, p. 95.
17   Mulligan 1991, pp. 94–5; Cardenal 2008, p. 76.
18   Conversation with Fernando Cardenal in Managua, Nicaragua, 1 March 2013.

movement.[19] While these students considered themselves socialists, they did not have the Stalinist and Fidelista or Guevarist politics of the original Sandinistas and they grew to represent a distinct Christian current of socialist politics within the FSLN. Though they did not have a very clearly elaborated socialist theory, they had their Christian principles, their common history in the MCR, and their shared commitment to the movement.

Some Catholic priests, such as Fernando Cardenal, became secret members and leaders of the FSLN while another priest, Gaspar García Laviana, actually joined the guerrillas and was killed in combat. He wrote: 'With a gun in hand, filled with faith and love for the Nicaraguan people, I must fight to my last breath for the advent of the reign of justice in our country'.[20] Many other priests worked with the Sandinistas and significant numbers of young Catholics eventually joined the Sandinistas, participated in guerrilla operations, or more typically supported the FSLN in one way or another. The FSLN Marxist-Leninist leadership put no obstacles in the path of Catholic activists who wished to join the Sandinistas, accepting them as full members and, as mentioned, in some cases as leaders.

By the 1970s, there were two strong political currents mingling in the FSLN: (1) the Stalinist and Fidelista politics of Fonseca and Borge; and (2) the Theology of Liberation or what could be called Nicaraguan Christian socialism. The former was far stronger than the latter. Few Marxist-Leninists became Christian socialists, but some Christian socialists did give up their faith and became Marxist-Leninists. Still, the revolutionary Christian current would continue to have a strong identity in the pre-revolutionary period, during the events leading up to the Triumph, and in the post-revolutionary phase. Later, many of the revolutionary Christians would break with the FSLN either during the 1990s or after 2006 when the Front returned to power.

Other Socialist Currents

The FSLN was the dominant left organisation throughout this period, but by no means the only one. Though the Soviet Union did not believe that the Sandinistas could overthrow Somoza and continued to hold their Popular Front position, by 1976 the Communist PSN, which for decades had so dutifully followed the Soviet line, also began to orient toward Cuba and the armed

---

19   Cardenal 2008, pp. 65–85.
20   Cited in Mulligan 1991, p. 99.

struggle.[21] This turn, however, did not lead to any examination or criticism of the Soviet Union or the Communist Party model of organisation. Some of these PSN members came to join the FSLN either individually or through organisational mergers. For example, Eva Sacasa joined the Communist PSN Youth in 1973 and in 1976 was sent to Cuba for military training. Meanwhile, the PSN and the FSLN had begun to work closely together in late 1976 and then merged in 1978. Sacasa thus became an FSLN member and after the Triumph she became part of the Ministry of the Intelligence.[22] The merger of the Communist PSN with the FSLN could only strengthen the core Stalinist and Castroite politics of the latter.

Other political tendencies also existed, though their organisations were not as large. At the National Autonomous University of Nicaragua, for example, there was a group of 'progressive professors' (jokingly known as the Pepes because so many were named José). The group included pro-Soviet Marxist-Leninists, but also Liberals, Maoists and Trotskyists, though the majority of its members were simply academics who opposed Somoza and wanted to achieve national sovereignty and social justice.[23] No doubt there were similar small clusters of progressives and leftists in other institutions throughout the country. Yet none of these other political currents, such as Maoism or Trotskyism, grew to be significant in numbers. Their impact on the FSLN or on society in general was negligible.

During the 1970s, a variety of new, leftist organisations had appeared. As mentioned earlier, the FSLN's study of Mao in the late 1960s and early 1970s had led to the split of the Workers Front (Frente Obrero – FO), an organisation that admired Mao and Enver Hoxha and which built its own base in the peasantry and working classes. The FO continued to be a critic and would-be rival to the FSLN. There was also the Marxist-Leninist Movement of Popular Action, which worked in the Popular Anti-Somoza Militias, as well as a small Nicaraguan Trotskyist group, the Revolutionary Marxist League, led by Bonifacio Miranda.[24]

A survey of leftist currents in Nicaragua on the eve of the revolution would not be complete without mentioning the brief presence of the South American Trotskyists. During the last year of the armed struggle and immediately after the

---

21   Paszyn 2000, p. 24, notes that when the Sandinistas achieved victory in 1979, it came as a complete surprise to the Soviet Union's leaders.

22   Baltodano 2010, Vol. III, pp. 99–106.

23   Hassan Morales 2009, pp. 87–8. Hassan himself, a leader of the Sandinistas linked to the GPP group and a member of La Junta, considered himself to be one of the non-ideological leftists.

24   Ortega 2010, p. 473.

insurrection, hundreds of socialists from Latin America, Europe and the United States also came to Nicaragua. Among them were scores of Trotskyists from South America organised in the Simón Bolívar Brigade. They were members of the Bolshevik Faction of the United Secretariat of the Fourth International led by the Argentine Nahuel Moreno. The group held critical views of both Stalinism and Social Democracy, and were also opposed to the 'glorification of "Che" Guevara and the Cuban Revolution'. Once in Nicaragua, the Morenistas succeeded in recruiting to the Fourth International a group of Nicaraguan Maoists and then together formed the Revolutionary Marxist League (LRM) mentioned above.[25]

The Morenistas' criticism of the Sandinista leadership brought swift repression after the Triumph. The FSLN, with its Stalinist origins, had no desire to have Trotskyists offering criticisms and alternative ideas to either FSLN cadres or the masses.[26] Immediately after the Triumph, the FSLN leadership had the foreign Trotskyists rounded up, put on planes, and shipped back to South America.[27] The remaining Nicaraguan Trotskyists succeeded in keeping the group alive through the 1980s as the Revolutionary Workers Party (PRT). While the PRT and several other leftist groups were present in Nicaragua during the period leading to the insurrection, it was the FSLN that had the 'moral authority' in society both because of its long history of struggle and because it had suffered torture, murder, imprisonment and exile in its thirteen years of struggle against Somoza.[28] But this is getting ahead of the story.

The FSLN Organisation of Women

Before moving on to discuss the split in the FSLN, we should note its organising among women. In the mid-1970s, the FSLN was involved in legal labour

---

25   Alexander 1991, p. 632; Bolshevik Tendency 1977. Also, an email communication from Michael Lowy, 21 June 2013 briefly summarises the Trotskyist presence in Nicaragua. Some sources say there were hundreds of South American Trotskyists in Nicaragua around 1979.

26   Reading memoirs of the period in which the authors discuss their reading in the pre-revolutionary period, there are few references to the works of Leon Trotsky or to other Troskyist writing. To cite an exception, however, Omar Cabezas mentions that Modesto, the pseudonym of Henry Ruiz, a *comandante* trained in the Soviet Union, read Ernest Mandel's *Political Economy* while up in the mountains in a guerrilla camp. Mandel was the leading intellectual of the Trotskyist Fourth International at the time. Cabezas 1982, p. 107.

27   Alexander 1991, p. 632. Ramírez 1999, p. 107.

28   Ortega 2010, p. 474.

and community organising, as discussed in the previous chapter, and part of that work also involved the organisation of women. The FSLN had attempted on a couple of occasions in the past to organise women without success. In April of 1977, *comandante* Jaime Wheelock suggested to Lea Guido that the group make another attempt. Guido had studied as a girl in the Colegio de la Divina Pastor, the Colegio Americano, and then in the Colegio Batista. At the university she studied sociology, earned a Master's Degree in Public Health at the University of Lyon and then a PhD in Public Health at the University of Toulouse. While in Europe she met theology of liberation worker priests in Switzerland who were organising Christian base communities among Spanish and Italian immigrant workers. Through conversations with her husband Xavier Langlade, a Frenchman who was a leader of the May and June 1968 strikes in France, she was also influenced by those events. While in Europe she also studied the writings of Karl Marx and Ernest Mandel, the Trotskyist economist. Through her husband's sister who was her friend, Guido met Roberto Huembes and other Sandinistas, principally of the Proletarian Tendency (PT), and joined the PT in 1976. When asked by Wheelock to undertake the creation of a women's organisation, she accepted the assignment.

The repression taking place at the time was terrible, so the Association of Nicaraguan Women Confronting the Nation's Problems (AMPRONAC) was initially begun as a human rights organisation. While at the beginning in the largest cities the organisation was initially quite small and made up primarily of wealthy women and professionals, gradually Guido and other organisers established a national network that succeeded in reaching working-class and peasant women in other cities, towns, and in the countryside.

AMPRONAC worked to organise and carry out campaigns in coordination with the FSLN related to the broader anti-somocista struggle. In 1977, the group, with only 25 members, organised a human rights campaign, demonstrating with posters and banners reading: 'Nicaraguans, Defend Your Rights'. The group participated in the protests following the assassination of Pedro Joaquín Chamorro in January 1978, joining in the support of the strike called by the business association that soon fizzled out. Around the same time, they took over the United Nations offices, extending the protest of the killing of Chamorro to others as well and raising a new slogan: 'Where Are Our Peasant Brothers and Sisters?' Working with the Christian base communities they reached out to mining communities in Siuma and to peasant women.[29] While the FSLN had

29   Baltodano 2010, Vol. III, pp. 74–98. Also Randall 1981, pp. 1–18.

secondary women leaders who engaged in organising women, the leadership of the party remained in the hands of an all-male group, committed to the liberation of women in society, but unable to fully practice it in their revolutionary organisation.

The FSLN's Three Rival Tendencies

While other leftist organisations existed, the FSLN was by far the largest, most ideologically coherent, best organised, and most important, and in the mid-1970s it was leading important campaigns. In 1975 and 1976, the FSLN actively recruited new supporters for its guerrilla operations and launched offensives in various parts of the country. But by late 1976, it was clear that the offensives had failed. A number of FSLN militants had been killed – including Carlos Fonseca, the founder – as well as some 2,000 peasants. The guerrilla operation as a whole had been virtually destroyed, though a few small guerrilla units remained and continued to fight on.[30] According to Humberto Ortega, by 1977, 'the National Guard had consolidated its total defeat of the Sandinista forces in the mountains'.[31] Increasing doubts about the guerrilla strategy, resulting from the Somoza regime's successful use of the National Guard to suppress the movement, led to the internal crisis in the FSLN.

Despite the ideological clarity of Fonseca and Borges and the original FSLN, built around their original Communist politics and their later conversion to Castro's revolutionary strategy, it is not surprising – given the Somoza dictatorship's repressive character and the difficulties of building a revolutionary movement under such circumstances – that there would arise rival tendencies with different analyses and strategic outlooks even within the FSLN. Though there had been some dramatic and highly successful operations, some Sandinistas, after thirteen of years of guerrilla struggle in the mountains, had come to believe that the group's original guerrilla strategy could not lead to a successful revolution and that in fact it would lead to defeat. Soon various individuals and groups began to put forward different strategies that would lead the FSLN to split into three rival organisations.

By 1975, three such tendencies had evolved each with different analyses, politics, and distinct notions of the appropriate class that would make the

---

30   Ortega 2010, pp. 315–46. He titles his discussion 'The Extintion of the Guerrilla Movement'. See also Nolan 1984, p. 46, on the 2,000 peasants killed.

31   Ortega 2010, p. 364.

revolution, and strategies for achieving it.[32] The first tendency, made up of the original founders of the group, was known as the Prolonged Peoples War (GPP) and was initially led by Carlos Fonseca, Pedro Arauz, Tomás Borge, Henry Ruíz and Carlos Agüero.[33] The roots of the GPP, as previously described, were in the old pro-Soviet Nicaraguan Socialist Party and its politics were Stalinist Communist or Marxist-Leninist as later revised by their adoption of the Cuban *guerilla foco*. Borge and his comrades subsequently modified the original Cuban *guerrilla foco* model, turning to Mao Tse-tung's Chinese experience and the theory of the 'prolonged peoples war'. So the GPP tendency remained committed to the idea of a guerrilla group operating in the mountains, organising the peasants and workers, but with the long-term strategy of gradually building a people's army that would eventually defeat Somoza's National Guard. Based in the mountains in the north of the country, they saw the guerrilla organisation drawing its strength from its relationship to the peasants. The GPP, they believed, would eventually lead peasant armies to surround and conquer the cities, as had happened in China.

A second tendency, led by Roberto Huembes, Jaime Wheelock, Carlos Núñez, and Luis Carrión, known as the Proletarian Tendency, argued that the FSLN must develop working-class organisations, especially in the agricultural labour unions, as the foundation for a revolutionary movement in arms. The PT argued that the GPP's view of peasant revolution was 'an anachronism', since the peasantry had been replaced by an agricultural proletariat.[34] The PT held a more classical Marxist view that a socialist party rooted in the working class would lead a revolutionary movement made up of labour unions and involving strikes and urban insurrections.[35] The PT's view was based on an analysis that showed that the labour movement had grown larger and that it had become more independent of Somoza. In 1979, there were eight national labour federations with a total of 133 affiliated unions and 27,000 union members in the country.[36] At the same time, the PT suggested that there was a tendency on the part of the FSLN to attempt to substitute itself for the working class and for a

---

32   For an extensive discussion of the similarities and differences among the tendencies, see
      Fonseca Terán 2005, pp. 86–140.

33   Ortega 2010, p. 354, gives the leaders of each of the tendencies. He has what I found to
      be the most complete and thorough discussion of the different groups and their ideas on
      pp. 347–64.

34   Nolan 1984, p. 55.

35   Nolan 1984, p. 52, discusses Jaime Wheelock's experience in Chile and in Communist East
      Germany where he travelled, lived, and developed his ideas.

36   Perez-Baltodano 2008, p. 564.

genuinely working-class party.[37] The PT had a following in the city of Managua and a meager presence among peasants in the countryside.[38] Relatively small and weak, the PT's one strength was having secured weapons in Europe. The GPP expelled the PT from the FSLN and even threatened to kill its members.[39]

Finally, the Third Tendency (*Terceristas*), also sometimes called the Insurrectional Tendency, argued that to successfully carry out a revolution it would be necessary to build a movement and a military force that could lead an armed insurrection in the cities and invasions from the borders of the country. At the same time, to lay the basis for such insurrections, it would be necessary to form alliances with other social classes and sectors of society – intellectuals, priests, professionals, landowners, and industrialists – as well as finding support from governments (including non-Communist governments) in Europe and Latin America. Unlike the GPP which emphasised organising the peasants, or the PT which emphasised organising workers, the Third Tendency saw its social base as 'all Nicaraguans opposed to Somoza'.[40] They believed that mass strikes and insurrections, culminating in a general strike and a final national insurrection, would be needed to overthrow Somoza.[41]

The GPP and the PT both looked forward to a prolonged struggle, while the Third Tendency believed that the organisation of a national insurrection should be put on the agenda at once. The full political position of the Terceristas was made clearer in 1978 when they published two documents, *Analysis of the Situation* and *The Tasks Before Us*. Humberto Ortega summarised the group's view that 'the Sandinista Popular Revolution should not be supported only by the humble masses, exploited and oppressed, but also by the rest of the comfortable and bourgeois groups of the nation whose political posture would tend to put an end to Somocismo and open up a democratic and popular process'.[42] While most Third Tendency leaders still shared the core Communist and Castroite politics of the other Sandinistas, they put forward a programme of a social-democratic character, in the immediate period calling for a mixed economy, political pluralism, and a foreign policy of non-alignment. When accused by the other Sandinista groups of being nothing more than social-democratic reformists, Humberto Ortega replied, writing:

---

37   Nolan 1984, p. 54.
38   Hassan Morales 2009, p. 191.
39   Nolan 1984, p. 58.
40   Ortega 2010, p. 362.
41   Ortega 2010, p. 374.
42   Ortega 2010, p. 422.

The fact that we [cannot] establish socialism immediately after overthrowing Somoza does not mean that we are planning a capitalist type
social-democratic and popular government; what we propose is a broad,
democratic, and popular government which, although the bourgeoisie
has participation, is a means and not an end, so that in its time it can
make the advance towards a more genuinely popular form of government,
which guarantees the movement toward socialism.[43]

Though it was not completely clear at the time, the Third Tendency then
seemed to envision something like what had happened following the revolutions carried out by the Red Army's invasions and Communist takeover of
Eastern Europe. There, as the Soviet Union's Red Army 'liberated' Eastern
Europe from Nazism in 1945, the Communist Parties took power and created
short-lived 'People's Republics' with capitalist and peasant party participation.
Not long afterwards, however, the Communists eliminated, absorbed, or completely subordinated those parties and became Communist governments and
one-party states.[44]

The Third Tendency ideology was at the time probably less important than
their new strategy and organisation and leadership. The leaders of the Third
Tendency were Daniel Ortega and his brother Humberto Ortega, though the
writer Sergio Ramírez also played a key role.[45] Based in San José, Costa Rica,
where they enjoyed the protection of President Daniel Oduber and ex-presi-
dent José Figueres Ferrer, the Third Tendency organised a military force that
between 1976 and 1979 numbered about 1,500 Sandinistas while at the same
time they claimed to have trained an estimated 15,000 insurgents among the
people.[46] The Third Tendency worked to convince other sectors of Nicaraguan
society, particularly the business groups, to join the revolutionary opposition,
and engaged in international diplomacy to win the support of political parties
and governments in Europe and Latin America. By mid-1978, the Third Tendency had also succeeded in winning support from the Cuban government,

---

43   Nolan 1984, p. 67, citing a letter written by Ortega, captured by the military and published
      in the press. See the important fn. 18, which argues against the possibility that the letter
      was a forgery.

44   Feijto 1971, *passim*. Czechoslovakia and Albania were exceptions to that process in Eastern
      Europe, though the result in the end was much the same. Yugoslavia was a distinct
      exception, though also a Communist one-party state under Josip Broz Tito.

45   Kinzer 2007, pp. 64–7; Ramirez 1999, pp. 89–90.

46   Ortega 2010, p. 393.

which until then had been backing the GPP.[47] Retrospectively, several FSLN leaders would look back at the Third Tendency, especially the Ortega brothers and Ramírez, as social democrats and opportunists all too prepared to make deals with the emerging bourgeois opposition.[48] At the time, however, they believed that they could dominate the bourgeoisie in the process of establishing a revolutionary government.

Faced with this challenge, Borge and the historic FSLN leadership expelled the Proletarian Tendency, detained some of its leaders, and even took some to foreign embassies in order to send them out of the country. At the same time, the Third Tendency developed its own organisation, so that by the mid-1970s the FSLN remained divided into three rival groups, 'each with its own leaders, structures, programme, policies, and philosophy of action'.[49] The three groups were not only separate, but antagonistic rivals. Humberto Ortega would write later that the Third Tendency had to drag the other two tendencies to accept the insurrectional strategy that would ultimately lead to the overthrow of Somoza.[50]

The Unification of the FSLN Tendencies

Things changed dramatically after 1975 as the result of several developments. The death in 1976 of Carlos Fonseca, who had returned from Cuba to rejoin the guerrillas in the mountains, put an end to an era. Meanwhile, the appearance of the Third Tendency with its policies of alliance with other social classes and capitalist groups presented a face of the Nicaraguan revolution more attractive to nationalist and social-democratic parties, as well as to foreign powers in Europe and South America. With its base safely ensconced in Costa Rica and its attractive public figures, such as writers Sergio Ramírez and Giaconda Belli, acting as its emissaries, it succeeded in winning support from the governments of not only Costa Rica but also Panamá, Mexico and Venezuela.[51] The Third Tendency also won complete support from Cuba and displaced the GPP from its position as the dominant leadership of the movement.[52] Finally the swearing

---

47   Ortega 2010, p. 483.
48   Ramírez 1991, pp. 114–15.
49   Téllez 2013, p. 14.
50   Ortega 2010, p. 363.
51   Both Belli 2002 and Ramírez 1999 discuss their roles as ambassadors among those parties and countries.
52   Hassan Morales 2009, pp. 184–94.

in of the Democrat Jimmy Carter in January 1977, a man who pledged to make human rights a touchstone of his foreign policy, raised the possibility of an administration in Washington, DC, that might be more critical of Somoza and perhaps more sympathetic to the opposition in Nicaragua, especially to the Third Tendency's fresh face.

Wanting to overcome the damage done to the image of the United States by its war against Vietnam, to pose a clear contrast between the behaviour of the United States and the Soviet Union, and to re-establish bipartisanship in foreign affairs, Carter promised to make human rights the centre of his foreign policy. He would initially raise this issue most clearly in Latin America and particularly Central America where military dictators ruled Guatemala, Honduras, El Salvador and Nicaragua, insisting that US military assistance would only come if those nations met human rights standards. President Gerald Ford, during his brief tenure, had already begun to distance the US from the Somoza government, but Carter was the first to threaten to withhold economic aid on human rights grounds. While 'the material impact [of this change in policy] was insignificant, the moral impact was enormous', writes historian William M. Leo-Grande.[53] With the United States no longer unconditionally backing Somoza, for the first time, the dictator's more moderate opponents could foresee the possibility of change. But as LeoGrande has also written: 'The Carter Administration's policy toward the Nicaraguan revolution was more than a little schizo-phrenic'.[54] When Somoza eased up on his repression, Carter in late 1977 sent $2.5 million in military aid and in a letter of 1 August 1978, he praised Somoza for having improved human rights.[55] As historian Walter LaFeber has written, Carter's policy was contradictory. 'He valued human rights, but he preferred Somoza to the FSLN'.[56]

While the Sandinistas' guerrilla strategy had failed, the prospects for revolution seemed to be improving; still the FSLN remained too deeply divided to carry the struggle forward. All three FSLN tendencies, though they recognised that the division into rival groups represented an impediment that threatened the revolution, proved incapable of overcoming their rivalries and uniting. They engaged in bitter recriminations and fortunately avoided more violent outcomes. It was finally Fidel Castro, perhaps the only figure admired and trusted by all three groups, who succeeded in bringing them together in 1979 by

53   LeoGrande 1998, pp. 16–17.
54   William M. LeoGrande, 'The United States and the Nicaraguan Revolution', in Walker 1982, p. 75.
55   LaFeber 1993, p. 231; LeoGrande 1998, p. 20.
56   LaFeber 1993, p. 20.

telling them that he was prepared to provide the FSLN revolutionaries with material support including arms, but only if they overcame their differences.[57] In March 1979, the FSLN announced that a new National Directorate had been formed made up of nine members, three from each of the factions: for the Prolonged Peoples War faction, Tomás Borge, Henry Ruíz, and Bayardo Arce; for the Proletarian Tendency, Jaime Wheelock, Luis Carrión, and Carlos Núñez; for the Third Tendency, Daniel Ortega, Humberto Ortega, and Victor Tirado.

The unification of the three tendencies represented a victory for the Third Tendency, which, by allying with the weak Proletarian Tendency, succeeded in relegating the founding Prolonged Peoples War tendency to a secondary position. Consequently, during the late 1970s, Daniel Ortega and his brother Humberto Ortega thus effectively became the leaders of the FSLN with Tomás Borge and Jaime Wheelock as their subordinates, a set of relationships that would endure until the 1990s.[58] While many others would play important roles as well, the dominance of the Ortegas – Humberto as military chief and Daniel as party leader – would remain unchallenged for many years. The Third Tendency's political strategy, based on seeking an alliance with the Nicaraguan bourgeoisie and petty bourgeoisie, became the FSLN's strategy, though the reunited FSLN retained its Marxist-Leninist party style of organisation. As Sergio Ramírez would later write, it was the Third Tendency's politics and strategy that would lead them to victory.[59]

With the FSLN now reunited, preparations were made to launch the final offensive. While each tendency had somewhat different politics, they all saw the reunited FSLN as a vanguard party, and all accepted the supposedly democratic-centralist, but in reality vertical, top-down, organisation of the FSLN. For all three tendencies, Cuba continued to provide the party's political model and revolutionary ideal.[60] The unification of the three tendencies represented fundamental change in military strategy, the end of the *guerrilla foco* model or

---

57   Kinzer 2007, p. 67, and Hassan Morales 2009, p. 190; but Ramírez 1999, pp. 171–2, dismisses the argument that Castro played the central role, arguing that it was the death of Chamorro that forced unity on the factions. And Ortega 2010, p. 364, does not mention Castro at all when discussing the reunification of the FSLN. Still, it seems clear from the evidence that Castro brokered the final reconciliation.

58   Hassan Morales 2009, p. 194.

59   Ramírez 1991, p. 114.

60   All of the memoirs of Sandinista leaders and activists refer to the enormous significance of Cuba for the Sandinistas, even if some thought they would have to deviate somewhat from that model to be successful in Nicaragua. Many also make clear that they saw themselves as part of the Soviet camp.

the Maoist prolonged popular war model, and the building of larger combat units capable of engaging National Guard troops. From Costa Rica, the group's new headquarters, the reunited FSLN would soon conduct genuine military manoeuvres as opposed to merely guerrilla operations.

Even after the FSLN reunited, the organisation remained quite small. In a nation of three million people, it had only about 400 cadres and 1,000 members, and never had more than 3,000 armed combatants in the field, though it exerted greater influence through the mass organisations in which it worked: student groups, community organisations, and unions.[61]

The Bourgeois Opposition

The Third Tendency strategy of building a broad democratic movement of all opposition groups and all social classes opposed to the Somoza dictatorship, now adopted by the FSLN as a whole, coincided with the growing rift in Nicaragua's capitalist class. The devastating Managua earthquake of December 1972 (described at the end of Chapter 3), and Anastasio Somoza Debayle's misappropriation of the financial aid that poured into Nicaragua from governments and non-governmental organisations around the world, marked a turning point in the country's already critical situation. Somoza took advantage of his control of the government and his embezzlement of foreign aid to expand his personal businesses and those of his cronies, leading to greater competition in the capitalist class. What other businessmen called 'unfair competition' led in turn to political divisions among the country's bourgeoisie.

The growing economic and political conflict caused by Somoza's behaviour in the wake of the earthquake shattered the coalition of interests that had formed the basis of the regime's rule since the 1930s. The Somozas' strength had never been simply military, but had always depended upon the political support of the country's wealthy financiers, industrialists, merchants, and landlords. By 1973, however, sections of the bourgeoisie were not only expressing their concerns about Somoza's aggressive economic behaviour, but also beginning to oppose his policies and to turn against the regime itself. At about

---

61   Regarding the size of the FSLN: Zimmerman 2000, p. 209, gives a size of 150 to 200 members
      in 1977. Ramírez 1999, pp. 111–12, mentions a meeting of about 400 FSLN cadres in Managua
      in September 1979. Téllez 2013, p. 21, says that the party only succeeded with great effort in
      distributing 1,000 membership cards at the beginning of 1980. At the time Nicaragua had
      a population of about three million. Fonseca Terán 2005, p. 100, quotes Daniel Ortega as
      saying the FSLN never had more than 3,000 armed fighters.

the same time, students and workers were becoming bolder. During 1973 and 1974, there were strikes not only by students, but also by construction workers, health workers, and teachers, as well as protests against government repression.[62]

The worsening economic situation – a result of both the international economic crisis and Nicaragua's own particular problems – led to disinvestment, as capitalists declined to invest or moved their money abroad. Unemployment grew, the government's debt grew, and inflation increased. The Nicaraguan government's debt to foreign nations rose from US$200 million in 1972 to an astronomical US$1.5 billion in 1979, with the payment on the foreign debt becoming both a burden and leading to greater dependence on foreign capital.[63] The economic crisis that had begun in the late 1960s thus, aggravated by natural disaster and Somoza's avarice, became a deep political crisis by the mid-1970s and a pre-revolutionary situation by 1978.

When, in 1974, Anastasio Somoza Debayle was elected to an unprecedented seven-year term, La Prensa publisher Pedro Joaquín Chamorro brought together leaders from the Conservatives, the Liberals, the Social Christian Party, and the Communist PSN to create the Democratic Union of Liberation (la Unión Democrática de Liberación or UDEL). The UDEL, which was backed by groups from the upper classes, the middle classes, and some organisations of workers and farmers, was a clear indication that the Somoza government no longer had the support of the country's capitalist class.[64] As the 1974 elections approached, UDEL, eight other organisations, and 27 well-known figures issued a pamphlet titled 'General Somoza is disqualified from being a candidate or Constitutional President'. At the same time, the 'Group of 27' raised the slogan: 'There is No One to Vote For'. All were arrested, one-by-one, and brought before a judge on the charge of encouraging a boycott of the election. The combination of the boycott propaganda and the repression of the boycott movement led to significant abstention in the September election.[65]

Around the same time, the FSLN carried out its spectacular raid on the dinner party at the home of José María Chema Castillo in December 1974, followed by Somoza declaring a state of siege, suppressing the press, and unleashing a wave of government terror that swept across the country. Somoza's National Guard not only arrested, tortured, raped and murdered individuals, but also

---

62   Zimmerman 2000, p. 209.
63   Ortega 2010, pp. 294–6.
64   Ortega 2010, p. 310.
65   Ortega 2010, p. 311.

burned and bombed entire villages. A special military tribunal was established to investigate the FSLN, and in a lengthy New Year's Eve broadcast, Somoza blamed Pedro Joaquín Chamorro, editor of *La Prensa*, for the country's troubles.[66] If Somoza's economic policies had divided the capitalist class, Matilde Zimmerman argues that the terrible and horrifying repression of 1975 and 1976 undermined the legitimacy of the government in the eyes of the middle classes as well.[67] The Somoza dynasty was becoming unmoored from the society to which it had been tied; detached from the upper classes that had supported it.

The next step in the unfolding crisis came on 10 January 1978 when *La Prensa* publisher Chamorro – a historic leader of the opposition Conservative Party, the likely candidate for president of the UDEL coalition in the coming 1981 elections, and the man whom Somoza had just publicly attacked – was assassinated. The murder of Chamorro, widely thought to have been ordered by Somoza, led to spontaneous protest demonstrations throughout the country while opposition business groups called for a national general strike.[68] Ignoring the business organisations' call to simply 'stay home', protestors took to the streets in violent demonstrations. Protestors in Managua focused their rage on Plasmaférisis, the Somoza-owned company that bought and sold the blood of the poor, setting the building on fire. The destruction of Plasmaférisis, so symbolic of the blood-sucking relationship of the Somozas to Nicaraguan society, was literally burned into the popular consciousness.[69]

A month later, the indigenous community of Monimbó in Masaya, just twenty miles from Managua, rose up in rebellion as FSLN clandestine activists rushed there to provide leadership.[70] Then in April, a national student strike closed 80 percent of the country's public and private high schools.[71] The Catholic Bishops issued a letter in 1978 criticising the way that public officials enriched themselves through politics while workers had no right to organise labour unions and put forward their legitimate demands.[72] The Catholic Church's withdrawal of support from Somoza was perhaps the most important political development until that point, surpassed only by the American government's final break with the dictator a year later.

---

66   Millet 1977, p. 245.
67   Zimmerman 2000, p. 211.
68   While Somoza may not have killed Chamorro, it has been difficult *to prove* that he did not.
69   Diederich 2007, pp. 153–75.
70   Kinzer 2007, p. 28; Diederich 2007, p. 164.
71   Zimmerman 2000 p. 212.
72   Pérez-Baltodano 2008, pp. 568–76.

With the crisis deepening and the business sector left without a political party to represent its interests, there developed at first a tacit and eventually an explicit alliance between the economic oligarchy and the Sandinistas. A significant factor in this developing relationship was the fact that many young people in the Sandinistas' clandestine and military operations were children of the oligarchy. Most studies have found that the business group had become strategic allies of the Sandinistas well before the Triumph. Some even suggest that the business class may have believed that it could take over the Sandinistas.[73]

As the anti-Somoza movement broadened from students, workers, and the usual political opposition to include businessmen and the Catholic Church, the FSLN leadership looked for a way to present a potential leadership that could appeal to all of the opposition forces in Nicaragua as well as to political parties and governments abroad. The first face of the Sandinista revolution that caught the attention of the public at large not only in Nicaragua, but also in the United States and throughout the world, was the appearance of 'Los Doce' or 'The Twelve'. The FSLN, following the strategy initially suggested by the Third Tendency, had chosen the Twelve because they represented significant sectors of middle- and upper-class Nicaraguan society. Their faces and roles, it was hoped, would show the world that the great majority of Nicaraguans had come to oppose Somoza.

In July 1978, the FSLN's Costa Rica headquarters presented Los Doce to Nicaragua and to the world. The Twelve were a group of intellectuals, businessmen, and religious leaders pulled together by the FSLN as a provisional government. The group included many prestigious Nicaraguans: as president, the businessman Felipe Mántica, owner of the La Colonial supermarket chain; Emilio Baltodano, a coffee exporter and owner of the Presto instant coffee factory; Joaquín Cuadra Chamorro, lawyer for the Banco de América group and the Nicaragua Sugar Estate; Ricardo Coronel, an agronomist at the San Antonio sugar plant; the architect Casimiro Sotelo living in California; the dentist Carlos Gutiérrez living in Mexico; attorney Ernesto Castillo Martínez living in Costa Rica; the economist Arturo Cruz, an official of the Inter-American Development Bank in Washington; Dr. Carlos Tünnermann, former rector of the National University; the writer Sergio Ramírez living in Costa Rica; the Maryknoll priest Miguel d'Escoto, chief of communications for the order in New York; and the Jesuit priest Fernando Cardenal. Two of Los Doce, Sergio Ramírez and Fernando Cardenal, were secret members of the FSLN. Los Doce had no FSLN *comandantes*, no labour union or peasant members; it was made up entirely of capitalists and professionals.

Los Doce had already agreed on a programme in May of 1977 that called for a democratic government with full civil liberties; the abolition of the National Guard and the creation of a new national army; the expropriation of all of the property of Somoza and his associates; an agrarian reform that would lead to a mixed economy of private, public and cooperative sectors; and a foreign policy of non-alignment, freeing Nicaragua from its long dependence upon the United States.[74] Los Doce presented to Nicaragua, to the United States, and to the world at large an image of an alternative Nicaragua, and one that was nothing like Cuban Communism. Here apparently was some sort of middle-class, democratic, reformist government. When ten of The Twelve arrived in Managua on 5 July 1978, with their slogan, 'the dictatorship is a corpse and we have come to bury it', they were met by huge crowds, just as they were in the provinces too. Those demonstrations started to create the political climate that would make possible the insurrections that followed.[75]

At about the same time, other elements of the FSLN (principally the Proletarian Tendency, but also the GPP) organised the United People's Movement (Movimiento Pueblo Unido of MPU) made up of community, student, and labour organisation. If Los Doce presented the face of upper-class Nicaragua, the MPU represented an alliance of the working people of Nicaragua. The MPU included the Communist PSN, the independent-General Confederation of Workers (CGT-independiente), and the recently founded Communist Party of Nicaragua – not to be confused with the Communist PSN – as well as a following in other labour unions.[76].

Even as this peaceful and legal jockeying for political position was taking place, in August 1978, in the most spectacular of all the FSLN actions, a group of commandos took over the National Palace, capturing and holding all of the congressional representatives present until Somoza agreed to free hundreds of political prisoners who had been in jail since December 1974. As the revolutionaries made their way to the Managua airport, tens of thousands of people came out to cheer them shouting 'Down with Somoza!'[77] In Matagalpa, there was another insurrection that same month led by high-school students, which

---

74   Ramírez 1991, p. 98.

75   Ortega 2010, p. 427.

76   Ortega 2010, p. 428. The Communist Party of Nicaragua, led by Elí Altamirano, was a critic and opponent of the FSLN.

77   Diederich 2007, pp. 176–88.

was only finally put down by aerial bombing and the occupation of the city by thousands of troops. The audacity of the seizure of the National Palace and the Matagalpa uprising opened the way to the final insurrection and the revolution.[78]

Carter, finally recognising the depth of the Nicaraguan crisis and the likelihood that Somoza would be overthrown – and fearing that a Cuban-style Communist government might come to power – worked through the Organisation of American States (OAS) to create a mediation committee.[79] In response to this new development, the opposition established another coalition called the Broad Opposition Front (Frente Amplio Opositor or FAO) involving all of the more moderate opposition groups: the UDEL, the Conservatives, the dissident Liberals, the Social Christians, and the PSN Communists, as well as Los Doce. Businessman Alfonso Robelo headed the FAO.

The OAS mediators and the FAO met and came to an agreement that Somoza would step down, while the National Guard would be kept intact, and the legislature would be divided between capitalist opposition parties and Somoza's National Liberal Party (PLN). When the OAS called upon Somoza to resign, however, he suggested a plebiscite, allowing the Nicaraguans to vote on who should govern through a traditional election. Carter liked the idea and pushed the FAO to continue talks with Somoza. For three months Somoza talked, believing that if the United States had to choose between him and the Sandinistas, they would choose their old ally. The negotiations eventually broke down, but by pushing the FAO to negotiate with Somoza, Carter had helped to undermine the credibility of the moderate opposition.[80]

Clearly Carter's plan was to eliminate Somoza while saving his government and keeping the Sandinistas from taking power. The new 'constitutionalist' plan called for Somoza to resign in favour of a constitutional successor who would in turn create an 'executive committee' of 'prominent, independent Nicaraguans and turn power over to them'. That committee would work with the National Guard, the Liberal Party, and the opposition to create an interim government and then hold elections in 1981.[81] In protest against this plan, which would have left the Guard intact, the FSLN left the FAO and with some other groups joined the MPU in creating the National Patriot Front (Frente Nacional Patriótico or FNP), an attempt to create a broad enough organisation to take power when

78   Zimmerman 2000, p. 212.
79   LeoGrande 1998, pp. 20–2.
80   LeoGrande 1998, pp. 21–2; Diederich 2007, pp. 205–26.
81   LeoGrande 1998, pp. 24–5.

Somoza fell. Despite the formation of these various coalitions, it was not clear in 1978 what organisation might take power in the event that Somoza was overthrown or fled.

'The Final Offensive' and the National Insurrection

The Sandinista preparations for the national offensive and final insurrection had been going on for some time. In late October 1978, the FSLN established the Sandinista Army of Nicaragua, headed by *Comandante Cero*, Edén Pastora, with the idea that this army would be a major factor in the insurrection and would replace the National Guard when the Somoza regime had been overthrown.[82] Thousands of internationalists had come through organisations in various countries to join the movement. Largest and most important of the internationalist organisations was the Simón Bolívar Brigade of 300 men, all of them Central and South American Trotskyists, led by the radical adventurer Dr. Hugo Sapadafora.[83] Chile's left – the Socialist Party, the Communist Party and the Movement of the Revolutionary Left (MIR) – sent 90 fighters. There were also fighters who came from Germany, England, Uruguay, Argentina, Spain, Mexico, and all of the countries of Central America. All told, there were, according to Humberto Ortega, who was the principal FSLN military leader at the time, some 5,000 internationalist volunteer fighters who came to join the FSLN in the final push to overthrow Somoza. They joined the Sandinistas in carrying out a combination of uprisings in the cities and invasion across the borders based on a three-step plan: the mobilisation of the principal fighting units; the calling of a national strike; and the uprising of the masses. The FSLN troops and voluntary organisations were organised in several fronts in different regions of the country.[84] While it did not take place exactly as planned, once the insurrection had begun, it developed a momentum and logic of its own and eventually became an unstoppable force.

In September 1978, the FSLN led a series of uprisings in Masaya, Chinandega, Diriamba, León, Jinotepe and Estelí in what it called the 'final offensive'. Somoza's response was to send airplanes to bomb and artillery to shell

---

82   Ortega 2010, p. 448. The US government and its allies, Ortega says, met secretly with Pastora and attempted to win him away from the FSLN. Ortega 2010, p. 450.

83   Ortega 2010, p. 493.

84   Ortega 2010, pp. 496–500, describes the fronts. He also gives detailed discussions of the plan and its implementation.

the rebellious cities, especially their working-class and poorer quarters, killing an estimated 5,000 people.[85] Three representatives of the Twelve – the writer Sergio Ramírez, the priest Miguel d'Escoto, and businessman Emilio Baltodano – met with the American ambassador to tell him that something must be done to stop Somoza's 'genocide'.[86]

Matilde Zimmerman argues: 'In these conditions of fierce repression and social crisis, growing numbers of Nicaraguans came to see the FSLN as their organisation and as the legitimate leadership of the fight against Somoza'.[87] While this may be true, virtually no one knew anything about the FSLN leadership, few knew much about its programme, and only a small minority had had any contact with the FSLN as an organisation. They identified with the FSLN simply for its consistent and courageous opposition to Somoza. In any case, by the end of 1978, a revolutionary period had opened up and the FSLN proved to be the most prepared and the best positioned to take advantage of it.

The struggle that ensued, culminating in the national insurrection of mid-1979, was a remarkable uprising by the country's youth – college students, workers, and many peasants – against the murderous Somoza dictatorship. Many of the fighters were teenagers and men and women in their early twenties who risked and by the thousands gave their lives in guerrilla warfare in the countryside and urban uprisings in the cities of Estelí and León, as well as in many other towns and villages. Somoza's National Guard continued its repression mercilessly and sadistically. The Guard raped, mutilated, castrated and beheaded the revolutionary fighters, many of whom were adolescents and some of whom were only children. Many recall that at that time 'to be young was a crime'. Students in the cities simply walking down the street or youth in the countryside might simply be rounded up and shot.

During the repeated uprising in Estelí and other cities, the National Guard bombed or dropped barrels of gasoline on the cities, destroying entire neighbourhoods and indiscriminately killing many people, particularly those in the barrios known to be political, usually the barrios of working people and the poor. The Sandinista fighters were joined by thousands of others who came out of their homes and fought the National Guard, defeating it first in the smaller cities and then finally in Managua. By June, the fighting raged in Managua with the National Guard using aerial bombings and tanks to destroy the barricades built by those who had risen up in rebellion. Guardsmen moved into

---

85   Zimmerman 2000, p. 213.
86   Ortega 2010, p. 447.
87   Zimmerman 2000, p. 213.

the neighborhoods, killing execution-style many of the young men they found there. They were taking no prisoners.

The Carter administration continued to seek a way to remove Somoza, while turning the state over to reliable pro-American politicians and preserving the National Guard, even if perhaps a purged Guard. But then an unforeseen event suddenly changed history. When National Guardsmen murdered Bill Stewart, a reporter for ABC News in Managua on 29 June 1979, an execution captured on camera and repeatedly played on American television, it became clear that the US would have to break not only with Somoza but also with his government and the Guard. Still the Americans, now prepared to dump Somoza, wanted to avoid recognising a Nicaraguan government that might include the Sandinistas. US Secretary of State Cyrus Vance, understanding that the Somoza regime was near collapse, proposed that the Organisation of American States send in a peacekeeping force. The OAS rejected that proposal, arguing that Somoza was 'the fundamental cause' of the country's turmoil and that he had to leave at once.[88]

Two weeks before Stewart was killed, the Sandinistas had announced that they had created a five person *Junta de Gobierno*, a provisional government. The five members of the Junta were: Violeta Chamorro, widow of the recently assasinated Pedro Joaquín Chamorro, the Conservative party leader and news-paper publisher; Alfonso Robelo, an entrepreneur who had organised strikes by the business sector against Somoza; Moïses Hassan Morales, a physicist and teacher who had earned his PhD at North Carolina State University; the writer Sergio Ramírez; and one FSLN *comandante*, Daniel Ortega. Like Los Doce, the Junta presented a cross-class government with a reform programme, intended to calm the fears of the Nicaraguan bourgeoisie and the Americans. Only later would it become known that, like Ortega, Hassan and Ramírez were also secret FSLN members, meaning that the Sandinistas always held a majority of three in the five-man Junta. The Junta drafted a political programme made up of five points: (1) the establishment of a democratic regime with civil liberties; (2) the abolition of the National Guard and the creation of a new army; (3) the expro-priation of the property of Somoza and his associates; (4) an agrarian reform and the distribution of landed property within the context of a mixed economy; (5) a non-aligned foreign policy.[89]

The US sent a new ambassador, Lawrence Pezzullo, to deal with the rapidly disintegrating situation. On 13 July, he met with Somoza, vice president Fran-

---

88   Kinzer 2007; pp. 47–8; Diederich 2007, pp. 269–80.
89   Ortega 2010, p. 394.

cisco Urcuyo, and congressional leaders and made it clear that the US demanded that Somoza resign and be succeeded by Urcuyo. On 16 July, Somoza read
his resignation to an assembly of congressional representatives; it was accepted, and Urcuyo was sworn in as president. Somoza, his mistress, and about one
hundred of his closest associates boarded a Nicaraguan jet and flew to a US air
force base in Florida. Urcuyo actually took office and held a press conference
declaring himself the new president, and it was only after a Deputy Secretary of
State Warren Christopher threatened Somoza with expulsion from the US and
Urcuyo with political abandonment by the United States that the latter agreed
to step down from his brief, 43-hour presidency. Guatemalan dictator, General Romeo Lucas García, sent three planes to take the rest of the old regime's
top officials out of the country. The FSLN forces deployed in a ring around
central Managua closed in on 18 July. The National Guard headquartered in
the Somoza bunker surrendered unconditionally. With Somoza gone and the
United States no longer supporting the regime, the National Guard disintegrated, as many Guardsmen fled to Honduras or Costa Rica for fear of their
lives.

The Nicaraguan people had triumphed over the dictator. The Junta de Gobierno created by the FSLN immediately became the new government of Nicaragua, assuming power on 19 July. The next day, the Sandinista guerrillas and the
civilians who had joined them in the final insurrections flooded into the city's
central square, now named the Plaza of the Revolution, to be joined by tens of
thousands of ordinary Nicaraguans who embraced the young revolutionaries
and celebrated them as the saviours of the country. The Junta, carried atop a
fire truck, arrived at the plaza to the uproarious cheers of the crowd to declare
the victory.

Estimates of those killed in the struggle against the Somoza dictatorship
range from 30,000 to 50,000; those who died left tens of thousands of widows,
widowers, and orphans. The revolutionary upheaval also left thousands of
maimed fighters, many of them amputees who had given an arm or a leg to end
the dictatorship. The physical and psychological toll of the dictatorship and
the struggle against it would be a public health burden that the country would
bear for years. Yet, while mourning and honouring the dead, the Nicaraguan
people were elated at the victory of the revolution and anxious to create a new
Nicaragua.

Conclusion

The Nicaraguan Revolution of 1979 was a tremendous accomplishment and most remarkable was the role of the FSLN. That such a small group, never more than a few hundred, operating as guerrillas in the mountains and as clandestine organisers in the countryside and the cities, and later as the organisers of a national, multi-class coalition against Somoza, after a little more than fifteen years had succeeded in becoming the leadership of the national insurrections of 1978 and 1979, and then in finally overthrowing Somoza and establishing a new government, was an amazing achievement. Their victory was testimony to the clarity of their objectives, their courage, and their tenacity. While other political parties had entered into opportunistic pacts with the government or occasionally engaged in conspiracies and attempted *coups d'état*, the Sandinistas had always maintained their political independence from the government and had consistently insisted that the only way to overthrow Somoza was through an armed struggle, and they actually engaged in that struggle, futile as it was for most of seventeen years.

The FSLN's founders and later the GPP Tendency remained true to the end to their commitment to guerrilla warfare, first modelling themselves on the Cuban experience of Fidel Castro and Che Guevara and the *guerrilla foco* as theorised by Régis Debray. Later, partly under the influence of the Chinese Communist experience, they modified that model, adopting the prolonged popular war theory, yet they *were never successful as a guerrilla organisation and never built a peasant revolutionary army*. They failed to establish a logistical infrastructure, they never established a significant social base among the peasantry, and they never held any liberated territory.

It was the clear failure of the guerrilla experience that led in the mid-1970s to the fragmentation of the group into three tendencies and the eventual rise of the Third Tendency which advocated alliances with other classes in Nicaragua, as well as seeking support from other Latin American and European parties and governments beyond Cuba, the Soviet Union, the Eastern Bloc and North Korea. The Third Tendency led by Daniel and Humberto Ortega became dominant and led the FSLN to victory by organising mass insurrections in urban areas while creating a provisional government.

The FSLN's founders and its leaders throughout the 1970s, including the Third Tendency, nevertheless remained under the political influence of the Soviet and Cuban models. Fidel and Che had been the FSLN's inspiration, far more than Sandino. Cuba had given them shelter when they were forced into exile and recovering from their wounds; it had provided financing, training, and political recognition to the FSLN. The Cuba they admired had by the 1970s structurally and politically assimilated to the Soviet Union and had adopted its state and party structures, its ideology and foreign policy. The FSLN also shared the ideology common to bureaucratic Communism.

The FSLN's programme of political education, which excluded all critical discussion of Stalinism, had hardly ever included the important questions of the relationship between democracy and socialism or other questions such as workers' control. The FSLN leaders and cadres of all tendencies by and large adhered to Stalinist views of 'democratic centralism', that is, the bureaucratically centralised, top-down party, as well as the necessity of establishing a Communist Party dictatorship, and the need for the complete state control of the economy as well as party control of all aspects of society.[90] The Third Tendency's alliances with different social classes – including landowners and industrialists – and with different political parties and social organisations was, at least in the beginning, simply opportunism in the strictest sense of the term, and did not represent a break with their fundamentally Communist or Castroite politics.[91] Like the *guerrilla foco*, coalition politics, as advocated by The Twelve and the Junta, represented only strategies, not principles.

The Somoza regime's National Guard and its fierce repression had made it extremely difficult for the Sandinistas to develop a well-coordinated and well-articulated political party before the Triumph of July 1979. The FSLN was, as its statutes said, 'a political-military organisation', not a political party. The FSLN had for years remained in a constant state of reorganisation, while its links to community groups and unions were repeatedly broken. Periodically shattered by the National Guard, the FSLN was constantly required to carry out reorganisations of both its guerrilla fighting groups and its clandestine organisations as they were decimated by arrests and murder or death in combat.

Since its founding in 1962, the FSLN had never been able to hold a convention or to elect its national leadership, and while there was much discussion at the local level, especially by the mid-1970s, it could not be transformed into debate within the organisation as a whole. The FSLN had at times engaged in industrial union organising, built peasant unions, and constructed community organisations, but the unions and community groups themselves were fragile organisations and the party's links to them were intermittent and tenuous. FSLN *comandantes* felt that they spoke and acted for, on behalf of, the Nicaraguan workers, peasants, and the poor, and while some of those people supported the

---

90   Pérez-Baltodano 2009, pp. 145–59.

91   Some individuals, such as Sergio Ramírez, may have held more social-democratic views.

FSLN, there had never been any way for ordinary people to control the party or even to have any influence on it.

The Somoza dictatorship and the FSLN's own choice to build a clandestine, armed, revolutionary organisation and to send their forces to the mountains had tended to keep the guerrilla organisation in its early years in a state of political isolation. Consequently, the Sandinistas did not – except for a couple of years in the early 1960s – develop relations with other political parties and social organisations until the late 1970s. Despite its call for building a 'front', and many failed attempts to do so, the FSLN remained until the mid-1970s a sect and had a sectarian character. The FSLN was at least until the late 1970s largely bereft of political experience in the ordinary sense – that is, the interplay between political parties and other social organisations – beyond building their own revolutionary organisation. Until the late 1970s, most of their political dealing had been with the PSN in Nicaragua or with the Cubans, North Koreans, and Palestinians or with other Marxist-Leninists abroad who shared their politics. Only after the appearance of the Third Tendency, with its proposal for building an alliance with other classes and social groups, as well as building bridges to European social democrats, would the FSLN find it necessary to negotiate with others with whom it did not agree.

All of which meant that in 1979, when the Sandinistas took power, it was not clear what they represented politically. Would they prove to be simply Cuban-style Communists? Or would they take on characteristics more like Mexico's nationalist, populist and social-democratic one-party state? What was the significance of the revolutionary Christians within the FSLN and the broader revolutionary movement? Would Nicaragua produce some sort of Christian socialist state and society? Equally important, what would be the reaction of the United States to this new revolutionary government within a historic American sphere of interest? Would the American government allow things to take their course? Or would the United States intervene?

The Sandinistas in Power (1979–84)

The Junta de Gobierno came to power on 19 July 1979 amidst tremendous euphoria at the overthrow of Somoza, even as the population mourned those lost in the war and grieved the tremendous destruction done to many of the nation's cities. The Sandinistas, who for eighteen years had led the guerrilla struggle and then the insurrectionary movement, were the heroes of the day. Their idealism, their courage, and their endurance had won them the respect of all but their most intransigent *somocista* adversaries. Everywhere the Nicaraguan people – not just the left and the Catholic revolutionaries but middle-class people, workers, the peasants and the poor – rallied to the new, youthful, revolutionary leadership. The Sandinista's great strength at that moment was that in the popular consciousness they were seen as embodying three ideals which had become generalised during the social and revolutionary struggles of the 1970s: national sovereignty, social justice, and popular democracy.[1] The Sandinistas had tremendous moral authority within Nicaragua and beyond, giving them enormous leeway in the beginning to influence the direction of the nation.

The Sandinistas, who dominated the Junta de Gobierno and represented the only strong political organisation in the country, faced tremendous challenges in the summer of 1979. The FSLN had been a revolutionary guerrilla organisation and now faced the challenge of transforming itself into a political party that could lead in the construction of a new state. While there was a great sense of hope and enthusiasm, there were few structures intact or economic resources available. The old state – the executive, the legislative and judicial branches, the army and the police – had been swept away by the revolution. Many of the richest Nicaraguans had fled the country, taking their money with them. The economy was in a shambles as a result of the combination of revolution and Somoza's bombing of the cities. Under Somoza, people had not been allowed to organise in their own self-interest, so, with the exception of the Catholic Church, there were few non-governmental institutions or organisations. Most Nicaraguans were poor and illiterate; few had any economic resources. Housing was inadequate and of extremely poor quality; sewer systems, running water, and electricity were rare in the countryside. The country had a weak edu-

---

1 Pérez-Baltodano 2008, p. 598.

cation system and little public healthcare; social services were minimal. The challenge facing the Sandinistas was enormous.

Unlike the Cuban Revolution of 1959 led by Fidel Castro, the Sandinistas could not look to the Soviet Union to solve their economic problems.[2] After the Cuban Missile Crisis of 1962, when the United States had used its naval forces to blockade the island and had forced the Soviet Union to remove nuclear missiles, the Russians had become more cautious. In addition, by 1979, the Soviet Union was engaged in an economically costly and politically damaging war in Afghanistan. While the Soviet Union would provide weapons and assistance in creating the Nicaraguan security system, it was not prepared to support the creation of a full-blown Communist state and society such as it had done in Cuba in the 1960s. China, which had entered into an alliance with US President Richard Nixon in 1972, was now in the enemy camp. And North Korea was too poor to be of much help. Dependent on the Soviet Union, Cuba, which was Nicaragua's closest ally, was in no position to provide the kind of economic assistance that Nicaragua would need. Sergo Mikoyan, the Soviet Union's Latin America specialist, suggested that the Sandinista government adopt Lenin's New Economic Policy of the early 1920s, a period of a mixed economy with state regulated capitalism.[3] The Sandinista government would have to find its own way forward, seeking assistance from a variety of countries with different economic and political systems.

How would the Sandinistas address the far-reaching problems they confronted? What political principles would guide the FSLN, no longer a guerrilla combat organisation but now a political party, in its attempt to build a new state and to address the nation's problems?[4]

The Sandinistas nine-man National Directorate – Daniel Ortega, Humberto Ortega, Víctor Tirado, Tomás Borge, Bayardo Arce, Henry Ruiz, Jaime Wheelock, Luis Carrión and Carlos Núñez – shared a common view of many issues. First, they all believed that the FSLN was the vanguard organisation that would have to lead the process of revolutionary transformation, and they were convinced that the National Directorate had the responsibility and the power to direct the FSLN. As Sergio Ramírez writes: 'The vertical command structure, based on a political and military hierarchy at whose head stood the National Directorate

---

2   Paszyn 2000. See the Introduction and Chapter 3, 'The Soviet Reaction to the Opportunities Created by the Nicaraguan Revolution'.

3   Paszyn 2000, p. 5.

4   A short, useful overview of the Sandinistas is Prevost's 'The FSLN as a Ruling Party', in Walker (ed.) 1991.

was the basis for the birth of the FSLN as a party'.[5] And it was not only their experience and past practice: it remained a dogma.

Second, the Directorate had inherited the Marxist-Leninist ideology, inculcated early on by Carlos Fonseca and Tomás Borge, which provided the common intellectual and political foundation for the group foundation, even though not all of them completely shared that worldview.[6]

Third, Cuba was their model and ideal. Sergio Ramírez wrote retrospectively: '... the Cuban revolution continued to be the political model *par excellence* and it never ceased to have a sentimental attraction'.[7] Henri Weber, a French Trotskyist, wrote at the time: '... Cuba represented for the Sandinistas what Lenin's Soviet Republic represented for the communists of the twenties'. Weber wrote: 'It was a revolutionary, Castroist organisation, then, that took power in Managua on July 19, 1979'.[8] Cuba, which had been their inspiration, the place where several of them had spent years in exile, and which had offered its political and military support to the Sandinistas, provided the example of the kind of political system, economic organisation, and society that they wanted to create.[9]

All of this was spelled out in the writing of the Sandinistas themselves. In September of 1979, the Directorate summoned its 400 cadres (virtually their entire national membership) to a three-day closed meeting where the leadership adopted 'The 72-Hour Document', a kind of party platform that left no doubt about the leadership's commitments. The document stated that: (1) the FSLN wanted to consolidate itself as a Marxist-Leninist party; (2) the goal was to

---

5 Ramírez 1999, p. 110.

6 On Fonseca's admiration first for the Soviet Union and then for Cuba, see Zimmerman 2000. She points out that in his book *Un Nicaragünse en Moscú*, published in 1958, Fonseca remained a Stalinist: he praised the Soviet Union as a workers' paradise, brushed aside the Khrushchev revelations of Stalin's crimes, praised Stalin as a great leader, and supported the Soviet crushing of the Hungarian Revolution. Zimmerman 2000, pp. 45–6, 77–80. While he never gave up those views, Fonseca did become a supporter of the Cuban guerrilla strategy and of the Cuban revolution. Zimmerman writes: 'The goal of the group that came together around Fonseca in Honduras was to duplicate the Cuban Revolution'. Zimmerman 2000, p. 78.

7 Ramírez 1999, p. 115.

8 Henri Weber 1981, p. 59 and p. 60. A Trotskyist and member of the Ligue communiste révolutionnaire (LCR) at the time he wrote, Weber later became a member of the French Socialist Party (PS) and its representative in the European Parliament.

9 Ramírez 1999, pp. 115, 118; Pérez-Baltodano 2008, p. 613, makes the interesting observation that the Sandinistas proposed to create a Cuban-style state at the very moment when changes in the global economy were making such a state obsolete, anachronistic, and, indeed, unworkable.

bring about the 'dictatorship of the proletariat' (i.e. a Communist state); (3) the road to that goal lay through temporary alliances with other classes and parties, such as the Junta de Gobierno, but understanding that those alliances were only temporary; (4) Nicaragua should become part of the Communist camp that included Soviet Union, Eastern Bloc, Vietnam and Cuba.[10]

While that statement represented their fundamental politics, the Sandinistas also understood that if they were to announce their views and political allegiances to the world, they would find themselves not only ostracised and attacked by the United States and many other Western states and parties, but also in conflict with the upper classes of Nicaragua with whom they were at least temporarily allied. So to hide their real objectives, the Junta, which the Sandinistas dominated, proclaimed to the public a completely different position based on three principles that, they said, represented the foundation of the new government. First, they pledged that Nicaragua would have a system of political pluralism, that is, one in which various political parties and other social organisations could have a role. Second, they promised that there would be a mixed economy made up of a public, a private, and a cooperative sector. Third, they proclaimed a position of non-alignment, that is, independence from both the capitalist and Communist blocs. The Sandinistas told the world, in effect, that they would create a liberal or Social Democratic government, economy and society, though in truth the leadership believed that these principles would only represent a phase, a brief transition stage to the fully Communist society that they planned to create: a one-party, Communist regime.[11]

Some historians, such as William M. LeoGrande, argue that after taking power the Sandinista leadership was divided into two factions: (1) the moderates led by brothers Daniel and Humberto Ortega; (2) the radicals led by

---

10 Summarised by Ramírez 1999, pp. 112–13; US State Department 1987.

11 Some orthodox Trotskyists have suggested that the Sandinistas held the Social Democratic or Stalinist 'two-stage' theory of revolution, that is, that first there would have to be a 'capitalist, bourgeois democratic revolution' and then a 'socialist revolution'. Those Trotskyists believe that the Sandinistas' belief in the two-stage revolution prevented them from completing the revolutionary process. Yet it seems clear that at the beginning the Sandinistas believed they were going to carry out a 'socialist revolution' to create a Communist-style state. They believed that Cuba had proven that one could go directly from a capitalist dictatorship in an underdeveloped economy to socialism, without passing through a democratic capitalist phase. All the Sandinistas' talk of 'political pluralism, mixed economy and non-alignment' was a façade that had more in common with the phony People's Democracies of Eastern Europe than with any two-stage theory. See, for example, Claudio Villas 2008.

Tomás Borge and Bayardo Arce who wanted to create another Cuba.[12] All of the Sandinista leaders were, however, held together by Carlos Fonseca's ideology, by the long experience of guerrilla warfare, and by the role of Cuba as model and ally throughout the revolutionary period. As a group they were not really committed to political pluralism. As LeoGrande himsef writes: 'They conceived of themselves as a political vanguard that would hold hegemony while directing a revolutionary transformation of Nicaraguan society'.[13]

The Sandinista's duplicitous politics – secretly holding the goal of creating a Communist state while publicly proclaiming that they sought to construct a social-democratic government – would lead to constant controversies and misunderstandings among their followers, their allies, and their opponents. At the same time, their contradictory Marxist-Leninist and social-democratic statements on all sorts of issues, combined with the presence of the revolutionary Catholics in the movement, would also create the illusion among the left around the world that the Nicaraguan government represented something fundamentally new and innovative, creative and different.[14] The swirl of that revolutionary rhetoric obscured the Sandinistas' fundamental politics which were ultimately Soviet and Cuban in origin. Such a smoke screen not only worked to fool their enemies, it also fooled their friends, and it could only make it more difficult for genuinely democratic and revolutionary socialist ideas and organisations to emerge in the Nicaraguan working class. Ironically, though, the balance of forces in the world and in Nicaragua would ultimately force the Sandinista *comandantes* to accept something very much like the social-democratic model they publicly proclaimed. They would be forced by circumstances to create a mixed economy, to tolerate a far greater political pluralism than they wished, and to pursue a non-aligned strategy. None of that, however, was what they initially desired. For, as historian Matilde Zimmerman has written, they wanted 'to duplicate the Cuban revolution'.[15]

The Transition

By 18 July 1979, the Sandinista forces had taken all of the major cities of Nicaragua, including the capital Managua, and were encircling the remaining National Guard units holed up in Somoza's bunker. Somoza, his mistress, and

---

12   LeoGrande 1998, p. 28.
13   LeoGrande 1998, pp. 28–9.
14   Ramírez 1999, p. 112.
15   Zimmerman 2000, p. 78.

his protégées had already fled the country and were on their way to Miami, Florida. Somoza's hand-picked successor, Francisco Urcuyo, who served as acting president for a couple of days, then also resigned and left under the pressure of the US Embassy. With Somoza gone, the National Guard collapsed and many Guardsmen crossed the borders into Honduras or Costa Rica while more than seven thousand were taken prisoner in Nicaragua.[16] While there was no doubt some settling of scores with old enemies, including one atrocity in which Sandinista soldiers killed 14 or more people, that was not the new government's policy. As one authority writes: 'After Somoza's overthrow, there were no verified accounts of a governmental policy of murder, torture, or disappearances in Nicaragua'.[17] The Sandinista government carried out no mass executions. Many Guardsmen were soon released into society, though some would go to Honduras or Costa Rica to join their confreres who were beginning to plot counter-revolution.

The FSLN had complete control of the country, unchallenged by any other military, political, or social force. This came as an utter surprise to the FSLN leadership which had presumed that it would have to share power either with some remnant of the Somoza government or with some party or coalition of parties of the bourgeoisie. Instead, the FSLN, operating through the Junta, held the reins of government entirely in its own hands and – while governmental forms and structures would change – it would continue do so until 1990.[18] The FSLN quickly became the hegemonic political power in the country, its small, compact, and highly centralised organisation dominating the country's political and social structures.

The FSLN saw itself throughout this period as the vanguard of the revolution with the right and the responsibility to set the Nicaraguan nation and its people on the correct course. The Sandinistas presumed that they would set up the government structures and new social structures, starting with the national government. They quickly took control over not only the national government but also all of the key posts in the new state administration at every level.

Throughout the period from its founding in 1962 until the triumph of 1979, the FSLN had defined themselves as a political-military organisation, not as a political party. As such a military organisation, the FSLN had a command structure, where orders from the central leadership were handed down to lower level regional organisations until they reached the base of its members.

---

16   West 1992, pp. 393–408. He says the Sandinista held between 7,000 to 8,000 prisoners (p. 398).

17   Michael Linfield, 'Human Rights', in Walker (ed.) 1991, p. 276.

18   Kinzer 2007, pp. 70–3.

Through most of its history from 1962 to 1979 the FSLN had been a small, cadre organisation made up of anywhere between 50 members in the early years and to about 400 members toward the end. Even after 1979, the FSLN did not become a mass political party, but rather maintained its definition as a cadre organisation, expanding to only 1,500 members by 1981, in a nation with a population of three million.

The Triumph presented the opportunity to transform the FSLN into the party and to democratise it by holding a convention, electing leaders, writing a party constitution and by-laws – but the Sandinistas did *not* do so. One could argue that their failure to do so was because of the pressing issues of national reconstruction, but given that the country was emerging from a dictatorship, perhaps nothing was more urgent than establishing democracy. Yet *because democracy was not a central value of the FSLN*, the National Directorate never considered establishing either a democratic party or a democratic state. A tremendous opportunity to create a more democratic politics and society was missed.

Surprisingly, upon taking power and assuming the leadership of the country, almost none of the FSLN's structures, leadership, or membership changed and would not change until the election of 1984. *The FSLN called no national party convention* and would not do so until 1990 after they had lost state power.[19] The National Directorate of nine commanders, *los comandantes*, continued as the party's leading body, handing down orders to the Regional Leadership Committees and the Zone Leadership Committees. Weber wrote at the time: 'So far the party has been created from the top down with little internal life below the level of the National Directorate'.[20] The concepts of the vanguard party, democratic centralism, and the absolute power of the National Directorate remained in place. As one scholar writes: 'Inevitably, all of this pushed the Sandinistas toward a vertical and centralised decision making process'.[21] Indicative of the commandist nature of the organisation was the use of the phrase *¡Dirección Nacional Ordene!* (By order of the National Directorate), which became common throughout the 1980s. The National Directorate was absolutely autonomous, responsible to no one else in the party, while the party organisations and members were permitted no autonomy. Cadres were expected to be absolutely loyal to the National Directorate and to other superiors in the party and to

---

19   The National Assembly of FSLN Militants was called in the wake of the FSLN defeat in the 1990 elections and was in effect the first party political convention held by the organisation since its founding.

20   Weber 1981, p. 79.

21   Martí I Puig 2010, pp. 79–106.

carry out the orders they had been given.[22] When the master of ceremonies at public events shouted *'Dirección Nacional!'* the public was expected to respond, *'Ordene!'*

After 1979, the FSLN leaders and members no longer constituted a military organisation, but now operated within the emerging state structures and the mass organisations under the party's control. Thus there was a tendency for the FSLN to fuse with the state, leading to a one-party-state structure. The FSLN's control of the incipient state institutions now became the principal source of its political power as well as providing the party with resources. Most of the FSLN leaders and members held government posts which paid their salaries and provided them in many cases with houses and automobiles. FSLN and government rhetoric and symbolism tended to blur the distinction between the party and the government: both were called 'Sandinista', both used the same red-and-black flag, and both within a year or two had the same personnel holding the top offices. As many analysts have commented, the system resembled that of Mexico's Institutional Revolutionary Party of that era, perhaps even more than Cuba's Communist Party.[23]

The Junta de Gobierno and Consejo de Estado

The question immediately facing the FSLN in 1979 was the creation of a new government. The Sandinistas, in a desire to keep together the broad forces which had supported the revolution, to take the first step toward creating new state institutions, and to create a democratic façade through which the Sandinista *comandantes* could rule, established in 1979 the *Junta de Gobierno de Reconstrucción Nacional* (the Governing Board for National Reconstruction), both a legislative and an executive body.[24] The Junta was initially made up of five members: Violeta Chamorro, the widow of the assassinated newspaper editor Pedro Joaquín Chamorro; Alfonso Robelo, a businessman; Daniel Ortega, the coordinator of the FSLN Directorate; Moïses Hassan, an academic and long-time FSLN member; and Sergio Ramírez, the author. Since Ramírez's FSLN membership was not public, the body had the appearance of balance between two FSLN supporters with leftist politics and two people from business

---

22   Martí I Puig 2010 pp. 52–4, 79–106.
23   Martí I Puig 2010, p. 84.
24   The word *junta* can mean a meeting, a board, council, or assembly, but it is also used for dictatorial ruling bodies.

backgrounds with more conservative politics, plus the supposedly independent Ramírez. In fact, however, the Sandinista-dominated Directorate through its three-member majority invariably took the initiative and determined the policy. The Junta came to power on the basis of a supposedly social-democratic programme of a mixed economy, political pluralism, and a foreign policy of non-alignment. As historian Willim M. LeoGrande writes: 'The platform's ambiguity reflected its origins as a compromise between the radicalism of the FSLN and the conservatism of the private sector. It was not the product of a consensus for social democracy'.[25]

Alongside the Junta, the Sandinistas established the *Consejo de Estado* (State Council), sometimes described as a co-legislative body and something like a national congress or parliament. The State Council was a corporative body made up of political parties, the Sandinista's mass organisations of workers, peasants, women, and youth, representatives of the Catholic and Protestant churches, and delegates from the business organisations.[26] The Council of State throughout most of its history had 47 seats, 12 for political parties and nearly all of the rest held by Sandinista mass organisations. Of those 12 political parties, only three were not aligned with the FSLN. The Sandinista Defence Committees (CDSs), which were a hybrid – part popular organisation and part Sandinista state security apparatus – had nine representatives on the State Council.[27]

The FSLN's stacking of the State Council led Violeta Chamorro and Alfonso Robelo to resign from the Junta in April of 1980. That same year, all of the non-FSLN parties and organisations withdrew from the Council, arguing that it was neither representative nor democratic. *Envío*, the Central American Jesuit publication, described the problem thus:

> While the parties of the Democratic Coordinating Committee wanted a Council of State governed by traditional criteria of representation [i.e. votes in elections], the FSLN used the criteria of representation based on participation in the struggle against Somoza and participation in the popular organisations of the reconstruction. Under this concept, the worker and *campesino* [peasants] organisations and the CDS's have significant representation for having been the most active sectors in the struggle both before and after the victory.[28]

25   LeoGrande 1998, p. 27.
26   Envío Team 1981b.
27   Black 1981, pp. 244–9.
28   Envío Team 1981b.

That is, the Council of State was not elected but chosen by the Junta.

In 1982, after the passage of the State of Emergency, *opposition parties were no longer given any representation in the council.*[29] Since the FSLN leadership laid down the line for its mass organisations, there was hardly room for any genuine democratic discussion and debate in the Council's deliberations. Clearly the Sandinistas were not interested in having a democratic parliament, but rather wanted a legislative body that would enact and carry out the FSLN's initiatives as presented from the Junta to the Council of State. Throughout its six-and-a-half year history, the Council of State never became a genuinely democratic, representative, or legislative body.

The Sandinistas sometimes argued that the State Council was intended to be a kind of parliament such as existed in the Western capitalist countries and at other times suggested that it was a council of the organisations of workers and peasants who had fought against Somoza and were now making the revolution. The problem was that it was neither one nor the other. Unlike governments in democratic capitalist countries, the representatives were not elected by district or at-large by the voters. Ultimately the FSLN leadership determined what organisations and what representatives would sit in the chamber. And unlike councils of workers and peasants that had arisen in some countries during revolutionary periods (Paris in 1871, Russia after World War I, or Spain in the 1930s), Nicaraguan workers' organisations had not created the State Council, but rather the FSLN party-state had created from above workers' organisations that were under its political control and brought them in the Council which it had also created. The State Council never played an important role in initiating legislation, but rather served as a vehicle for handing down positions and projects from the FSLN and the Junta.

In any case, it was the *Junta* and the Council which voted for the first major legislation of the revolution: the abolition of the old Constitution, the dissolution of the National Guard and the intelligence agencies of the former state, the expropriation of Somoza's property and the property of others in his circle, and the nationalisation of the country's most important banks. The *Junta* and the Council passed all of the country's laws between 1979 and 1985 establishing the government's new education and health programmes and dealing with many other matters. Throughout those years it was the FSLN Directorate, acting through the *Junta* and the Council, which led Nicaragua. Only in November of 1984, when elections were held for President, Vice-President, and a new National Assembly, would the governmental system change, though then too

---

29   Williams 1994, p. 177.

the FSLN would continue to head the government with Ortega as president and the FSLN as the dominant party in the Assembly.

While the FSLN strove to control the highest echelons of the government it also wanted to give the government the appearance of being pluralistic, so the Sandinistas put a number of political moderates in positions of some significance and apparent power in their administration. *Comandante* Edén Pastora, who had led the famous 1978 takeover of the National Palace, not a Marxist-Leninist, was made deputy minister of the interior under Minister Tomás Borge. Haroldo Montealegre, University of Chicago and Columbia trained economist, served as minister of reconstruction finance. Arturo Cruz, an economist who had worked at the Inter-American Development Bank in Washington, DC, became the Nicaraguan ambassador to the United States. Jaime Pasquier held the position of Nicaraguan ambassador to the United Nations. Businessman Alfonso Robelo had been part of Los Doce, though he later resigned. José Esteban González had served as the national coordinator of the Nicaraguan Permanent Commission for Human Rights. These and many other businessmen and professionals with moderate politics – neither FSLN Marxist-Leninists nor counter-revolutionary Contras – would by 1981 or 1982 turn against the FSLN government, claiming that despite their titles they had been excluded from the inner circles of power in what they came to recognise as a Marxist-Leninist government that intended to end capitalism and democracy and to suppress civil liberties. While that may have been true, it was also the case that these businessmen and professionals recognised that their property interests and their political power were being undermined, so they eventually rebelled and became opponents of the government. (Some would later become Contras, but that was not where they began). Be that as it may, their early collaboration with the FSLN government helped to create the false impression that the Nicaraguan government was pluralistic.[30]

The Army, the Ministry of the Interior, and the CDS

The Sandinistas' most successful state-building project was the creation of the security apparatus – the Ministry of the Interior, the Sandinista Police, and the Sandinista Popular Army – with the assistance of Cuba, East Germany and Bulgaria.[31] The Communist countries, past masters at building police states,

---

30   Christian 1986, pp. 310–33.
31   Kinzer 2007, p. 185.

provided the Sandinista government with their model of police and military organisations, loaned advisors to train the Sandinistas in their methods, and supplied arms, vehicles, communications equipment as well as other materiel. Tomás Borge, Minister of the Interior, was in charge of the police and fire department, state security, the intelligence apparatus, the prison system, the press censorship office and the nationwide network of Sandinista Defence Committees. Over time he also brought several Army units under his command. The Ministry of the Interior took responsibility for dealing with the former National Guard and the right-wing opposition in Nicaragua, many of whom were linked to the Contras and their military attacks.

Humberto Ortega, brother of the head of the FSLN Directorate, became the head of the Nicaraguan Army. The Army grew out of the guerrilla forces that had led the struggle against Somoza, altogether about 1,300 soldiers. Initially they were intended to form the core of an army of 25,000 troops, though during the Contra War the army grew to 80,000 troops, plus tens of thousands of militia members. With its hardened guerrilla core and training for new recruits provided by Cuban, Soviet, and Eastern Bloc advisors, as well as modern military equipment from the Soviet Union or Eastern bloc nations, the Sandinista Popular Army became a very effective fighting force. The Army and the Interior Ministry would prove the most durable state institutions created by the Sandinistas, lasting through the revolution and later incorporated remarkably smoothly into the neoliberal capitalist state in the 1990s–2010s.

Also related to the state security institutions were the Sandinista Defence Committees (CDS) established in 1979 and clearly modelled on the Cuban Committees in Defence of the Revolution (CDRs). Part mass organisation and part state security institution, the Nicaraguan CDSs were intended to organise around community issues, but also to act as Sandinista intelligence gathering organisations that reported to the Ministry of the Interior. The CDSs engaged in surveillance first of former National Guard members and then later of pro-Contra activists, but also of ordinary citizens. The CDS in 1980 had 500,000 members (out of a total national population of three million) organised in 12,000 neighbourhood level organisations throughout the cities and the countryside of Nicaragua, making them the largest of all of the Sandinista mass organisations. The FSLN National Directorate organised the CDSs from the top-down, providing them with materials for political education and laying down the political line. The CDSs had responsibility to organise Nicaragua's citizens for educational and health campaigns. They also sometimes organised the class struggle in the neighbourhood, mobilising their members against businessmen or landlords seen as exploiting the public, though occasionally CDS leaders or members also used them to settle personal scores.

The experiences of the Contra War and the privations that came with it, as well as disappointment in the government, led to a general demoralisation in the population, and by the mid-1980s the CDSS had become hollowed-out, weak organisations with little popular participation. The independent, Jesuit-run Central American magazine *Envío* reported: 'A 1985 study by the Nicaraguan Institute for Social and Economic Research (INIES) found that in the four *barrios* studied, grassroots participation was minimal. Neighbourhood and block meetings were poorly attended, if they were held at all. People preferred to stay home and watch the 7 pm TV soap opera'.[32] The decline of the CDSS was part of a general demoralisation of the population that only worsened between 1985 and 1989.

The Sandinistas' Mass Organisations

While busy creating state institutions, the Sandinistas were also creating the state's social base of support through what were called popular or mass organisations. Almost immediately upon taking power, the Sandinistas began to create 'mass organisations' like those in Cuba for workers, women, youth, and other groups. Marxist-Leninist theory held that a vanguard party, such as the FSLN, transmitted its policies and programmes of action through these organisations to the masses. Ideally perhaps (as in the Communist countries that were the Sandinistas' model) these mass organisations would include all the members of a particular social group and would face no competing organisations led by other political organisations. In Cuba, for example, the Cuban Communist Party controlled the only labour federation to which all unions must belong and no other federations or unions were allowed to organise nor could workers themselves create unions.

Early supporters of the Nicaraguan revolution argued that these mass organisations were 'real schools of democracy with all of the attempts and failures that accompany the early learning process'.[33] Yet from the beginning these were organisations principally created and directed from above. *The Sandinistas wanted participation, not democratic control from below.* The creation of such monopolistic and exclusive organisations in Cuba had been made possible by the complete nationalisation of the economy, which had eradicated the bourgeoisie as a social class, as well as the extreme controls placed on the

---

32   Envío Team 1982b and Envío Team 1989.

33   Luis Serra, 'The Sandinista Mass Organizations', in Walker 1982, p. 96.

petty-bourgeois economy, and the outlawing of all parties, labour unions, and other groups of any sort not controlled by the party.[34] The Sandinistas, however, faced a completely different situation. While the commanding heights of the economy were nationalised, much remained in private hands, and while the FSLN was the dominant political party, other parties did continue to exist and each had its own labour unions and social organisations.

The Sandinistas proved quite effective in quickly building mass organisations, a reflection both of the weakness of previous organisations because of the 40-year Somoza dictatorship, and also of the desire of the Nicaraguan people for new organisations that could represent their interests and really bring about change. Many Nicaraguans hungered for organisations through which they could fight to change the balance of power in society and improve their lives. The FSLN's party-led mass organisations were the Association of Rural Workers (ATC) with 40,000 members, the farmers unions (UNAG) with 70,000 members, the Sandinista Workers' Confederation (CST) with 100,000 members, the 'Luisa Amanda Espinoza' Association of Nicaraguan Women (AMNLAE) with 70,000 members, the National Association of Nicaraguan Educators (ANDEN), the Sandinista Children's Association (ANS), and the '19 of July' Sandinista Youth with 50,000 members. (There were also the two mass organisations linked to the military and security forces, which have already been mentioned, the Sandinista Defence Committees with 500,000 members, and the Sandinista People's Militias (MPS) with at least 35,000 members). While the FSLN directed these organisations, it never enjoyed the monopolistic and exclusive character of Cuban organisations. The result was a kind of Mexican model. The state-party led corporate mass organisations, just as the Institutional Revoutionary Party did in Mexico, but in addition, also as in Mexico, they sometimes faced competition in the social arenas from the right and the left.

Were the Sandinistas' mass organisations democratic? Luis Serra argued in the early 1980s: 'In the mass organisations, the people were developing the capacity to govern themselves through their elected representatives'.[35] Yet, writing in a book published at the beginning of the 1990s, Serra offered a far more critical view, noting the corporative character of the institutions and their lack of real democracy. Membership in the popular organisations became automatic, with dues deducted from workers' wages for membership in a rural cooperative or an urban community organisation. Elections in the mass organisations lost their significance as there might be only one candidate,

---

34   The Cuban model, like the Soviet model, reflects the bureaucratic collectivist societies' hostility towards both capitalism and socialism.

35   Luis Serra, 'The Sandinista Mass Organizations', in Walker 1982, p. 96.

or sometimes only the leadership could vote in the election, or in other cases non-FSLN candidates were not permitted to run, or the FSLN simply appointed leaders. Most leaders of mass organisations were either FSLN members or aspiring members (*militantes* or *aspirantes*). 'Despite the collective organs and democratic procedures based in law, certain directors concentrated too much decision-making power in their own hands, thereby inhibiting the growth of new leadership and participation by the masses', Serra wrote in his later article.[36] The FSLN leadership 'sent down' the chain of command instructions for the mass organisations. As Serra concluded: 'this vertical system for the transmission of goals and plans kept the masses and the primary and intermediate directorates dependent and relatively powerless, particularly in regard to the formation of work plans appropriate to actual conditions'.[37]

The purpose of the mass organisations was to allow the Sandinistas to encourage mass participation, to carry out mass indoctrination, and to make possible mass mobilisation. There is no doubt that the mass organisations did draw some groups, in particular women, into greater social and political participation. These organisations, however, were never genuinely autonomous. The Sandinista leadership remained, for example, 'suspicious of a "women's"' organisation.[38]

The words 'democracy' and 'democratic' in both Spanish and English have several related but distinct meanings.[39] The weak meaning of the word 'democratic' is that anyone can participate. In this sense, the Sandinista organisations were democratic; anyone in the various sectors (labour, women, and youth) could participate. The stronger sense of the word 'democratic', however, is that people actually control their organisations through running candidates and by voting on decisions about the organisations' policies and activities. The Sandinista organisations were not fully democratic in that sense, since in general their line was set from above by the FSLN directorate.

Under the Sandinista government there were elections with candidates for office in the unions or other mass organisations and membership votes, and while there were debates and discussions sometimes leading to votes on issues, all of these tended to be orchestrated by the Sandinista leadership, with

---

36   Luis Serra, 'The Grass-Roots Organizations', in Walker 1991, p. 57.

37   Luis Serra, 'Grass-Roots', in Walker 1991, p. 57 and p. 60.

38   Susan E. Ramírez-Horton, 'The Role of Women in the Nicaraguan Revolution', in Walker 1982, pp. 147–59.

39   I think, for example, of how I have heard people say in Spanish, 'Es un restaurante democrático' ('It's a democratic restaurant'), meaning that its prices are low enough that anyone could afford to eat there. It is open to all.

clearly circumscribed parameters. In the end, the leaders made the important decisions about leaders and the line. The idea of democracy in the strong sense, the right of people to control their own organisations through democratic discussion of alternative leaderships and policies, debate and voting, did not form part of the Sandinistas' theory or practice. Workers and peasants did sometimes raise their own views, attempt to use the Sandinista organisations as their own, to fight for their own demands, and there were occasionally outbursts of militancy from below independent of the FSLN initiatives. These upsurges from below, however, were quickly brought under control by the Sandinista union and party leadership, who directed such militancy into the party's approved channels.

As David Close writes in *The Years of Doña Violeta*, the Sandinistas were only interested in the 'democracy of results' as measured in greater social equality. The FSLN Directorate would determine the process through which it worked to achieve the democratic – that is, egalitarian – results it wanted.[40] The Sandinista leaders saw themselves as social engineers directing society from above to achieve equality below. Independent worker organisations, which might come up with their own ideas, could only interfere with the engineers' project.

By the mid-1980s, the mass organisations began to decline in strength as a result 'of the decomposition of the proletariat and the peasantry that resulted from the war and the economic crisis'. More than 300,000 peasants had been forced by the war to move from rural areas in the zones of conflict to other regions in the countryside or into the cities. At the same time, with the decline of production, many workers lost their jobs or saw their wages fall. Demoralised by the war, the economic decline, and the draft, between 1985 and 1988 many workers, peasants, women, and young people declined to participate or participated only half-heartedly in the popular organisations. Still, the mass organisations continued to serve as the Sandinistas' base of social support and mobilisation, even if in a weakened form.[41]

Women, Feminism, and its Limits

While Nicaraguan women came to play a significant role in the Sandinista revolutionary movement, being mobilised through the 'Luisa Amanda Espi-

---

40   Close 2005, pp. 314–15.
41   Luis Serra, 'Grass-Roots Organizations', in Walker (ed.) 1991, p. 65.

noza' Association of Nicaraguan Women (AMNLAE) to defend the revolution, the FSLN set definite limits to women's self-organisation and democratic participation. Women in significant numbers had joined the guerrilla movement and the insurrection and after the Triumph they moved optimistically into greater roles in the economy, in society, and in politics. The 1987 Constitution made important legal advances, providing for equality for women in many areas of life, and even if the law was often ignored in practice, it established a higher standard at which to aim. The FSLN wanted to mobilise women to support the revolution, but did not necessarily mobilise the revolution's power for women or allow women to organise to fight for themselves.

Socially women's greatest successes came through the work of AMNLAE members in the Agricultural Workers Union (ATC) where women had come to number 40 percent of the membership. A Women's Secretariat was created and in 1986 the union put forward a list of social demands for childcare, maternity subsidies, collective laundry facilities, and children's cafeterias, as well as more opportunities for women in union and technical training programmes and more women in the union leadership. Yet for a variety of reasons – traditional values, male chauvinism, domestic responsibilities, occupational segregation, the society's lack of economic resources, opposition to women's autonomous organisation, and others – women still faced barriers in the FSLN, in government, at work, and in society.

Women's organisations, like other mass organisations, lacked autonomy. The top leaders of AMNLAE were FSLN members who brought the party line to the organisation and handed it down to the women, though not without sometimes finding their views contested. In other organisations, such as the Sandinista Workers' Federation (CST), women 'tended to be excluded from leadership positions'. In the CST, where one-third of the members were women, 'Women workers were characterised as dependent, submissive, docile, obedient, emotional, and unfit for leadership, and, unlike the ATC, the CST tended to view sexual harassment and other issues of particular concern to women as "women's issues"'.[42]

The Sandinista organisations and government were by no means progressive on women's reproductive rights. The Sandinistas glorified motherhood and encouraged women to have babies while at the same time promoting a traditional view of women's role in society. President Daniel Ortega made a public declaration against abortion, stating: 'One way of depleting our youth is to promote the sterilisation of women in Nicaragua ... or to promote a policy of abor-

---

42   Patricia M. Chuchryk, 'Women in the Revolution', in Walker (ed.) 1991, pp. 143–65.

tion'. Women were expected to take on new roles in the Nicaraguan military, government, and economy, but to also continue to be mothers. As Tomás Borge declared: 'How can we not guarantee that a woman can be *both a mother and an artist* ... both fulfil all the tasks the revolution demands of her and at the same time fulfil the beautiful work of a *self-sacrificing, capable and loving mother?*'[43]

The Control of the Working Class and the Left

The FSLN, both as ruling party with control of the state and as the director of the mass organisations, worked to prevent popular upsurges from below that would threaten its control and its national project. After the Triumph, many workers wanted to take over the farms and factories of their bosses, sometimes bringing them into conflict with the Junta's policy at the time and with the FSLN which quickly moved to stop the takeovers. While there would later be strikes organised by unions with links to conservative and even counter-revolutionary organisations, in 1980 the FSLN was suppressing strikes and occupations led by other leftist organisations or militant workers.

When, in January 1980, the FSLN faced a strike wave and illegal land occupations supported by the Frente Obrero (FO) and its newspaper *El Pueblo*, the government dissolved the FO and sentenced four of its leaders to two years of 'public labour'. Similarly, in February, when the Nicaraguan Communist Party (PCN) and the Confederation of Union Action and Unity (CAUS) were involved in a mass demonstration critical of the government, a number of their leaders and members were arrested. Some of them received prison sentences that ranged from 7 to 29 months.[44] At other times, the Sandinista militants known as *turbas*, that is, hooligans, were sent to attack non-Sandinista labour federations or the homes of rival union leaders.[45]

While Nicaraguan workers enjoyed the right to strike in theory and did strike in practice on many occasions, the Sandinista mass organisations did everything possible to restrain strikes, arguing that they would endanger the regime's stability or later that they would result in losing the war against the Contras.[46] The Trade Union Coordinating Committee, made up of nine of the

---

43   Patricia M. Chuchryk, 'Women in the Revolution', in Walker (ed.) 1991, p. 153 and p. 155.

44   Weber 1981, p. 104 and p. 107; Envío Team 1981a.

45   Christian 1986, p. 294.

46   Since the Sandinistas never promulgated a labour law, workers had no idea of exactly what their rights were. For a discussion of why there was no labour law, see *Envío*, No. 134 (September 1992) at: http://www.envio.org.ni/articulo/2546.

Sandinista and other labour federations, passed a resolution at its meeting in Managua in November 1980 that reaffirmed the right to strike, but said that it should be used as a last resort and only when other procedures had been exhausted.[47] Journalist Shirley Christian writes: 'Strikes were forbidden by the FSLN, as were, for the most part, wage increases'. When workers at the Pellas family's Nicaraguan Sugar Estates threated to strike, '... the Sandinistas changed the workers' minds by threatening to send in the army'.[48]

In these and other cases, the Sandinista unionists argued that there was no need to strike against employers or the government because the FSLN would look out for the workers' interests. Of course, by the mid-1980s the Sandinista government was really concerned that disruption in the workplace and in society could weaken the war effort and lead to a Contra victory and the return of a *somocista* government. In 1988, when the Sandinistas had become disappointed by the failure of peace negotiations, angered by the continuing war, and furious at internal opponents, Sandinista workers were mobilised to suppress the strikes of other workers.[49] But that was only later. From the beginning, the FSLN government strove to achieve control of the unions and that meant both eliminating rival unions and preventing strikes, both of which they failed to achieve.[50]

The Soviet and Cuban models to which they aspired and the exigencies of the economic and military problems faced by the country drove the Sandinistas to try to control the unions and the workers, but the accommodations they had made to the capitalist class and the strength of other political organisations, on the left and on the right, meant that the FSLN only achieved something like Mexico's corporate regime, not Cuba's totalitarian system. At the same time, it should be made clear that the Sandinistas, while they sometimes engaged in repression and in cooptation of their opponents, never imposed a dictatorship that suppressed political and social opposition groups once and for all. Nor, after the initial imprisonment of about 3,000 National Guardsmen, did the FSLN government imprison large numbers of its opponents, and torture had been abolished, as had the death penalty. Nicaragua was no model of democracy, but nor was it a brutal dictatorship.

---

47   Weber 1981, p. 125.
48   Christian 1986, p. 293.
49   Kinzer 2007, p. 365.
50   Christian 1986, p. 294.

The Literacy Campaign

While the Sandinistas had little commitment to democracy, they had a very serious commitment to social equality. They believed in what they called the 'logic of majorities', that is, that society's priorities should be organised around the needs of the working class, the peasantry and the poor. The FSLN, even as the state's governing institutions were being established and mass organisations being founded, began to undertake an ambitious programme of social reforms aimed at improving the lives of the Nicaraguan people. Among their most immediate goals were to bring education and healthcare to Nicaragua, especially to its working people and to the poor.

The National Literacy Campaign represented in many ways the highpoint of the Sandinista Revolution and of the government of 1979–90. Morally inspiring and uplifting, pedagogically innovative, and logistically challenging, the campaign of 1980 involved 100,000 volunteers, most of them youths from 14 to 18, in the education of 400,000 illiterate men, women and children in the cities, towns and in the countryside. It was conceived of as a second liberating army, but far larger and with a far greater scope than the guerrilla army that had fought in the mountains or even the masses who had participated in the insurrection. The National Literacy Campaign created a tremendous élan as the country's youth confronted and defeated the great enemy before them: ignorance. In a mere five months, according to the campaign's reports, Nicaragua reduced illiteracy from more than 50 percent to less than 13 percent. Never in the world's history, not in the great literacy campaigns of Soviet Russia in the 1920s, revolutionary Mexico in the 1920s, or Cuba in the 1960s, had there been such a remarkable achievement involving such a large percentage of the population and with such remarkable results in such a short time.[51] The literacy campaign would provide a model for other projects such as the inoculation campaigns against polio and other diseases, the coffee brigades of the 1980s, and the initially voluntary military mobilisation against the Contras. The Sandinista Revolution would, however, unfortunately prove incapable of repeating such an extraordinary national sense of commitment, mission and accomplishment. Nor would subsequent governments be able to maintain high literacy rates.

Never in Nicaragua's history had a government or any other organisation undertaken to bring literacy to the entire nation. General Sandino's Defender

---

51   I base this entire section principally upon the memoirs of Fernando Cardenal, s.j. the head of the National Literacy Campaign. Cardenal 2008, Vol. II, pp. 9–105. For a short account, see Valerie Miller, 'The Nicaraguan Literacy Crusade', in Walker 1982, pp. 241–58.

of National Sovereignty Army (EDSN) had had a department in charge of teaching peasants to read, though the EDSN's resources and its influence were limited. And Sandino's beleaguered guerrillas had none of the wherewithal to accomplish such a goal. Under the Somoza dictatorship, religious schools and other private schools had educated the rich, as they had done since colonial times, while his expanded public education system provided basic education to some in the large cities and small towns. Most of those in the countryside had very little, if any, education. Few students went beyond primary school and most did not finish sixth grade, while only a handful attended and fewer finished high school. University education was almost exclusively for the children of the elite only. Consequently, illiteracy in 1980 was estimated to be more than 50 percent, and probably significantly higher, since few of those polled wanted to admit they were illiterate.

Carlos Fonseca, the founder of the Sandinista Front for National Liberation (FSLN), had adopted the slogan 'And also teach them to read'. The initiative for the National Literacy Campaign came from the Sandinista government almost immediately after the Triumph of July 1979. The new government asked Fernando Cardenal, a Jesuit priest, to assume leadership of the campaign under the aegis of the Ministry of Education headed by Carlos Tünnerman, who gave it his full support and bestowed upon the campaign virtually complete autonomy. Cardenal created a leadership team made up of people who were his friends and associates, volunteers who stepped forward, and others who were assigned by the government.

From the beginning, the campaign leadership had a truly international character. The first person chosen was his fellow Jesuit Robert Sáenz, who had a background in literacy education in El Salvador and in Nicaragua during the guerrilla war. Cardenal also invited his sister Ana Sáenz to work on the project. Others volunteered: Katherine Grigsby, a Canadian educator; the American volunteer Valery Miller; the Mexican documentary film-maker Citali Rovirosa; and many other internationalists. Knowing that Cuba had had a literacy campaign in the 1960s, members of that team travelled to Cuba to meet with the Ministry of Education. Cuba decided to loan the Nicaraguan campaign the Vice-Minister of Education, Raúl Ferrer, who had been the vice-coordinator of the Cuban literacy campaign.

Cardenal also sought out and won the support of a variety of educational organisations and individuals in Latin America for this work, among them: the Latin American Commission of Christian Education (CELADEC); Dimensión Educativa, a Colombian organisation; Francisco Lacayo Parajón, a professor of sociology at the Jesuit University of Central America (UCA); and Nicaraguan educators Carlos Támez and Luis Alemán. While Cardenal invited the

Nicaraguan Bishops Council, the official leadership of the Catholic Church in Nicaragua, to become more involved in the work, they declined, though they did appoint a representative to the National Commission for Literacy that Cardenal had created.

The Sandinista government and Cardenal worked to create an air of excitement and enthusiasm about the campaign. The government declared 1980 'The Year of Literacy'. The campaign itself was officially called 'The National Literacy Crusade: "Heroes and Martyrs of Nicaragua"'. Carlos Mejía Godoy composed a Crusade's hymn with the famous line, 'Fist held high! Book open!' The volunteers who would go forth to conduct the campaign were called 'The People's Literacy Army' (El Ejército Popular de Alfabetización or EPA). This would be a second army and a second revolution. The campaign held a series of events to publicise the activities in the media and printed posters in various designs with different slogans, and not only in Spanish, but also in English and the indigenous languages of the Atlantic Coast. Once the official poster had been printed, other organisations and individuals made their own literacy campaign posters that appeared throughout the country.

The Sandinista National Director appointed *comandante* Carlos Carrión, the head of the newly formed '19 of July' Sandinista Youth, to be the liaison to the Crusade. Under his direction, the Sandinista Youth organisation took on much of the responsibility for training the People's Education Army. All of the volunteers would have to be at least 14 years old and to have signed permission from their parents to participate. Paulo Freire, the famous Brazilian educator, was brought in to advise Cardenal and the other organisers of the campaign. Freire argued that the educational campaign was also a political and consciousness-raising campaign that would be carried out in large part through dialogues with the peasants and themes of their everyday lives.

Fund-raising for the campaign would be an ongoing process. The Venezuelan Jesuits were the first to donate, contributing $20,000. Freire, who while in exile had been working with the World Council of Churches, convinced the Council to contribute a million dollars. During the campaign, Cardenal sent representatives to Europe who spoke to European governments and labour unions and raised more money. The Sandinista government meanwhile gave Cardenal a blank cheque, letting him draw on the campaign's account while awaiting the donations from abroad.

The chiefs of staff of the Literacy Campaign were Cardenal, Luis Carrión, and Douglas Guerrero, who would oversee the entire operation. The first stage of the literacy campaign was to carry out a national census to determine the number of illiterates in the country. The Sandinista Youth were appointed the task of carrying out the census throughout the entire country, and would have to ask: (1) Who could and could not read and write? (2) Who was interested in learning? (3) Where did the people live? (4) Who was available to help teach people to read and write? (5) What level of education did the potential teachers have? Finally the census takers would have to make a map of each area so that later, when the Literacy Campaign arrived, they could find those who could teach and those who needed to learn.

Cardenal's Literacy Campaign organising team and Luis Carrión's Sandinista Youth leadership brought together 300 young people for a four-day training session in El Retiro, the former home of the dictator Somoza. Sleeping throughout the rooms and gardens of the mansion, eating whatever could be found, and meeting in its drawing rooms the students were instructed in how to carry out the census. In December of 1979, they were sent out to every region of the country from the mountains of Matagalpa to the swamps of the Atlantic Coast. In some areas, the Sandinista Youth recruited and trained other young people to help them. In two weeks, they turned to Managua with the census fulfilled. A UNESCO expert told Cardenal that it had been a remarkable success. The census indicated that illiteracy in general was 50 percent or more, while illiteracy in the countryside was 75 percent.[52]

Cardenal's leadership team decided that they should have a political education academy. The idea was that since they all came from different political backgrounds – FSLN members, some Christians, some Communists from the PSN, others from other Marxist groups, and some with no political education whatsoever – it would be useful to attempt to create a common political understanding based on the Sandinista ideology.[53] Cardenal records a very interesting incident at the time when they were creating the Campaign leadership's political education academy. He explains that they also asked the Cubans to join the academy, but the Cubans declined saying that they understood that every country had its own culture and religion, and that Cubans had one political line and the Nicaraguans another, and that they believed that they wouldn't feel right participating. The Cuban and Nicaraguan governments both recognised that Cuba's role had to be limited. Cuba sent teachers to help as advisors with the campaign, enough to put one or two in each department. But no Cuban teachers actually participated in the campaign as teachers.

Departmental and municipal commissions were established throughout the country. In order to be able to travel to all of these locations, Cardenal boldly

---

52   Cardenal 2008, Vol. II, p. 24.
53   Cardenal 2008, Vol. II, p. 27.

asked Mexican President José López Portillo to give him helicopters for the campaign. López Portillo gave him the helicopers, Mexican pilots, and paid for the fuel. The helicopters and a couple of planes provided by the Nicaraguan Air Force made it possible to visit the departments to supervise the work as well as to respond to emergencies.

The sheer scale of the operation was daunting. The Campaign would send 60,000 volunteers into the countryside and 40,000 adults and young people into the cities. Everything to be supplied to these 100,000 volunteers had to be purchased outside of Nicaragua and usually outside of Central America. The campaign sent an American volunteer – John McFaden, known as 'The Viking' on account of his huge size and red complexion – to Miami to purchase ten tons of equipment including: 120,000 pairs of pants, jackets, and patches with the campaign insignia, 60,000 pairs of boots, backpacks, and hammocks. The campaign had printed some one million primers and 100,000 teachers' manuals. Then too there were the hundreds of thousands of notebooks and pencils. Each team would also have a blackboard made of material that could be rolled up and unrolled to be hung on the wall of a factory, a house, or a tree.[54] Businessman Lenín Medrano, manager of the huge La Perfecta Milk Company, and Humberto Collado, the son of a Nicaraguan businessman and a former activist in Young Christian Encounters (Encuentros Cristianos Juveniles), took on the responsibility for logistics.

The primer titled 'Morning of the People' contained 23 lessons organised around Nicaraguan history and issues. Each class would begin with a general discussion, followed by the reading lesson. The lesson might deal with 'Who was Sandino?' or the word 'revolution'. One lesson dealt with the Church, with a sentence reading, 'There is religious freedom for all churches that defend the interests of the people'.[55] Since many of those who could not read were also incapable of counting, adding or subtracting, in addition to the reading primer there was also a book to teach arithmetic. There were special materials for the Atlantic Coast where people were taught to read in their native languages: Creole English, Miskito, Sumo and Rama.[56]

The campaign had the support not only of the Sandinista leadership, but also of all of the Sandinista mass organisations: Association of Rural Workers (ATC), the Sandinista Workers' Confederation (CST), the 'Luisa Amanda Espinoza' Association of Nicaraguan Women (AMNLAE), the Sandinista Defence Com-

---

54   Cardenal 2008, Vol. II. p. 37.
55   Cardenal 2008, Vol. II, p. 46.
56   Cardenal 2008, Vol. II, p. 94.

mittees (CDS), the National Association of Nicaraguan Educators (ANDEN), the Sandinista Children's Association (ANS), and the '19 of July' Sandinista Youth, the Sandinista People's Militias (MPS). Unlike the Cuban experience, where the mass organisations had actually carried out the literacy campaign, in Nicaragua they were only the supporters of the youth who would carry out the work.

The training programme, which eventually trained 200,000 literacy workers, was based on what has come to be called a 'train the trainer method'. A group of 80 teachers from ANDEN and 80 youths from the Sandinista Youth trained the first 200 trainers, who in turn went off in groups to train others, the numbers expanding geometrically until they trained 200,000 literacy workers, of whom 100,000 participated in the campaign.

The young volunteers of the People's Literacy Army were loaded up on buses and trucks and sent throughout the country, most of them going to the rural farming areas. There each day for five months they worked alongside the farmers and their families doing the daily chores and in the afternoon they held their classes. Most of the volunteers came from Nicaragua's cities and this was their first encounter with the peasantry and with rural poverty and hunger. The National Literacy Campaign provided food for the volunteers, 120,000 rations of rice, corn and beans per month, but the volunteers often shared the food with the families, just as they shared the medicines in their first aid kits. Many of the young people formed strong attachments to their host families while living in the towns and villages, working alongside the families, and teaching them to read, write and count.

Throughout the campaign, Cardenal and the other directors boarded their helicopters and flew to cities, towns and rural areas to deal with problems and emergencies. The campaign was not without its tragedies. The Contras murdered a number of the volunteers; altogether seven volunteers were killed, 41 died in accidents, and eight died of natural causes. Yet despite the murders intended to demoralise and disorganise the campaign, not one of the volunteers asked to return home.[57] When the five months had been completed, the Literacy Campaign had taught 400,000 Nicaraguans to read and write and had lowered the illiteracy rate from 51 percent to 12.9 percent, Cardenal reported. For ten days, returning volunteers were greeted in Managua's Plaza of the Revolution by family and friends, an army of returning veterans of the war against ignorance.

---

57   Cardenal 2008, Vol. II, p. 66.

The Literacy Campaign, which in one way or another involved 500,000 people or one-sixth of the country's entire population, had a profound impact on the nation, creating a sense of national unity around the commitment to improve the lives of working people and to uplift the poor. Because it involved such a large proportion of the country's population and the mobilisation and transportation of 100,000 people to the rural towns and urban neighbourhoods of the entire country, it created a tremendous new national consciousness and a strong sense of patriotism. Led by the Sandinista government, the campaign also tended to strengthen the FSLN and the government and the party-state's influence throughout the country. The Literacy campaign became the model for vaccination campaigns and coffee harvest campaigns throughout the 1980s, though no other event would have as great an impact on society.

The National Health Program

Under the 35 years of the Somoza dictatorship, the wealthy had been able to purchase healthcare for themselves from private hospitals and physicians, and a small number of government and private sector workers were covered by the social security system (established in 1957), while many Nicaraguans' health needs were very inadequately served by religious and private charities. In truth, many Nicaraguans could never afford to go to the doctor, purchase medications from a pharmacy or seek attention in a hospital. In 1978, the social security system covered only 16 percent of the economically active population and only 8.4 percent of the total population. At the time of the Triumph, there were only 189 primary care units and only 1,311 doctors, more than 80 percent of whom practised in urban areas. Rural healthcare was inadequate at best and in many areas there simply was none. Before the revolution, the official infant mortality rate was a very high 42 per one thousand births, though the actual rate was an alarming 120 per thousand. With the Triumph, in certain ways the situation immediately deteriorated, as wealthy health professionals fled the country, among them some 646 doctors and 886 health technicians between 1979 and 1986.[58]

Twenty days after the Triumph, the new government created the Single National Health System (SNUS) incorporating two-dozen existing institutions operating in the public health area. SNUS adopted six guiding principles:

---

58   Envío Team 1988a.

(1)   Health is the right of all and the responsibility of the state.
(2)   Health services should be accessible to the whole population, with priority given to the mother/child relation and to workers.
(3)   Medical services have an integral character: both individuals and the environment are to be treated.
(4)   Health work should be carried out by multidisciplinary teams.
(5)   Healthcare activity should be planned.
(6)   The community should participate in all of the health system's activities.[59]

The Sandinista government made healthcare a priority, putting significant resources into medical education and services.[60] The Ministry of Health expanded the healthcare budget tremendously, increasing it between 1978 and 1980 by an astounding 344.6 percent. During the early 1980s, the Sandinistas dedicated about 11 percent of the total national budget to healthcare.[61] New hospitals were built in Managua, Masaya, Rivas, Matagalpa and Bluefields, bringing healthcare to thousands who had never had access before. The Sandinista government undertook to train hundreds of doctors and nurses leading to a four-fold increase in medical school enrolment between 1979 and 1984. By 1984, there were residency programmes for 16 specialties, as well as master's degrees in epidemiology, public health and hygiene.[62]

In the first years of the government, there were vaccination campaigns that paralleled the literacy campaigns. In 1980 and 1982, more than one million vaccinations were given against polio, measles, and tetanus, almost 150 percent more than had been administered in 1978. There were campaigns against dengue and malaria, the latter reducing the number of cases by more than 500.[63] Through government control of the salt plants to provide iodine, levels of endemic goiter because of iodine deficiency were reduced from 33 percent of the population before 1979 to 20 percent in 1982.[64] More important than the construction of hospitals and the vaccination campaigns was the commitment to creating a genuinely national healthcare system.

---

59   Envío Team 1988a.
60   For an early, short account, see Thomas John Bossert, 'Health Care in Revolutionary Nicaragua', in Walker 1982, pp. 259–72.
61   Envío Team 1982a.
62   Slater 1989, pp. 646–51.
63   Envío Team 1982a, citing the *World Development Report of the World Bank*, the annual report of the Health Ministry, and the annual report of the Junta of the National Reconstruction Government.
64   Envío Team 1983b.

As in the National Literacy Campaign, so too in health, large brigades of enthusiastic and idealistic volunteers were mobilised in the first years to carry out a variety of health-related tasks. The 'People's Workday for Health' (*Jornadas Populares de Salud*) involved trained volunteer health brigades that participated in wide-ranging projects such as vaccination campaigns and cleaning up open sewers. In November of 1981, for example, a massive health campaign against malaria involved 80,000 trained volunteers. These volunteers distributed therapeutic doses of anti-malarial drugs to an estimated 75 percent of the nation's population.[65]

The Ministry of Health reported in 1986 that the 189 primary healthcare units in existence in 1979 had grown to 606. Some 468 of those were health posts, smaller than health centres and located in the more isolated zones. It also reported more health professionals: the number of doctors increased by 58 percent and nurses by 211 percent. Medical consultations rose 300 percent while infant mortality dropped from the shocking 120 per thousand in Somoza's time to 69 per thousand. Life expectancy reportedly increased from 53 years in 1979 to 63 in 1986. Giuseppe Slater, M.D., a foreign doctor who worked in a hospital in Estelí, wrote an article about Nicaragua's healthcare system for the *American Journal of Public Health* in 1989. He concluded:

> Nicaragua, in the nine years since the Sandinista revolution, has developed a medical system that is physically and financially accessible, offers care that is very uneven in quality, is generally adequate for most common problems, and is sub-optimally coordinated with preventative health efforts ... The present system is an immense improvement for the great majority of Nicaraguans, who previously had limited or no access to health care.[66]

He also noted the system's egalitarianism: 'Socioeconomic status is not a consideration in treating patients, nor is there any subtle prejudice against the poor'.[67] This represented quite an achievement.

Yet at the same time, the country faced a healthcare crisis created by the war with huge numbers of casualties and the dislocation of large numbers of peasants. President Daniel Ortega reported on 24 June 1987 that 43,176 people on both sides had been killed, wounded or kidnapped in the Contra War. Of that

65   Envío Team 1983b.
66   Slater 1989, pp. 649–50.
67   Slater 1989, p. 651.

total, 22,495 were deaths, including 2,327 women, 2,210 children, 179 teachers, 52 doctors and 15 nurses. The war also created 11,000 war orphans and more than 250,000 displaced peasants.[68]

The Contra War tended to undermine the Sandinistas' attempt to create a healthcare system for all. The war not only competed at the highest level of government for economic and personnel resources, but also created a dramatic need for healthcare at the front, while at the home front it deposited large numbers of wounded and maimed who would need treatment for years. At the same time, the population dislocations and the large number of orphans left behind created new needs for social and medical services. The Sandinistas would find that it would be very difficult to move ahead while overwhelmed by the war's new healthcare challenges.

While the Sandinista government made immediate and important advances in literacy and health, other social problems proved more difficult.[69] Take housing, for example. Nicaragua had never had adequate quality housing and the rapid urbanisation of the 1960s and 1970s, followed by the earthquake, had tremendously exacerbated the problem. Somoza's bombing of working-class neighbourhoods in an attempt to eradicate the Sandinistas' supporters had devastated yet more urban housing. Most housing construction was done by small companies or private individuals, and there was no way to quickly construct sufficient housing.[70] While the Sandinistas established a housing plan, with the exception of the repair of several thousand homes, it had little immediate impact on the housing shortage. The Contra War would undermine any progress on this front throughout the Sandinista years in power.

The Problem of Corruption in the First Years

The Sandinista leaders, as we have seen, began their revolutionary careers as selfless leaders prepared to sacrifice their careers, their personal lives, and even their lives for the revolution. When they first took power, the FSLN leaders seized property from wealthy landowners, business owners, and former government officials in order to redistribute it to the country's working people. Yet, almost from the beginning, the FSLN leaders, perhaps unconsciously at first, began to acquire not only political power, but also economic wealth.

---

68   Envío Team 1988a.
69   Harvey Williams, 'The Social Programs', in Walker (ed.) 1991, *passim.*
70   Harvey Williams, 'Housing Policy in Revolutionary Nicaragua', in Walker 1982, pp. 273–90.

The FSLN government was tainted with corruption almost from the beginning, not only in the sense that each *comandante* attempted to enhance the power of his own Ministry, but also in the sense that they began to take advantage of their positions of power to acquire property and wealth for themselves. The government's earliest decrees nationalising property included Decree Number 59 of September 1979 that transferred the 'luxurious mansions and residences' to the National Reconstruction Trust (later transferred to the Area of Property of the People), while 'summer houses' were transferred to the Nicaraguan Institute of Social Security.[71] In fact, however, the *comandantes* and other Sandinistas in positions of power – arguing that the *comandantes* had to live and work somewhere – took over many of the most luxurious homes for their own use as offices and residences.

While these homes ostensibly remained property of the state, in fact, to all intents and purposes, they became the homes and private offices of the *comandantes*, and in 1990, at the time of the *piñata* (which will be discussed later), the titles of the homes were transferred to the *comandantes*. Daniel Ortega took over for himself two city blocks, including the community park. His brother Humberto took over about forty upper-middle-class houses on the road to Masaya, an area where later real estate values rose rapidly. The most notorious of these cases was that of Tomás Borge who took over five luxury homes and reconstructed them into one enormous mansion. When that created a scandal, he moved to a house in a more modest neighbourhood and remodelled it, adding a swimming pool. He had the refurbished house lowered so that it could not be seen from the street.[72] Borge's real estate in Managua and other cities would eventually, after the return of the right to power, make him a multimillionaire.[73]

The Sandinista *comandantes* and other officials expropriated the Mercedes-Benz automobiles that had been used by Somoza, his family and friends, and which were so common among the upper class. The Mercedes-Benz became in the public's consciousness the typical FSLN party leader's car. On a smaller scale, government agencies, such as the Ministry of Internal Commerce, charged with insuring that basic necessities were met and that consumers did not face price gouging, found that officials or workers stole from the agency and sold goods on the black market.[74] The Contra War led to scarcity of goods and poverty which encouraged such petty corruption. The FSLN leaders' use of

---

71   Decree Number 59, *La Gaceta*, No. 13, Sept. 13, 1979, cited in Hassan Morales 2009, pp. 53–4.
72   Hassan Morales 2009, pp. 52–6.
73   Enríquez 2011.
74   Kinzer 2007, p. 155.

the luxurious homes and automobiles of the old Nicaraguan bourgeoisie did not immediately change their Marxist-Leninist politics or their commitment to workers and the poor, though in the long-run it would contribute to their transformation into a new ruling group.

The Economy – The Expropriations

One of the most immediate problems facing the Sandinistas was that they were entirely unprepared to run a government. The FSLN cadres had spent years – in some cases decades – in a revolutionary guerrilla movement, and for many their only experience was military struggle. While there were some well-educated Sandinistas, many had little or no formal higher education and no professional experience. As Dionisio Marenco later wrote:

> All of us were prepared to die ... None of us was trained or prepared to live or for what to do after the victory. I was a cabinet minister in the first revolutionary Cabinet. They said to me: 'You're going to be minister of construction' and I got to know the construction ministry the day I walked into it. Each of us did what we could.[75]

The lack of politically reliable, trained and competent administrators represented one factor that obstructed the development and implementation of an economic plan.

The key to the future of Nicaragua would be the FSLN's ability to develop the economy and to do so in a way that they hoped would benefit the great majority of the population. Nicaragua, small, backward, and sparsely populated, had always been one of the poorest nations in the Caribbean and Latin America; only Haiti was poorer. While the Somoza dynasty had carried out a largely successful modernisation of the state and the economy, it had principally benefitted the wealthy. Before the revolution, the per capita income was $800, but that was strongly skewed toward businessmen and landowners, and most Nicaraguans lived on about a dollar a day – less than half the per capita income.

When the Sandinistas took power, the economy entered a new sort of crisis resulting from the revolution, the flight of the Somoza coterie, and the Contra War. First, Somoza had carried off tens of millions, perhaps hundreds of millions, of dollars. Other wealthy Nicaraguans had similarly sent their money to

---

75   Marenco 2008.

banks abroad. Second, many regions of the country had been ravaged by revolutionary warfare, including the destruction resulting from Somoza's bombing of several of the country's major cities. Third, the Sandinistas faced the US-inspired and US-backed Contra War, which by 1989 had resulted in almost 31,000 dead, another 30,000 injured and maimed, and damages amounting to 1.9 billion dollars. Finally, the United States, which had been a major trading partner, imposed an embargo forbidding all trade that was intended to strangle Nicaragua economically. The embargo is estimated to have cost the economy at least 642 million dollars. The Sandinistas would have to rapidly develop policies and carry out measures to rebuild the country's economy in the midst of destruction, war and embargo.[76]

The Sandinistas did not attempt to take over the many multinational corporations (some American and some European) that operated in Nicaragua. While the United States government attempted to get US-based corporations to pull out of the country, it largely failed. In the mid-1980s, there would still be 43 multinationals in the country, including American giants such as Caterpillar, Exxon, IBM, and Texaco. Their investments totalled approximately 87 billion dollars and represented a quarter of the nation's production.[77] Despite their ideology, the Sandinistas did not have the political, economic, or administrative capacity to take over these companies' facilities, and doing so, they understood, would only have further antagonised the United States and alienated sympathetic European countries.

The Sandinistas initially carried out what was from a revolutionary point of view a rational policy regarding the Nicaraguan capitalist class. The Junta government issued Decree Number 3 that expropriated the Somoza family and Somoza insiders who owned a total of over 100 corporations and over two million acres of farmland.[78] The Somoza properties represented one-fifth of all cultivable land in Nicaragua. In addition, the FSLN passed the Absentee Law, much like that passed during the French Revolution of 1789, which declared that anyone who left the country for more than six months – virtually always because they opposed the revolution and had joined the opposition – would lose their property. The law was first applied to Juan Ignacio González, the owner of the Victoria Brewing Company, who, like many other wealthy Nicara-

76   Pérez-Baltodano 2009, p. 611, quoting Daniel Ortega's advisor Paul Oquist for figures on cost of embargo and war.

77   La Feber 1993, p. 307.

78   A summary of the Sandinista economic programme can be found in Mayorga 2007, Chapter III, pp. 42–55. See also Kinzer 2007, p. 76; Ramírez 1999, p. 233.

guans, had fled to Miami and supported the Contras.[79] On 13 October 1979, the Sandinista government also nationalised the country's few mines located in northeast Nicaragua and mostly owned by US companies.[80] The government nationalised all banks, credit agencies, and insurance companies, and the lumber industry as well.[81]

Agrarian Reform

Agrarian reform, which stood at the head of the FSLN's agenda, began almost at once, and took the form of the redistribution of land from wealthy landlords to poor peasants.[82] The confiscation of the Somoza properties meant that the government had enough land for the first stages of the agrarian reform to allow the Sandinistas to avoid a confrontation with the rest of the country's capitalist class, most of whom were agricultural producers. The Sandinistas recognised that they did not have the power to expropriate the entire landlord class, nor did they have the capacity to manage such large enterprises. As Baumeister puts it: 'The most significant element in this Sandinista equation is the break with a principal tradition of previous revolutionary processes: the association between increments of war against counter-revolutionary forces and "Jacobinisation" (radicalisation), as seen in a majority of revolutions over the past two centuries'.[83] That is, the Sandinistas resisted pressures to expropriate, nationalise, and distribute land.

The expropriation of the properties of Somoza and his cronies was for the moment sufficient to satisfy the peasants' appetite for more land and made it unnecessary for the Sandinistas to immediately confront other major landowners.[84] The nationalisation of Somoza's property, while not touching most other landlords (except the absentees), provided the economic basis for a tenuous accommodation with the country's large plantation owners who had to be encouraged to keep producing. The FSLN's desire to maintain an amicable rela-

---

79   Ramírez 1999, p. 177 and p. 233. González later broke with the Contras, arguing that they were created by the CIA.
80   Ramírez 1999, pp. 233–4.
81   Kinzer 2007, p. 76.
82   An overview of the Agrarian reform can be found in Eduardo Baumeister, 'Agrarian Reform', in Walker (ed.) 1991, pp. 229–45.
83   Eduardo Baumeister, 'Agrarian Reform', in Walker (ed.) 1991, p. 235.
84   For an early and realistic account of the agrarian reform, see David Kaimowitz and Joseph Thome, 'Nicaragua's Agrarian Reform: The First Year (1979–80)', in Walker 1982, pp. 223–40.

tionship with those capitalists was constantly threatened, however, by the government's occasional nationalisation of some new kind of property as well as by the party's rhetoric, a discourse often more radical than the government's actual actions.

Consistent with their public face and their discourse intended for consumption by the Nicaraguan upper classes, foreign governments, and the media abroad, the Sandinistas put forward the position that they intended to establish a social-democratic mixed economy, something like those that existed in Scandinavia, that is, an economy based upon private, public, and cooperative sectors, together with strong social welfare programmes. But in reality, in line with their concealed Marxist-Leninist convictions, they desired to establish a bureaucratic communist political economy based on the example of Cuba, the Soviet Union, and the Eastern Bloc. They wanted an accommodation with the bourgeoisie in the short-run to prevent the collapse of production, but in the long-run they planned to expropriate it and eliminate the capitalists as a social class.

Sandinista leaders recognised that they could hardly rebuild the country without finding a way to incorporate these wealthy groups into the economy and the society, though they would never prove successful in doing so. The Sandinistas' ambivalent attitude toward the capitalist class sometimes led to behaviour that undermined their own plans and caused Nicaraguan financiers, capitalists, and landlords, who feared for their property, investments, and profits, to either withdraw from the economy or to go into opposition politically or sometimes militarily. The Sandinista rhetoric attacking the 'bourgeois traitors' only exacerbated the capitalists' anxiety. The Sandinista policies also caused the alienation of the peasantry who did not receive titles to their land, as well as leading to the disaffection of many radicalised workers who were disappointed by the bosses' continued ownership and control of the factories, as well as by the low wages, the impact of inflation, and unemployment.[85]

In early 1981, for example, following a visit to the Soviet Union to seek both increased military assistance and economic aid, *comandante* Humberto Ortega declared that Marxism-Leninism was to be the model of the Nicaraguan revolution.[86] Not long afterwards, on 23 June, Daniel Ortega added to the list of expropriations and nationalisations the confiscation of the property of any person declared to be counter-revolutionary, or of anyone who engaged in de-capitalisation, and of any property of more than 500 *manzanas* in the most

---

85   Pérez-Baltodano 2009, pp. 605–8.
86   Christian 1986, p. 316.

important provinces that was left idle or inefficiently exploited, or of any such property in the rest of the country of more than 1,000 *manzanas*.[87] Some businessmen hearing these declarations and edicts quit producing, decapitalised their firms, and withdrew from the economy altogether, leading the state to expropriate another fifteen industrial companies.[88]

Still, the truth was that though there were significant expropriations and nationalisations, the private sector remained significant in agriculture, industry and services, and, in fact, most of the economy still remained in private hands. State ownership and control represented 25 percent of agriculture; 25 percent of manufacturing; 70 percent of construction; and 30 percent of commerce. The state had significant control in mining (30 percent) and financial services (100 percent). The government had hoped to control 41 percent of GDP by 1980 and succeeded in achieving 49 percent by 1984. The greatest government impact was in agriculture where the great plantations were reduced to just six percent of the total land under cultivation, while medium and small producers owned 40 percent of the land. Some 48 percent of all agricultural land had been affected by the agrarian reform in one way or another; 12 percent were owned by the state and 36 percent by cooperatives.[89] The Sandinistas came to control about half of the economy, and one could even say the most important half.

The 129 industrial enterprises nationalised by the Sandinista government (most of them related to agricultural processing) were consolidated in the Industrial Corporation of the People (COIP) under the Ministry of the Industry. In 1982, while the state controlled 31 percent of industry, large- and medium-sized private businesses still controlled 54 percent, while small businesses and artisans possessed 15 percent. Private enterprise was hardly annihilated. These many important private enterprises, however, no longer operated in a free market capitalist economy. The state tended to monopolise certain crucial sectors of the economy, such as agricultural inputs and outputs, through the Nicaraguan Enterprise of Agricultural Inputs (ENIA) and the PROAGRO, the state distribution company. The state also controlled the importing and distribution of agricultural machinery. The Ministry of Foreign Commerce controlled exports through the specialised industrial organisations: ENAL for cotton; ENAZUCAR for sugar; and ENCAFÉ for coffee.[90] Many of the capitalists who stayed in

---

87   One manzana equals 10,000 square varas and one vara equals 0.6987 square metres or 7.521 sq ft, while one *manzana* equals 6,987 square metres or 1.727 acres.

88   Solà i Montserrat 2008, p. 368.

89   Mayorga 2007, pp. 42–3.

90   Solà i Montserrat 2008, p. 368.

Nicaragua kept their businesses and farms, but the government controlled financing, distribution, and marketing.

The Sandinista revolution had a tremendous, diverse impact on the capitalist class, temporarily dividing and fragmenting it. During the first few years, some former members of the capitalist class became part of the Nicaraguan government, bringing their technical and professional experience to tasks such as the agrarian reform. While some capitalists lost ownership of their land, through their role in government they were frequently able to remain the managers of it, and thus preserved, to some extent, the continuity of their class and its role in Nicaraguan society.[91] Other capitalists took their wealth to other Central American countries and to the Caribbean and South America or to the United States, becoming a *force majeure* as transnational capitalists. After the 1990 election of Violeta Chamorro, many of these would return to Nicaragua even richer, more powerful, and much better connected internationally than they had been before the revolution.[92]

Within Nicaragua then there remained big and small business people who formed a capitalist opposition within the society, some willing to go along with the Sandinistas as long as they did not see an immediate threat to their interests, others hostile either for ideological reasons or because their interests had been affected. Some members of this capitalist class, especially those in the oligarchy who were connected by family ties, maintained ongoing economic and political relations with their fellows who had fled to Miami, Florida, or who were in Central America or the Caribbean. The Nicaraguan business class – divided between those in Nicaragua and those abroad, and also between those who formed part of a loyal opposition at home and those who supported the Contras – represented not simply a threat, but also a standing economic, social and political alternative to the Sandinistas. If the Sandinistas should fail to construct a new state and to improve conditions in the society for the masses, that bourgeoisie would be waiting in the wings to try its hand with the help of its allies in the United States.

Nicaragua did not have a capitalist free market economy, but neither was it a Communist state-directed economy, nor could it be called a socialist worker-run economy. Throughout the period of Sandinista power from 1979 to 1990, the economy remained in some sort of intermediate stage, half capitalist and half run by the state bureaucracy, but challenged from time to time by the workers,

---

91   Carlos Vilas, 'Asuntos de familia: clases, linajes y política en la Nicaragua contemporánea', *Desarrollo Económico*, Vol. 32, No. 7, cited in Mayorga 2007, p. 52 and fn. 62.

92   Mayorga 2007, Chapter III, pp. 42–55. See also Vilas 1984.

a stage in which all three outcomes – capitalism, bureaucratic Communism, and revolutionary, democratic socialism – remained possible. The continued existence of a powerful capitalist class, not only in Nicaragua but also abroad, as well as the challenges of the Contra War, and the US embargo, would work to abort the chances of either Cuban-style Communism or revolutionary, democratic socialism. While the capitalist state had been abolished, the capitalist class at home and in exile continued to exist and with US support would ultimately reassert its control of the economy and the government. The working class, controlled by the Sandinistas, failed to find a way either to take control of the FSLN or to organise an independent party.

The Role of Loans and Foreign Aid in Nicaragua

No discussion of the economy would be complete without mentioning foreign aid, which played an enormous role. During the Carter administration, which attempted to reach a *modus vivendi* with the Sandinistas and hoped to influence their behaviour, the United States provided in the immediate aftermath of the insurrection some $15 million in emergency relief to shelter and feed the thousands displaced by the war. That was followed up in September 1979 with another $8.5 million in economic assistance. The State Department also created an $80 million supplemental aid package for Central America for 1980, with $75 million going to Nicaragua, but only after Carter certified that Nicaragua was not supporting 'international terrorism' – that is, military aid to the revolutionaries in El Salvador.[93] After Reagan took office in 1981, American aid flowed not to the Sandinistas, but to their political opponents, both political and military.

　　Throughout the 1980s, the Sandinistas were dependent upon hundreds of millions of dollars of foreign aid in the form of gifts, loans, in-kind aid (cargo ships full of grain, for example), and foreign staff support for all sorts of state projects. Most of the aid came from Mexico, Venezuela and Cuba, as well as from Columbia, Peru, Brazil, and Argentina, though the Eastern Bloc nations and the Soviet Union also contributed, as did nations such as Libya. Much aid also came from Sweden, Germany, and other Western capitalist countries, in some cases from Social Democratic political parties and trade unions, as well as from the World Council of Churches and individual religious denominations, the United Nations and its agencies, and the Red Cross. The Soviet

---

93　LeoGrande 1998, pp. 30–1.

Union's emergency aid to Nicaragua was, according to one expert, 'negligible', though later the Soviets would provide large shipments of wheat. In 1981, after a visit by Interior Minister Tomás Borge to Moscow, the Soviet government offered Nicaragua a $ 50 million credit loan to purchase Soviet agricultural, construction and transportation equipment. In terms of military assistance, the Soviet Union sent hundreds of millions in tanks, helicopters and other hardware between 1981 and 1984.[94] Thousands of American, Latin American, and European leftists also visited or went to live and work in Nicaragua, many of them bringing material aid of some sort or another.[95] The tremendous amount of material aid for the Sandinista Revolution coming from abroad, which represented more than half of the country's total resources, helped it to survive the long, difficult and painful 1980s.

The Communist and Social Democratic governments were motivated to try to shape the Nicaraguan Revolution in the direction of their principles and projects. The Communists – Soviet, Eastern Bloc and Cuban – who were closest to the FSLN leadership, provided large amounts of military assistance, amounting to hundreds of millions of dollars, as well as aid for other government projects. Their aid not only supported the Sandinista government, but also in some cases fundamentally shaped the nature of its state institutions, as in the case of the Ministry of the Interior and its various security and police forces. Those nations and their contributions also played a major role in shaping the economy, either through their model of nationalisation of industry and agriculture or through their interest in certain mega-projects. While foreign aid helped to hold the Sandinistas' state-building project together, they could not ultimately save it.

The Problem of Administration and the Mega-Projects

The extensive nationalisations challenged the Sandinistas to create an administration to competently manage all of these many industries and firms, a challenge for which they were ill equipped. The Sandinistas' Marxist-Leninist ideology led the new government to create a national economic plan. Ideally, following the historic Soviet model, this would have been a five-year plan, but the leadership opted to simply draft a one-year plan. The December 1979 state

---

94   Paszyn 2000, pp. 41–9.
95   I was one of those in 1985 bringing medical supplies to a hospital in Estelí with friends, Dr. Bruce Bernard and Dr. Sherry Baron, whom I later married.

reform (following the break-up of the FSLN alliance with the business class) created an expanded and centralised state bureaucracy charged with planning.[96]

The Economic Programme to Benefit the People and the Strategy for Industrial Development of 1980 put the emphasis on consumer goods such as food, clothing, and construction materials. The second area of emphasis would be export products. The One-Year Plan document adopted in 1981, a mere twenty-some pages long, hardly represented a comprehensive economic plan, though it established a framework for planning.[97] Under the early economic plans, the economy remained more or less stable until 1984 when the combination of the Contra War, the lack of hard currency for foreign exchange, and then the US embargo in 1985 brought the economy to a virtual standstill and then caused it to shrink.[98] Yet, even before the Contra War made it altogether impossible, the Sandinistas were challenged to fulfil their economic plan.

Despite the plan and the planning organisation, none of the FSLN *comandantes* was prepared to have a central state organisation deprive them of their ministry's power to distribute political and economic power.[99] Each *comandante* controlled some division of government, a ministry that became a fiefdom, and each made his own decisions about how to allocate resources, many of those made on the basis of self-interest (and as we will see later, often involving corrupt practices). As Andrés Pérez-Baltodano suggests: 'Much of the energy that might have been used to create a vision of a truly socialist politics was squandered in maintaining a balance between the spheres of power of each of the *comandantes*'.[100] If the state plan proved incapable of controlling the state-owned enterprises, it had even less control over private business.[101]

The new Sandinista state economy quickly became distorted by a series of mega-projects either foisted on Nicaragua by its Communist allies or cooked up by one or another of the *comandantes*. The Soviet Union signed an agreement to send Nicaragua a fleet of MIG fighters and the Cubans were designated to build the huge airport to accommodate them, with a 3,000 metre runway, control tower, administration building, hangars, and housing for personnel. While the Cubans did most of the actual construction, still the project consumed hundreds of millions of dollars, an enormous part of the national budget, and contributed to runaway inflation. In the end, under pressure from the Reagan

---

96   Pérez-Baltodano 2009, pp. 614–16.
97   Hassan Morales 2009, pp. 113–17.
98   Solà i Montserrat 2008, pp. 368–9.
99   Sergio Ramírez 1999, p. 235.
100   Andrés Pérez-Baltodano, private communication, 15 January 2014.
101   Sergio Ramírez 1999, p. 235.

administration, the Soviet Union backed out of the deal and sent no planes, the Cuban engineers and construction workers left, and the airport was never finished.[102]

   Another project, a favourite of Fidel Castro, was a trans-Nicaragua highway, named the Tuma-Waslala-Siuna highway, which would connect the Caribbean and the Pacific, a development that Castro believed was of great geopolitical significance. While Cuba provided an elite, armed, military construction team, the highway was never finished.[103] There was also the July Victory (Victoria de Julio) sugary refinery, built at a cost of $200 million, $73.8 million from Cuba. Finished in 1985 but never a financial success, it changed hands various times and finally went into bankruptcy and closed in 2001.[104] Jaime Wheelock, Minister of Agriculture, also proposed to create automatically irrigated sugar cane fields on a massive scale. And among other such projects were: a Pacific Coast Railroad conceived without consideration of what cargo it would carry or where it would be taken; a deep water port to be built by Bulgarians in Bluff on the Atlantic Coast; and the proposed introduction of the African palm to produce palm oil (a project which would later prove successful).[105] Most of these 'white elephant' projects, as they came to be known, never really panned out. The mega-projects promoted by Communist allies or various *comandantes* conflicted with any sort of national plan, distorted the economy, wasted a large portion of the national budget, and contributed to inflation, while they failed to further economic development.

The Land Problem

The revolution's promise to the majority of Nicaraguans was an end to the dictatorship and land to the peasants. Yet this proved far more difficult to carry out than they had foreseen. The Sandinistas' inability to resolve the land problem was their biggest and most costly economic failure because of its social and political implications, ultimately leading to the disillusion and alienation of a large portion of the peasantry, significant numbers of whom went off to join the Contra forces.

   The Sandinista government nationalised tens of thousands of acres of farm-land that had previously belonged to Somoza, his family and cronies, and

102   Hassan Morales 2009, p. 163; Ramírez 1999, pp. 158–9; LeoGrande 1998, pp. 376–80.
103   Hassan Morales 2009, pp. 158–61.
104   Hassan Morales 2009, pp. 161–2; Fonseca L. 2001.
105   Hassan Morales 2009, p. 118.

to those who had abandoned the country and joined the opposition. Altogether, about 20 percent of arable land was expropriated and nationalised. The Nicaragua government had promised the country's predominantly rural and agricultural population that they would receive this land, expecting to have it deeded over to them as individual landowners. The idea of creating agrarian cooperatives along American lines was also raised, but rejected. Following its Marxist-Leninist principles, the government nationalised the land in the form of Agricultural Production Units (UPA) intended to become complete agricultural communities with their own childcare centres, schools, and health clinics. Peasants were expected to work together for their common good and for the common good of Nicaragua. As Sergio Ramírez writes, the creation of these state farms was intended to avoid the creation of an inevitably conservative petty bourgeoisie of small farmers, and instead to strengthen the rural working class. The Marxist-Leninist FSLN wanted to enlarge the proletariat, not to create more farmers, petty-bourgeois by definition. The peasants, however, felt betrayed because the government refused to deed the land to them. Their disappointment in and anger at the Sandinista government led many peasants to join the Contras in their effort to overthrow the new regime.[106]

When the Sandinista government realised that its policies had driven the peasants into the arms of the Contras, it decided that indeed it would deed over the land to the peasants, but these deeds forbade the holder from either leaving the land to his children or selling it to others. The peasants, who actually wanted to own their own land and to be able to bequeath it to their children or to sell it, found this an equally unacceptable policy. After the Sandinistas lost power in 1990, peasants received full title to the land, allowing them to dispose of it as they wished, though without adequate government support for credit and help with marketing, and with normal capitalist relations reasserting themselves, it was hard for many to hold on to their land, which tended to become concentrated in the hands of larger landowners.[107]

Just as the Sandinistas had imposed wage and price controls on the economy in general, so too did they on the rural economy. Ranchers could not dispose of their cattle and farmers could dispose of their crops only as permitted by the government. Cattle ranchers unable to do as they liked with their cattle in Nicaragua drove large herds into Honduras or Costa Rica.[108] The Sandinista government's one rural success story was the expansion of credit to small

106   Ramírez 1999, p. 227.
107   Ramírez 1999, pp. 228–43.
108   Kinzer 2007, p. 157.

farmers who had never before been able to access credit. Good as that was, it was the exception. The Sandinista government officials and party leaders in the countryside, almost all from urban backgrounds and trained in the crudest sort of Marxism, generally approached the peasantry with suspicion, prejudices, and without the slightest understanding of peasant culture.[109] On top of the government's hated policies, the condescending attitudes of the Sandinista government officials could only further antagonise the peasantry.

The Labour Problem

Labour is one of the biggest and most difficult problems facing any revolution. Revolutions are usually fought from below by the classes of people who have been oppressed and exploited and who fought in part in the desire to end those conditions. Revolutions therefore almost invariably see demands on the part of workers to reduce their workday and to improve their conditions, wages and benefits, and gradually to improve their standard of living. Yet, at the same time, especially when revolutions occur in underdeveloped countries, in order for the revolution to survive and for the new revolutionary order to prosper, it is important to establish some sort of labour discipline, because the nation must increase productivity or succumb to economic dependency. One of the great debates in revolutionary history has been the question of whether one can rely on moral incentives, that is, persuasion to convince workers that they are serving the revolutionary cause and their own people, or whether it is necessary to use material incentives, as well as the threat of being punished in some way, perhaps by dismissal, demotion, or reduction of wages.[110]

With the Triumph, the Nicaraguan Revolution also faced exactly these issues that affected two different groups of workers: professional and technical employees on the one hand, and skilled, semi-skilled, and unskilled workers on the other. With the tremendous strains put on the economy as a result of the period of violent struggle against the dictatorship, the vast expropriations of property, then the Contra War, and after 1985 the US embargo, the country's professional and technical workers struggled to keep jobs, find new jobs, and protect their middle-class social status and incomes. The Sandinista government needed to keep these essential workers relatively happy if the economy

---

109   Ramírez 1999, p. 229.
110   Influenced by the Chinese Revolution, Ernesto 'Che' Guevara had advocated moral rather than material incentives in the early years of the Cuban Revolution, with disastrous economic consequences.

was to continue to function even at the low level to which it had fallen, yet the government's Guevarist version of Marxist-Leninist ideology combined with its penury kept it from offering significant material incentives, that is, higher salaries, to these professional and technical workers. The leadership was not prepared to make what it considered to be concessions to middle-class professionals.[111] Moreover, these essential employees were frequently berated by Sandinistas in the workplace as 'reactionaries, bourgeois, exploiters, or even counter-revolutionaries'.[112] Some of these professionals and highly skilled workers, unable to make a living in their fields, became self-employed small business people engaged in commerce, while others joined the emigration of hundreds of thousands from the upper and middle classes who left the country in the 1980s, ending up in other Central American or Caribbean countries or in Miami.[113] In any case, the Sandinista government failed to find a way to make use of their talents and skills to the fullest and the economy suffered.

The problem was equally serious or perhaps more grave when it came to the ability to deal with industrial, service and agricultural workers, the latter group being the most numerous. The productivity of state companies was lower than that of privately owned companies, required enormous resources, but did not result in a higher proportion of production.[114] After the Triumph and the expropriation of agricultural lands, Jaime Wheelock, Minster of Agriculture, reported that the workday had fallen to just two hours of not very serious labour.[115] Moïses Hassan, who had been a member of the governing Junta, and who, though not a Marxist-Leninist, had held other high posts in the Sandinista government, wrote in his letter of resignation from his office and from the FSLN in 1985 that, as a result of the leadership's 'demagoguery and adulation of the masses', there had been a 'deformation of consciousness among wide sectors of Nicaraguan workers' who failed to understand that only through dedicated and continuous labour could they find a solution to the country's economic problems. Consequently, 'the productivity of labour in Nicaragua since the revolutionary Triumph has descended, one of the most alarming phenomena at the moment'. The government, he wrote, had lost the ability to administer 'the coercive mechanisms that guarantee productivity'.[116] The Sandinistas' revolutionary government, though inspired by a vision of Soviet- or Cuban-style

111   Hassan Morales 2009, pp. 97–109.
112   Hassan Morales 2009, Appendix I, Letter of Resignation, p. 434.
113   Kinzer 2007, p. 132; Orozco 2008.
114   Solà i Montserrat 2008, p. 370.
115   Hassan Morales 2009, p. 66.
116   Hassan Morales 2009, Appendix I, Letter of Resignation, pp. 434–6.

communism, proved incapable of either imposing labour discipline through penalties and rewards, or of inspiring workers through exhortation. Nor was the government prepared to let the market determine salaries and wages. The Sandinistas proved unsuccessful in getting people to work harder and as labour productivity fell, so did the national economy's output.[117]

The Sandinista government's attempt to deal with the labour problem through price and wage controls in order to protect workers' real wages only exacerbated the issue. The government established prices and wages without any comprehensive economic plan, and consequently the numbers they set were often arbitrary. The Sandinista unions complained of 'salary anarchy'.[118] Both employers and workers found the wage system failed to work for them: employers were sometimes required to pay too much to unproductive workers or not allowed to pay more to keep more productive workers, while the workers found that they often could not live on the wages they were paid. In the private sector, professionals, technical workers and ordinary wage labourers gave up regular jobs to engage in *bisnes*, that is, to enter the growing informal economy as self-employed entrepreneurs, vendors or contract laborers.[119] The formal, private sector economy began to unravel. During the Sandinista period from 1979 to 1990, the government never succeeded in establishing a labour policy that could increase labour productivity and also meet workers' needs.

The Unions at an Impasse

The Nicaraguan Revolution had given a tremendous impetus to union organisation, though in the context of the revolution and Contra War, these state-party-led and highly politicised organisations were far from our ordinary conception of labour unions. At the time of the Triumph, there were some 133 unions with 27,000 members, a labour movement constantly threatened with repression. By 1983, there were almost ten times as many organised workers, 1,103 unions with 207,000 members. These various union organisations included some loyal to the Sandinistas, some independent leftist unions, and some unions linked to conservative or even Contra organisations, though the majority were Sandinista-led organisations.

---

117 Labour productivity in the long-run is determined by capital investment and more productive machinery, but in the short-run, as in Nicaragua at the time, the question was getting people to work harder and to produce more.

118 Envío Team 1984.

119 Kinzer 2007, p. 154.

The dominant union organisation was the Sandinista Workers' Confederation (CST), a national union founded after the 1979 victory out of the merger of all pro-Sandinista factory unions. Next in importance was the Association of Rural Workers (ATC), founded by the Sandinista Proletarian Tendency before the Triumph, which organised agricultural labourers throughout the country. The Sandinistas also led the Federation of Health Workers (FETSALUD), a national union representing health workers. Usually allied with the Sandinistas were a group of three independent, Marxist-led confederations: the General Confederation of Labour – Independent (CGT-i); the Confederation for Action and Labour Union Unification (CAUS); and the Workers' Front (FO).

In November 1981, the CST, ATC, FETSALUD, FO, CAUS, CGT-I and the CUS joined together to found the Nicaraguan Labour Union Coordination (CSN) in an effort to promote the construction of a single union confederation. Also participating in the CSN were the Nicaraguan Journalists' Union (UPN), the National Association of Nicaraguan Educators (ANDEN) and the National Union of Public Employees (UNE), all three of which supported the revolution. The conservative opposition to the Sandinistas also had its labour organisations. The Nicaraguan Workers' Confederation (CTN) and the Confederation of Labour Union Unity (CUS) worked with the business organisations and the right-wing parties in the 'Ramiro Sacasa G. Nicaraguan Democratic Coordinating Group' (*Coordinadora*).[120]

The central issue facing the Sandinistas and their unions throughout the entire period from 1979 to 1990 was how to both defend the revolutionary government, its progressive measures and social programmes and still respond to workers' demands for higher wages. These were highly contradictory responsibilities. The Sandinista unions basically gave up on the ideas of trying to defend the workers' standard of living until after the Contras were defeated, arguing that '[g]iven the political decision of US imperialism to liquidate this revolution, we must all now get used to living in a war situation'. That is, it would be impossible to significantly raise wages until the war was over. Or as they said: 'This war is difficult because it means that, instead of bread, the workers get politics'.[121]

The Sandinista government suspended the right to strike, and the Sandinista CST defended that decision, arguing that strikes only served the counter-revolution. Most workers may have understood the situation and supported it, but that did not solve the problem of low wages. The conservative unions linked

---

120   Envío Team 1984.
121   Ibid.

to the employer associations and right-wing Democratic Coordinating Group argued that the Sandinistas should give up their centralised economic model and implement the social-democratic mixed economy that they claimed to support. The conservative unions, interested in bringing down the revolutionary government, engaged in strikes in the hope of creating enough strain to cause the government to collapse.[122]

The Sandinistas' attempt to continue to both carry out the war and to provide social services eventually led to runaway inflation. During the first half of the 1980s, the annual inflation rate averaged 30 percent. After the United States imposed the trade embargo in 1985, the inflation rate rose dramatically to an annual 220 percent. That tripled the following year, reaching almost 700 percent, and by 1988 inflation had reached the astronomical 14,000 percent. Such runaway inflation not only destroyed any attempt at either government or private sector planning, but also completely undermined wage and price policies. The economy was collapsing. As we will see, the Sandinistas were compelled by this situation to change their policies drastically.

---

122   Ibid.

CHAPTER 7

The Sandinistas and the Contra War (1985–90)

Republican Ronald Reagan was elected president of the United States in 1980 on the basis of a conservative platform that stated, among other things: 'We deplore the Sandinista takeover of Nicaragua'. And it went on to say: 'We oppose the Carter administration's aid programme for the government of Nicaragua. However, we will support the efforts of the Nicaraguan people to establish a free and independent government'.[1] Implicit in the last sentence was the idea that the new Republican Party president wanted to remove the Sandinista government and might support an armed movement that would do so. From the time he came into office until he left eight years later, Reagan pursued a policy of support for the Contra War aimed at overthrowing the Sandinista government in Nicaragua, a policy that took thousands of lives, many of them the lives of non-combatants.[2] Reagan continued this policy even when it led him to do so illegally in violation of the US Constitution and American law.

Like many Republican and Democratic Party presidents and politicians before, Reagan was an ideological anti-Communist who saw the Sandinista revolution as an extension of the Communist system of the Soviet Union and Cuba (a point of view with which the Sandinistas themselves would have privately agreed). His policies represented a continuation – with his own particular right-wing twist – of the historic, bipartisan US foreign policy that treated Central America and the Caribbean as part of a larger US sphere of interest in Latin America, and that worked to protect US economic and geopolitical interests in the region. Under the guise of anti-Communism, the United States often intervened in Latin America not so much to fight Communism as to protect American investments from any radical social movement from below. Reagan was a fervent anti-Communist who surrounded himself with like-minded cabinet members and advisors who would work with him to bring down Communism in the Soviet Union and Eastern Europe, to continue the isolation of Cuba, and to destroy the Sandinista Revolution.

Before Reagan, President Jimmy Carter's administration, recognising that it had 'limited leverage', had had rather modest aims in Nicaragua. It worked to establish normal relations with the Sandinistas with the goal of exerting

---

1 Kinzer 2007, p. 87.
2 The case is made in LeoGrande 1998 and Walker 1987.

some influence on the course of developments. Carter believed the Sandinistas' friendly relationship with Cuba would have to be accepted, and he expected the Sandinistas to aid the Salvadoran revolutionaries, but he hoped to prevent Nicaragua from becoming 'a major factor in El Salvador's revolutionary war', and – until Reagan's election – that 'strategy worked reasonably well'.[3]

Ronald Reagan and his foreign policy team believed that 'the Sandinistas were Marxist-Leninists', and that if they remained in power 'they would guide Nicaragua inexorably toward a one-party Leninist dictatorship, alliance with the Soviet Union, and subversion of their neighbours'. They also believed that 'No incentives from Washington or anywhere else would dissuade them from this trajectory'. If it sometimes seemed otherwise, the Reaganites argued, the Sandinistas were merely engaged in short-term tactics, buying time 'while the Leninists consolidated themselves'.[4] (Once again, we might note, the Sandinista leadership, while it would not have said so, would have agreed). Reagan broke with Carter's policy of attempting to work with and influence the Sandinistas, convinced that it was necessary to overthrow them and to bring to power a new government more amenable to the United States' influence. The Reagan administration therefore pursued a two-pronged strategy: first, to destabilise the economy, and second, to support an armed opposition to the Sandinistas.[5]

Reagan's most immediate concern was ensuring that the Sandinista Revolution did not spread to other countries in Central America, and it was with the hope of preventing such a development that he sent Assistant Secretary of State Thomas Enders to Managua to make the Sandinistas a one-time-only offer. Enders demanded that the Sandinistas make two concessions that could avert a war: first, that the Sandinistas stop providing military assistance to the Farabundo Martí National Liberation Front (FMLN) in El Salvador and to other Central American guerrilla movements; and second, that the FSLN cut or at least substantially reduce its military ties to Cuba and the Soviet Union. Enders told the Sandinistas: 'You can do your own thing, but do it within your borders, or else we are going to hurt you'.[6] When Enders told the Sandinistas that they were at 'a fork in the road', Daniel Ortega replied: 'We, too, have seen the crossroads. We are resolved to defend this revolution by force of arms, and if we are pushed, to carry the war to all of Central America ... But we are not suicidal. I regard your proposal as reasonable'.[7]

---

3   LeoGrande 1998, p. 32.
4   LeoGrande 1998, pp. 108–9.
5   LeoGrande 1998, pp. 108–11.
6   LeoGrande 1998, pp. 118–19.
7   LeoGrande 1998, p. 120.

Though Enders had apparently convinced Ortega, he was unable to convince the hardliners in the Reagan administration, who at once cut off all economic aid permanently, announced they would carry out military exercises with Honduras, and made increasingly severe arms control demands.[8] The Sandinistas, knowing only too well the long history of US imperialism in Nicaragua and aware that Reagan was working to crush them, ultimately rejected the American demands, refusing to allow the United States to dictate their foreign policy. They were also aware that if they ceased to assist the FMLN, the Central American revolutionary movement as a whole would be weaker, undermining their own government, and they knew that without Cuban and Soviet arms, they had no hope of defending themselves.

Not long after Reagan's inauguration, on 20 January 1981, the US Central Intelligence Agency (CIA) invited former Somoza loyalists, National Guardsmen, and conservative Nicaraguans in exile in Miami to a meeting in Guatemala. Harvard-educated Edgar Chamorro, a distant relative of the murdered newspaper editor Pedro Joaquín Chamorro and leader of the moderate group, wanted nothing to do with the National Guard, but the CIA made it clear to Chamorro and the moderates that they would have to unite with the former Guard officers and soldiers or they would not receive US assistance.[9] Chamorro knuckled under and the two groups united in a new organisation, the Nicaraguan Democratic Force (FDN), headed by Adolfo Calero Portocarrero. The FDN provided leadership to the Contra movement that for several years would make war on Nicaragua, while Chamorro, who became the FDN's public face, set up headquarters in Tegucigalpa, Honduras. The Reagan administration allocated an initial $19 million to the Contra forces. The CIA began to train troops in Florida and to send them to Honduras for deployment in Nicaragua.

The war could be said to have begun with the bombing of bridges in northern Nicaragua on 15 March 1982. The Reagan administration and the US Congress took the position that the US funds to the Contras would *only* be used to interdict arms shipments to El Salvador. In fact, as everyone was aware, the United States created and financed the Contras with the sole objective of overthrowing the FSLN government in Nicaragua. To show his support for the project, President Reagan stopped in Tegucigalpa, capital of Honduras and the CIA operations centre for the Contras, to express his support for the Contra effort. His Ambassador John Negroponte was put in charge of directing the Contra War.

---

8   LeoGrande 1998, p. 122.
9   LeoGrande 1998, p. 115.

The Problem of the Caribbean Coast and the Miskitos

The Sandinistas had committed two major policy mistakes that contributed to the growth of the Contra forces and undermined their own position. The first, which has already been discussed, was the failure to individually deed over to the peasants the land that had been expropriated from Somoza, his cronies, or other capitalists. Disappointed with and angered by the FSLN, significant numbers of peasants began to go over to the Contras. Some had more complicated motives. Many of those who first founded the Popular Anti-Sandinista Militia (or MILPA, the acronym forms the word meaning cornfield in Spanish) were somewhat better-off farmers who earlier had fought in the FSLN Northern Front against Somoza. But when the FSLN came to power, they felt threatened by the expropriations, by government regulation of the economy, and by the mobilisation of the poor, all of which put in jeopardy their own economic situation, their social status, and their aspirations. They also resented that they were passed over for government posts in the region filled by FSLN members form the cities.[10] Other peasants in other regions of the country, mostly because the government would not give them deeds to their property, also joined the Contras, and most of these local anti-Sandinista militias became part of the Contras. The implications of this for the FSLN were terrible, since not only did the Contras have a significant and growing number of troops, but they also could claim to be the voice of the Nicaraguan people and of its poorest people, the peasantry.

The second issue that undermined the Sandinistas was their handling of what is called the Atlantic or Caribbean region of eastern Nicaragua, and particularly the way they dealt with the indigenous Miskito people and other Amerindian groups.[11] The Nicaraguan Caribbean coast had a history quite distinct from that of Pacific Nicaragua. While Pacific Nicaragua had been conquered by the Spanish, Caribbean Nicaragua had been allied since the eighteenth century with the British and the region was later strongly influenced by the United States. Pacific Nicaragua resembled most of Latin America, being mostly Spanish-speaking and Roman Catholic, while Caribbean Nicaragua was English-speaking and Protestant, principally Moravian. It had more in common culturally and linguistically with Jamaica than it did with the rest of Nicaragua.

---

10   Horton 1998, pp. 95–124.
11   While often referred to as the Atlantic, it is actually the Caribbean region. In their own
      language, the largest Atlantic indigenous group uses the name Miskitu, though Miskito is
      more common.

Those in the Pacific region believed that Nicaragua was a mestizo (Spanish-Indian) nation, denying the profound African racial component and cultural influence throughout the country.[12] For the Pacific Coast Nicaraguans, the notion of *mestizaje* meant not just the mixture of the Spanish and Indian races, but also their total annihilation in the historic crucible that produced the new *mestizo* race, a new ethnicity that the Pacific region folk believed formed the social and cultural basis of all of Nicaragua. Clearly such a racial ideology could hold no attraction for the people of the Atlantic coast, which was largely made up of indigenous people, Creole blacks, and Garifunas (mostly migrants of African descent from Honduras), all proud of their ethnic and cultural heritages. Except for Mosquitia, the largely indigenous Atlantic Coast region that overlapped Honduras and Nicaragua, Atlantic Nicaragua more closely resembled the British Caribbean islands with their large Afro-Caribbean populations than it did Latin America.

The Atlantic region remained throughout its history extremely isolated, with no highway or road that connected it to the Pacific Region, and it remained much less economically developed, except for America-owned industrial enclaves; in part for those reasons, it was much poorer. The region's isolation meant that the Pacific and Atlantic Nicaraguans had little direct experience with each other. The Nicaraguans from the Pacific region, by and large, knew little about the history and culture of the Atlantic region. And that was true of the FSLN leadership as well. Yet Pacific region Nicaraguans did often have strong racial and cultural prejudices against both the indigenous and the Creole blacks, believing that they were in general less capable. And because of the Atlantic's Anglo-American history and ties, the Pacific Nicaraguans tended to believe that those groups were not loyal and could not be trusted. There was some element of truth in this, since Atlantic Nicaraguans had favourable attitudes towards the US government and the American companies operating in their region. At the same time, the Atlantic peoples feared the Spanish-speaking Pacific Nicaraguans who for centuries had attempted to conquer them; in fact, this was what had originally led the indigenous people in the region to ally themselves with the British in the seventeenth century. There was a mutual cultural antipathy between Pacific and Atlantic Nicaraguans that made each group fear and mistrust the other, a wariness most justified on the side of the Atlantic Nicaraguans who had been the victims of several invasions and eventually of forced incorporation into Nicaragua.

---

12   Ramírez 2007, *passim*. The subject of this book is the forgotten, suppressed, and denied history of African peoples in Nicaragua.

The problems, however, did not stop there. As Marxist-Leninists, the FSLN believed that a socialist revolution and economic development would over-come the backwardness of the Atlantic region and lead to its full integration into Nicaragua as a whole. Many of the FSLN leaders believed that the advance of socialism would tend to make ethnicity and culture irrelevant. Even the best-intentioned Sandinista leaders tended to see Indian history as ultimately flowing forward, dissolving into the mainstream of mestizo Nicaragua, and disappearing. Jaime Wheelock, in his book *Raíces indígenas de la lucha anti-colonialista en Nicaragua* (Indigenous Root of the Anti-Colonial Struggle in Nicaragua), offered a variation on that idea. He praised the indigenous peoples in all regions of Nicaragua for their courage in the fight against the Spanish and later the *criollo* conquerors, but saw that the loss of their communal lands and then later the loss of their small farms and plots had brought them into the common popular classes, transforming them into wage workers. For Whee-lock, the destruction of the Indians as a people was their good fortune because they became part of the proletariat, the chosen agent of historical change in the modern era.[13]

Despite these latent ideological and political differences, many Atlantic peoples initially sympathised with the revolution. Two Miskitos who were studying together at the National University in Managua at the time of the insurrection, Steadman Fagoth Müller (who went by Fagoth) and Brooklyn Rivera, had taken over the pro-Somoza indigenous organisation ALPROMISU. They changed its name to MISURASATA, an acronym made up of the three tribal names, Miskito, Sumo, Rama, and the word Sandinista. Sympathising with the goals of the revolution, a MISURASATA platoon supported the Sandinista mil-itary organisation and supported the literacy campaign which offered classes in the Atlantic coast languages. MISURASATA was included in the Council of State, though unlike other mass organisations, it was never under the con-trol of the Sandinistas. Attitudes toward the FSLN began to change when por-traits of Lenin and Ho Chi Minh began to go up on public buildings and the Sandinista Defence Committees (CDS) offices and homes and leaders started using Marxist-Leninist rhetoric. The Caribbean coast residents, who had ten-ded to be more conservative and pro-American to begin with, began to turn away from the revolution.

Oblivious to the concerns of the peoples of the Caribbean region and com-pletely obtuse when it came to the indigenous people, the FSLN made a series of grave errors that drove thousands of Miskitos into the opposition, mistakes that were then capitalised on by the CIA working with conservative organisations

---

13   Wheelock 1980, *passim*; Hale 1994, pp. 87–90.

and religious leaders in the area. First, the FSLN initially assigned Spanish-speaking mestizos to fill many party and government posts in the Caribbean region. Second, the FSLN sent troops – by 1981, some 7,000 of them – from Pacific Nicaragua into the Caribbean region, leading residents of the region to feel that they were under military occupation. Third, the FSLN assigned Cuban teachers and health workers to the area, that is, the Sandinistas placed among the Caribbean Coast peoples Communist foreigners who were mistrusted and disliked because of their ideology, culture, and language. Fourth, the FSLN discussed land distribution to peasants in the area, but in terms that were completely alien to slash-and-burn agriculturalists who already believed themselves to be the historic owners of all of the land and who felt they needed no title from the government. Finally, the FSLN acceded to the demands by indigenous organisations for autonomy, in terms of language, and did make some concessions in terms of political power sharing, but not in terms of control of the territory or its resources.[14]

The FSLN, anxious to secure the area politically and militarily, made a series of clumsy and costly mistakes leading to repression and violence. The arrest in September 1979 of some thirty Miskito young men in Puerto Cabezas (also known as Bilwi) who were accused of anti-government activities led to the first anti-government protests. A year later, in September 1980 in Bluefields, there was a demonstration by local Afro-Nicaraguans against the presence of hundreds of Cuban teachers and healthcare workers. The protestors tore down Cuban flags and stole guns, leading the government to call for dialogue, but when a delegation arrived to talk to the authorities, they were beaten and arrested by national security police. There were similar protests against and boycotts of Cuban-run facilities by the Miskitos. Then, in January of 1981, Sandinista troops shot and killed a 19-year old Miskito man in the Puerto Cabezas town park, leading to a public parading of the body and militant demonstrations. The turning point came in February of 1981. First, Fagoth and MISURASATA broke with the Sandinistas and left the Council of State, leading to his arrest in mid-February. Then a few days later in the town of Prinzapolka, just south of Puerto Cabezas, Sandinista troops attempting to arrest another MISURASATA leader, Elmer Prado, entered a Moravian church where in a confrontation four Miskitos and four soldiers were killed. At that point the Sandinistas and the Misktos were effectively at war.

The Sandinistas began breaking up MISURASATA offices and arresting young men they believed to be associated with the organisation. The Miskitos repor-

---

14   Dunbar-Ortiz 2005, pp. 94–7.

ted that Sandinistas were executing many held in custody. At the same time, perhaps as many as 3,000 Miskitos fled to Honduras. Fagoth was released but went to Honduras where he and several thousand young men joined the National Guardsmen there who formed part of what would become the Contra forces. By 1982, the Contra forces in Honduras, largely made up of Miskito fighters, were receiving training and support from the CIA and Argentina. The Sandinistas responded to the situation by three large forced relocations, one in January 1982 involving 8,500 Miskitos, another later in 1982 involving about 7,000 Miskitos and Sumos, and a third in October 1983 of about 5,000 Miskitos. The Sandinistas argued that they were carrying out these relocations in order to protect the indigenous people from harm as a result of Contra incursions and the Contra-Sandinista conflict. Yet it was also clear that they were attempting to keep the Miskito communities from becoming Contra bases within Nicaragua. Still the indigenous people kept flowing out of the country, mostly to Honduras but in some cases to Costa Rica as well. Eventually, as many as 25,000 indigenous people were in exile, most living in the Honduran Misquitia.[15] As Sergio Ramírez later wrote: 'This represented one of the most tragic errors of the revolution …'.[16]

Jeanne Kirkpatrick, Ronald Reagan's foreign policy advisor, member of the US National Security Council and fervent anti-Communist, worked closely with Fagoth who had become a Contra leader. As the exiles and refugees came across the border into Honduras, the Contras recruited the young Miskitos to their military units. On the ground in Nicaragua and Honduras, the CIA, conservative American organisations, and some Protestant churches joined in a propaganda campaign among the Miskitos intended to make them even more fanatical in their opposition to the Sandinistas. In these campaigns, CIA agents and other Americans described the Sandinistas as Russian, Soviet, or Cuban Communists and atheists who would take the indigenous peoples' lands and destroy their families and culture. Indigenous people reported that they had been told that the Sandinistas would skin them and make shoes out of their skin and make soap out of their babies, and investigators reported that some believed the stories.[17] By late 1982, the Miskitos had become an integral part of the larger Contra War against the Sandinistas.

The Sandinistas moved quickly to rectify the situation, establishing dialogue with the Miskitos and other indigenous peoples remaining in Nicaragua, as well

---

15   Christian 1986, pp. 295–309; Hale 1994, pp. 145–9, which deals with one Miskito community in Sandy Bay, a microcosm of the general situation.
16   Ramírez 1999, p. 148.
17   Hale 1994, p. 151.

as with Creole blacks and Garifunas of the Atlantic region. Through a combination of diplomatic and military measures, they succeeded in keeping the Atlantic region, including Nicaraguan Mosquitia, under their control. In 1985, they adopted an autonomy law which, while failing to meet all the demands of the Miskitos and other local peoples, was accompanied by a new policy of accepting ethnically based political power that went further in establishing what became peaceful and cooperative relations between the FSLN central government and the Atlantic region. Meanwhile, between late 1981 and 1985, thousands of Miskitos had joined the Contras in their war on the Sandinista government.[18]

The United States on one side and the Soviet Union, the Eastern Communist Bloc, and Cuba on the other were financing and supplying opposite sides in Nicaragua, but this was not simply a proxy war; it had become a genuine civil war. At the same time, the Contra War was *not* a war of rich against poor, of capitalists against workers and peasants, but, as Ramírez wrote, financed from outside, 'it ripped from top to bottom, like a knife stuck in the country's guts, cutting through all social classes and dividing them'.[19] There were rich and poor on both sides. Or as former *New York Times* reporter Steven Kinzer wrote: 'Nicaragua, with eager help from outside powers, was tearing itself apart'.[20]

As in many wars, the first victim was domestic liberty. In response to the Contra War, the Sandinistas declared a state of emergency in 1982, abrogating many of the rights that the people had fought for and won when they overthrew Somoza. War and the necessity of winning the war led the Sandinista government to assume emergency powers and to take actions that it deemed necessary even when they encroached on hard-won freedoms. With the country under siege, meetings of citizens, the distribution of literature critical of the government, workers' strikes and peasant protests all became threats to order, to production and to the winning of the war. The war strengthened the National Directorate's military-style control over the FSLN and the FSLN's control over society, though the rebellious attitudes of peasants, the indigenous, and some workers frequently made it difficult for the Sandinistas to maintain that control.

---

18   Hale 1994, pp. 112–14. The text of the Autonomy Law can be found in Hale 1994, Appendix C, pp. 231–9.
19   Ramírez 1999, p. 140.
20   Kinzer 2007, p. 342.

The Contra Offensive

The US-backed Contra War was an international effort. The American, Honduran, and Argentine governments cooperated in financing, organising, and arming the Contras. The CIA delivered the arms, the Honduran government provided facilities, and the Argentine military dictatorship sent officers who provided military training.[21] The Contra War eventually took place in a military theatre that extended over 47 percent of the national territory of Nicaragua, principally near the Honduran border and in those areas where the Nicaraguan state had always been weakest, such as the Caribbean Coast.[22]

The Contra's strategy was to dispatch troops from their bases in Honduras, making attacks not principally on military installations, but on Sandinista government programmes such as cooperatives, health clinics and schools. A number of doctors and teachers lost their lives in such attacks.[23] The strategy therefore tended to take the lives of non-military personnel and non-combatants, mostly killing civilians, and not only young men and women, who were particularly targeted, but also sometimes the elderly and children. The Contra campaign was intended to weaken Sandinista institutions and to demoralise the population with the goal of undermining support for the Sandinista government.[24]

The US government also pressured Costa Rican President Luis Alberto Monge into allowing the CIA to set up a base in that country near the Nicaraguan border. The CIA began flying in supplies to the base from which it planned to launch a 'Southern Front'. At the same time, the CIA carried out economic sabotage directed at 'oil storage tanks and pipelines, port facilities, communication centres and military depots, causing hundreds of millions of dollars in damages. As a propaganda ploy, the Contras claimed credit for these attacks; in reality they played no part'.[25]

Nicaragua stood at the centre of Ronald Reagan's broader war against the left throughout Central America and the Caribbean. Throughout this period

---

21   Calero Portocarrero 2010, p. 81.

22   Pérez-Baltodano 2008, p. 660.

23   Slater 1989, pp. 646–51. He mentions the Contra attacks on health facilities, doctors and other health workers. Many other reports on Nicaraguan health at that time also mention the Contra attacks on health workers.

24   Calero Portocarrero 2010 insists that the Contras 'gave orders to respect the civilian population', but virtually all accounts suggest that in fact the Contras actually targeted civilian populations.

25   'Intervention and Exploitation' 1945.

Reagan also provided assistance to the military governments in Guatemala and the right-wing government in El Salvador in their struggles against the left-wing guerrilla organisations in those countries. Then on 31 October 1983, Reagan ordered US Marines to invade the tiny Island of Grenada to overthrow the left-wing government of Maurice Bishop. All of this was intended to help tighten the noose around Nicaragua.

The Contra War sorely tested the FSLN government and the Sandinista Popular Army. Believing that they needed to strengthen their forces, in 1983 the Sandinista government made one of its most important and ultimately disastrous decisions, adopting a policy of military conscription called Patriotic Military Service. All males between the ages of 17 and 26 were required to perform two years of military service. While on the one hand this policy provided more troops, on the other hand it was bitterly resented by much of the population. Many young men evaded the draft, some fleeing to Honduras or Costa Rica to escape it. Conscription would be one of the important reasons that the Nicaraguan people deserted the FSLN in the 1990 election.

The reality of the US threat to the Sandinista government was accentuated by the American invasion of the tiny island of Grenada in 1983. Formerly a French and then a British colony, Grenada only became independent in 1950 under the leadership of Sir Eric Gairy. The New Jewel Party led by Maurice Bishop overthrew the elected government of Gairy in 1979 and established the People's Revolutionary Government. Bishop's government, clearly influenced by Cuba, established a one-party revolutionary government that worked to improve health, education, and the general welfare of the island's working people. However, much like Cuba it held no elections, permitted no opposition parties, and created labour and women's organisations subordinated to the government.[26]

With a total area of 133 square miles and a population of about 100,000, the little island of Grenada in itself represented no threat to the US government, but Reagan and his team feared that Cuba, Nicaragua, and Grenada were creating a new and dangerous trend in the Caribbean and Central America. The Marxist-Leninist politics of Bishop's New Jewel Party government provided the pretext for the American invasion. The Reagan administration was from the beginning also hostile to the presence of heavily armed Cuban troops on the island, as well as advisers from the Soviet Union, East Germany, Bulgaria and North Korea, and

26   Payne, Sutton and Thorndike 1984 gives a sympathetic account of Bishop, the New Jewel
     Movement, and the People's Revolutionary Government. A conservative and critical view
     is provided by Sandford 1984. Searle 1983 represents more or less the view of the Bishop
     government itself.

claimed to have discovered large arms caches. President Reagan told the media that Grenada had become 'a Soviet-Cuban colony being readied as a major military bastion'.[27] Reagan, anxious to show that the US defeat in Vietnam would not inhibit the United States from engaging in military action against its Communist and other enemies, decided to make an example of Grenada.

Bishop was overthrown by an internal military coup on 15 October 1983, arrested, and executed by the officers who had seized power. The Organisation of Eastern Caribbean States (OECS), Barbados, and Jamaica appealed for US intervention. The US justified its invasion by arguing that the Bishop government had allied itself with Cuba and the Soviet Union, and asserted that recent improvements in the Grenada airport were intended not to facilitate tourism but to serve Cuban and Soviet military aircraft. The Reagan administration also claimed that it was rescuing American students studying at St. George's University Medical School. Despite objections from Prime Minister Margaret Thatcher's government and from the British Commonwealth, on 25 October, 8,000 US troops and 350 troops from Barbados and other Caribbean islands invaded Grenada and swept away the military government. The US supported an interim government until elections could be held and those elections brought to power a new government allied with the United States.

No strangers to US invasions and occupations, the US invasion of Grenada put the Sandinista government on alert and frightened the Nicaraguan people. The Sandinistas, already at war with the Contras, felt even more besieged and beleaguered. The FSLN now feared for its survival.

The Nicaraguan Election of 1984

Reagan's principal charge against the Sandinistas was that they were establishing a Communist government in Central America, and that, like Fidel Castro's Communist government in Cuba, the FSLN government had never held elections and never allowed the people of Nicaragua to choose their own leaders. Faced with this criticism of their government, not only from Reagan but also from their domestic critics, American liberals, and European and Latin American social democrats, the Sandinistas decided to create a government along more liberal-democratic lines. Already in 1982 the Sandinistas had passed a Law of Political Parties that conceded the right of other political parties to contest for political power and through elections to remove the FSLN and replace it

---

27   Gwertzman 1983.

with another political party. Sure that they had massive political support from the majority of the population and above all from the peasants and workers, the Sandinistas decided to hold elections in 1984 for president and vice-president and for a congress made up of elected representatives of political parties. This would be the first elected leadership since the triumph of the revolution five years before and it opened the first major public, society-wide debate over the revolution's success or failure.

Archbishop Miguel Obando y Bravo, a very popular figure in a country that was 95 percent Catholic, played the leading role as spokesperson for the anti-Sandinista forces throughout the entire election period, mobilising the Church as an organisation to oppose the Sandinistas. He received economic assistance from USAID and secret funds from the CIA and other foreign sources to help finance the Church's anti-government activities. Obando attacked the Sandinistas for suppressing political liberties and for challenging the church's authority as well as for drafting the country's youth to fight the Contras. On the other hand, he never criticised the Contras, despite emerging reports of their many atrocities, including the murder of health workers and schoolteachers.[28] His attitude exacerbated the division among Nicaraguan Catholics between those loyal to the institutional Church and those who supported what they called the 'popular church' and backed the Sandinistas.[29]

The split in the Church had come into the open in March of 1983 when Pope John Paul II, a staunch anti-Communist, visited Nicaragua, clearly giving support to Obando and the anti-Sandinista opposition. The Christian Base Communities of the popular church prepared for the Pope's visit with the slogans: 'Welcome to free Nicaragua, thanks to God and the Revolution' and 'Between Christianity and Revolution, there is no contradiction'.[30] The Pope responded by condemning the popular church as 'absurd and dangerous' and demanding obedience to the bishops. The differences became public when during the Pope's open air mass members of the popular church shouted slogans such as 'Popular Power!' and 'We Want Peace!' and, though the Pope called for 'Silence!', the mostly poor congregations continued their chants. The public confrontation with the Pope proved a public relations disaster and political problem for the Sandinistas. The Pope elevated Obando to the rank of Cardinal in 1985.[31] Archbishop Obando led the right in its attack on the

---

28   LeoGrande 1998, pp. 413–17.
29   LeoGrande 1998, p. 368.
30   Envío Team 1983a.
31   LeoGrande 1998, p. 369.

Sandinistas, raising the dominant themes of the campaign: the lack of political freedom, the decline of the economy, and the draft.

The FSLN National Directorate chose Daniel Ortega, who already functioned as its informal leader, to be the party's candidate, a choice that increased his stature in the party and in society enormously. Ortega, who would become the dominant figure in the FSLN for the next thirty years, had been born on 11 November 1945 to a working-class family in La Libertad, a town in the Chontales province in central Nicaragua. His parents Daniel and Lidia Ortega were opponents of Somoza and his mother had been jailed for political activity. Daniel Ortega, the son, became involved in politics as a youth, was first jailed at the age of 15, and joined the Sandinistas shortly after its founding in 1962.

In 1967, Ortega was arrested for his role in an armed robbery at the Bank of America and imprisoned until 1974. When the Sandinistas raided the house of Chema Castillo in December of that year and captured many high level government officials and Somoza relatives, they exchanged their hostages for fourteen imprisoned Sandinistas, among whom was Daniel Ortega. Free from prison, Ortega went to Cuba for military training and then secretly returned to Nicaragua and to clandestine military work. Later, based in Costa Rica, he helped design the Third Tendency's strategy of alliances with other social classes and organisations. After the Triumph, he became coordinator of the Junta de Gobierno and then of the FSLN Directorate. Always ambitious, in seeking to be his party's nominee Ortega pushed aside other possible FLSN candidates for president. As his running mate he and the FSLN leadership chose Sergio Ramírez, the writer and intellectual, who had also served in the Junta de Gobierno.[32]

The domestic civic opposition to the Sandinistas, as opposed to the armed Contras, was deeply divided between ten different political parties, none of which had much of an organisation on the ground. Aware that they could not effectively challenge the Sandinistas in an election, some groups in the civic opposition preferred not to participate in an election at all, fearing that doing so would legitimate the government they opposed. Reagan's administration, itself initially somewhat divided on the question, decided to urge the opposition to unite and fight for the best election conditions possible.

The opposition came together under the banner of the National Opposition Union (UNO, which in Spanish means 'one') and put forward as its presidential candidate the US State Department's choice, Arturo Cruz, who had revolution-

---

32   Barcelona Centre for International Affairs 2011a.

ary credentials, having been one of Los Doce (he had replaced Alfonso Robelo when Robelo resigned from the Junta de Gobierno).[33] The Reagan administration liked Cruz in part because he was popular with foreign government and especially with liberals and social democrats in Latin America, Europe, and the United States.[34] Later the *Wall Street Journal* revealed that Cruz had been on the payroll of the CIA; he received $6,000 a month, as he himself later admitted.[35] Cruz initially faced constant harassment and sometimes violence at the hands of FSLN militants, though in the end the Sandinistas restrained their overzealous supporters and allowed him to campaign. The United States, however, since it was clear that Cruz could not win, convinced him that he should withdraw from the campaign, in order to delegitimise the election. Cruz did so and consequently there was no credible and popular opposition candidate. On election day, 75 percent of eligible voters went to the polls and Ortega won 67 percent of the votes, the rest being divided among six minor party candidates. The FSLN also won 61 of the 96 seats in the National Assembly. Ironically, since Cruz, the UNO candidate had withdrawn, the United States argued that the elections were not free and fair and continued to condemn the FSLN as a Communist government.[36]

The 1984 elections gave revolutionary Nicaragua its second governmental structure since 1979, while the Junta and the Council of State were dismantled, making way for an elected president and National Assembly. These governmental changes were later made into the law of the land in the Constitution of 1987 which established a democratic government, though with a typically Latin American presidentialist character. Under the 1987 Constitution, the president's powers were virtually unlimited: he had the right to impose taxes, to control the federal budget, and to spend public money as he saw fit. He could also by decree create new laws about anything he wished. The new constitution created the National Assembly, which meant an end to the Council of State and a reduction in the political power of the Sandinistas' mass organisations. The Constitution 'was second to none on the rights of women, native peoples, and prisoners'. Yet, because the FSLN had continuously controlled the state institutions and the mass organisations, because it had won the presidential election and a majority of the congress, and because of the wartime emergency powers that the government had declared in 1982, under this new structure

---

33   LeoGrande 1998, p. 371.
34   LeoGrande 1998, p. 372.
35   Andrew W. Reding, 'The Evolution of Governmental Institutions', in Walker (ed.) 1991, p. 27.
36   LeoGrande 1998, p. 375.

the Sandinistas had more power than ever. While now a nominally democratic state, Nicaragua still retained many of the characteristics of a one-party state.[37]

The Rise of the US Central American Peace Movement ...

During the early 1980s, Americans began to organise a movement in opposition to the Reagan administration's policies in Central America and in particular against the Contra War in Nicaragua. Providing the political weight and economic support for the movement were some 28 religious denominations that had joined together in the Inter-Religious Task Force on Latin America, including almost all the major denominations – Baptists, Catholics, Friends (Quakers), Methodists, Presbyterians, and United Church of Christ – which opposed aid to the Contras. Similar coalitions formed among liberal rights groups, such as the American Civil Liberties Union and Common Cause, and even a few of the more liberal labour unions.[38] Liberal Democrats generally tended to be critical of the war, with their representatives in Congress sometimes lagging behind popular opposition.

Many of the religious activists were inspired by their faith's religious teaching, whether Catholic, Protestant, or Jewish. Decades of missionary work had given many of these groups a personal connection to and psychological investment in Central America.[39] Many Catholics in the United States had also been inspired by the Theology of Liberation that motivated Central Americans in their revolutionary movements.[40] The assassination in 1980 of the Archbishop of San Salvador, Oscar Romero, while giving mass in his church, followed by the rape and murder of three nuns and a lay missionary in the same country that same year, was a compelling motivation for Catholics to become involved and especially for the activism of religious women.[41]

The US Central American Peace movement's main organisations were Sanctuary, Witness for Peace, and the Pledge of Resistance which together mobilised tens of thousands of Americans in anti-intervention activities.[42] At the grassroots these organisations were built on local chapters and affinity groups in

---

37   Reding, 'The Evolution of Governmental Institutions', in Walker (ed.) 1991, p. 31.
38   LeoGrande 1998, p. 420.
39   Smith 1996, pp. 141–3.
40   Smith 1996, pp. 145–58.
41   Smith 1996, pp. 148–9.
42   Smith 1996, p. 60.

scores of communities throughout the United States.[43] Following the pattern set during the anti-Vietnam War movement, the Central American peace movement pressured Congressional representatives, working with liberals on a few of the key committees.[44]

Some religious and secular activists were involved in the sanctuary movement, moving immigrant victims of the Central American Wars, some of them revolutionaries, into the United States without inspection at the border, through what they themselves described as a kind of underground railroad. The religious and secular activists transported these immigrants to cities throughout the United States, providing them shelter, clothing, and food until they could establish themselves and then often working to help them fight for asylum status. Some of the American activists involved in these activities were arrested, tried, convicted, and spent time in prison for their activities.[45]

In addition to these religious anti-war organisations, there were also secular groups which were not so much anti-war as supporters of the Central American revolutionary movement. The Committee in Solidarity with the People of El Salvador (CISPES), for example, founded in 1980, functioned as an arm of the Farabundo Martí National Liberation Front. The small but quite active American far left of Communists, Maoists, and Trotskyists, most of which supported the Sandinistas and the FMLN, even if critically, were also active in the anti-Contra War movement. All of these groups from the churches to the political support groups of the far left organised protest demonstrations, symbolic actions, civil disobedience, and engaged in lobbying. While the movement was significant, it was swimming against the stream of conservative American politics in the Reagan era and had difficulty impacting on US government policy.

... and Yet More War

While the anti-Contra War movement was growing, Reagan remained extremely popular, more so than ever before following the attempt on his life on 30 March 1981. Re-elected in 1984 in a landslide victory, Ronald Reagan was determined to continue aiding the Contras in overthrowing the Sandinista government in Nicaragua. The United States continued to fund the Contras at the rate of approximately $20 million per year until 1985 when reports of the US mining of Nicaraguan ports began to turn the American public and the

---

43   Smith 1996, p. 125.
44   Smith 1996, p. 99.
45   Smith 1996, pp. 60–70.

Congress against the war. In the fall of 1985, Congress passed a budget allocating $100 million to the Contras. But by the mid-1980s, the tide was beginning to turn against the President and the Contras. In 1985, the US House of Representatives passed the third Boland amendment, named after its author, Democrat Edward P. Boland of Massachusetts, which cut off all US government aid to the Contras, whether from the State Department, the CIA, or any other agency. That should have ended US funding to the Contras and led to their rapid collapse.

Reagan and his executive staff, however, were determined to find a way to continue to finance the Contras, and they had a number of creative ideas, many of them illegal, seeking as they did to circumvent Congress. He and others in his administration raised some money directly from American private citizens. Reagan personally met with King Fahd of Saudi Arabia in 1984 to arrange a $1 million per year contribution, and again in February 1985 when the contribution was increased to $24 million per year.[46] The Israelis also contributed $10 million in military equipment.[47] Reagan succeeded in getting the Taiwanese government to pressure businessmen to contribute $2 million to help the Contras.[48] Finally, Col. Oliver North arranged for the sale of weapons through Israeli brokers to the Islamic government of Ayatollah Khomeini in Iran, the proceeds of which were then passed on to finance the Contras. In this way, some $3.8 million was raised.[49] The Iran-Contra affair, as it came to be known, was clearly in violation of the US Constitution, bypassing as it did the US Congress which is the only American government body with the power to declare war and to allocate funds.

The story began to come to light when, on 5 October 1986, shortly after Congress voted for the $100 million to the Contra War, a Sandinista soldier firing a Soviet anti-aircraft weapon brought down in Nicaragua a C-123 cargo plane named 'The Fat Lady'. The plane was carrying 10,000 pounds of arms and ammunition to the Contras. Crew member Eugene Hasenfus, a former US Marine employed by the CIA's Air America Company, candidly explained that he had been transporting arms to the Contras. In the plane, the Sandinistas found many documents that revealed a secret supply operation and Hasenfus's wallet contained phone numbers linking him to Col. Oliver North of the US National Security Council staff. Shortly thereafter, on 25 November 1986, Attorney General Edwin Meese revealed that profits from the sale of weapons to Iran had been used to finance the Contras. Yet, even after these revelations, CIA pilots

---

46   Woodward 1987, p. 1.
47   LeoGrande 1998, p. 387.
48   Associated Press 1987.
49   LeoGrande 1998, pp. 407–8.

still made over 300 supply missions over Nicaragua following the Hasenfus crash, delivering tons of arms that made it possible for the Contras to continue and even intensify the war throughout the rest of 1986 and into 1987.[50]

The Sandinistas Change their Economic Policy

Ronald Reagan, while still continuing to try to find ways to fund the Contras, turned to other means to crush the Sandinistas, initiating an economic embargo in 1985. In part as a result of the embargo, the Nicaraguan economy shrank 14 percent between 1981 and 1990, the worst performance in Latin America. Threatened with a declining economy, in February of 1985 the Sandinista government adopted its first economic plan to deal with the crisis by imposing austerity. Later, in February of 1988, an even more stringent programme, the Stabilisation and Adjustment Programme, was adopted in an attempt to gain control over what was by then a crumbling economy. The plan was similar to the structural adjustments being imposed by the International Monetary Fund around the world, consisting of a neoliberal model of open markets, free trade, cuts in social spending, and a clamping down on labour unions.

The FSLN plan was intended to re-establish state control over the economy, reduce inflation, rationalise prices, increase efficiency, promote exports, and thus in the end to revive the purchasing power of the working class.[51] What this meant in practice was a dramatic devaluation of the currency by over 3,000 percent, deep cuts in government subsidies to transportation and food, and a severe cutback in social services accompanied by massive layoffs of public employees. Though workers received a 400 percent wage increase, this was possible only because of the currency devaluation that entirely negated it. By the end of 1989, per capita income had been reduced by half from what it had been in 1970.[52]

As many men volunteered or were drafted to fight the war, women's participation in the labour force grew proportionally, resulting in a 'feminisation of the labour force both in industry and in agricultural work'. While women worked in factories, services, and in the fields, they held few management positions. At home they continued to be responsible for domestic labour and childcare. Employers discriminated against pregnant working women and few women

---

50   Kinzer 2007, p. 341; LeoGrande 1998, pp. 476–80.
51   Pérez-Baltodano 2009, p. 649.
52   Close 2005, pp. 195–8, provides a useful summary of Sandinista economic policy between 1984 and 1989.

with children had access to childcare centres. Women came to make up 40 percent of the Agricultural Workers Union (ATC) and made their voices heard there and through the National Union of Domestic Workers made strides towards the ten-hour day. Yet, with the general deterioration of the economic situation, women too suffered lay-offs and a decline in their incomes and standards of living.[53]

While cutting subsidies for food and fuel for workers, the Sandinistas offered economic incentives and subsidies to business: a reduction of import taxes and port charges; lower taxes (by 50 percent) for employers who improved workers' living conditions; an extended grace period on tax payments for coffee producers and cattle ranchers; price incentives for coffee producers whose production increased by 25 percent; reduced long-term interest rates for cattle producers; and forgiveness of 50 percent of unpaid loans for producers of rice, sorghum, basic grains, sesame, and produce, as well as a special subsidy for cotton producers. These gifts to capital were accompanied by a 'renewed affirmation of established property rights'.[54]

The government dictated these ukases without a democratic consultation with the mass organisations or the public in general. The working class and peasantry did not universally accept these measures without complaint. When a construction workers' union went on strike against the FSLN wage freeze, accompanied by a hunger strike as well, the Sandinista Police surrounded their offices, cutting off lights and water, and starved them out. Though the government continued to provide the population with a basic food package of rice, beans and sugar, the stabilisation measures were a severe blow to the peasantry, to working-class families and particularly to the women who so often sustained them.[55] While the measures did help to end the economic chaos and inflation, they did not lead to a significant revival of the economy. With the Contra War continuing, there was no economic policy decision that on its own could solve the country's problems.

Peace Negotiations and Treaty

The Sandinistas had been looking for a political solution to the Contra War at least since 1983, when Daniel Ortega succeeded in convincing the govern-

---

53   Patricia M. Church, 'Women in the Revolution', in Walker (ed.) 1991, pp. 143–66. Quotation from p. 148.
54   Spaulding 1994, p. 111.
55   Babb 2012, p. 159; Envío Team 1988b.

ments of Mexico, Panama, Venezuela and Colombia to create the Contadora Group which he hoped would facilitate negotiations leading to a peace agreement. While the Contadora Group remained part of the background for several years, it failed to bring about any negotiations. Spanish Prime Minister Felipe González and other European leaders, as well as the secretaries-general of the Organisation of American States and the United Nations, also attempted to bring the warring parties to the peace table, but without success.

The principal problem facing any negotiated peace settlement was the Sandinistas' refusal to deal with the Contras who, they argued, were a creature of the United States, no more than American mercenaries. The Sandinistas demanded to negotiate directly with the United States government. As Sandinista spokesman Bayardo Arce frequently said: 'We want to negotiate with the owner of the circus, not with the clowns'.[56] The United States refused to deal with the FSLN, declaring that it was not their war and insisting that the Sandinistas negotiate with the Contras. Events in late 1986 and 1987, however, changed the situation. First came the Iran-Contra Affair which undermined the Reagan administration's credibility, followed by the midterm elections of November 1986 that gave the Democrats control of the Senate and a stronger grip on the House, and then the death of CIA Director William Casey from a brain tumour in May 1987. These events, which significantly weakened the position of the Reagan administration, were seized upon by the newly elected president of Costa Rica, Oscar Arias, as an opportunity to make peace.

Arias broke with the policies of his predecessor Luis Alberto Monge who had secretly aided the Contras, refusing to support the CIA or to permit the Contras to operate from Costa Rica. Despite strong pressure from the White House, Arias had the police arrest Contras living in Costa Rica and shut down the Contra airbase, ending the CIA's plans for a 'southern front' in the war. Having established Costa Rica's political independence from the United States, in February of 1987 Arias then invited the presidents of Guatemala, Honduras and El Salvador to San José, Costa Rica, for a regional summit meeting. There he proposed a new framework for ending the war, a regional peace for *all* of Central America – recall that guerrilla wars were going on in Guatemala and El Salvador as well as Nicaragua – based on the negotiation of a ceasefire, amnesty for all political prisoners, and free elections. His plan also called upon foreign powers to end arms shipments to all 'irregular forces', that is, it would end CIA support for the Contras as well as Cuban aid to Nicaragua and other Central American revolutionary groups. All four presidents accepted the proposal which Arias

---

56   Kinzer 2007, p. 342.

then took to European leaders and to the Democrats in the US Congress seek-ing support. Under his compelling argument that he was proposing peace and democracy, the US Senate voted support for his plan by 97–1. A second Cent-ral American summit held on 24–5 May at Esquipulas, Guatemala, was joined by Daniel Ortega, a signal development. Even though the five nations accom-plished little more than a pro forma statement in favour of democracy and human rights, that was an important step, made more important by the fact that they agreed to continue meeting.

When Arias made an unofficial visit to the United States shortly afterwards, Ronald Reagan summoned him to the White House where Arias was con-fronted with Reagan's top national security figures. Reagan told Arias that he was 'undermining US policy toward Nicaragua', but the confrontation, and the threat implicit in any such dressing down from the United States, failed to make Arias change his mind.[57] In an attempt to out-manoeuvre Arias, Reagan hur-riedly put together a peace plan of his own, but this only served to stiffen the resistance of the Central American presidents. Arias continued to move ahead, calling another regional summit, Esquipulas II, on 6 August. To the surprise of nearly all observers, in an extraordinary demonstration of political independ-ence, the five Central American presidents meeting in Guatemala City agreed to a regional peace plan (the Esquipulas II Accord), signed on 7 August 1987. The agreement called for freedom for all political parties, freedom of the press, a pledge to hold regular elections monitored by the OAS and the UN. Most attractive to Ortega and the FSLN was the declaration that 'irregular forces' like the Contras were not legitimate. It also called for an end, by 'regional or extra-regional governments', to the provision of assistance and arms to such 'irregular forces or insurrectional movements'.[58]

What impressed everyone was that Ortega had also agreed to dramatic changes in the internal regime of Nicaragua. Steven Kinzer, the former *New York Times* reporter, makes this observation: 'By accepting these provisions, Daniel Ortega was making astonishing concessions. He was agreeing not only to ease pressure on dissidents, but to reshape the nature of Sandinista rule. The political system outlined in the Guatemala accord was not at all the one that Sandinistas had originally envisioned. It was, in fact, the "bourgeois democracy" that they had scorned for years'.[59] One could argue that bourgeois democracy had already come to Nicaragua with the 1984 elections that involved opposition

---

57   Kinzer 2007, p. 348.
58   Kinzer 2007, p. 350.
59   Ibid.

parties from Conservative to Communist contesting for the presidency and for seats in the National Assembly, though, behind the democratic forms, the Marxist-Leninist FSLN National Directorate remained in power. The new agreement though would be different, committing the FSLN to a full transition to a liberal democracy.

Consequently, when Ortega returned to Nicaragua, he found the National Directorate, dominated by the figure of Tomás Borge, in virtual rebellion against the decision that he had unilaterally made. Faced with the intransigency of the Directorate, Ortega flew to Cuba to seek the backing of Castro. Ortega explained his visit to Cuba, saying he had had to discuss with Castro the withdrawal of Cuban military advisors in Nicaragua, officially 800 of them but possibly as many as 2,000. Castro agreed with him that the war had to be ended and gave his blessing to the agreement. When Ortega returned to Nicaragua with Castro's approval of the treaty, and notice of an end to Cuban military advisors, the Directorate fell in line and the FSLN newspaper *Barricada* declared: 'Sandinista Front Monolithically Supports Accord'.[60] The FSLN members, who had never been consulted, followed the dictates of their leaders. Another missed opportunity for democratic discussion, debate and decision making by the FSLN, the legislature, and the Nicaraguan people.

Ronald Reagan meanwhile refused to accept the Central American governments' agreement. His Secretary of State George Shultz announced that, unrelenting in its anti-communist crusade, the administration was seeking $270 million in new aid for the Contras. The Central American presidents, now operating under the new peace agreement, declared their opposition to such aid, stymying Reagan for the moment. When the Scandinavian Nobel committee awarded its Peace Prize to Arias for the Central American peace agreement, it only confirmed that much of the European elite also opposed Reagan's policy.

The FSLN, to show its commitment to the Esquipulas II regional peace agreement, proclaimed a series of measures to end the wartime repression of the opposition together with the first steps toward the transition to a different political system. First, Ortega announced the formation of a National Reconciliation Commission headed by his political adversary Cardinal Obando y Bravo. Second, the FSLN government permitted the reopening of *La Prensa*, the Conservative opposition press that had been closed for sixteen months, as well as allowing the Catholic radio station to return to the air. The FSLN also declared a unilateral ceasefire in three regions, though everywhere else fighting continued and the Contras even launched a new offensive. Still the FSLN was refusing

---

60   Kinzer 2007, p. 351.

to negotiate directly with the Contras and was continuing to fight on, still for a while advised by the Cubans and largely armed by the Soviet Union, though that aid was about to dry up.

In the Soviet Union, Mikhail Gorbachev had been elected general secretary of the Communist Party of the Soviet Union in 1985, making him the de facto head of state. He soon introduced the reforms known as *perestroika*, that is, the 'restructuring' of the economy to make it more productive, and *glasnost*, meaning 'transparency' but signifying a new political opening offering greater rights to the Russian people. To any observer it was clear that the Soviet Union was undergoing a series of momentous changes, though almost no one foresaw that the Soviet Union would soon break up and the entire Communist Eastern Bloc collapse by 1991. Gorbachev was interested in reducing tensions with the West, in particular the United States, and in ending regional conflicts which drained and distorted the Soviet economy. Still, Gorbachev supported Nicaragua at the time of Daniel Ortega's April 1985 visit and continued to do so with expanded military aid up to 1987.[61] However, when Ortega had visited the Soviet Union in October 1987 and saw what was happening there, he drew the conclusion that the Sandinistas had to move more quickly to reach a negotiated settlement. Revealing the bad news that the Soviets would not continue to arm the FSLN as in the past, he succeeded in convincing the National Directorate to support his latest strategic turn, and on 5 November he announced at a Managua Sandinista rally to surprised supporters that the FSLN would negotiate with the Contras, though only through a mediator.

With Congress continuing to debate the $270 million in funding for the Contras, there was tremendous pressure on the FSLN. The talks between the FSLN and the Contras taking place in the Dominican Republic and mediated by Cardinal Obando broke down in early December, when the Sandinistas refused to include in the agreement a general amnesty, press freedom, and an end to the state of emergency. So once again the five Central American governments met at a summit, this time in Costa Rica. There, Ortega agreed to end the six-year-old state of emergency. At the same time, on 3 February 1988, the House of Representatives rejected any further aid to the Contras, a historic decision that would soon lead to their collapse.

Daniel Ortega, speaking for the FSLN, now changed his position again and agreed to *direct* negotiations with the Contras. The offer was accepted and the two sides met together at the Nicaraguan village of Sapoá on the Costa Rican

61   Paszyn 2000, pp. 56–87.

border on 21–4 March. Adolfo Calero, leader of the Contras, declared that the United States, by cutting off their funds, had dealt the Contras a devastating blow, leaving them no alternative but to negotiate. On 23 March 1988, the two sides announced a ceasefire and read the short Agreement of Sapoá, which 'embodied most of the demands the Contras brought to the bargaining table'.[62] The agreement called for an immediate ceasefire, a general amnesty, full freedom of expression, the right of return of all Nicaraguans with full political rights, and a Truth Commission to be headed by Cardinal Obando.[63] Then, the Contras and the FSLN shocked the two hundred reporters and other onlookers by joining together in the singing of the Nicaraguan National Anthem. Daniel Ortega told the reporters: 'We are after all sons of the same mother, of the same fatherland'. The war was over.[64]

The decision of the US Congress to end its aid to the Contras, and the Soviet Union's suggestion that it would not continue to arm the Sandinistas, represented enormous factors in bringing an end to the conflict which had been so devastating to Nicaragua. The Contra War had had a tremendously destructive and deadly impact on Nicaragua. It took an estimated 30,865 lives, while leaving approximately 30,000 more injured or maimed, and eventually costed $1.9 billion, while the embargo's impact on the financial sector is put at $642 million and in the commercial sector at $459 million.[65] Nicaragua took its case against the United States for deaths and damages incurred during the war to the World Court in the Hague which in 1986 ordered the US government to pay the Sandinistas $17 billion in war reparations, though the American government refused to pay a penny. The US government's combination of the Contra War and the economic embargo of Nicaragua proved quite successful, if not in driving the Sandinistas from power, then in destroying the economy and undermining their popular support.[66]

The Contras were not defeated on the battlefield alone; other circumstances played an important part: the Iran-Contra revelations; the American mid-term elections that gave a majority to the Democrats in the Senate and strengthened their hold on the House; the coincidental illness of CIA Director William Casey, diagnosed with a fatal brain tumour; and finally by Oscar Arias's courageous and creative decision to seek a regional peace agreement. While the agreement failed to bring peace to Guatemala and El Salvador, it did end the war in

---

62   LeoGrande 1998, p. 537.

63   A facsimile of the Sapoá agreement can be found in Calero 2010, pp. 267–70.

64   LeoGrande 1998, pp. 536–7.

65   Pérez-Baltodano 2009, p. 611.

66   Leogrande 1996, pp. 329–48.

Nicaragua. Yet, though the Contras had been militarily defeated, they did not disappear as a political force and would reappear in the 1990s, and take power politically in 1997, ironically in partnership with the FSLN.

The Sandinista Government: What Kind of State?

The Marxist theory of state and revolution – put very simply – holds that a genuine revolution destroys the previously existing state, representing one class, and replaces it with a new state representing another class. The classic example is the Russian Revolution of October 1917 when the Bolsheviks, a working-class party, led mass working-class and peasant organisations to take power, destroying the old Czarist police, army, and government bureaucracy and creating a new state at least initially (1918–27) based on the working class. For nearly a century, this has been the Marxists' classic model of socialist revolution. The fact that the Bolshevik Revolution of 1917 was later overthrown by a counter-revolution led by Joseph Stalin at the head of the party-state bureaucracy in no way alters the fact that initially the revolution itself had been a root-and-branch destruction of the Czarist state followed by the creation of a new (though short-lived) workers' state.[67]

Another genuine revolution, though of a different sort, is the Mexican Revolution. In Mexico between 1910 and 1920, a narrowly-based bourgeois government, the dictatorship of Porfirio Díaz, was overthrown by a broad populist movement of workers and peasants led by a modernising bourgeoisie; again the army and the government bureaucracy were destroyed and replaced, but in this case by a government representing the interests of the capitalist class.[68] The Mexican Revolution has been called a Bonapartist revolution, since neither the capitalist class on the one hand nor the workers and peasants on the other proved strong enough to seize and wield state power. A Mexican general, Álvaro Obregón, resolved the problem by taking power, basing his

---

67   There is an enormous debate about the Russian Revolution of 1917. I subscribe to the notion that it was initially a workers' state which was overturned by a bureaucratic counterrevolution as described and analysed by Trotsky 1937 and Shachtman 1962. Though, as Victor Serge's writings suggest, the workers' state had already degenerated considerably by the early 1920s. Historian Moshe Lewin's books offer an academic interpretation similar to this theory.

68   The argument that Mexico had a genuine revolution has been made by Tannenbaum 1968; Gilly 2005; and Knight 1986.

government on both the capitalist and working classes, while preserving capitalist economic institutions.[69]

The Cuban Revolution, the one most admired by the Sandinistas, was also a genuine revolution that destroyed not only the Fulgencio Batista dictatorship but also the capitalist state and economy, erecting in its place a new government led by Castro and his M-26–7 guerrilla organisation. In the early 1960s, Castro declared that his was a socialist government, but by 1970 the Cuban government had completely assimilated to the Soviet Union politically and economically. M-26–7 merged with the old Communist Party organisation to form the new Cuban Communist Party and no other political party was permitted. Cuba became a one-party state. The state nationalised all property, to be managed by the Communist Party leadership which formed the nucleus of the new bureaucratic collectivist ruling class. Castro's role as a *caudillo* gave the regime a distinctive character, though it was fundamentally a bureaucratic collectivist state and economic system identical in fundamentals, if not in flavour, to those of Eastern Europe. Like the Communist Soviet Union, Eastern Bloc, China, and Vietnam, it was a political system fundamentally opposed to both capitalism and to socialism, that is, it was inimical to both capitalist rule and to democratic workers' power.[70]

The Sandinista revolution of 1979, which became the FSLN government of the 1980s, was not identical to any of these earlier revolutions. Unlike the Bolshevik Revolution of 1917 in Russia, it did not arise out of a working-class political movement, but rather came out of a small guerrilla organisation. Unlike Mexico, the Sandinista state was not a Bonapartist government, because it did not rise above relatively evenly balanced and contending social classes. Its failure to reach a modus vivendi with the bourgeoisie made that impossible. While the bourgeoisie, the working class, the peasantry, and the urban poor were all weak, the Sandinista government did not succeed in balancing itself above them by placing its weight on and gaining support from all of them, including the capitalist class, but rather sought to organise from above to dominate the workers, the peasants, and the poor and to transform them into its social base with the objective of creating a Cuban-style bureaucratic collectivist state. That objective was thwarted principally by the bourgeoisie's independence and active resistance, but also to some extent by the existence of rival organisations and ideologies in the labour and social movements. The

---

69   The theory of Bonapartism is developed by Karl Marx and explained in Hal Draper 1977. Trotsky 1938 applied the theory to Mexico.

70   See Farber 1976, Farber 2006, and Farber 2011.

Sandinista revolutionary leadership proved incapable of creating the state they desired, and what was the incomplete core of a bureaucratic collectivist state came to exist alongside equally incomplete capitalist economic and political institutions, while the entire hybrid social structure was in turn suspended on a web of relations based on national and international ties to various classes, parties and states providing economic support.

Nicaragua recapitulated neither the history of Soviet Russia, nor of Revolutionary Mexico, nor of Castro's Cuba. When we look at the Nicaraguan experience, we find something that does not fit any of these cases but requires us to ask how, within just one decade, we would see first a capitalist state in the form of a dynastic dictatorship overthrown through revolution, and then a revolutionary government established by a Marxist-Leninist party that – in just a decade – was transformed into a liberal-democratic state with a capitalist economic system. One could say that in just over a decade there was an *ancien régime*, a revolution, and then a counter-revolution, three different social systems in little more than ten years. How could the situation remain so fluid? States do not usually just come and go so quickly, leading us to ask: What was it about the Sandinista state, which governed Nicaragua from 1979 to 1990, that made these rapid changes possible?

The Sandinistas without a doubt destroyed the old state in what was a genuine revolution and then began to attempt to create a new state and society. The Sandinista government that came to power was based on the approximately 400 cadres and 1,000 members of the Sandinista National Liberation Front, who had led no more than 3,000 armed men and women in the insurrection and the final Triumph in a nation with a population of three million people. Thousands more participated in the insurrection, but as individuals or as members of small, spontaneously formed bands, with only the most tenuous organisational structures or connection to the FSLN. The FSLN, while it had historically based its military operation on the peasantry, could not be said to have led a peasant army, nor did it have a large or well-organised following in the working class. The FSLN was neither a workers' nor a peasant party.

While many peasants, workers, and the poor rallied to the revolution, as did significant sections of the middle class and even some of the capitalist class, the popular forces did not have the organisation, political consciousness, or leadership to create new state institutions, political parties, or other autonomous organisations. That is, at the beginning there was no working-class movement; there were no unions, and there was no working-class party. The FSLN by itself did not have the ability to form a new state; it was simply too small and too narrowly based, and though the majority of Nicaraguan society – and certainly the lower classes – rallied to the FSLN, it was initially without the organisational structures or capacity to create a state. The small ruling group that took power had no army, no treasury, and virtually no administrative capacity. It did, however, have the will to take and wield state power, which was its greatest strength.

The Sandinistas, as they themselves, their allies, and their detractors universally agree, modelled themselves on Cuba. They foresaw the FSLN, as Castro had done twenty years before, establishing an alliance with the Soviet Union and the Eastern Bloc. While the Sandinistas proclaimed their belief in 'political pluralism', which meant permitting the continued existence of the Conservative and Liberal parties, the pro-Soviet Socialist Party, and the Christian Social Party, they were never sincere. Some took this pluralism to represent a novel political approach, and others thought it represented the FSLN's real social-democratic politics, but in fact the Sandinista policy paralleled the Stalinist policy in the Eastern Bloc countries in the late 1940s and early 1950s, and Mao's in China in the early 1950s, where for a few years after taking power the Communists permitted a variety of labour and peasant parties to exist before they were eliminated and all independent parties prohibited. Similarly with the economy, where in the Eastern Bloc countries and China, a mixed economy with a capitalist sector was briefly tolerated only to be suddenly extinguished and replaced by an economy almost totally nationalised and managed by the Communist Party.[71] The Sandinistas expected to euthanise their capitalist partners and rival political parties as soon as they established a stable government with a strong popular base, but that moment never came.

While the FSLN government permitted the existence of opposition parties, in fact only the Sandinistas played any role in the building of the new state, in administration, in policy decisions, or in establishing the parameters permitted to labour unions and social movements. First in the Junta de Gobierno through their secret majority, and then in the new government of 1985, the FSLN constituted the ruling party, and though it was harassed by the loyal opposition and menaced by a disloyal internal opposition tacitly allied with the Contras, political pluralism was largely a façade.

The situation in the economic and social spheres was somewhat different. The Sandinistas also worked to build a Communist-style state through the creation of state-party controlled mass organisations of workers, peasants, women, and youth. The Soviet Union, the Eastern Bloc countries, and Cuba all provided models of such mass organisations, and the Sandinistas' organisations were clearly modelled on them. Yet, unlike in Cuba or the Soviet Union,

---

71   See Harris 1978; François Fejtö 1971; Fontaine 1968–9.

these state-party organisations never achieved a monopoly in each of those sectors, nor were the organisational vehicles consistently capable of carrying out the party's line. The FSLN, for example, failed to find a modus vivendi with the indigenous people until the late 1980s, after MISURASATA, the indigenous organisation, had seceded from the State Council, while thousands of indigenous people either left the country or joined the Contras and went into full scale rebellion.

Most important was the FSLN relation to the labour unions. The labour unions in general were dominated by the FSLN, though various other labour federations and unions existed both on the left, led by small Marxist groups, and on the right, where unions were linked to either the loyal conservative opposition or to the Contras and the CIA. The most important of these organisations, the Sandinista-led ATC, which represented agricultural workers, faced the contradiction of being told to carry out a policy – the creation of state farms – rejected by the peasantry at large, a policy which ultimately drove thousands of peasants into the arms of the Contras. Nor did the Sandinistas have a strong enough base in other social classes or the strength through the police power to simply force the peasants to accept the policy (as Stalin had done in Russia). The apparent pluralism that existed in the labour movement did not represent a commitment to democracy, but was simply the result of the Marxist-Leninist leadership's failure to achieve the party monopoly of mass organisations that they sought. While the FSLN organisations did provide a social base for the party and the state, they were not strong enough to contribute to the formation of a new state given the tremendous economic problems.

The Sandinista leadership, despite its claims of political pluralism and desire for a mixed economy, wanted and attempted to build a state based on the Soviet-Cuban model. The core of that state was the FSLN itself, constructed from the beginning on the Marxist-Leninist model of a vertical, top-down command structure. With the revolution, the FSLN fused with the emerging new state structure to become a one-party state, permitting the existence of other small, insignificant parties, some of them satellites of the FSLN and some independent, but largely irrelevant. The state offices provided the Sandinistas with both levers of power and with income, housing, automobiles, and salaries for its cadres and some of its members, all of those highly desirable and politically significant in such a poor country suffering from mass unemployment. The Sandinistas could also use their control of the state to hire, laying the basis for a political patronage machine.

The Sandinistas built the Ministry of the Interior, the state security apparatus, and the Army on the Communist model. Cuba, Bulgaria, East Germany, and the Soviet Union, which suggested the organisational structure and functions of the Interior's Secret Police and the Army, also provided the advisors and the material for those institutions. The Ministry of the Interior and the Army were both solid organisations that could have formed the core of a new state. Yet, while the executive, the police, and the army are necessary in the creation of a new state, they are not sufficient, and it was in building the other essential elements of the state that the Sandinistas failed.

The Sandinista's greatest failure (in their own terms) was their inability to create a state with institutions that could really manage the economy: a treasury, a state bank, and a solid currency. While the Sandinistas created a treasury department and, following the Communist model, nationalised the banks and foreign commerce, many corporations, and much of the nation's farmland, other corporations and farms were not nationalised and the new state economic institutions never solidified into a functioning system. With the continued existence of a private market and half the economy still in private hands, it was impossible to create a Communist-style collectivist system based on bureaucratic state planning. Despite some initial success in the early 1980s, the FSLN never succeeded in creating a real national economic plan and never had either the management or the labour organisations capable of making the state enterprises run efficiently.

At the same time, the FSLN government failed to provide the framework for profitability and accumulation for the quite significant private capitalist sector of the economy which might have created the possibility for peaceful co-existence with the bourgeoisie until it was possible to euthanise the remaining capitalist businesses. There was neither a nationalised economy with bureau-cratic planning nor a functioning capitalist market. The Sandinistas created not a mixed economy but rather a half-capitalist, half-Communist system, a mixed-up economy. Their attempts to improve the economy were, of course, made virtually impossible after 1982 by the Contra War which took up both capital and labour. As the US trade embargo and above all the Contra War put even greater strains on the economy, the Sandinista government turned to printing worthless money, leading to the terrible inflation of the late 1980s, and nearly to the total collapse of the economy.

Socialism based on working-class power exercised democratically through institutions of genuine representative and popular democracy, where rival political parties put forth their alternatives to the people, was never contem-plated by the FSLN. Such a democratic socialist system never became a pos-sibility because of the FSLN's political domination of the mass organisations, such as the trade unions and women's organisations. Somoza had dominated the labour union movement before the revolution and the Sandinistas domin-ated it after the revolution, and no independent workers' movement, much less one with a revolutionary socialist programme, ever appeared. The Maoist sects active in the working class and the peasantry that opposed the Sandinista government were unfortunately even more Stalinist than the FSLN itself, while the Trotskyist groups, themselves not without authoritarian deformations, never achieved a significant foothold in the working class.

Throughout this period, the Sandinista government and its economy became extremely dependent on foreign grants, gifts, and loans. While much of the aid came from the Soviet Union, the Eastern Bloc and Cuba, a good deal also came from Venezuela, Mexico and Western European nations, as well as from religious organisations, international aid agencies, and the United Nations. Sweden, for example, the largest Western donor and the organiser of assistance to Nicaragua, provided tens of millions of dollars each year, as well as grain shipments and other aid. Consequently the state's economic institutions and the country's economic and social system never became fully formed along Marxist-Leninist lines, while at the same time, Nicaragua, despite the economic embargo of the US, remained tied to the capitalist world through foreign government assistance, low level trade, and dozens of international aid organisations. The Nicaraguan proto-state stood suspended on a safety net, the ends of which were held by different classes, parties and governments around the world.

Carlos Vilas, the Argentine sociologist who worked in the Sandinista government, astutely observed in his book *The Sandinista Revolution: National Liberation and Social Transformation in Central America* that rather than a transition to socialism, the Nicaraguan revolution was 'entangled in a difficult transition to development' in which the emphasis was on the expansion of small and medium-sized private producers in association with the state. Vilas concluded at that time that the process could best be characterised as 'a popular, agrarian and national liberation revolution', rather than as a proletarian or socialist revolution.[72] Not only was this an accurate description at the time, but it also helps us to understand the tentative character of the Nicaraguan revolutionary state, since a 'popular' state is by definition a state of undefined class character.

The FSLN succeeded between 1979 and 1990 in creating a proto-state with many of the elements that go into the making of a state, but without all of the necessary elements, and without achieving sufficient strength or durability to actually create a fully formed new state. The Sandinista proto-state also failed to develop a clear class character, that is, to become either a bureaucratic collectivist state like those of the Soviet Union, the Eastern Bloc, Cuba or China,

---

72   Vilas 1986, p. 268.

or a capitalist state ruled by a European-style social democracy. Forced by circumstance to accommodate the capitalist class at home, its foreign policy was also compromised; it depended not only on the Communist states, but also on political relationships with a range of ruling parties in a variety of capitalist states around the world whose financial aid was vital to the regime's survival.

The Sandinistas faced the enormous problem throughout the period from 1979–90 that the old capitalist ruling class, with the assistance of the US State Department and the CIA, continued to exist and to organise both within Nicaragua and in Miami. The old oligarchy succeeded in creating a network that constituted a shadow state, a version of the old capitalist state without Somoza, that involved both the domestic loyal opposition and the Contras who took up arms to overthrow the Sandinistas. The presence of the vestiges of the old elite and the phantom of an alternative state represented a persistent threat that tended to undermine the power of the FSLN's fragile and contradictory proto-state. The persistence of the Miami-Nicaragua capitalist ruling class and of its state-on-the-shelf waiting to be shipped and reassembled in Managua, posed a threat to the Sandinistas as great as the Contra War, and, of course, directly linked to the Contras who were carrying out that war. That ruling-class-waiting-in-the-wings eventually returned to Nicaragua, but found that it could not simply install the state-on-the-shelf it had created. Ironically, President Violeta Chamorro would find that, in order to govern, she would have to work with the Sandinistas and the proto-state that they had created, and a new Nicaraguan state could only be the result of collaboration between Chamorro and the FSLN, between the old capitalist class and the former guerrilla revolutionaries.

Violeta Chamorro: A New Ruling Class, a New State, a New Economy (1990–96)

The transfer of power from Daniel Ortega and the FSLN to Violeta Chamorro and the National Opposition Union (UNO) coincided with several international developments that completely changed the world context, most importantly the collapse of Communism in the Soviet Union and the Eastern Bloc in 1991, leading in Cuba – which was economically dependent on the Soviet Union – to a severe economic crisis known as the 'Special Period'. China, an inspiration to the early FSLN, had already entered into an alliance with the United States in 1972 when Mao embraced Richard Nixon, and by 1978 Deng Xiaoping was leading China to adopt reforms that within a few decades would transform China into one of the world's most powerful capitalist countries, albeit with the continuing rule of an authoritarian Communist Party.[1] Vietnam pursued reforms similar to those adopted in China, also under continued Communist Party domination. These events taking place on a world scale signalled the end of bureaucratic Communism as an alternative to capitalism. The whole world had become capitalist; little of the world was democratic. These developments also meant that no longer could revolutionaries in the capitalist world look to Cuba or the Soviet Union for political, military and diplomatic support, such as they had once found there. By the 1990s, there was one capitalist world economy with only two bureaucratic Communist exceptions: Cuba and North Korea (though several governments in the developing world resembled bureaucratic Communism).

Within the capitalist world, the elections of Ronald Reagan in the United States and Margaret Thatcher in Great Britain signalled a new turn to the right in the 1980s, with reductions in the social welfare budget and attacks on labour unions in those countries. The Anglo-American leaders promised that they would dismantle the welfare state and return to free market capitalism. On a world scale, this right turn was transformed into what was called the 'Washington Concensus' or what came to be referred to as 'neoliberal' policies aimed at promoting more competition, higher productivity, and greater profitability through more open markets and greater competition on a world scale.

---

1   La Botz 2012 and Yu 2012.

The major capitalist countries, operating through the International Monetary Fund (IMF), the World Bank, and the General Agreement on Trade and Tariffs (GATT – subsequently the World Trade Organisation – WTO), used loans, development assistance, and trade policies to impose on developing countries 'structural adjustments' that required them to lower trade barriers, such as tariffs and quotas, to reduce government-owned enterprises through privatisation, to open their markets to foreign investment, to reduce the national budget's social welfare programmes, to create an export platform based on free trade zones, and to pass labour law reform to weaken labour unions.

There were enormous economic and political pressures on developing nations to adopt these neoliberal policies, though generally the capitalist politicians and bankers found willing partners among the politicians and businessmen of those economically dependent countries, many of whom had been educated in American Ivy League business schools. The result of these new policies taken together was 'globalisation', a new model of world finance and investment, production and distribution, marketing and sales, accompanied by parallel developments in telecommunications and mass culture. The United States supported the international financial institutions – the World Bank, the IMF, and the GATT/WTO – in establishing a global capitalist system. Within this context, American, European, and Japanese corporations projected their power as never before.

Neoliberalism became the ruling ideology and political economy in practice virtually everywhere on Earth. The FSLN, in dealing with the Contra War and the Nicaraguan economic crisis of the 1980s, had already begun to apply such neoliberal politicos, though they would only be fully implemented in Nicaragua with the administrations of Violeta Chamorro, Arnoldo Alemán, and Enrique Bolaños during the sixteen years from 1990 to 2006.[2]

The 1990 Election of Violeta Chamorro

Ronald Reagan's policy of supporting the Contra War, isolating Nicaragua through the embargo, and – as former President Richard Nixon had said of his efforts in Chile – doing everything possible to 'make the economy scream', had created a tremendous economic crisis which in turn led to a deep polit-

---

2   William I. Robinson, 'Nicaragua and the World: A Globalization Perspective' in Walker (ed.) 1997, pp. 23–42. Robinson provides a sophisticated and complex overview of Nicaragua, the United States, and the larger context of the world economy in this period.

ical crisis in Nicaragua. By 1989, the Nicaraguan government was bankrupt, the economy was collapsing, the common diet was reduced to rice, beans and tortillas, there were tens of thousands of dead and maimed, and much of the population had become tremendously demoralised. Above all, the continuing Contra War and the government's adoption of conscription in 1983 led many to become disillusioned with the Sandinista government and willing to consider other alternatives. While most Nicaraguans may still have supported the Sandinistas and the revolution, and opposed the Contras, it soon became clear that they would be willing to vote for some other political option.

The legal framework for competitive elections already existed. The precedents for the 1990 election had been set by the Law of Political Parties of 1982, by the national elections held in 1984, by the Esquipulas agreement that had ended the Contra War in 1987, and by the Constitution adopted that same year, all of which had already given Nicaragua a formally democratic electoral system. The FSLN was also well prepared to participate in a genuinely competitive parliamentary and presidential election; it had already reorganised itself for the 1984 elections, functioning since then less as a Marxist-Leninist cadre party and more as a traditional electoral party.

The situation of the opposition, however, was initially far from clear. Nicaragua, as we have seen, had never enjoyed a durable democratic political system and had never had robust political parties. The country's two major party traditions, Conservative and Liberal, had failed throughout the twentieth century to develop modern political ideologies and party platforms.[3] Anastasio Somoza García had very effectively split both of those already weak parties into pro- and anti-Somoza factions, further debilitating them. Finally, the FSLN's dominance over the entire political system for a decade had demoralised the old parties, while the mass emigration of much of the business and professional class and the old political elite had left them without a cohesive class structure and without a strong resident leadership. In 1989, as the election approached, there were some two dozen opposition parties, stretching from the far left to the far right, among which no one had been able to rise above the others, nor had the parties together been able to unite throughout the decade of Sandinista rule. And with the election on the horizon, the opposition parties 'fell to squabbling among themselves'.[4] There was no obvious political alternative; and

---

3 Andrés Pérez-Boltodano 2009, *passim*. The ideological weakness of the Conservatives and Liberals is one of the *Leitmotivs* of the book.

4 Eric Beaver and William Barnes, 'Opposition Parties and Coalitions' in Walker (ed.) 1991, p. 134.

there was no outstanding candidate. Certainly no single party had anything like the capability to challenge the FSLN for dominance in the coming election.

Clearly then, the only way to defeat the FSLN at the polls was through the creation of a political coalition. A centrist group within the opposition, rooted in the elite of the historic capitalist class and led by businessman Antonio Lacayo, worked to bring together a coalition of fourteen parties that stretched from the Liberals and Conservatives on the right to the Communists on the far left. The strategy, approved and supported by the US Central Intelligence Agency (CIA), was not intended to create a genuine political alliance based on a common programme, but rather simply to achieve a numerical majority that could defeat the FSLN. Deeply divided internally, the coalition was held together only by their common opposition to – and one could even say hatred of – the FSLN, and by the political and economic support of the United States. The coalition took the name 'National Union of the Opposition' with the acronym UNO, the Spanish word for one, suggesting, contrary to the reality, that the opposition had united as one.

With none of the parties in a dominant position and none of their candidates acceptable to the others, Antonio Lacayo and his American backers succeeded in September 1989 in winning the nomination as UNO's presidential candidate for Lacayo's mother-in-law, Violeta Chamorro, the widow of the famous Conservative leader and publisher of *La Prensa* who had been an outspoken opponent of the Somozas, Pedro Joaquín Chamorro. Her participation in the Junta de Gobierno for nine months in the first post-revolutionary government gave her political credentials in the post-revolutionary period, while the fact that she had not been active in politics since then also gave her a neutral political image. Supporters and critics alike agree that she had little political experience or ability, and her political vision could be summed up in her support for the Catholic Church, for a laissez-faire capitalist system, and for the unity of Nicaragua in a democratic government.[5] Her modest image of housewife, mother, and grandmother allowed her to be seen by many as a comforting maternal figure of an anguished nation, the grandmother of all Nicaragua. After suffering an injury from a fall during the campaign, she was pushed about in a wheelchair, allowing many who had suffered injuries during the war to identify and feel sympathy with her pain as they imagined that she felt sympathy for theirs.

Funding for the opposition came overwhelmingly from the US Central Intelligence Agency (CIA) and the US National Endowment for Democracy (NED), which together spent about $48 million on the election arrangements, as well

---

5 Close 2005, p. 121.

as from the political opposition within Nicaragua. The CIA, which had contributed about $25 million to the internal political opposition between 1984 and 1988, provided another $5 million in 1989. The NED spent between $11 and $15.5 million on its activities in Nicaragua in 1989, part of it given directly to the UNO coalition.[6] While many capitalists in exile were reluctant to support Chamorro and her coalition because they disliked its broad character and inclusion of leftist parties, still UNO was able to raise millions of dollars in contributions from wealthy Nicaraguans in Miami and from conservative contributors in the United States. Though the US Republican Party had handled the Contra War, it was principally the Democratic Party that managed the political opposition. Antonio Lacayo, Chamorro's campaign manager was mentored in his new role by Michael 'Goose' McAdams, a campaign specialist of the National Democratic Institute of the Democratic Party, who had run over 200 political campaigns in the United States.[7] The National Republican Institute also sent campaign advisors to offer suggestions to Lacayo, though they did not play as important a role.[8]

President George H.W. Bush and his administration played a large part in the propaganda surrounding the campaign. Bush met with the candidate on several occasions and appeared beside her in photographs taken both in the United States and in Costa Rica. The President and other officials declared on more than one occasion that if the FSLN won the election, the US-backed Contra War would continue, and that, on the other hand, if Chamorro won, the United States would contribute economically to rebuilding the country. The message to war-weary Nicaraguans was clear: If you want to end the war, the draft, and the economic crisis, you should vote for Chamorro; otherwise hunger will continue and your children will go on dying.

Daniel Ortega campaigned in 1990 as he had in 1984 as the leading *comandante* of the Sandinistas who had led the successful revolution which had ended the Somoza dictatorship. He wore his military fatigues, appearing on platforms bedecked with the red-and-black FSLN flags, speaking in the revolutionary rhetoric of the 1980s. While he personally and the FSLN as an organisation were capable of mobilising tens of thousands of their supporters to massive rallies, Ortega's revolutionary discourse and military image only reinforced the fears of many uncommitted voters and even some Sandinistas that his election would mean a return to war, continued military conscription, and more economic

---

6   LeoGrande 1998, pp. 560–1; Wilson 1990; Lacayo 2006, p. 62 and p. 73.

7   Lacayo 2006, p. 52.

8   Lacayo 2006, p. 67.

hardship. Nevertheless, Ortega, the Directorate, and the FSLN cadres believed that they were going to win the election by a significant majority.

The Nicaraguan election of 1990 was one of the most closely supervised and scrutinised in world history. The United Nations (UN), the Organisation of American States (OAS), former US President Jimmy Carter's Carter Centre, as well as European and Latin American governments and political parties sent election observers. While these organisations were ostensibly neutral, their massive presence tended to suggest that the FSLN government could not be trusted to run a fair election. The partisan character of some of the observers can be seen in the case of the United Nations delegation which was led by Elliott Richardson, who had briefly been Secretary of Defence in the Nixon administration.

While the pre-election polls had all shown the FSLN to be in the lead, they were misleading; in a situation of civil war, Nicaraguans feared telling the truth about their political views. The truth, it would turn out, was that Nicaraguan people had grown tired of the war, angry about the draft, and disheartened by the economic crisis. It has also been suggested that the party leadership had grown distant from its own membership and more importantly had alienated its base. On 25 February 1990, 86 percent of Nicaragua's registered voters turned out to cast ballots and gave a victory to Violeta Chamorro that stunned her opponents and supporters alike.[9] She won 54.74 percent of the vote, while Daniel Ortega received 40.82 percent, a stinging defeat for the FSLN. In the legislature, the UNO coalition took 51 seats while the FSLN won 39 in the 93-member assembly. The fact that the FSLN could be defeated by such a weak and divided coalition suggests how strongly Nicaraguans wanted change.[10] It also reveals just how effective the Contra War had been in wearing them down and how successful the CIA and the NED had been in helping to shape the vote.

The General Situation on the Eve of the Transition

The election of Violeta Chamorro did not signify a victory for counter-revolution. Nicaragua in 1990 was not the Nicaragua of Somoza. The Sandinista mass organisations – labour unions, women's organisations and other movements – had come into existence and continued to play an important role in the society and in politics. The agrarian reform that had finally in 1985 given land titles to

9   LeoGrande 1998, p. 562.
10   Close 2005, p. 62.

the peasants created, virtually for the first time in the country's history, a class of small landowners or family farmers. As a result of the 1984 and 1990 elections, political pluralism was now an established fact in a country with democratic political institutions. The Sandinista government – while it certainly had had authoritarian tendencies – had never created an actual dictatorship, had only occasionally jailed its critics, and, as a rule, had not executed its political opponents. The Sandinista Army and the Sandinista police were in fact both strong and well respected organisations in society at large. While the Sandinistas may have failed to achieve their political project of creating a Communist society like Cuba's, they had, despite war and economic crisis, left Nicaragua better than they had found it in many respects. Ironically, they had laid the basis for a liberal, democratic state.[11]

In other respects, the situation was disastrous. Violeta Chamorro's government took power over a country that had been ravaged by war, almost asphyxiated by the embargo, had become deeply politically polarised and psychologically traumatised. Production was virtually paralysed by the disruptions of war and embargo. Many technical and professional workers had left the country and gone into exile abroad. Much of the labour force had been mobilised in the military while a significant part had joined the contras or fled abroad for safety. Inflation was rampant and the currency had become virtually worthless.[12] Ten years of revolution and war, the loss of tens of thousands of lives, and the privations of hunger had left much of the population damaged, depressed and demoralised. The war had created thousands of widows and many widowers, left thousands of orphans, and many men, women and children physically maimed and psychologically afflicted with post-traumatic stress disorder.

While the United States ended its support for the Contra War and lifted the embargo, it failed to provide all of the economic support that it had promised and that the Chamorro government expected. At the same time, world market prices for commodities such as coffee fell, reducing the country's potential income, while simultaneously the country suffered years of drought. Cotton, which together with coffee had been one of the country's two great export products, declined greatly in significance. The repeated changes in the economic situation, especially in property relations and land titles, made capitalists leery of investment. Perhaps most important of all, the lack of clarity about the political situation – the election of Conservative Violeta Chamorro to

---

11   Close 2005 p. 64.
12   Mayorga 2007, p. 56.

the presidency while the Sandinistas still controlled the army and the police –
made foreign governments as well as domestic and foreign capitalists hesitant
to commit themselves.

Creating a Centre Bloc Coalition to Rule: The Triumvirs

Chamorro's UNO coalition had won the election, but it was a disparate and
deeply divided collection of parties ranging from Conservatives and Liberals
to Christian Democrats, Social Democrats, and Communists. Almost from day
one of her administration, the UNO coalition fragmented into pieces, meaning
that she would never enjoy the backing of UNO representatives in the legislature. A political spectrum emerged in the legislature that had three broad
bands: on the left, the FSLN; in the centre, the Chamorro supporters who
were moderate conservatives; and, on the right, the *somocista*-Contra groups
who were counter-revolutionaries and wanted to return to the *status quo ante*.
Chamorro's own vice-president, the erratic Vigil Godoy, became a leader of the
right-wing band, constantly attacking and mobilising against her. Ironically,
while carrying out the transition to a capitalist society, Chamorro's administration could seldom get the support of COSEP, the employers' association.
Chamorro's political weakness, and her lack of organised support in Congress
or in society, led her to seek an alliance with the FSLN leaders and legislators
who held the congressional majority. She had no other choice. The first post-
revolutionary government at the beginning thus had a hybrid character: it was
a capitalist restoration carried out by a Conservative president and supported
by the leftist FSLN. As Chamorro was forced by circumstance to rely on the
left, the left moved to the right to join hands with her. While Nicaragua's situation was unique, this was not so different from the transformation of the Social
Democratic parties and later even former Communist parties into champions
of neoliberalism as occurred in Europe during the same period.

The Sandinista leadership was in a position similar to Chamorro's. The
FSLN left – or perhaps it would be better to say the Sandinista rank-and-file
made up of peasants and workers – had won its freedom from the Somoza
dictatorship and won a degree of social power through its enormous sacrifices,
and now wanted to see fulfilled its desires for land, jobs, higher wages, and
improvements in education and healthcare. Yet the FSLN leaders could not
simply lead struggles to fulfil those demands or the society would quickly
return to deep social struggle and inevitably to a civil war that, as had just
been proven, they could not win against the Contras and the US. The FSLN
Directorate then had to lead struggles intended to protect some of the gains

of the revolution as well as to let off steam and reduce the social pressure while not actually threatening the possibility of reaching an agreement with the Chamorro leadership and the social classes that it represented.

During the transition period between the Sandinistas stepping down and Chamorro becoming president, Violeta Chamorro for the UNO coalition and Daniel Ortega for the FSLN both sent trusted family members on their behalf to negotiate the transition. Chamorro sent her son-in-law Antonio Lacayo, while Daniel Ortega, when not present himself, sent his brother Humberto Oretega, head of the Sandinista Popular Army. The key political deal between the Chamorro government and the Sandinistas was arranged by Lacayo in collaboration with Humberto Ortega. Violeta excluded from the negotiations Vigilio Godoy, the vice-president, who represented the intransigent right wing of UNO that wanted to sweep the Sandinistas off the political map. Daniel Ortega, for his part, excluded from the negotiations the more radical elements in his party who wanted to continue the struggle for socialism and equality.[13]

Lacayo held a series of meetings with the Ortegas that laid down a mutual understanding that the new government would be a kind of partnership between Chamorro and Lacayo, who controlled the executive branch of the government and foreign affairs, and the two Ortegas, who controlled the army and the police, held the largest bloc in the National Assembly, and controlled the mass organisations of workers and peasants. Lacayo reports that when he met with Humberto Ortega, shortly before Chamorro took office, Ortega argued that both UNO and the FSLN had radicals in their respective camps, the UNO radicals on the right and the FSLN radicals on the left, who threatened the transition to a new government and the future of Nicaragua, and 'therefore it would be absolutely necessary that the moderates in both groups take leadership in this new stage of the country's history'.[14] Humberto was clearly proposing that as head of the army he would not only work with the Chamorro government, but would also become a full partner in it. Lacayo drew the conclusion that having Humberto continue as head of the army 'became attractive because of his offer to control the radicals among the Sandinistas with the only organisation that they respected, the EPS [the Sandinista Popular Army]'.[15] In another conversation involving Daniel Ortega, Violeta Chamorro and Lacayo, and a few other

---

13   Lacayo, 2006, pp. 125–32; Close 2005, p. 112.

14   Lacayo 2006, pp. 111–12. Lacayo's memoir of the period is particularly valuable. While there is no other source to confirm Lacayo's accounts of his conversations, his memoir coincides well both with what we know of the behaviour of the two Ortegas and with other interpretations such as that of Moïses Hassan.

15   Lacayo 2006, p. 140.

UNO and FSLN leaders, FSLN leader Sergio Ramírez suggested it was important to keep Humberto as the head of the army because 'it can't be permitted that control of the Front pass into the hands of the radicals'.[16] That is, the FSLN leaders wanted to be sure that the legislature would not pass into the hands of the party's left and society's underdogs.[17]

The conversations between Lacayo, Humberto Ortega, and Daniel Ortega on the eve of the Chamorro government represented the foundation for what would be an evolving partnership between the three that has been characterised by Moïses Hassan as the 'triumvirate'.[18] The triumvirate represented an alliance between UNO's centre-right led by Chamorro and the FSLN's former Tercerista or Third Tendency, now the centre-left. Beyond the triumvirs, Sergio Ramírez also played a central role as the leader of the FSLN representatives in the National Assembly. The implicit and evolving arrangement between Chamorro's government and the FSLN represented a key step in the transformation of all of the parties involved and of Nicaragua's government, economy and social relations.

The Creation of a New State

One could say that just after the 1990 election there was almost a kind of dual power in Nicaragua. Certainly power was deeply divided and would have to be united in a new state in order for a new class to rule. In effect, Chamorro and the FSLN Directorate each controlled a fraction of the institutions that would have to be assembled and put together into one governmental machine in order to create a new state. The Sandinistas controlled the army, the Ministry of the Interior, the State Security (DGSE), the Supreme Court and all other courts, and

---

16   Lacayo 2006, p. 154.

17   It has been suggested, though not substantiated, that Humberto Ortega may have actually financed Lacayo's political operation. Morris 2010, pp. 175–6 and p. 263, fns. 11, 12 and 13. Morris makes the weakly supported assertion that Humberto Ortega provided a 'slush fund' of $300,000 per week to Lacayo, principally to pay bribes to legislators. He alleges that the 'slush fund' came from the Army and especially the Navy which generated the funds from payments by Colombian drug dealers. The documentation for these accusations is rather thin, and is based on two items: (1) the testimony of Antonio José María Ybarra-Rojas, a reputed US citizen and former Nicaraguan vice-minister who was accused of embezzlement by the Chamorro government; (2) a London *Times* article. See also Hernán Zaballos 2012 and Strange 2010.

18   Moïses Hassan, *La maldición*, p. 275, p. 279.

had 39 of the 92 delegates in the national assembly, and led the mass organisations of workers and women. Ortega and the FSLN would be capable at any
moment of moving powerful levers to defend their interests. On the other hand,
Violeta Chamorro controlled the executive branch of the government, including the fiscal power and the treasury, and she was supported by the United
States and the international financial institutions that controlled the flow of
government and private sector money from abroad. Any new political power
would have to arise out of the unification of these institutions. The Chamorro-
FSLN coalition laid the basis for constructing not just a new government, but a
new state.

The Transition Pact

As the effective leader of the Chamorro government, Lacayo's goal was not to
go back to the days before the revolution, but rather to establish a government
that could create a full-blown capitalist system based on private property and
the free market. Uninterested in settling scores or in revenge, Lacayo wished
to create a new regime of capitalist accumulation which he understood could
only be done with the Sandinistas, not against them. Lacayo headed up the
Chamorro administration's team in a series of meetings with the Sandinistas
that, on 27 March 1990, halfway between the elections and the new government
taking office, produced the Executive Branch Transition Protocol. Key to any
and all future developments, this Transition Agreement (as it was also called)
provided that: (1) the Contras would be demobilised and disarmed; (2) the
Sandinista Popular Army's integrity would be protected as it became a non-
political and professional force; (3) the government would respect the property
rights of those who had received land from the revolutionary government; (4)
public employees would be shielded from political reprisals. Central to this
agreement was the idea of a new government that would give amnesty to
returning Nicaraguans and create an ambience of national reconciliation.[19]

Without a doubt the most important point in the transition was the question
of the Sandinista Popular Army. Under both Somoza and the Sandinistas, the
army had been the principal foundation of the power of the government. The
Sandinistas understandably feared that if the right-wing intransigents either
took command of or abolished the army, it would be possible for the right
to simply erase all of the political and social reforms that had resulted from

---

19   Lacayo 2006, pp. 130–2; Close 2005, pp. 79–85.

the FSLN's period of rule. The Sandinistas therefore demanded that the army remain intact and that it continue to be commanded by Humberto Ortega, propositions that were anathema to the intransigent wing of the UNO coalition. Lacayo and the moderates insisted that there would have to be a dramatic reduction in the size of the army from the 86,000 soldiers it had in January 1990. Ortega agreed that as the army's commander he would carry out the reduction in forces. So – with her *somocista* allies driven to frenzy by these proposals – Chamorro announced in her inaugural address that she would assume the post of Minister of Defence and that Humberto Ortega would continue as head of the Sandinista Popular Army. This decision signalled a definitive split in the UNO coalition between the conservative moderates and the somocista intransigents, and effectively spelled the end of UNO as a political force, making the FSLN the dominant power in the legislature.

The Piñata

With Violeta Chamorro's election victory, the Sandinistas feared being stripped of their political power and worried that the gains of the revolution, particularly the expropriation and nationalisation of land and property, would be reversed. So, during the transition period, that is, after the election but before Chamorro became president, the Sandinista majority in the legislature passed a series of laws intended to implement the transition agreement, but also to protect the FSLN as an organisation, as well as to defend the mass organisations and social institutions created by the revolution and the gains won by workers and peasants through the revolution. The most important of these laws were: the Law of General Amnesty and National Reconciliation, for acts committed during the period from 19 July 1979 to 13 March 1990; the Law of Administrative Careers and Civil Service protecting the rights of public employees; the Reforms to the Labour Code protecting the rights of private sector workers and union members; the revocation of the Law of the Means of Social Communication, ending the state monopoly of the media (some of which then passed into the hands of FSLN organisations or individual Sandinistas); and the Decree of University Autonomy increasing the university's independent management.[20]

The Sandinistas' greatest political preoccupation was with the nationalised property: farm land, processing plants, and urban real estate. These related preoccupations led the Sandinistas in March of 1990, shortly before Chamorro was

---

20   I have taken this list of laws from Close 2005, p. 87.

to take office, to pass Laws 85, 86, and 88 transferring legal title to thousands of properties that had been turned over to peasants as well as protecting the cooperative ventures of peasants and workers. The fundamental thrust of these laws was to protect the economic and social gains of the working classes.

This political concern was also linked to the personal anxiety of many Sandinistas who served in the government, the party, or in a mass organisation, but who had no personal property, often had no education or profession, and who feared that they would be unable to make a living in the post-revolutionary world. Since the Triumph of 1979, the Sandinista leaders, as mentioned earlier, had been living in homes and mansions seized from the dictator Somoza, his family, his inner circle, and from others who had fled the country and gone into opposition to the regime. Some other urban and rural property had been expropriated as well. So, when in March of 1990 the Sandinistas passed Laws 85, 86 and 88, they also thereby gave themselves titles to the houses that they had been occupying for a decade.[21] Daniel Ortega had taken over for himself two city blocks, including a community park. His brother Humberto took over about forty upper-middle-class homes on the road to Masaya, which was an area where real estate values rose rapidly. His real estate holdings would lay the basis for what would later become a significant fortune. Most notoriously, Tomás Borge took over five luxury homes and reconstructed them into one enormous mansion. When later criticised for his avarice, he moved to a house in a more modest neighbourhood and remodelled it, adding a swimming pool. He later had the refurbished house and lot lowered so that it could be seen from the street.[22] Borge's real estate in Managua and other cities would eventually make him a multimillionaire.[23]

The Sandinistas, however, not only received titles to their homes, they also became the proprietors of at least thirty businesses as well as the owners of TV and radio stations.[24] Their ownership of properties transformed them into junior members of the capitalist class, while their domination of the communications industry would be crucial to the future of the FSLN as a political party. They became capitalists overnight, even if not very powerful ones, a step in their transformation into a section of the capitalist class and later into the new hybrid capitalist class of the old wealthy families and the Sandinista businessmen-politicians that rules Nicaragua today.

---

21   Ramírez 1999, pp. 53–7; Lacayo, 2006, pp. 144–5 and 297–8; Pérez-Baltodano 2008, p. 670.

22   Hassan Morales 2009, pp. 52–6.

23   Enríquez 2011.

24   López Castellanos 2013, p. 22.

In addition to the houses and business that were deeded over to the top FSLN leaders in 1990, Sandinistas at all levels of government took whatever they could from the government before leaving. They spent down the national budget and the budgets for the various ministries and national companies, much of that money going into the hands of the party, party leaders and their supporters. Sandinista officials bought up Ministry vehicles, paying a nominal price of $100, and leaving various government agencies without transportation. They also stole from government offices furniture and equipment, stripping some of them completely. Even President Chamorro arrived in office to find the president's rooms stripped.[25] All of this distribution of property to themselves came to be known as the *piñata* after the *papier maché* effigy which is broken open at a child's birthday party, spilling out the candy, for which the children scramble and jostle to collect as much as they can.

The original *piñata* was followed later by other transfers of property to both the Sandinistas and Chamorro loyalists. In August of 1991, during the negotiation of the *Concertación* pact with the Chamorro government, the Sandinistas also convinced the government to deed over 25 percent of the stock in government enterprises to the Sandinista labour unions in exchange for agreeing to the government's economic plan and devaluation of the currency. The Sandinistas' labour union officials, an emerging labour bureaucracy, thus became shareholders in the new Nicaraguan capitalism.[26]

A 'second *piñata*' took place in June of 1994 when other state properties were once again privatised into the hand of the triumvirs – Lacayo and the Ortega brothers – and of their followers. While the new owners were supposed to pay a sum equal to the income generated by the property, many of them failed to do so.[27] Economic historian Roser Solà i Montserrat writes: 'The privatisations enriched a small group with ties to the armed forces, to the FSLN, and to big business linked to the conservative oligarchy, which thus maintained its systems of privileges and perquisites at the cost of the public'.[28]

Finally, the *comandantes* used their control over state resources, their reputations and their national and international connections to establish nongovernment organisations. 'Sometimes state institutions morphed into NGOs: the Agriculture and Agrarian Reform Ministry's Centre for Research and Studies on Agrarian Reform (CIERA) was awarded to its director, sociologist Orlando

---

25   Lacayo 2005, pp. 169–70.
26   Ramírez 1999, p. 55.
27   Hassan Morales 2009, pp. 281–2.
28   Solà i Montserrat 2008, p. 371.

Núñez, in its entirety (land, buildings, files and staff) and became the Centre for Research and Promotion of Rural and Social Development (CIPRES)'. At the same time, other *comandantes* used their reputations and connections to create their own NGOs. Former *comandante* Jaime Wheelock created the Institute for Development and Democracy (Instituto para el Desarrollo y la Democracia – IPADE), while Monica Baltodano established Popol Na Foundation for the Promotion and Development of the Municipality. Others did the same.[29] The new NGOs provided their owners with staff jobs, economic resources, and continuing influence in the society. If not all became part of the new bourgeoisie, they became part of an emerging petty bourgeoisie made up of NGO directors and their professional staff.

The original argument had been that the deeding over of state property to Sandinista leaders would safeguard the revolution's social gains, particularly protecting the social property from the depredations of the old bourgeoisie; in fact, there was much truth in that. Some agricultural and industrial properties were protected to the benefit of the workers. But the other and equally important aspect of the *piñata*, as well as the other transfers of property, was quite different from the ostensible rationale. The Sandinista *comandantes* and other FSLN leaders, many of them of humble origins or middle-class backgrounds, were able to lift themselves out of the working classes into the petty bourgeoisie or even into the capitalist class. Top FSLN leaders, such as Humberto Ortega, Bayardo Arce, and Francisco López Centeno, became wealthy capitalists, the owners of major enterprises. The *piñata* and the various other property transfers representing hundreds of millions of dollars in property served as the original political primitive accumulation for the Sandinista bourgeoisie. Later, through their political alliances first with the Chamorro administration, and then with the Alemán government, the Sandinistas would gain entrée to the old bourgeoisie, the older and richer group entering into economic deals with the younger group on the make during the succeeding decades.

Establishing a New Government and a New State

The Sandinistas' state-building project had failed largely because of the Contra War and the US embargo, but also because of their own mistakes. They succeeded only in creating an Army and Ministry of the Interior, and that was prin-

---

29   Rocha 2011.

cipally the work of Cuba, East Germany, and the Soviet Union. The Sandinistas' social welfare system dealing with health and education had had significant success, especially in the early 1980s, but the Contra War and embargo had kept it from fulfilling its ambitious goals. When the Sandinistas lost the election, the country was bankrupt and the economy was collapsing, and most of the social programmes that the FSLN had launched could not carry out many of their essential functions. The state-building project also failed, however, because of the FSLN Directorate's errors in judgement, such as the decision not to distribute land directly to the peasants. Consequently, during the revolutionary decade, Nicaragua had become utterly dependent upon assistance from the Soviet Eastern Bloc and Cuba, as well as aid from the Western European social democracies and Latin American allies. Foreign aid, foreign advisors, and organisational staff in large measure either supplemented or substituted for the Sandinistas' failed state.

The issue facing Violeta Chamorro and her administration then was not simply a change of government, but rather the construction of a new regime and of a new state. Nothing remained of the Somoza state, so the new state would have to be constructed out of the pieces that could be salvaged from the Sandinista proto-state, together with whatever she and her government could create. The building of the state was itself dependent upon the reconstitution of the business classes and of their political parties. If there were to be a new capitalist state, there would have to be a cohesive and robust capitalist class.

The old bourgeoisie as a class and the Conservative and Liberal parties as political powers, which had never completely abandoned Nicaragua, were reinforced after the 1990 election by the return in the next few years of 300,000 Nicaraguan refugees and exiles; this represented a remarkable tenth of the country's total population.[30] Some of these were *somocistas*, but not all of these returning Nicaraguans were either rich or politically conservative; still, they were people who had either rejected or escaped the revolution and had gone to live in the United States or other countries, an experience that influenced their outlook. The construction of a new Nicaraguan state would be based on the reuniting of that section of the old oligarchy that had stayed in Nicaragua and the part that had gone abroad, together with their new junior partners, the Sandinista bourgeoisie which had enriched itself through the seizure of property both from the old bourgeoisie and from the Sandinista government. The fall of Somoza and the victory of the Sandinistas had ended one regime and led to another; similarly, '[t]he victory of the UNO didn't just change the gov-

---

30   Núñez 1997. He gives the figure of 300,000 exiles on the right who returned.

ernment, but rather created a new regime'.[31] Since strong military and security organisations already existed and could be appropriated by the new government, the key task then would be to reconstruct the state treasury, to ensure the functioning of the market, to strengthen capitalist property relations, and to provide for profitability and capital accumulation. The new regime would be based on a free market and a representative government, though in the new neoliberal era this would be in many respects a new political economy.

Together with the cohering of this new capitalist class, there would also have to be a new political alliance or coalition that could bring together both the old capitalists represented by the various Conservative and Liberal parties as well as by the leaders of the Contra forces, and the Sandinistas. Based on the reunification of the oligarchy, this political alliance would be able to rule effectively as long as it could prevent disruption of its political project by either a militant *somocista*, bourgeois right wing or a radical plebeian left wing. The centre-left/centre-right alliance did not preclude a certain level of inevitable conflict, but it did require that such conflict be contained and subordinated to the larger goals. The Chamorro government and the FSLN would have conflicts over policies, but they would not necessarily be class conflicts between the bourgeoisie and the working class and its allies, but rather limited inter-class conflicts between the old oligarchy and the new bourgeois social democratic bloc that the Sandinistas were becoming. That is, the Sandinistas, many of whose leaders were becoming capitalists, now became a social democratic party sharing power in a kind of government of national unity whose function was to attenuate class conflict. Over time, as the old bourgeois bloc accepted the existence of the new order and as the country's working class and poor became more demoralised and disheartened under the new regime, class conflicts would diminish, though at the very beginning they would be intense.

Governing From Below: The Strikes and Riots of May and June 1990

Shortly after the election of Chamorro, Daniel Ortega made a famous speech to a mass meeting of Sandinistas during a rally in Managua in which he pledged the FSLN party's commitment to continue to defend the revolution and its social gains, particularly its social property. In the most important and oft-

---

31   Pérez-Baltodano 2008, p. 671; Close 2005, pp. 65–6. Both argue that this was a new regime, but not necessarily that it was a new state, as I am arguing here.

quoted line of his speech, Ortega stated that though Chamorro had won, 'The Nicaraguan people will continue to govern from below'.[32] What Ortega meant by this was that Chamorro's fragile UNO coalition would be unable to stand up to the power of the Sandinista unions and other mass organisations fighting in defence of the revolution's gains. What future events demonstrated, however, was that Ortega would now use the unions not only to fight for workers' interests, but also as a force with which to negotiate the conditions of his partnership with the Chamorro administration, and, at a deeper level, his Sandinista leadership's partnership with the old bourgeoisie. He was not simply defending the gains of the revolution, but rather strengthening the political power and economic interests of the Sandinistas as a social group and a political party. This was demonstrated in the strikes and riots of May and June 1990.[33]

While Lacayo and the Ortegas were coming to an agreement, they were also testing each other and being tested by their own organisations and social bases. Just before leaving office, the Sandinistas had carried out a currency devaluation of 200 percent; consequently, when the Chamorro administration took office, the new administration faced demands from several of the Sandinista unions for wage increases. In addition to the wage demands, there was also opposition to the proposed suspension of the Civil Service Law, which put in jeopardy the jobs of all public employees, and resistance to the first stages of the restitution of property to its previous owners. The Sandinista CST private sector and UNE public sector union leaders decided to launch a series of strikes both for the wage increases but also more importantly to oppose Chamorro's decrees that would end civil service protections and return previously expropriated and nationalised property to the original owners. Some of the union leaders went so far as to demand that Chamorro accept a formal 'co-government' with the Sandinistas, unaware that there was already a co-government, though not on the terms they desired.

The various wage and political demands led to a series of strikes by 70,000 CST and UNE workers in May and June of 1990, accompanied by the seizing of public buildings, the blocking of city thoroughfares, the erection of barricades and the burning of tires in the streets, as well as rioting that led to significant destruction of property. Two months later, the FST union of 40,000 went on strike, but when the Chamorro administration refused to make concessions, another 90,000 workers joined them in solidarity. Through these strikes, the

---

32   Fonseca Terán 2005, p. 458. He has an extended discussion of the speech on pp. 456–72.
33   Close 2005, pp. 157–61 and 176–7.

unions won wage gains of 100 percent that broke the Chamorro administration's first attempt to establish a policy of wage restraints. Daniel Ortega, who played the leading role in directing the strikes, was both giving in to the pressures of his own working-class left wing, but at the same time controlling it and channeling it to serve his own interests. Ortega both tested the will of the new government and proved that even if no longer the president, he still had the power to paralyse Managua and to menace Chamorro's administration.

The Chamorro government called upon his brother Humberto Ortega, head of the army, to deploy the necessary troops and equipment to sweep the streets clean of the barricades. As Sandinista mass organisations retreated before the Sandinista Army, Daniel Ortega called in the union leaders to sign the agreement that accepted the government's wage offer, a pact that also ended the indexing of wages to the rate of inflation. Whether this confrontation between the two Ortegas was an unforeseen development or a carefully orchestrated event remains an open question, but in any case each brother gained in the process. Humberto proved he could lead the army in defence of the new state, while Daniel showed that he still controlled the party and the unions.

The wage gain was a short-term victory, while the loss of cost of living indexing represented a long-term defeat for the unions, as the Chamorro government devalued the currency by another 500 percent in March of 1991, while wage gains were kept to between 35 and 200 percent.[34] The May–June and August strikes of 1990 represented an important benchmark in the transition of the unions as a workers' social movement led by a left party to the unions as bureaucratic organisation, and to finally becoming – after a short flurry of independent direct action – part of the FSLN political machine striving to increase its power within the new capitalist state. The strikes had shown that Daniel Ortega still had the ability to mobilise the mass organisations, even if he could not necessarily secure long-term gains for the workers.

To bring the chaotic situation under control, the Chamorro government worked to create a kind of national social pact between the government, businesses, and the unions. The *Concertación* was based fundamentally on a mutual agreement to accept the neoliberal measures being proposed by the government in line with the demands of the United States, the World Bank, and the IMF. After many meetings with the various parties and a conference of all of them together, the Sandinistas agreed to the *Concertación*, though COSEP, the principal business organisation, refused to sign.[35] The result of the informal

---

34   Close 2005, p. 158.
35   Lacayo 2006, pp. 197–210.

conversations between Lacayo and the Ortegas, the Transition Protocol together with the resolution of the strikes and riots of May and June 1990, and the adoption of the *Concertación* agreement, laid the foundation for both a functioning state and the neoliberal order that would continue under the conservatives and the Sandinistas through five presidencies from 1990 to 2012 and beyond.

Throughout this period, Daniel Ortega and other leaders of the FSLN would publicly criticise or oppose measures being taken by the government to return property to its original owners, to privatise other companies, and to create a free market, though privately they would meet discretely with Lacayo and other representatives of the Chamorro government and agree to the very deals that they were publicly decrying. In this way, Ortega and the FSLN were able to maintain, for quite some time and among much of the public, their image as defenders of workers, peasants and the poor, while actually participating in the creation of a new political system that would grind those social classes to produce profit for the country's new capitalists, including the Sandinistas themselves.[36]

The FSLN Convention of 1991

In the midst of the controversies, social protests, and violent incidents of the first years of the Chamorro administration, the Sandinistas throughout the country engaged in heated debates about the way forward under new circumstances. These discussions and debates held by thousands of FSLN members throughout the country represented a genuinely democratic experience; one might say the first in the organisation's history. The differences of opinion at the local and regional level seemed so great that they might tear the organisation apart. The FSLN members had been shaken by the electoral defeat, by the coming to power of Chamorro and the UNO coalition, by the *piñata*, and by the FSLN's negotiations with Lacayo. Members were asking themselves what role the FSLN and its mass organisations should have in the new situation in which they suddenly found themselves. A meeting of 300 FSLN members in Crucero (Managua) drafted an analysis and critique of the Sandinistas' history and current situation, as well as a series of resolutions for improving the organisation;

---

36   Both the conservative Antonio Lacayo and leftists, such as Moïses Hassan and Sergio
      Ramírez, comment on the duplicity of Daniel Ortega, his two faces, one public and one
      private.

they also called for a national convention, a proposal accepted by the National Directorate and initially scheduled for February 1991 but then postponed until July.[37]

Though the Sandinista Front for National Liberation had been founded in 1962, it had never, in its almost thirty-year history, held a convention. This was in part understandable and perhaps even justifiable because of the repressive character of the Somoza dictatorship that ruled until 1979, though it should be noted that in similar circumstances other revolutionary organisations in other countries and times found a way to hold meetings and conventions in locations abroad. Even after it took power, the FSLN called no convention throughout the decade of the 1980s. Finally, after losing the 1990 election, the National Directorate called the First National FSLN Congress attended by 581 delegates on 19–21 July 1991.

To prepare the convention, the FSLN organised local meetings throughout the country. Everywhere FSLN members participating in the pre-convention discussions criticised the National Directorate's centralised organisation and top-down relationship to the members. The Crucero document mentioned above, while proud of the organisation's history and appreciating its strengths, criticised the Sandinista leadership for its 'authoritarianism', 'lack of sensitivity to the suggestions and concerns of the members', 'gagging critics', as well as its 'bureaucratic style of leadership and imposition of leaders and organisational schemes'.[38]

Various political positions emerged from the discussions around the country; the two dominant ones were described at the time as the Social Democratic or pragmatic perspective led by Sergio Ramírez, and opposing it that of the group that called itself the 'rank-and-file' (*basistas*) or 'principled position' (*principistas*). The so-called Social Democratic Tendency based its view on the collapse of Communism in the Soviet Union and Eastern Europe, arguing that no such Communist left project was possible any longer anywhere in the world. Therefore, the pragmatists said, the FSLN should give up its Leninist and *guerrilla* image and its confrontational style, repudiate social and labour union violence, and build a new party that would operate through civic engagement and parliamentary action. The Social Democratic Tendency argued that the country should seek a rapprochement with the United States.

---

37   The Proclamation and Resolutions of the Crucero meeting can be found in Envío Team 1990.

38   Envío Team 1990.

The Rank-and-File Tendency, most of whose leaders and activists came from the National Federation of Labour (FNT), took an altogether different point of view. They criticised the National Directorate for its attempt to insert itself in the emerging post-revolutionary economic and political system without adequately representing the interests of the working class. At the same time, they criticised the Social Democrats for advocating 'a petty-bourgeois utopia of class collabouration'. The FNT activists' 'principled' tendency wanted more support from the FSLN for the labour unions' everyday struggles, including for the militant strikes and street demonstrations of workers. They wanted the party to recognise that its power should be based on the people and not in the state.

Before the convention, the National Directorate and the Sandinista Assembly made up of 81 members presented the local meetings with two alternative proposals for electing a new leadership, the first by voting for or against a slate presented by the leadership, and the second by voting for the leaders as individuals. These options tended to become the focus of much of the debate in the local meetings, often distracting from the broader issues. The Sandinista Assembly also proposed that 80 'historic cadres' of the FSLN, who had not been elected by their local organisations, be seated and given a voice and a vote at the convention. Both the voting by slate and the seating of the 'historic cadres' passed, giving a strong indication that the National Directorate had a firm grip on the convention.

Speaking at the convention, *Comandante* Joaquín Villobos, quoting the recently deceased Dr. Guillermo Ungo, the Salvadoran social democrat, told the delegates that 'there's no democracy without revolution, and there's no revolution without democracy'. Villalobos, echoing issues that had been raised in the pre-convention discussions, criticised the vanguard party model and stated that 'Democracy begins at home and as leftists we must overcome all involuntary vestiges of Stalinism that our revolutionary movements sometimes have'.[39] These were noble sentiments, but the FSLN was unprepared and unable to break with its own Stalinist, Guevarist, and vanguardist traditions.

Humberto Ortega, who had declined to continue as a member of the National Directorate since he was now to head the Army under the new Chamorro government, told the convention: 'We are in a world convulsed by change in which all theories, all schemes, all models that have been put forward in this century need to be reconsidered and analysed in order to find the best of them for our peoples and for Nicaragua'.[40] Ortega had perfectly captured the sense

---

39   Envío Team 1991a.
40   *Envío* Ibid.

of crisis in the left around the world at that moment of the collapse of Soviet Communism, yet there was no serious reevaluation of the theory and practice of the Sandinista Revolution in the convention.

Daniel Ortega's position began to emerge before the convention in the spring. 'Towards the end of May, Daniel Ortega began to take part publicly in the ideological debate that had enveloped *sandinismo*, putting all of his prestige on the side of mass action and clearly identifying *sandinismo* with the cause of the dispossessed. In his discourses and declarations, he warned that the FSLN could not fall into the trap of those who desired in the name of modernisation to change the nature and the *raison d'être* of the Frente Sandinista'.[41] Ortega defended the right of the people to rebel, and the right of workers to strike and to take to the streets. He also criticised those who wanted the FSLN to give up its opposition to US imperialism. In his speech to the convention, Ortega put emphasis on the need of the Sandinistas to 'unite its ranks' in the struggle, to be in the *barrios* with the workers and in the fields with the peasants, but also to learn how to be more effective in the elections. Yet at the same time, Ortega motivated the inclusion in the National Directorate of Sergio Ramírez, his longtime collaborator and leader of the Social Democratic Tendency, saying that he was a loyal and effective leader of the Sandinista delegation in the National Assembly.[42] In the end, Ortega placed himself in the centre, bringing together both of the major tendencies in the organisation, and reconfirming his role as the FSLN's preeminent leader.

Despite Ortega's reassertion of FSLN orthodoxy, the convention also voted to affiliate with the Socialist International (SI) of socialist and social-democratic parties around the world. This was a signal decision, since historically the FSLN had identified with the parties of the Communist International and its traditions, particularly the Soviet Union and Cuba. The collapse of the Soviet Union and the Eastern Bloc between 1989 and 1991, and rapid orientation of those states to neoliberal capitalism, had eliminated Communism as a viable international political pole. The decision to affiliate with the SI reflected the influence of Ortega and Ramírez who had developed strong political connections to the leaders of several of the European Social Democratic Parties. The convention re-elected Daniel Ortega to the top post of General Secretary by acclamation, and, voting by slate, re-elected six of the sitting members of the National Directorate, and added Ramírez and another new member. Despite a campaign

41   *Envío* Ibid.
42   *Envío* Ibid.

in her favour from both men and women in the FSLN, the convention did not elect *comandante* Dora María Téllez. Machismo won out and the Directorate remained a nine-*man* body.

Despite the earlier debates, there was no fundamental change in the FSLN as a result of the convention. The Directorate remained in power. The democratic centralist organisation and top-down command structure remained in place. The ideology, originally inspired by Soviet and Cuban Communism, was masked, as it from the beginning of the revolution in 1979, with social-democratic rhetoric. The FSLN convention did not attempt to carry out a thorough and genuinely self-critical examination of its theory and practice in either the pre-revolutionary period or the ten years of the revolution. Even more importantly, the convention ignored the reality that Ortega and the Directorate were engaged in a pragmatic attempt to find a way forward for their political organisation through their negotiations with the Chamorro government, a path that involved not simply opportunism and pragmatism, but inter-class collaboration and violations of their own fundamental Marxist-Leninist principles. The very real issues involving the questions of power, democracy, and social justice that it posed never came up for discussion in a frank way. At the same time, the convention did provide a first opportunity for the FSLN cadres and ordinary members to begin to think of themselves as a political party, rather than the revolutionary military organisation that they had been, and out of that new consciousness would come in the next couple of years a real debate about the issues of theory, organisation, and politics that the convention had neglected.

The Violence

While the convention was debating the future of the FSLN, the country was dealing with the problem of widespread violence. The Chamorro government, and the Lacayo-Ortega alliance which undergirded it, faced throughout their administration outbreaks of criminal violence and, more importantly, armed challenges from both the right and the left. War and poverty had undermined the social fabric and morality of the society. Serious criminal acts in Nicaragua – murders, rapes, and armed assaults – increased from about 30,000 in 1985 to almost 49,000 in 1995.[43]

---

43   Close 2005, p. 148.

Much more significant was the political violence. The end of the war saw the demobilisation of 78,000 soldiers of both the Contras and the Sandinista Popular Army (sometimes called the *Compas*, short for *compañeros* or comrades), some 56,000 officers and elements of the Army and 22,000 Contras, referred to by themselves and by the government as the *Resistencia*, the Resistance. While 17,000 arms had been collected from military personnel and 15,000 from civilians, still many high-powered weapons remained in the hands of demobilised soldiers from both sides.[44] The former Contras, now dubbed *recontras*, and the former Sandinista army *compañeros*, now known as *recompas*, demobilised and, without land or jobs, turned to both political rebellion and crime. *Recontras* attacked Nicaraguan army units, while both *recontras* and *recompas* seized land. Toward the end of this violent period of uprising, the two groups with their origins in the rival armies of the civil war merged in the *revueltos* (the scrambled), joining together in an armed political movement that demanded jobs, land, agricultural credits, the restructuring of the peasant cooperative debt and the removal of land mines from Honduras.[45] The peak of this violence occurred in 1993 when there were 554 violent incidents that took 422 lives.

The violence included challenges to the Chamorro-FSLN alliance from the left. The *recontras*, who had as Contras simply acted under the direction of the CIA and therefore had no political experience, had little capacity to create a political programme or articulate their demands.[46] Many of the *recompas*, however, were disillusioned Sandinista workers and peasants who resented Ortega and the FSLN for having yielded power to Chamorro. While the Sandinista and Chamorro governments had promised land to the Contras who laid down their arms, there was initially no land distribution to the Sandinista Popular Army veterans who were demobilised, leading to a new political movement. One group of former Sandinista veterans formed the Revolutionary Front of Workers and Peasants (CROC), led by Victor Manuel Gallegos, a former major in the Sandinista Popular Army. The CROC seized the city of Estelí in August of 1993, but this worker-peasant insurgency was quickly suppressed by the Sandinista Army, leaving at least 40 dead.[47] The Chamorro government called upon the army to suppress all armed movements of disappointed workers and peasants, while at the same time offering social programmes such as land, seeds, and loans on a case-by-case basis to those who laid down their arms.

---

44   Lacayo 2006, pp. 329–32.
45   López Castellanos 2013, pp. 50–1; Lacayo 2006, pp. 329–33.
46   Close 2005, p. 152.
47   'Qué pasa en Nicaragua?' 1993.

All of these arrangements were initially made on an ad hoc basis, with the government threatening to treat those who did not accept the deals as common criminals.[48]

The New Economic Policy

The Chamorro government, deeply committed to private enterprise and the reduction of the role of the state, introduced a neoliberal economic model on its own initiative, even before entering into any agreement with the major international financial institutions such as the World Bank and the International Monetary Fund (IMF). The Chamorro government was committed ideologically to such measures as open markets, privatisation, and the reduction of the social budget, as well as an end to subsidies on such items as food and fuel for workers, peasants, and the poor. On its own initiative, the Chamorro administration would carry out neoliberal policies, but it would also be obliged to do so because of the agreements it signed with the international financial institutions in order to become eligible for loans at lower interest rates.

The Chamorro administration inherited in 1990 from the Sandinistas an economy that was a shambles, in much worse shape than it had been before the revolution of 1979. The 1980s, known throughout Latin America as the 'lost decade', began when the fall in oil prices led to an economic crisis in Mexico and then in several South American nations, and proved equally disastrous for Central America and especially Nicaragua. In Nicaragua, the lost decade was also the revolutionary decade during which manufacturing had declined significantly. Cotton production, previously one of the most important crops, had collapsed, with only about one-fifth as many acres under cultivation. The biggest issue of the decade of the 1980s, of course, had been the war.

The war had left 30,000 dead and it had devastated the economy. There had been $2 billion in damage, $1.1 billion lost due to the embargo, $1.9 billion spent on Defence, and reduced national consumption estimated at $4.1 billion – a total of $9 billion in losses.[49] Nicaragua's total debt in 1990 was estimated at $4 billion to the Soviet Union and between $6 and $8 billion to Western nations and international financial organisations. The worst economic problem resulting from the war, however, was inflation, which had peaked in 1988 at 33,000

---

48   López Castellanos 2013, pp. 50–1; Lacayo 2006, pp. 329–33; Close 2005, pp. 155–6.
49   Close 2005, p. 194.

percent before declining to 1,600 percent in 1989, though it spiked again in 1990 to 13,000 percent. Such extraordinary inflation made the economy impossible for everyone: bankers, capitalist investors, farmers, and workers. The Chamorro administration's first goal – and in reality its only economic success in six years – was to restrain inflation.

The economic situation in 1990 is perhaps best understood in human terms. The University of Central America estimated unemployment to be at 32 percent. About 34,000 of an existing 40,000 small businesses had failed. Some 75 percent of the population lived in poverty and 46 percent in extreme poverty, defined as less than the minimum number of calories needed for subsistence. In children, extreme poverty leads to stunted physical and mental development. In rural areas, the situation was even worse: 63 percent of the population were poor and 78 percent were living in extreme poverty. Infant mortality rates were among the worst in the region.[50]

The initial attempt by Dr. Francisco Mayorga, president of the Banco Central, to create a new currency, the *córdoba de oro*, failed. Inflation accompanied by 25 currency devaluations in the government's first few months continued, leading to an increase in the cost of living and a decline in the standard of living of Nicaraguan working people. While the Sandinista-led strikes attempted to keep up with the spiral of inflation followed by devaluation, they could not succeed. Over time, the Chamorro administration's austerity budgets did succeed in ending inflation, though at the same time the country slid into economic stagnation. If there was declining inflation it was partially because there was no economic growth; the country's economy in 1990 produced less than it had done in 1970.

The other major economic issue facing the country was its foreign debt, which amounted to US$11 billion or six times the country's gross domestic product, owed principally to the Soviet Union, Mexico and Costa Rica. Of that sum, US$4 billion were debt service arrears. The Sandinistas had been unable to make progress on dealing with the debt because of the decline in exports as a result of revolution and the Contra War, as well as the impact of the fall in commodity prices and the devaluation of the US dollar.[51] Before it left office, the Chamorro administration would be able to reduce the foreign debt principal somewhat, though only through foreign assistance and debt relief.

As one study noted, during the Chamorro years, Nicaragua was 'completely dependent on external aid, not only to cover its deficit shortfall, but also to

50   Close 2005, pp. 223–4.
51   Brooks 1998.

finance its internal investment ...'.[52] Between 1990 and 1995, Nicaragua received some US$3.2 billion in foreign economic assistance, 80 percent of which went towards servicing the foreign debt. Some 41 percent of the country's total budget came from foreign aid, according to the World Bank.[53] While Nicaragua had been counting on a good deal of assistance from the United States – some $300 million had been approved – Senator Jesse Helms succeeded in convincing the US Senate to stop the aid principally because Chamorro had failed to remove the Sandinista Humberto Ortega from his role as head of the Nicaraguan National Army. Consequently $104 million was stopped in 1992 and was not finally given to Nicaragua until 1994.

Neoliberal policies adopted by Chamorro were not a novelty in Nicaragua. The Sandinista government had already in the 1980s introduced neoliberal measures – government budget cuts and layoffs – in response to the crisis of the war, embargo and hyperinflation. The Chamorro government followed similar policies, though they went far beyond anything the Sandinistas had imagined. Almost from its first day in office, her administration began to reduce the state sector and lay off state employees. The army furloughed by far the largest number of workers on the public payroll. The Sandinista Popular Army, which in 1986 had 120,000 troops, by January 1990 was reduced to 86,000, and by November 1990 to 27,864; by 1996, it had only 14,000 soldiers.[54] The government also created an Occupational Conversion Programme to encourage government employees to leave the public sector for private employment. Some 3,798 workers were given an average of $1,443.40 each to resign their jobs.[55]

Property and the Market

The Chamorro government's most important goal by far was to re-establish the capitalist market and capitalist property relations – a system which if not totally eradicated by the FSLN government had become utterly non-functional. Chamorro and Lacayo wanted to make it possible for capitalists to make a profit and accumulate capital. They were particularly anxious to re-establish the

---

52   Latin American Studies Department of the University of Stockholm report of 1994, cited
      in Close 2005, pp. 216–17.
53   Close 2005, p. 217.
54   Close 2005, p. 164.
55   Lacayo 2006, p. 308.

private banking system that is so central to any capitalist economy. At the government's initiative, in early 1991 the National Assembly passed a new bank law, in accord with the *Concertación*, that permitted the operation of private banks. Joaquín Cuadro Chamorro, an attorney who worked for Nicaragua's major banks and corporations, commented: 'This law puts an end to the Sandinista popular revolution'.[56] The privatisation of the banks would lead within a few years to the establishment of several new banks each at the centre of an economic group with its conglomeration of financial, commercial, industrial, and agricultural businesses. Almost all of these banks would develop a strong international presence in Central America, the Caribbean, and other regions.[57]

Another step in the process, complying both with the *somocista* right-wing demands and with the international financial organisations' neoliberal policies, was the re-privatisation of state enterprises. While most of those properties belonged to Nicaraguans, included among those properties were 908 belonging to Americans.[58] The process of privatisation created financial opportunities for government officials, bankers, brokers, and others in the re-emerging capitalist class. In short order, the Chamorro government sold off major industrial enterprises: the railroad, the national airline, the merchant marine and the fishing fleet. One of the saddest, most irrational, and most lamentable of these privatisations was the sale of Nicaragua's picturesque and, though antiquated, still functioning freight and passenger railroad system – locomotives, rolling stock, and the rails themselves were all sold as junk, leaving a series of railroad terminals standing in front of dusty lots as monuments to the victory of personal avarice over social good.[59] Chamorro's administration opened an office in Miami so that former *somocistas* and other exiles could reclaim the property, land, businesses and homes that had been expropriated by the Sandinistas, and thousands made claims at the offices both in Nicaragua and in Florida.

The privatisations merit some detailed attention. The state's agricultural properties, organised in the public corporations Cafenic (coffee), Hatonic (cattle), and Agroesco (cotton), were the largest and most important. Lacayo mentions the guidance of the World Bank and the Inter-American Development Bank (IDB) in dealing with the privatisation of land 'with the need to establish a "free market" in this sector so that those who wanted to sell land could do so,

56   Lacayo 2006, p. 261.
57   Mayorga 2007, pp. 66–71.
58   Lacayo 2006, p. 654.
59   López Castellanos 2013, p. 48.

and so permit greater fluidity in the economy'.[60] The coffee plantations would be redistributed: first, to the former owners of the Somoza era; second, to the Association of Rural Workers (ATC); third, to the Contra fighters; and fourth, it was finally decided, to the demobilised officers and soldiers of the Sandinista Popular Army (EPS). According to Antonio Lacayo, it was the government's idea to use the vast Somoza properties which had been nationalised by the Sandinistas to meet the needs of the ATC, Contras, and EPS soldiers. The ATC actually controlled all of these lands which were considered part of the Area of the Property of the People, so the Chamorro administration would have to negotiate with the ATC's parent organisation, the FSLN.

The actual negotiations were carried out with Jaime Wheelock, former Sandinista Minister of Agriculture, who had organised the original confiscation, nationalisation, and operation of the Sandinista government's agricultural ventures. COSEP, the business association, represented the interests of those interested in reclaiming their property.[61] The privatisation of the land was finally agreed to by accepting the Chamorro government's offer to deed to the labour unions 25 percent of stock in the plantations, farms and processing plants.[62] In the end, out of 599 plantations with 310,000 *manzanas* (1 *manzana* = 1.72 acres), demobilised soldiers of the Sandinista Popular Army received 54,000; the former Contra soldiers received 24,000; 97,000 were turned over to the workers; and only 154,000 were returned to their former owners.[63] While the privatisation of land had not fundamentally affected the broad outlines of the Sandinista agrarian reform, over time market pressures led to the gradual restoration of the *latifundos* of the past.

Wheelock met personally with such large landowners as Carlos Pellas, the Lacayo Montealegre family, and the McGregor family to assure them that the FSLN would not oppose the return of their land and their processing plants.[64] The return of the San Antonio sugar mill to Carlos Pellas, a capitalist who had never left Nicaragua during the revolution, represented, because of his name, wealth and stature, a particularly significant and symbolic privatisation of industry. The process moved along rapidly. On the anniversary of her second year in office, Violeta Chamorro made a tour of the country during which she visited the sites of fields and plants which had been returned to Coca Cola and Pepsi Cola (bottling), La Colonia (supermarkets), Camas Luna

60   Lacayo 2006, p. 378.
61   Lacayo 2006, p. 301; Close 2005, pp. 212–16.
62   Lacayo 2006, p. 377.
63   Mayorga 2007, p. 62.
64   Lacayo 2006, p. 356.

(furniture), Eskimo (ice cream), La Perfecta (dairy products), and Fogelsa (refrigeration for bottling plants).[65]

To get a sense of the pace of developments, CORNAP, National Corporations of the Public Sector, had 351 enterprises when the government took it over, but by the beginning of the third year, 46 had been returned to previous owners, 20 had been privatised, and 25 others were in the process of being privatised.[66] By 1993, out of some 351 state enterprises, 289 had been privatised; and by 1998, the process was practically complete.[67] A few state enterprises were not privatised, such as COFARMA, the pharmaceutical company that became part of the Ministry of Health.[68] But other state social services were privatised, such as some health, education and pension programmes.[69] Antonio Lacayo notes that when they were dealing with large and important properties that involved new investors, they always worked 'under the tutelage' of organisations such as US Agency for International Development (USAID) and the Inter-American Development Bank (IDB).[70] Later, the government also privatised slaughterhouses that exported beef to the United States.[71]

As Nicaragua entered into agreements with the International Monetary Fund and the World Bank, they insisted that the government privatise the largest enterprises, such as the state-owned telephone company (TELCOR), electrical company (INE), and water company (INNA). These firms had been state enterprises under Somoza, so this was an entirely new development, putting even more of the economy into private hands.[72] The IDB played the leading role in organising the privatisation of these utilities.[73] Over the protests of the labour unions, all of them were privatised by the end of 1997, though with the unions having the right to purchase as much as 25 percent of the stock.[74] Decisions were also made that would lead to the eventual privatisation of the ports, airports, the mail service, the water system, and other public companies as well.[75]

---

65   Lacayo 2006, p. 374.
66   Lacayo 2006, p. 377.
67   Mayorga 2007, p. 65.
68   Close 2005, p. 213.
69   Mayorga 2007, p. 57.
70   Lacayo 2006, p. 377.
71   Lacayo 2006, p. 640.
72   Mayorga 2007, p. 56.
73   Mayorga 2007, p. 74.
74   Close 2005, pp. 212–15.
75   Mayorga 2007, p. 59.

As the privatisations took place, there were, of course, conflicts that involved the government, the previous owners or new buyers, and the workers. Workers at the Jabón Prego soap factory in Granada occupied the factory, but it was nevertheless returned to its owners. La Fosferera, the national match company in Managua, was divided equally between the workers and a previous owner, Pedro Ortega Macho. When Ortega Macho fired the workers and decapitalised the plant, the courts decided in favour of the workers and issued a warrant for Ortega Macho's arrest.[76] While there were many such conflicts, and occasionally the unions or the workers' collective won, the general trend was that property was being returned to the previous owners.

What was the final upshot? Who owned the former state property in the end of the process?

> Between 1990 and 1996, 47 percent of the values of private stock had been given to the business sector, two-thirds through restitution. Only 13 percent was privatised in favour of the workers, and only 1.5 percent to veterans of the war. Some 28 percent was turned over to various government ministries and other state entities (the Tourism Institute, for example) where it could be managed until problems relating to property rights had been solved.[77]

Chamorro government officials themselves were frequently the beneficiaries of the process of return of properties, indemnification, and privatisation. Many Nicaraguan businessmen believed that the government was rife with corruption and was working to benefit family members and political allies.[78] In September 1994, it was revealed by *La Prensa* that Lacayo himself, Chamorro's chief of staff and the man most responsible for these arrangements, had received a payment of $14 million when Lehner of Boston and Borgonovo of El Salvador, the original owners of Punta Ñata on the Cosgüina Peninsula, were indemnified. While claiming that he had had nothing to do with those specific negotiations, he expressed his surprise and delight that the original owners of the property had been properly compensated – not to mention the boon to his personal bank account.[79]

---

76   Close 2005, p. 214.
77   Mayorga 2007, p. 65.
78   Spalding 1997, p. 256.
79   Lacayo 2006, p. 645, citing *La Prensa*.

Establishing a Capitalist Economy in the Neoliberal Era

Violeta Chamorro's administration, in addition to privatising the economy, worked with the IMF and the World Bank to carry out a series of structural adjustments that were in line with the government's own policies. Subsidies to food and fuel for workers and peasants were reduced, while small farmers lost access to credit.[80] The national budget was cut, partly through reducing the number of government ministries and also by reducing government programmes. Price controls were ended, while the government worked to hold down wages.[81] Tariffs were dramatically reduced, opening Nicaragua to foreign competition within its own markets.

The privatisation of formerly state-owner enterprises led to a 'dramatic fall in employment'.[82] Industrial employment in the 1980s, which had reached 106,000 people, fell to 86,000 in 1990, and then to 60,000 in 1996. This was 14 percent below the levels of the disastrous years 1985–9. The decline of industrial employment led to a deskilling of the working class, making it more difficult to contemplate the reactivation of the economy with the quality production demanded by international competition. In 2001, Nicaragua's industry was using dilapidated and obsolete equipment, lacked adequate financing, and was totally dependent on the importation of intermediate inputs and capital goods. At the same time, it had high operating costs, inadequate physical structures, poor public services, and few well-trained professionals and workers.[83]

Violetta Chomorro initiated the reintroduction of the free trade zone and maquiladoras. Somoza had actually first introduced these policies in 1976. When the Sandinistas came to power, they nationalised the maquiladoras under the name Zona Industrial de las Mercedes run by the Industrial Corporation of the People (COIP). Chamorro, with the help of the Central American Bank for Economic Integration (BCIE), privatised them within a new legal framework. Some were returned to their old owners, some – at least initially – were taken over by workers and unions, while others closed and new ones opened. The government, using BCIE loans, invested millions of dollars to refurbish the industrial park and the plants. Investors were offered ten years with no taxes and after that a 40 percent reduction in taxes.[84] In 1995, the free trade zone of Las Mercedes in Managua had 18 factories employing 7,000 workers, while by

---

80   Enríquez n.d.

81   International Monetary Fund 1997 and International Monetary Fund 2001.

82   Solà i Montserrat 2008, p. 371.

83   Solà i Montserrat 2008, p. 372.

84   Lacayo 2006, pp. 640–1; Vukelich 1994.

1997 several more factories had opened and the workforce had grown to 12,878. Many of the new workers came from state-owned factories that had been closed by the Chamorro administration. At the end of the Alemán administration in 2001, there were 40 factories employing some 34,476 workers.[85] While this represented a tremendous expansion of the maquiladora industry in the free trade zones, Nicaragua lagged far behind other Central American countries in the development of enterprise zones, maquiladoras, and production for export.

Nicaragua's free trade zone maquiladoras produced for US name brands and stores such as Walmart, K-Mart, and JC Penney. They paid workers 15 cents per hour; employees worked six or seven days a week and between 8 and 12 hours a day and took home between US$9.00 and US$12.00 per week. The Nicaraguan Ministry of Labour and the employers, later joined by the Sandinista labour unions, worked together to prevent workers from joining independent unions that might have improved their pay, benefits and conditions. A crisis in the Sandinista trade unions in 1994 led women workers who were CST members to create the Working and Unemployed Women's Movement 'María Elena Cuadra', a group that succeeded in organising several thousand women in the plants and won some improvements in conditions but without being able to develop the sort of workers' power movement that could really change the situation fundamentally by affecting the free trade zone's low-wage economy. While the María Elena Cuadra movement continued to exist as a non-governmental organisation with support from foundations in the US and Canada, it later turned from workers organising for power to education, job training, and micro-financing.[86] With the Sandinista party able to control its labour unions and keep them from organising broad fights for higher wages and better benefits and conditions, workers remained subject to the low-wage economy of the new Nicaragua.

What was the immediate impact of the Chamorro economic policies? *Envío* reported in November of 1992:

> According to United Nations data, 53% of the economically active population is under- or unemployed; 70% of all Nicaraguans have trouble satisfying their most basic needs; infant mortality is 71.8 per 1,000 live births; social security only covers 18% of the employed population; rural illiteracy is an estimated 40%; 3 out of 4 Nicaraguans do not have access to sewage services or even latrines; 62.5% have inadequate housing and

---

85 Solà i Montserrat 2008, p. 373.
86 Bickham Méndez 2005, pp. 25–59; 205–25.

no consistent access to potable water; 12.5% live in dangerously over-crowded conditions; and 70% have a calorie intake below the minimum considered necessary for normal development.[87]

For many, perhaps most, Nicaraguan people, the new regime was proving to be an unmitigated disaster.

Debates within the FSLN

The combination of continuing political turmoil, violence, and the calamitous economic and social situation meant that the FSLN continued to be under tremendous pressure from both the wealthy elites above and the working class and the poor below. The political tendencies that had emerged at the time of the FSLN First Congress held in 1991 developed into full-blown factional organisations over the next few years, creating a genuine debate over theory, politics, and strategy within the organisation. These factions first begun to debate their positions at the First Congress's Extraordinary Session held in 1994. Subsequently, Sergio Ramírez, leader of the FSLN National Assembly delegation, *comandante* Dora María Téllez, Carlos Fernando Chamorro, editor of the FSLN daily paper *Barricada*, and the poet-priest Ernesto Cardenal wrote a document titled 'For a *Sandinismo* that Returns to the Majorities', leading their tendency to be called 'The Majorities' (though they would prove to be a minority). Daniel Ortega, Tomás Borge, René Nuñez, and Henry Ruíz, all members of the National Directorate, joined by the party ideologue Julio López Campos, called their group the 'The Discussion Forum of the Sandinista Democratic Left' and produced a set of documents laying out their positions. The title of their document led them to be called (one is tempted to say, ironically) 'The Democratic Left'.

The Majorities, who were in essence social democrats, wanted to build a party capable of winning elections and, beyond that, building a new social consensus for democracy and socialism. Ramírez and his comrades criticised the FSLN leadership's historic tendency to see the statification, that is, the nationalisation of property, as the solution to the country's problems. The Democratic Left, on the other hand, still inspired by the Soviet Union and Cuba, defended state property and the organisation of the working-class and peasant masses in a socialist and anti-imperialist movement that would return to power through mass actions and electoral success. The Democratic Left put great

---

87   Envío Team 1992.

emphasis in the language of its document on representative and participatory democracy, though these had never been strong points in the FSLN leadership's practice.

Stripping away the rhetoric, the 1994 debate was one between the social-democratic critics led by the party's outstanding intellectuals such as Ramírez and Cardenal, and the historically Stalinist and Guevarist leaders of the FSLN such as Ortega, Borge and Ruiz. The latter won the votes and were reconfirmed as the FSLN leadership, strengthening the historic tendencies of vanguardism, democratic centralism, and the top-down dictation of directives to the party membership.[88] The debates within the FSLN led directly to the debates over the Constitution taking place in the Chamorro administration and the National Assembly, and from there to a Constitutional crisis.

The Struggle over the Constitution

In 1992, Violeta Chamorro's critics on the right, led by Cardinal Miguel Obando y Bravo, the right wing of the UNO, and a number of wealthy businessmen, had called for a new Constitution, but their effort fizzled out and the conservative opposition collapsed. A year later, frustrated and disappointed with the Chamorro administration's way of running the government, and with its politics which had failed to bring any improvement to the lives of the Nicaraguan people, a group of moderate legislators, led by Luis Humberto Guzmán of the Christian Democratic Union (UDC), began to meet to discuss how the Constitution of 1987 might be changed to create a more democratic and effective government. The combination of the UNO leadership's heavy-handed attempt to manage its congressional delegation and the crisis caused by Violeta Chamorro's dismissal of Humberto Ortega as head of the military in 1995 broke a number of legislators free from their previous allegiances, making a Constitutional revision possible.[89]

In late 1993, the FSLN and the UNO agreed to discuss Constitutional changes, but when those talks failed, the ever more independent moderate legislators began to put forward a call for 100 constitutional reforms. The proposed amendments dealt with everything from economic and property issues to political rights and the reform of state institutions. The discussion of these issues

---

88 Fonseca Terán 2005, pp. 475–90. While Fonseca Terán was a supporter of Ortega's so-called Democratic Left, he was in a faction that was critical of its political rightward drift. See p. 477, fn. 250.

89 Close 2005, pp. 233–6.

threatened the power of both Chamorro and the FSLN and had implications for the country's coming presidential elections. These struggles over the Constitution led to what was perhaps the most democratic moment in Nicaragua's recent history.

In 1994, Sergio Ramírez, leader of the Majorities faction and of the FSLN bloc in the National Assembly, led virtually the entire FSLN delegation in an open rebellion against Daniel Ortega. The struggle originated in part in the ambitions of Antonio Lacayo, Daniel Ortega and Sergio Ramírez, all of them possible contenders for the presidency in 1995, but it also reflected the serious political differences that had emerged between Ramírez on the one hand and Ortega and Lacayo on the other.[90] Ramírez, his bloc of thirty FSLN National Assembly delegates, and his other followers left the FSLN and created a new, independent organisation, the Sandinista Renovation Movement (MRS).

Suddenly, because of the FSLN split, the legislature became an institution of real discussion, debate, and decision-making, a parliament of real power. The MRS legislators in the Assembly were joined by other legislators from various parties – left, right, and centre – who also rejected the Lacayo-Ortega triumvirs. For the first time in modern Nicaraguan history, there was a genuinely independent legislature that was not controlled by the president. While this opposition only lasted from mid-1994 to January 1997, it passed a number of laws and Constitutional amendments intended to democratise Nicaraguan politics. Presidential powers were drastically curtailed. The president could no longer impose taxes, manage the budget, spend money, or create new governmental departments. The National Assembly recognised the rights of indigenous communities, banned censorship, and dropped 'Sandinista' from the names of the police and the army. The Supreme Court was expanded from seven to twelve members and organised into four divisions with different specialties. This turned out to be a political division of the court, however, rather than a genuine reform of the court. The Assembly also passed a law against nepotism, preventing blood relatives and in-laws of the president from running for the office of president, a law specifically intended to prevent Lacayo, son-in-law of President Violeta Chamorro, from being a candidate for president in 1996.[91]

The rewriting of the Constitution, however, was not solely about creating a genuine liberal state; it was also about creating a *magna carta* that was congruent with capitalism. Most importantly, the amended Constitution permitted

---

90   Lacayo 2006 pp. 644–5.
91   Lacayo 2006, p. 639; Fonseca Terán 2005, p. 494.

private property, whether personal property, real estate, or the instruments and means of production, while prohibiting confiscation and calling for compensation in cases of imminent domain. With these constitutional changes, the Sandinista's attempts during the revolutionary era to construct a Soviet- or Cuban-style bureaucratic collectivist regime were definitively reversed, and Nicaraguan capitalists were given the full backing of the state.

President Violeta Chamorro, however, refused to have the constitutional amendments and bills published in *La Gaceta*, the official government record, a step necessary to officially make them the laws of the land. She argued that the National Assembly had in fact gone far beyond its authority, acting more like a Constituent Assembly and undertaking what was in fact the writing of a new constitution. Therefore, she refused to publish the National Assembly's decisions and make them law. She also refused, as did the National Assembly, to abide by a decision of the newly restructured Supreme Court. Faced with this intransigence, Luis Humberto Guzmán, President of the National Assembly, decided to publish the new laws in *Nuevo Diario*, the newspaper of the independent left, and in the conservative *La Prensa*, the Chamorro family newspaper. Nicaragua suddenly had two rival constitutions, one supported by the president and the other by the legislature. The constitutional crisis continued until June 1995 when Cardinal Obando y Bravo negotiated an agreement providing a framework for the implementation of the new amendments and laws. With these constitutional changes, the legal framework for a new Nicaraguan state was created, combining the police and the army that the Sandinistas had created with the new government institutions and bureaucracy that emerged under Violeta Chamorro.[92]

The founding of the MRS and the political reforms of 1994–7 represented a brief democratic moment in the Assembly and in Nicaraguan political life, but they failed to advance either a democratic or democratic socialist movement in the country. The MRS leaders, many with long histories in the guerrilla movement and in the FSLN leadership, were principally intellectuals, such as Sergio Ramírez, Ernesto Cardenal and Giacondo Belli, or legislators of the FLSN bloc in parliament. Ortega and his group, however, were party leaders who had control of the FSLN party machinery and of the mass organisations. Consequently, when the MRS representatives later ran for office under their new party name, they found that they had virtually no electoral support. Nor did the MRS do any organising among workers, peasants or the poor. They did not build a social movement; they were a purely electoral party. Their

---

92   Close 2005, pp. 246–51.

opposition to what they perceived as Ortega's dictatorship even led them by the 2000s to attempt to ally with the right, moving the MRS farther away from the social-democratic politics of the founders.[93] The failure of the MRS to build a social movement and an electoral base meant that Nicaragua had no left political party in the twenty-first century, except the corrupt FSLN of Ortega.

The New World of the NGOs

While the MRS failed to create a new political party, some new progressive social forces were emerging in Nicaragua. The development of neoliberalism and globalisation and the collapse of Communism, together with the defeat of the revolutionary left of the 1960s and 1970s, led to the development of three new social phenomena: civil society; non-governmental organisations (NGOs); and the new social movements. The idea of civil society first developed in Eastern Europe in the struggle against Communist totalitarianism and later spread to Latin America, particularly to Brazil, where the left adopted the concept as it resisted the military dictatorships in the southern cone. Civil society referred to social spaces and groups not controlled by the state, which, simply by existing, represented a political alternative.

The civil society concept was less significant in Nicaragua because since the fall of Somoza there had not been a totalitarian state that had succeeded in eliminating other social forces. Still, because the FSLN and its mass organisations had so dominated politics and society, the concept of civil society had some utility in the new neoliberal period in legitimising voluntary associations, independent organisation, the right to protest, free press and free speech. Within civil society there developed three broad currents: first, the Movement for Nicaragua associated with the opposition, particularly the Liberal Constitutionalist Party (PCL); second, the Civil Coordinating Committee that inclined towards the positions of the MRS; and third, the Social Coordinating Committee that was made up of the FSLN and its mass organisations. Each of these constellations had the capability of mobilising around social and political issues.

Non-governmental organisations (or NGOs) were not-for-profit groups and institutions funded by foundations that took up work on specific issues such as economic development, women's health and welfare, or environmental issues.

---

93   Envío Team 2001 and Rogers 2011a.

While there had been some NGOs in Nicaragua before, the majority of Nicaragua's NGOs were established in the 1990s. The NGOs responded in part to the shrinking of the state's social welfare organisations – for example, they provided alternative institutions and sources of funding to meet health and education needs – and they were a response to the disappearance of revolutionary left organisations to which they offered a reformist alternative.

Church groups, corporations, and political organisations created NGOs, some state institutions became transformed into NGOs, and former Sandinista *comandantes* established their own NGOs.[94] While some of the NGOs had a social-democratic political outlook, most were simply do-gooder organisations working on some particular issue or project. Many of the NGOs came to accept the dominance of conservative politics and neoliberalism, becoming adjuncts to the existing political economy. Others even became advocates of neoliberalism, working to help entrepreneurs establish themselves and succeed in the competitive world of the open economy. Some of the NGOs became corrupt, raising funds abroad to provide their directors and staff with middle-class lives, while ostensibly working to address some social issue.

The term 'new social movements' referred to movements other than the traditional class movements of the left: the workers and peasants. In many countries, feminists and women's movements, the gay and lesbian movements, and the environmental movement began to appear in the 1970s. The most important social movement to emerge in Nicaragua in the 1990s was the women's movement. The defeat of the Sandinistas and the election of Chamorro tended to break the stranglehold of the FSLN's hold over its mass organisations, and in particular it led the breakup of the Luisa Amanda Espinoza Association of Nicaraguan Women, many branches of which became autonomous. By 1992, there were 200 local women's collectives, centres, associations and institutions.[95] Later in the 1990s, many other women's NGOs, centres and collectives were formed by women who had never been part of the FSLN or its mass organisations. The Working and Unemployed Women's Movement (Movimiento de Mujeres Trabajadoras y Desempleadas 'María Elena Cuadra' or MEC), which dedicated itself to organising, educating and training working women in the maquiladoras, is an example that has already been mentioned.

The new women's movement took up issues that had been off-limits in the Sandinista Association of Nicaraguan women, such as 'violence against

---

94   Rocha 2011.
95   'Women's Social Movements in Nicaragua' n.d.

women, homophobia and lesbianism, the need for nonsexist education, and the autonomy of the women's movement vis-à-vis the party'.[96] Many women's organisations dedicated themselves to women's issues, such as domestic violence, women's reproductive health, women's psychological health, and women's economic needs. These organisations not only carried out important social work, but some also advocated reforms and engaged in lobbying the government. The Women's Network Against Violence, founded in the mid-1990s, for example, brought together about twenty women's organisations, including women's collectives, women's groups in labour unions, and women's church groups to deal with domestic, social and political violence against women. Perhaps the most significant group established, because of its strong position in favour of women's autonomy and its willingness to stand up to the political parties and the state, was the Women's Autonomous Movement (MAM).[97]

The neoliberal economic policies of Chamorro and the other conservative governments had a particularly adverse effect on women. With the closing of state factories and privatisation, there were massive layoffs and many women lost their jobs while others tried to survive in the informal economy. Women who had jobs found that their wages could not keep up with rising prices, even if those prices were rising more slowly than before. Cutbacks in health and education had a disproportionate impact on women and their families. While women's organisations helped women with some of these issues, they proved incapable of leading a collective resistance to the neoliberal assault on women. Throughout this period, as conservative and patriarchal values and capitalist competition reasserted themselves, despite many extraordinary educational and organising efforts by the groups described here, women generally lost economic and political power as well as social status and found themselves reduced in many areas to a second class status behind men.

The development of civil society, the new social movements and the NGOs did have progressive aspects, defending as they often did issues such as political democracy, women's rights, and protection of the environment. They did not, however, have the power to pose a political alternative for the nation as a whole. They were too dispersed to have the social weight necessary to produce significant change. They did not represent the independent socialist party that would have been necessary to challenge both the right and the pseudo-left which the FSLN had become. Power remained with the triumvirs.

---

96   Santamaría n.d.
97   Santamaría n.d.

The Chamorro government, having allied with the FSLN, did not bring democracy to Nicaragua, but rather brought a return to government by pacts intended to enhance the power of the elites and to exclude the majority of Nicaraguans. Nor did Chamorro bring about a return to competitive capitalism, open markets, and the neoliberal promise of prosperity. The privatisation of state industries benefitted the old oligarchy, foreign corporations, and the Conservative and Sandinista leaders; at the same time, unemployment and falling wages brought destitution, hunger and ill health to the majorities. The most significant achievement of the Chamorro administration was its success in creating enough political stability to attract the old oligarchy to return to Nicaragua, claim its previously owned property, and begin to reconstruct a capitalist class. Politically, the Chamorro administration proved to be a transition not to modern capitalism, representative government, and democracy, but rather to continued authoritarianism and even greater corruption.

CHAPTER 9

Alemán and Bolaños: Corruption in Power (1996–2006)

The period from 1996 to 2006 witnessed the return to power of the *somocistas*, that is, of the Somoza family's close friends, economic partners, and political collaborators who had helped to run and had benefitted from the Somoza dictatorship. The two men who presided over the country during this period, Arnoldo Alemán and Enrique Bolaños, both part of the old regime and virulent opponents of the Sandinista revolution, learned in different ways that it was impossible to rule without the support of Daniel Ortega, the leader of the Sandinista Front for National Liberation. The FSLN that they dealt with now, however, was not the one they had fought years before. Once a revolutionary organisation, by the 1990s the FSLN had become a part of the liberal state, just as several of its leading members had become a part of the new bourgeoisie that emerged in the post-revolutionary period. When necessary, the FSLN was willing to be a partner with the old *somocistas*, while always trying to make the other party into the junior partner.

The combination of the Washington Consensus of open market policies that dominated the world economy throughout this period, the return to political pacts between the major parties in Nicaragua, and the avarice of the political leaders of all parties make this one of the most corrupt and sordid periods in Nicaraguan history. The struggles over political power and wealth in this era transformed both the national political institutions and the parties. Political struggles ceased to revolve principally around political programmes to set the direction for the country and its people, and instead came to revolve around the fight to win political offices, to control of government departments and agencies where deals could be made with the private sector, and to gain access to the public treasury. While the FSLN was not itself the principal initiator or perpetrator of political corruption in this period, its alliance with Alemán, who was the most notorious culprit, further sullied the FSLN's already tainted reputation and alienated and demoralised many of its followers. The Nicaraguan people, disappointed in the parties and their leaders, became cynical about politics, and cynicism made them apathetic. In non-election periods, fewer than half of all voters identified with any political party. This new stage in the degeneration of Nicaraguan politics began with the election of 1995 that brought Arnoldo Alemán to power.

Arnoldo Alemán had been a supporter of the Somoza dictatorship right up until its fall in 1979, after which he became an active opponent of the Sandinista government. It is not surprising that he would have found himself on that side. Alemán, born in Managua in 1946, was the son of Arnoldo Alemán Sandoval, an official in the Somoza government. Alemán, the son, attended the La Salle School and then studied business law at the National Autonomous University of Nicaragua, becoming a lawyer for a variety of commercial firms and banks. One of them, Inversiones Nicaragüenses de Desarrollo, s.a. (INDESA), was one of the first companies nationalised by the Sandinistas following the revolution. The Sandinistas also expropriated property owned personally by Alemán, and in 1980 the Sandinista government arrested him in a roundup of supposed counter-revolutionaries. Alemán spent nine months in prison, preventing him from attending his father's funeral in Miami, Florida. These experiences deeply embittered him against the Sandinista government.[1]

After release from prison, Alemán left Nicaragua to live briefly in the United States, but then soon returned to become involved in the leadership of several business organisations, including the High Council of Private Enterprise (COSEP), an organisation that resisted the policies of both the Sandinistas and the Violeta Chamorro government. His political opposition to the Sandinistas led him to become active in the right-wing Liberal Constitutionalist Party (PLC). The PLC had been founded in 1968 by Ramiro Sacasa Guerrero, Somoza's Secretary of Labour, as a current within Liberalism arising out of the Somoza regime but critical of the Somoza dictatorship.[2] Alemán became head of the party and in 1990, running on an anti-Sandinista platform, he won election to the municipal council which then chose him to be Mayor of Managua.

Known as *El Gordo*, that is, the Fat Man, Alemán was a larger-than-life figure who joked and laughed with reporters. A hand-waver and baby-kisser, he was personable and gregarious: an easy man to like. As mayor, his public works programmes, such as paved streets, traffic circles and fountains, and his support for the private development of shopping malls, gas stations and fast food restaurants made him extremely popular with all classes in the national capital. He also had city workers paint over dozens of Sandindista murals in Managua, obliterating the country's revolutionary history and angering FSLN supporters, while at the same time putting up new billboards that proclaimed: 'The Mayor gets things done'. The people mostly seemed to agree. At the same time, he kept up a barrage of criticism of Violeta Chamorro for her alliance with

1   Barcelona Centre for International Affairs 2011c.
2   For a history of the PLC, see Nuñez 2005.

the FSLN, suggesting that he would return Nicaragua to a mythical period of peace and prosperity before the revolution.

In 1995, as required by law, Alemán resigned as mayor to run for president. He brought together several branches of the Liberal family of political parties into a new electoral coalition called the Liberal Alliance, a genuine coalition unlike Chamorro's UNO. His own Constitutionalist Liberal Party (PLC) created a national grassroots organisation similar to the Sandinistas' and, like it, based among the poor. It was especially strong in the less populous Atlantic Coast region where the PLC became the leading party.[3] His presidential campaign won the backing of the wealthy Nicaraguans living in the country, but was also strongly supported financially by wealthy Nicaraguans and Cuban exiles in Miami, people who hated the Sandinistas and who hoped to see not only a right-wing victory over the left, but also expected to benefit personally and financially from Alemán's election.[4]

The Election of 1996

When the official pre-election period began in 1996, Alemán carried out a vigorous campaign, travelling in a fleet of four-wheel vehicles filled with US-trained campaign organisers, distributing tons of caps and t-shirts emblazoned with his logo to cities and towns throughout the country. He was populist in style, running against the economic and political elites and their subservience to international financial organisations. His slogan was 'War on unemployment and poverty', promising to overcome them through foreign investment that would enable a modern and growing economy.

Unlike Liberals of the past, Alemán adopted a religious rhetoric and sought and received the support of the church hierarchy. Cardinal Obando y Bravo performed a mass with Alemán in the church as a way of giving Alemán his blessing, and gave a sermon comparing Daniel Ortega to a snake. Alemán suggested throughout his campaign that if his opponent Daniel Ortega and the FSLN were elected and returned to power, they would take the country back to war and economic crisis, while he would lead the country into a peaceful and prosperous future. An attempt on Alemán's life on 25 January by a group of armed men (presumably pro-Sandinistas) that left one of his bodyguards dead and

---

3 Katherine Hoyt, 'Parties and Pacts in Contemporary Nicaragua', in Close and Deonandan 2004, p. 19.
4 Mayorga 2007, p. 97; Hazel Plunkett 2002, pp. 33–5.

three others wounded may have worked in his favour, casting his leftist opponents in a bad light and winning sympathy for him as a victim.[5]

There was no doubt that Daniel Ortega would be the candidate of the FSLN, but, under the country's new election laws, parties were required to hold primary elections and Vilma Nuñez, a long-time FSLN activist, disappointed and angered by the party's authoritarianism, decided to run against Ortega in the primary. Nuñez brought impeccable revolutionary credentials to her campaign. Born on 25 November 1938 in Acoyapa, Chontales, the daughter of a leader of the Conservative Party who was an opponent of Somoza, she attended Catholic Schools in her hometown and then in Managua before going on to the University of Nicaragua in León in 1958. There she joined the Committee to Free Political Prisoners, participated with Carlos Fonseca in the student meeting with Anastasio Somoza García, and later survived the student massacre of July 1959. At first a member of the Conservative Party and later a specialist in penal law and human rights, she gradually became involved with the FSLN, formally joining the party in 1975. In the months before the triumph of 1979, she was arrested, jailed, tortured, and condemned to prison as well as fined millions of dollars for arms trafficking. She was freed by the Sandinista revolution. During the revolutionary decade, she served in the Supreme Court and became its vice-president in the period from 1979–87; from 1987–90, she headed the Nicaraguan Human Rights Commission; and after the Sandinista defeat in 1990, she founded the non-governmental Nicaragua Human Rights Centre. Her candidacy was not only a dissident protest against the party's lack of democracy, but also a statement about its failure to include women in the leadership.[6] While Ortega easily defeated her, Nuñez's candidacy represented a contribution to a growing democratic opposition to the FSLN leadership.

Having won the primary handily, Daniel Ortega transformed himself completely for the 1996 election. Ortega adopted a new image, a new style, and a new rhetoric. He and other FSLN leaders gave up their olive green *guerrilla* uniforms emblazoned with Sandinista logos, and adopted civilian dress. For the first time, Ortega appeared in public with his wife Rosario Murillo and their children, presenting the image of a respectable family man. He began to include religious language in his speeches. He referred to the United States as Nicaragua's 'great neighbour', rather than as its implacable enemy, and he called

---

5   Pérez-Boltadano 2008, pp. 706–26.
6   Vilma Nuñez de Escorcia, 'Firmeza y dignidad de la mujer sandinista' (interview), in Balto-
    dano 2010, Vol. 2, pp. 393–407.

for national unity, not class struggle against the rich. Ortega told the press: 'As Sandino said, "Neither extreme right nor extreme left. The United Front is our slogan"'.[7] Ortega remained, however, an advocate of social programmes for working people and the poor.

The contest presented the public with a clear choice, at least at the level of discourse, between Ortega's social democratic rhetoric and Alemán's right-wing oratory. The vote on 20 October 1996 revealed the degree to which Nicaraguan politics had changed since the revolution of 1979 or even since the election of Chamorro. Alemán won a landslide victory, defeating Ortega by a vote of 50.9 percent to 37.8 percent. His Liberal Alliance also did well, with 42 Liberal representatives out of a total of 93 holding seats in the National Assembly, as well as 12 other reliable votes from other parties. The *somocistas* were back in power. Alemán became president of Nicaragua on 10 January 1997, ushering in an era of not just reactionary but notoriously corrupt practices.

Alemán had few political ideals and the PLC, though it claimed the heritage of Liberalism, was not really an ideological party. Liberalism luckily turned out to be the order of the day. The Liberal principles of yesteryear corresponded more or less to the neoliberal economic policies that, under the leadership of the United States and the international financial institutions, had become dominant since the 1980s in countries around the world: open markets, privatisation, reduction of the social budget, and anti-labour policies. In contradistinction to the Liberals' historic anti-clericalism, however, Alemán established a firm alliance with Cardinal Miguel Obando y Bravo and the conservative hierarchy of the Catholic Church, ties that held up even as revelations of the new president's corruption began to surface. While neoliberalism and Catholic providentialism are profoundly different social philosophies, each conservative in its own way, they proved to mesh well together.[8]

As president, Alemán's pragmatic objective was to strengthen and especially to enrich the Liberals who had not benefitted politically or financially as the Conservatives and the Sandinistas had during the Chamorro years. His method for achieving these goals was to use the government, its institutions, its funds, and its employees for his private purposes.[9] Chamorro's neoliberal economic policies from 1990 to 1996 had succeeded finally in her last years in office in initiating a very modest revival of the Nicaraguan economy. Alemán continued

---

7   Cited in Pérez-Boltadano 2008, p. 708.
8   The phenomenon of an alliance between providentialism and neoliberalism was international. For example, religious conservatism and neoliberalism came to power together in Turkey under Prime Minister Recep Tayyip Erdogan in the same period.
9   Pérez-Baltodano 2008, p. 707.

those policies and during his administration the economy continued to gain momentum, though this was more a result of the American economic boom and the general improvement in the world economy than of any particular policies that he adopted.

Alemán's government invested in infrastructure while the private sector put its money into finance, commerce, industry, and, above all, agriculture. Alemán encouraged foreign investment, foreign trade, export processing zones with their maquiladoras, hotels for tourists, and shopping centres for the country's better off. Nicaragua's economy grew at an average rate of 5 percent a year while inflation remained low, there was a growth of employment, and wages even rose. Poverty fell from 75.7 percent of the population in 1993 to 72.6 percent in 1998; there was also some decrease in malnutrition among children.[10] The government, however, instituted no new social programmes to deal with unemployment and poverty. There were no improvements in education or public health programmes. Those matters were not part of Alemán's concerns.

Alemán, like Chamorro before him, sought the assistance of the International Monetary Fund through Structural Adjustment Programs, but his relationship with the IMF broke down because of flagrant corruption in the privatisation programmes, the failure to fulfil the requirements and carry out the necessary procedures, and his evasion of required meetings with IMF officials. On the other hand, international donor nations and organisations, though they had become dubious about giving assistance to the Alemán government because of its lack of democracy and transparency, still continued to contribute because of the country's dire need. In 1999, the country received $554 million in foreign aid, not including contributions from foreign NGOs. Just as under the Sandinistas and Chamorro, foreign aid remained a significant and essential part of the national economy.[11] There was little time to focus on the country's economic and social problems, however, once the corruption scandals began.

The Alemán Corruption Scandals

The neoliberal programme of deregulation and privatisation that had begun under Chamorro meshed wonderfully with the methods of Alemán and his

---

10 David R. Dye and David Close, 'Patrimonialism and Economic Policy in the Alemán Administration', in Close and Deonandan 2004, pp. 119–28.

11 Dye and Deonandan 2004, pp. 127–33.

associates and their predilection for embezzlement. Every government transaction provided opportunities for political graft, misappropriation, and pilfering. The continuing privatisations of the telecommunications and energy industries, as well as the social security system, gave ample opportunities for decisions made on the basis of nepotism, friendship, and party loyalty. So too did government oil leases, land policies, and concessions to use natural resources. Each of these opportunities was seized upon to enrich Alemán and his associates.

Comptroller General Agustín Jarquín was among the first to discover and disclose the corruption in the Alemán administration, finding irregularities in the central bank, the state television station, the state-owned electric company, the grain distributor, and the Ministry of Finance. Both dissident Liberals and the FSLN leader in the National Assembly accused Alemán of corruption and demanded an investigation. The comptroller carried out an audit of the president's accounts and found that his personal wealth had increased from $26,118 in 1990, to $300,000 in 1995, and to almost $1 million in January 1997. The report said the president had acquired real estate, bank accounts, and stock. It also found that he used government funds and public employees to perform work on his properties.[12]

While Alemán denied the allegations, investigations continued. In August 1997, the comptroller annulled the privatisation of 51 percent of the stock of the Nicaraguan Bank of Industry and Commerce (BANIC) whose directors had illegally given themselves $1.5 million in bonds, pay, and salary overdrafts. BANIC had also made unjustifiably large loans to Alemán's cronies. In addition, it was learned that public employees were being required to contribute to Alemán's Constitutional Liberal Party. In late October of 1998, the ongoing media reports of the corruption scandal were interrupted by the arrival of Hurricane Mitch.

Hurricane Mitch, the largest hurricane of the 1998 season, though it never actually entered Nicaraguan territory, brought tremendous rainfall – between 25 and 50 inches – leading to flooding and mudslides that devastated many areas of the country. The storm, which hit Central America in October, affected two million Nicaraguans, destroyed almost 30,000 houses and damaged nearly another 20,000, while also affecting 340 schools and 90 health centres. Over 90 bridges were damaged and roads in many places were washed away. Some 3,800 people were killed, over 300,000 people displaced and total damage was estimated at $1 billion. Foundations in the United States and Europe directed

---

12   López Castellanos 2013, p. 55.

millions of dollars to non-governmental organisations in Nicaragua, creating new ones and revitalising and strengthening others, and they provided much assistance after the storm.

For Alemán, Mitch represented yet another opportunity for graft. As funds poured into the Nicaraguan government, Alemán used them to strengthen political patronage and to reinforce his ties with the Catholic Church hierarchy. Reconstruction funds were diverted to his loyal supporters, and tax division director Byron Jerez used reconstruction money to build himself a beach house. Alemán sent his cabinet and family members on a European vacation under the pretext of participating in the Stockholm Summit to aid Central America held by the Inter-American Development Bank. He also brought Nicaragua into the Highly-Indebted Poor Countries (HIPC) initiative as a way of increasing his own legitimacy. In a ten-year retrospective of the storm's impact, *Envío* wrote: 'The abuses committed with the reconstruction funds were the massive trunk that broke the back of a camel already bowed under enormous loads of corruption. Even international cooperation could not help but see and condemn it. Comptroller General Agustín Jarquín documented and denounced it and sent it to court, which landed him, not the perpetrators, in jail as a result of the then embryonic FSLN-PLC pact'.[13]

The arrest of Jarquín and his colleagues proved to be a mistake. Foreign ambassadors, international financial organisations, businessmen and economists criticised the government; some even visited Jarquín in jail. On International Human Rights Day, 10 December, thousands of Nicaraguans marched to protest against the comptroller's arrest. On Christmas Day, Alemán released Jarquín and the other prisoners who had spent 45 days in jail.[14] Corruption not only caused a political backlash, but also contributed to the failure of a number of banks in 1998, among them BANIC and the Sandinista-run Interbank.[15]

Backed by his party and the Liberal Alliance, supported by wealthy businessmen who either profited from the corruption or feared to challenge him, and sustained by Cardinal Obando y Bravo and the Catholic hierarchy, Alemán was able to keep his grip on power throughout 1998 and 1999, despite continuing and expanding allegations of malfeasance. But, by 1998, the defection of some Liberals and other allies in the National Assembly had eroded his majority, and he found that to pass legislation he needed the support of the FSLN. With his political power slipping away, and fearing that he might be impeached,

---

13   Rocha 2009. See also Pérez-Baltodano 2008, pp. 719, 726.

14   Hoyt, 'Parties and Pacts', in Close and Deonandan 2004, pp. 21–4.

15   On the Interbank problems, see Nitlápan-Envío Team 2000.

indicted, and imprisoned, he sought an alliance with Daniel Ortega who, as it happened, also found himself in potential trouble with the law.

The Pact of 1999

Alemán's problem, as we have explained, was the threat of indictment and prosecution for his corrupt practices. Daniel Ortega's problem was the accusation made in 1998 by his step-daughter Zoilamérica Nerváez, a 30-year old FSLN member, sociologist, and director of the Center for International Studies (CEI) in Managua, that he had sexually, physically, and psychologically abused her. The accusations shocked and outraged many in Nicaragua and abroad. Ortega had secretly married his wife Rosario Murillo in 1979 and had legally adopted her daughter in 1986, though little was known about the reclusive first family until he brought them into his election campaigns in the 1990s. In 1998, Nerváez released a 48-page report asserting – and detailing – that Ortega had molested her from 1979 when she was 11 and had continued doing so until 1990 when she turned 21. She duly filed charges in court against Ortega.

Ortega and his wife Murillo both denied the accusations and the Nicaraguan courts could take no action because as a legislator Ortega enjoyed immunity from prosecution. Still, the legal situation was complicated. The Inter-American Court of Human Rights accepted Nervéz's case on 15 October 2001, while on 18 December the Nicaraguan courts removed the charges against Ortega, though the Inter-American Court was still considering them. With Nerváez pursuing the matter in international venues, Ortega could not feel secure unless he maintained his congressional majority. Both Alemán and Ortega feared that if they lost political power they might be prosecuted and imprisoned; it was that shared sense of insecurity and imminent danger that united them in a political pact.

The Pact of January 2000 between the FSLN and the PLC, involving the revision of the Nicaraguan Constitution and Electoral Law, distributed more or less equally to both parties positions and power in the Supreme Court, the Supreme Electoral Council, the High Council of the Controller, the Attorney General's Office, and the Superintendent of Banks. This was done by expanding the number of members of these institutions and by adding new members as needed to balance the FSLN and PLC. There was also a new property law that protected the Sandinistas' real estate, homes, and businesses received at the time of the piñata of 1979. And Alemán, without having to run for election, was given a seat in the National Assembly, so that now both Ortega and Alemán enjoyed parliamentary immunity from prosecution. The law also increased the number of votes needed in parliament in order to remove protection of immunity from a representative. Finally, the pact established that in the event that no candidate had a majority in presidential elections, a new and lower threshold of 35 percent would be sufficient to declare a winner without a runoff.[16] This was just about the percentage (37 percent) that Ortega had received in the last election.

Like the pacts of the Somoza years, the Alemán-Ortega Pact of 1999 represented a deal between the country's economic and political elites intended to exclude the mass of Nicaraguans from the most important political decisions being made, starting with the pact itself. It also created in effect a two-party system, eliminating any significant role for minor parties on the right or on the left. It reinforced the extreme centralism in both the PLC and the FSLN, and it increased the power of the parties' respective *caudillos*, Alemán and Ortega. Daniel Ortega and the FSLN emerged from the negotiations of the pact as the real winners, their position strengthened and with Alemán now dependent upon them (some said he was their prisoner). Moreover, the Pact of 1999 committed the FSLN not only to the bourgeois political system, but also to an undemocratic and corrupt version of parliamentary politics.

The 2001 Election

The Pact of 1999 laid the legal and political basis for the coming elections of 2001. The damage done to Alemán's reputation by the corruption charges made it impossible for him to consider a run for presidency, but he continued to control the PLC and the Liberal Alliance and chose a successor whom he believed that he could dominate: his vice-president and head of the Committee of National Integrity, Enrique Bolaños Geyer. Many took it for granted that Bolaños was merely a placeholder for Alemán who planned to return to the presidency in 2006. The old cotton farmer did not turn out to be the man that Alemán thought he was, nor was the future the one that he expected.

Bolaños, born in 1928 in Masaya, was the descendant of Spanish and German immigrants who had become successful farmers. Educated in Catholic schools in Masaya and Granada, he then attended the University of St. Louis in Missouri, graduating in 1962 with a bachelor's degree in engineering. He subsequently studied advanced management at the Central American Institute of

---

16   Pérez-Baltodano 2008, p. 727; Fonseca Terán 2005, pp. 536–47.

Administration and Business (INCAE) which trained the presidents and CEOs of corporations throughout the region. Already in 1952 Bolaños had begun to plant cotton, becoming one of the developers of the cotton industry and a partner in the Bolaños-Saimsa Group. His family was Liberal by tradition, and he joined the somewhat critical PLC wing of the Liberal family, though he was careful to keep his own counsel. By the 1970s, he had risen to become one of the country's leading capitalists, the director of the Eastern Cotton Growers Association, the Nicaraguan Chamber of Industry, and the High Council of Private Enterprise (COSEP).[17]

On 16 June 1979, as the FSLN was in its final push to take power, Bolaños was driving his jeep between Masaya and Granada when he was stopped and arrested by a Sandinista patrol. In what must have been a terrifying experience in the midst of the revolution, he was taken before a popular tribunal and tried but found innocent, presumably because he had no direct role in the Somoza government. Following the revolution, the Sandinista government expropriated many of Bolaños's factories and cotton farms, turning over the farmland to landless peasants. The Sandinistas harassed the Bolaños family repeatedly and Enrique Bolaños himself was arrested and jailed for short periods on three occasions for activities related to his role as a leader and spokesman for Nicaraguan business organisations. While an outspoken opponent of the Sandinistas and an organiser of the domestic opposition, he was not directly associated with the Contras.[18]

With his governmental experience as vice-president and as a leader of the Nicaraguan business organisation, Bolaños – though completely colourless and lacking in personal charisma – was a strong candidate. He campaigned on a programme of opposition to the Sandinistas and a promise to end government corruption. Bolaños, like Chamorro and Alemán before him, had the backing of Cardinal Obando y Bravo and the Catholic hierarchy and, while the United States government was officially neutral, President George W. Bush made clear his opposition to the FSLN and the other parties and his support for Bolaños. Just before the elections, *La Prensa* ran a banner headline proclaiming 'PRESIDENT BUSH SUPPORTS BOLAÑOS'.

At the end of 2000, as the FSLN was discussing the coming presidential election, Humberto Ortega wrote a public document in which he urged Daniel Ortega not to run again for the presidency. Humberto argued that the FSLN should develop into a modern political party with 'a collective leadership'.

---

17   Barcelona Centre for International Affairs 2011b.
18   Barcelona Centre for International Affairs 2011b.

In private conversations with his brother, Humberto told Daniel that it was impossible for the FSLN to win the election and that he would be better to sit this one out rather than risk a reversal, that is, a defeat and perhaps an even lower percentage of the vote. And, Humberto argued, if, while still remaining the head of the FSLN, Daniel declined to run, he would appear to be a more democratic leader.[19]

Despite his brother's shrewd advice, Daniel Ortega decided to run for president and had no difficulty in winning the backing of the party that he had come to dominate. In 2001, Ortega ran as an opponent of the neoliberal policies and the corruption of the Alemán government of which Bolaños had been an integral part. Once again Ortega abandoned the Sandinistas' black-and-red banners, hung up his *guerrilla* uniform, and wearing civilian clothes, campaigned beside his wife. He adopted a discourse that was both social-democratic and religious. The FSLN, now quite an experienced electoral party, organised its members across the country to get out the vote for Daniel Ortega. In this election, the FSLN had no fear of candidates to its left since the Supreme Electoral Council, controlled by the FSLN and the PLC, had disqualified the Sandinista Renovation Movement (MRS), as well as YATAMA (literally 'Sons of Mother Earth'), the Miskito Indian party, and four other small parties.

Try as they might, Ortega and the Sandinistas could not shed their revolutionary *guerrilla* warrior image. Bolaños repeatedly accused Ortega and the FSLN of being violent revolutionaries who had been aligned with Communist Cuba and the Soviet Union. On 11 September 2001, when terrorists attacked the World Trade Center and the US Pentagon, the Bolaños campaign seized on the event to serve their campaign, accusing the FSLN of maintaining relations with countries and organisations – such as the Palestinians – that engaged in terrorist activities. The PLC's vice-presidential candidate warned that Nicaragua should not allow itself, by electing the FSLN, to be linked to countries and parties with dubious reputations at a moment when the United States was proclaiming a war against terrorism.[20]

Bolaños and the PLC won the November 2001 election with 56.3 percent of the vote, while the FSLN recieved 42.3 percent. The parties of Ortega and Alemán had completely dominated the election, with the MRS having been kept off the ballot and the Conservative Party, paralysed by internal conflicts, receiving a scant 1.4 percent. Although Bolaños was now president, he had no base of support in the legislature; the alliance between Alemán and Ortega and

19   Ortega 2013, pp. 205–6.
20   Pérez-Baltodano 2008, p. 746.

their parties remained intact, a fact that would frustrate the nation's new leader throughout his term.

Bolaños continued the neoliberal policies that had guided Nicaragua for more than a decade. The Washington Consensus – free trade policies, deregulation and privatisation, cuts in the social budget and attacks on labour – had become the international norm. Enforced as they were by the IMF, the World Bank and the WTO, there was little way for any country to avoid these policies if it wanted loans from foreign banks. Faced with a foreign debt of US$6.5 billion, Bolaños willingly carried out the programme of the World Bank and the IMF, imposing further structural adjustments on Nicaragua. Acting in concert with Washington, he also brought Nicaragua into the Central American Free Trade Agreement (CAFTA).[21] Like his Conservative and Liberal predecessors, he had nothing to offer in terms of new social programmes to deal with the country's endemic poverty and high unemployment.

Bolaños vs. Alemán

Quite quickly Bolaños found himself at war with Alemán. Alemán wanted to continue to control the party and the government for his own political and economic purposes, but Bolaños would not allow himself to be Alemán's puppet. Threatened by his predecessor, Bolaños struck back. With the support of the United States, he launched an anti-corruption campaign against Alemán and others involved in his administration.[22] In 2002, the Attorney General indicted Arnoldo Alemán and thirteen of his relatives and associates for embezzling US$96.7 million during the previous administration. Alemán was also accused of charging US$1.8 million in personal expenses to a credit card of the Central Bank to purchase jewels and carpets, bills for stays in hotels in Bali and India, as well as checks from a Paris nightclub. That represented four percent of the country's GDP and was the equivalent of the entire health budget.

Speaking at the public meeting where the Attorney General outlined his charges, Bolaños said: 'Arnoldo, I never dreamed you would betray your people like this. You took pensions from the retirees, medicine from the sick, salaries from the teachers. You stole the people's trust'.[23] Yet it would be remarkable if

---

21   With the addition of the Dominican Republic, the CAFTA agreement finally became the DR-CAFTA.
22   Mayorga 2007, p. 97.
23   'Waiting for the fat man to sing' 2002.

Bolaños, who had been both vice-president and chairman of the Committee of National Integrity, had himself been unaware of the corruption, especially since the Comptroller had identified a series of problems and the media had discovered others while Alemán was in office. In 2002, Alemán revealed that while serving as vice-president Bolaños had received, in addition to his salary, US$7,000 per month and another US$40,100 per month in expenses – a total of $565,200 per year – provided by the National Democratic Front (the Contra's political arm), ostensibly for the training of election watchers.[24]

The Bolaños government arrested Alemán in December of 2002, but the court permitted him house arrest, rather than jailing him, while he awaited the completion of his trial. A year later, on 7 December 2003, Alemán was convicted of corruption, embezzlement, and money laundering and sentenced to 20 years in prison. Nevertheless, because of health problems, again the court did not imprison him, but instead permitted him to serve his sentence under house arrest. In July of 2005, the courts ended his 'arrest' altogether and allowed Alemán to serve the rest of his sentence in his home on probation. The responsibility for these lenient policies – tantamount to allowing Alemán to go free – lay with Daniel Ortega, the FLSN and the PLC leaders who dictated to the court.[25] Alemán found himself completely dependent upon Ortega, who could always send his political ally back to prison if he proved obdurate.

Bolaños's conflict with Alemán put him at odds with both the PLC which Alemán still controlled and Ortega's FSLN which was allied with Alemán. With no power base of his own, Bolaños was impotent. With a group of followers in the PLC, he attempted to create his own political party, the Alliance for the Republic (APRE), which defined itself as a third way between Alemán's PLC and Ortega's FSLN, but it never really took off and soon failed altogether. By 2005, the situation had become acute; the National Assembly, dominated by the PLC and the FSLN, began an impeachment process against Bolaños while passing legislation that effectively stripped him of power. For example, all of his appointments from the cabinet down had to be approved by a two-thirds majority in the National Assembly. The Nicaraguan government ground to a halt.

With the government paralysed by the conflict, the United States government became concerned, as did Latin American governments. Cardinal Miguel Obando y Bravo and Dante Caputo, an Argentine representing the Organisation

---

24   López Castellanos 2013, p. 5.
25   Finally, in January 2009, to the shock of legislators and the public, the Supreme Court – controlled by the PLC and the FSLN – overturned Alemán's convictions.

of American States, intervened and opened negotiations between the president and the National Assembly to try to resolve the problem.[26] The Bolaños administration and the National Assembly reached an agreement called the Framework for Governability that required the Assembly to suspend the laws that had stripped Bolaños of his presidential powers until January 2007, that is, until the next presidential term. The fracas was over. Little of substance was accomplished during the Bolaños years, almost nothing for most Nicaraguans, 70 percent of whom lived on two dollars a day.

The effects of corruption on Nicaraguan society were profound and demoralising. As the former Sandinista *comandante* Dora María Téllez wrote in *Envío*, the newsletter of the Jesuit University of Central America, in its December 2005 issue:

> Our society is now at extremely high risk. The decomposition has reached the lowest rung of the social ladder, because the corruption of the upper echelons promotes it at all levels. People from top to bottom are looking for their piece of the action, their bribe. Many people are becoming demoralised and are now in a desperate search for fast, easy money any way they can get it. Chains of swindlers are operating in Nicaragua today, preying on a desperate society that has seen unleashed ambition for power and easy money and has lost the value of public service, of volunteerism. Nobody wants to work as a volunteer anymore. Such values are scorned in an individualist society that has put a price on everything. This country won't go anywhere with this contempt for public service, solidarity, and citizenship.[27]

The situation was bleak indeed.

The Reconstituted Capitalist Class

The Chamorro, Alemán, and Bolaños governments, together with Ortega and the FSLN, oversaw the economic fusion of the old bourgeoisie of the Somoza era with the Sandinista *nouveau riche*. There was never much of a social fusion since the old oligarchy did not admit into its circles those who had not been part of them before the revolution. At the same time, these three administra-

---

26   Ortega 2013, pp. 207–8; Barcelona Centre for International Affairs 2011b.
27   Téllez 2005.

tions constructed a new state made up of the Army and Ministry of the Interior, created by the Sandinistas, and a Treasury Department created by the post-revolutionary governments with the support of the international economic institutions (IMF, World Bank, GATT/WTO) of the neoliberal era. The Liberal leaders able to win enough votes to secure the presidency proved unable to govern without the FSLN votes in the National Assembly, and without the FSLN's willingness to keep its unions at bay. Consequently, the Liberal governments were forced to enter into a partnership with the FSLN to install and maintain neoliberal policies.

Under these Liberal governments – despite their weakness and corruption – the Nicaraguan business class established a relatively stable and secure market economy, making it possible once again to make a profit and to accumulate capital. Francisco Mayorga, the Nicaraguan banker and economist, has demonstrated how, in the period from the 1990s to 2010, the Nicaraguan capitalist class was transformed and strengthened, not only reasserting its economic power in Nicaragua, but also becoming a power throughout Central America. During the Sandinista era, many wealthy Nicaraguans had moved their money to offshore tax havens, such as the Cayman Islands, and had invested in other Central American countries. Some of them, all from the families of the old oligarchy, proved to be extraordinarily successful, principally in the international market in agricultural commodities, but in other areas as well. When Chamorro came to power, they returned to Nicaragua, many of them richer and more powerful than before the revolution. With the return of their Nicaraguan property and their participation in the privatisation of the public utilities, they ascended to new economic heights.[28]

At the heart of the new economic order were four banks, each the armature of a financial group: Grupo Promérica dominated by the McGregor and Eduardo Montealegre families; Bancentro (which includes Lafise); Grupo BAC, also known as the Grupo Pellas for its principal figure, though a number of other wealthy families are also involved; and Grupo UNO. Each of these financial groups was a conglomerate with interests in a variety of areas from finance and commerce to agriculture, construction, and tourism. In addition to the four, albeit not so powerful, were the businesses of the Nicaraguan Army (Instituto de Previsión Social Militar – IPSM) and of the Sandinistas, the most important of which is Agricorp, founded and headed by Amílcar Ybarra-Rojas, a company in which Bayardo Arce is involved. While during the period from 1979 to 2009 there was an enormous amount of change – one could argue that a revolution

---

28   Mayorga 2007, pp. 23–103.

and a virtual counter-revolution had taken place – still the traditional oligarchy had returned to dominance.[29]

Nicaragua, despite all of these changes under the neoliberal governments, remained a fundamentally agricultural country producing export crops such as beef, lobster, shrimp, tobacco, sugar, and coffee, as well as gold. Total exports in 2005 amounted to $1.55 billion. The United States received 34.9 percent of Nicaragua's exports, while El Salvador received 14.5 percent, Honduras 7.5 percent, and Costa Rica 6.7. Though the economy recovered somewhat after 1996, Nicaragua's growth rate was not very high, except during the reconstruction in the aftermath of Hurricane Mitch in 1998. The GDP grew at a rate of about three percent per year throughout the 1990s and early 2000s. GDP grew from $1 billion in 1989 to $9.3 billion in 2011. The growth in the GDP went principally to the capitalist class, with Nicaragua's workers, peasants, and urban poor making little improvement in the new capitalist economy.[30]

The weakness of government social programmes in this era encouraged the growth of non-governmental organisations. NGOs not only substituted for the state, but some also substituted for the lack of a left political party, since the FSLN had become part of the political establishment. Most NGOs were funded by foundations in Europe, the United States or Canada. In 2004, European NGOs placed a significant part of their total project portfolio in Latin America, particularly Central America. 'Between 1995 and 2005, Guatemala, Nicaragua, El Salvador and Honduras (along with Peru and Bolivia) were the top six priority countries for European NGOs in Latin America, with what was ... both the largest European NGO presence and the greatest allocation of funds'.[31] The NGOs donated tens of millions of dollars to Nicaragua, making them a significant factor in the country's economy as well as in its social life.

The Lives of Ordinary People

While there was economic growth in the Alemán and Bolaños years, it was not continuous, and little of it trickled down. The benefits, such as they were, were distributed very unevenly, with all growth contributing to maintaining and amplifying the unequal relations between property owners and working people. Formal unemployment averaged about 10 percent, while close to 50

---

29   Mayorga 2007, pp. 69–95.

30   USAID 2006. The report notes the economic inequality with half the country living in poverty.

31   Rocha 2011.

percent of the population lived below the national poverty line. The neoliberal administrations spent little on healthcare, which translated into a weak healthcare system with poor provision of healthcare services. Primary school enrollment was low, though it showed signs of improving. The youth literacy rate was appalling, being lower than in all other comparable economies, and insufficient resources were devoted to secondary education.[32]

Workers' labour unions provided them virtually no protection in the private sector during the Alemán and Bolaños years. The United States Trade Representative reported at the time:

> Although the current Labour Code made it easier to organise, there is evidence that workers continue to face significant obstacles in forming unions. The American Federation of Labour and Congress of Industrial Organisations (AFL-CIO) and the Union of Needletrades, Industrial and Textile Employees (UNITE) allege that workers who attempt to establish independent trade unions operate in a climate of fear and face harassment, retaliatory firings, and competition from company-sponsored unions. Union organizing drives have reportedly encountered particularly strong employer opposition in the FTZs [free trade zones].[33]

When factory workers attempted to organise the Chentex plant, nine leaders of the campaign and 17 others were fired; the company attempted to blackmail or bribe union leaders, and threatened to close the plant and move elsewhere. While they eventually won a Supreme Court decision returning some of them to their jobs, it was not altogether satisfactory to the workers. There were also accusations that employers created company unions or suborned legitimate unions.[34] Workers were frequently denied permanent employment, being kept in the status of probationary employees, even though they had worked at some companies for years. International Labour Rights Forum reported in 2004:

> Continuous contracting is common in Nicaragua and allows employers to avoid Nicaragua's labour standards. Workers are hired for short periods, no longer than three months. The contract is not extended beyond that time if the worker tries to defend their rights, join a union, sign a collective bargaining agreement, or support the declaration of a strike in a workers'

---

32   USAID 2006.

33   US Trade Representative 2005.

34   US Trade Representative 2005.

assembly. Workers are often fired under the pretext of 'just cause' which is permitted by Nicaraguan law, and without asking for authorisation from the Labour Inspectorate. Thus employers can avoid paying compensation and benefits to these workers.[35]

The situation of working-class women remained particularly difficult in the Alemán and Bolaños years, with high unemployment and low wages. While there was some improvement in access to contraception, abortion remained illegal. Women suffered domestic violence, and rape was increasingly common, while courts and police tended in general to handle such cases poorly; many cases were never brought to their attention because of women's fear of the rapists. One health study published in 1999 concluded: 'Wife abuse constitutes a major public health problem in Nicaragua, requiring urgent measures for prevention and treatment for victims'.[36] Men continued to abandon women with whom they had fathered a child, and incest remained all too common, generally a result of male family members imposing themselves on adolescent girls and female children.[37] During these conservative and corrupt years, the government did little to improve social services for women and their children.

The Elections of 2006

Nicaragua's population had grown slowly in the 1980s due to emigration, war deaths, and the economic crisis, but in the 1990s and early 2000s population growth had accelerated. In 1980, the country had only 2.5 million inhabitants, while by 2005 it had grown to 5.4 million. The country's population was young; there were hundreds of thousands of new citizens, and new voters had been born and had come of age during the post-revolutionary period. Many had been small children at the time of the revolution and some had been born only after the revolution, during the Contra War. While they learned of Nicaragua's recent history from their families, in their schools, and from discussions on television and in the newspapers, this was a new cohort of voters in what was virtually a new society created by the experiences of living through the Chamorro, Alemán, and Bolaños years. Ortega shrewdly began creating a political organ-

---

35   International Labour Rights Forum 2004.
36   M.C. Ellsberg et al. 1999, pp. 241–4.
37   López Vigil 2000.

isation with which to sweep up not only his own older cohort of supporters and independents, but also these new and inexperienced voters.

Even before the struggle between Bolaños and Alemán reached it final crisis, Daniel Ortega, seeing an opportunity arising from the split in the PLC, had taken action to improve his political prospects. First, in 2004, he renegotiated and renewed the pact with Alemán to insure that together they would maintain control of the National Assembly. Second, he called a quite irregular meeting of the FSLN at which he announced that he would be the FSLN candidate for president. As Victor Hugo Tinoco, a former FSLN leader, former Deputy Minister of Foreign Affairs, and later an MRS activist, wrote:

> Nearly two years before the 2006 elections, in a final anti-democratic spasm, Daniel Ortega announced the suspension of the FSLN's primary elections, and that he would be the sole candidate. He made this announcement in Matagalpa, with the 'support' and 'approval' of some 400 previously selected people, 95% of whom are party or municipal workers, and all of whom have salaries of $2,000–$3,000 a month and are not going to dare to dissent and risk their personal economic prospects. In this way, Daniel Ortega and 400 others decided that the other 600,000 Sandinistas do not have the right to an opinion or to elect their chosen candidate.[38]

Ortega's alliance with Alemán had not gone down well with all of those in the FSLN. In 2005, Herty Lewites, a long-time, dissident FSLN leader who, with the backing of the MRS, had been elected mayor of Managua, decided that he would put himself forward as a contender for president in the coming election. Daniel Ortega, who still controlled the FSLN leadership and the great majority of its membership, blocked Lewites, and expelled him from the FSLN, labelling him a traitor. Lewites left the FSLN and together with other historic FLSLN *comandantes*, such as Victor Tirado and Henry Ruiz, formed a new political organisation called the Movement for the Rescue of Sandinismo (MPRS). The new MPRS, together with the MRS (the Movement for Sandinista Renovation of Sergio Ramírez and Dora María Téllez) and the Christian Alternative, another political organisation, joined together to back Lewites, who ran on a left-wing programme emphasising democracy and socialism. Lewites began to rise in the opinion polls, with support from both former Sandinistas and some who had never been Sandinistas at all. But when Lewites suffered a heart attack and died in July 2006, the opposition was suddenly bereft of its strongest candidate,

---

38   Tinoco 2005.

and though Edmundo Jarquín, a former Sandinista ambassador to Mexico and Spain and later a functionary of the Inter-American Development Bank, and his running mate Carlos Mejía Godoy, the enormously popular activist, musician and singer, attempted to carry on in Lewites's place, the movement had lost its momentum.[39]

Ortega had been drifting in a conservative direction in both substance and style throughout the 1990s, but in the campaign for the presidency in 2006 he made a great leap to the right. The Sandinista red-and-black flags disappeared to be replaced by pink and turquoise regalia and bunting. The campaign theme song was a Spanish language version of John Lennon's 'Give Peace a Chance'. Ortega again wore civilian clothes and appeared on the campaign trail with his wife and family, an image of respectability that was all the more important following his step-daughter's accusations that he had sexually abused her.

To show that he was trying to overcome differences and was willing to work with those on the right, Ortega chose as his running mate Jaime Morales Carazo, a banker and former member of the Nicaraguan Democratic Front, that is, the Contras, and one of its spokesmen. Carazo had left Nicaragua during the revolutionary decade, and when he returned in 1996, he had become a member of Alemán's PLC and was elected a member of the National Assembly in 2001. Ortega's choice of Carazo nauseated many old Sandinistas who saw it as the ultimate betrayal of the cause for which they had fought in the 1970s.

Religion played a more significant role in the campaign than it had done in the past. In 2005, Ortega and his wife of almost 20 years, Rosario Murillo, were married in a Catholic wedding performed by Cardinal Miguel Obando y Bravo. Ortega also made a public 'confession' to Obando y Bravo for the sins committed by the Sandinistas during the revolution. In return for Ortega's complete ideological capitulation, the Cardinal reversed his previous political position and appeared on television on several occasions and – without endorsing Ortega – gave Catholics permission to vote for Ortega, saying that it would not be a violation of Catholic principles. Ortega, who had already become an outspoken opponent of abortion before the elections, led the FSLN representatives in the National Assembly to join with the Liberals and Conservatives in passing a total ban on abortions by a vote of 52 to 0, eliminating long-standing exceptions for rape, malformation of the fetus, and risk to the life or health of the mother. It was the most restrictive abortion law in the Americas.[40] The FSLN's vote on the abortion law angered many women in the FSLN and former FSLN

---

39   Tinoco 2005; Ortega 2010, pp. 208–9.
40   Vargas Llosa 2006.

members, as well as other progressive women in Nicaragua. Progressive women in countries around the world were shocked and horrified to learn about the new law.

Without explicitly endorsing Ortega, Cardinal Obando y Bravo had made very clear his support for the Sandinista leader. In late October of 2006, just before the elections, the Cardinal gave a sermon during mass on 'the prodigal son', which was widely interpreted as an implicit endorsement of Ortega.[41] How had Ortega come to win the support of Obando y Bravo, who throughout the period from 1990 to 2006 had supported his opponents? Most well-informed observers, as well as the media and the general public, believed it was because Ortega had blackmailed the Cardinal. In a confidential communication, the American Ambassador Paul A. Trivelli wrote to the US Secretary of State Condoleezza Rice reporting on his visit with the Papal Nuncio Jean Paul Gobel:

> In Gobel's view, Ortega clearly maintains some sort of hold over Obando y Bravo. NOTE: Rumors have long suggested that Ortega is blackmailing Obando y Bravo with information proving that the Cardinal fathered children with his secretary and that he has engaged in corrupt practices in his management of the private Catholic University (UNICA).[42]

Trivelli reported that Gobel had told him that an actual endorsement of Ortega by Obando y Bravo would be a 'red line' that the Pope would not tolerate. Whatever Ortega's hold on Obando y Bravo, it would keep the Cardinal in line until health issues forced him from public life.

The principal theme of the Ortega campaign was the call for a Government of Reconciliation and National Unity to be achieved through peace and dialogue. He wanted to assure Nicaraguan and foreign capitalists that the economy would be governed by the market and that their property would be safe. He met with more than 100 American investors and real estate developers on 29 September, and pledged: 'Confiscations are not even being considered'. He also signed a 'governability pact' with the Nicaraguan Chamber of Commerce promising to respect free markets and property rights.[43] At the same time, he criticised the neoliberal model, the privatisation and the corruption that had accompanied it, and called for a mixed economy. He advocated partnerships between government and private enterprise, including foreign investors.

---

41   Gooren 2010, pp. 47–63.
42   Trivelli 2005.
43   Azul and Martin 2006.

Ortega took up the Theology of Liberation's slogan of a 'preferential option for the poor', saying he would lift the Nicaraguan people out of poverty. The economic and social programme that he presented could be called neoliberalism tempered with social concern, what some have called social liberalism.[44] Unlike the Sandinistas' socialist programmes of the 1970s and 1980s, this combination of support for business and concern for the less fortunate was a far cry from the calls for socialism in the 1980s.

Where Ortega's views were quite different from those of his opponents were on the questions of international trade issues. While he did not call for leaving CAFTA, he argued that it should be renegotiated in order to improve its terms. More significantly and controversially, he called for Nicaragua to join ALBA, the Bolivarian Alternative for the Americas created by Venezuela and Cuba as an alternative to the US project, the Free Trade Area of the Americas (FTAA). Ortega believed that with the assistance of Venezuela and Cuba, Nicaragua would be able to make large strides toward dealing with issues in the areas of health and education. Venezuelan President Hugo Chávez invited Ortega to appear on his show *Aló presidente* and made clear his support for the Sandinista leader. At the Third ALBA summit in Havana in May 2006, Ortega joined Fidel Castro, Chávez, and the newly elected president of Bolivia, Evo Morales.[45] That is, while proposing a social liberal programme for Nicaragua, he wanted to become part of the alliance with the leftist governments in Latin America and in particular to get close to Chávez. Political rhetoric and posturing aside, there was little doubt that he wanted the support of oil-rich Venezuela for his government once it won the election.

By the time of the election, the fight within Alemán's Liberal Constitutionalist Party had led to a split. Eduardo Montealegre, a former banker who had held important cabinet positions in both the Alemán and Bolaños cabinets, driven by his own ambition and angered by the dictatorial control of the party by Alemán – who was after all a convicted criminal and technically a prisoner – led a rebellion by a group of PLC legislators and party leaders.[46] Expelled from the PLC, Montealegre and his associates organised the Nicaraguan Liberal Alliance (ALN-PC, later the Independent Liberal Party or PLI) in 2005 and put forward Montealegre as their candidate. Alemán's PLC put forward his vice-president José Rizo, a lawyer and businessman, but above all a politician. Also running

44   Barcelona Centre for International Affairs 2011a.
45   Barcelona Centre for International Affairs 2011a.
46   Montealegre had been Alemán's presidential secretary and chancellor, and later served as presidential secretary and secretary of finance in the Bolaños administration.

for president was Edén Pastora, the former FSLN *comandante* and former Contra as the candidate of the Alternative for Change (AC).

The administration of President George W. Bush in the United States, acting through Ambassador Paul Trivelli, attempted to determine the outcome of the election. Trivelli, violating the norms of foreign ambassadors, openly opposed Ortega and advocated support for Montealegre. The US Agency for International Development, the National Democratic Institute, the International Republican Institute and the International Foundation for Election Systems spent a total of $15 million on training election observers. According to Ivania Vega Rueda, a programme officer for the International Republican Institute (IRI), her group had spent $10 million in Nicaragua for political education, civil society organisations, and protest activities against the FSLN and the PLC. Jeane Kirkpatrick, former ambassador to the United Nations in the Reagan administration, Otto Reich, head of Latin American policy in the first years of the George W. Bush administration, the president's brother and outgoing Florida Governor Jeb Bush, and Assistant Secretary of State for Western Hemispheric Affairs Tom Shannon all travelled to Nicaragua during the campaign to throw their support behind Montealegre. All of these efforts failed, in large part because of accusations, widely publicised by his opponents and generally believed by much of the public, that he had profited illicitly during the banking crisis of the early 2000s.[47]

On 5 November 2005, Daniel Ortega of the FSLN received 37.99 percent of the vote; Eduardo Montealegre of the ALN-PC, 28.30 percent; José Rizo of the PLC, 27.1 percent; Edmundo Jarquín of the MRS, 6.29 percent; and Edén Pastora (AC) with just 0.29 percent. The Liberals had been deeply divided, splitting 55 percent of the vote between their two rival candidates, and while there had been division on the left as well, it had not been nearly as significant. Alemán's refusal to back Montealegre was in fact a way of throwing his support behind his ally Ortega. In the end, Ortega had only a plurality of a little over a third of the votes cast, but because of the Pact of 1999 that had established 35 percent as the threshold needed to avoid a runoff, the Sandinista leader became the president of Nicaragua.

In the elections to the National Assembly, the FSLN elected 38 representatives, just nine short of a simple majority. At the same time, it maintained its alliance with the PLC which had 12 representatives, so Ortega's FSLN and

---

47   The extremely complicated issue of the bank liquidations and the Central Bank's issuance
      of paper known as CENIs (Certificados Negociables de Inversión), and of Montealegre's
      role in these matters, is explained in Mayorga 2007, Appendix, pp. 162–84.

Alemán's PLC were in control of the National Assembly at the start of Ortega's presidency. Montealegre's ALN, the future PLI, won 29 representatives while the MRS won 14, a significant minority. While the FSLN and PLC together had a majority, if they flagged in their efforts they could lose control to the opposition parties. Ortega's challenge would be to consolidate his alliance with the conservative forces while rebuilding the FSLN and its mass organisation, not to make a socialist revolution, but to continue the neoliberal counter-revolution.

CHAPTER 10

The Ortega Government (2006–)

Daniel Ortega took office on 10 January 2007, and it was obvious that this term would be dramatically different from his 1985–90 presidency.[1] Most surprisingly, it became apparent early on that he planned to be a co-president, sharing power with his wife Rosario Murillo. Traditionally in Latin America, the first lady functioned as the figurehead of the ministry in charge of women's and children's affairs, but this was different. Rosario Murillo would not simply be an ornament or even the head of a department; she would govern. She would rule. As one analyst wrote at the time: 'Rosario Murillo is much more than just First Lady. She exercises real decision-making executive power and veto power. In practice, she's functioning more like the head of government, with her husband acting like a head of state'.[2]

Murillo became government spokesperson, taking charge of publicity and communications for all ministries as well as of the President's agenda, trips, and meetings with the media. She also handled the coordination of the social ministries – health, education, and culture – as well as the national, departmental, and local organisations of the 'direct democracy' councils; and the government's public ethics office and its departmental and regional secretariats. Her pet project, the Council on Communication and Citizenry, grew rapidly in resources, personnel, and importance. Many Nicaraguans considered her the real power behind the throne.[3] The arrangement was very reminiscent of Anastasio Somoza García and his wife Salvador DeBayle: 'Nicaragua was very much a family business. The high command of the Somoza dictatorship was always Tacho and Salvadora'.[4] But there had not been a Latin American presidency such as this since Juan and Eva Perón had ruled Argentina.

---

1 Throughout this chapter I have relied a great deal on *Envío*, the monthly magazine published at the Jesuit University of Central America (UCA) in Managua since 1981 (see: http://www .envio.org.ni/quienes_somos.en). *Envío* publishes news, analysis, and many original articles by Nicaraguans from a wide spectrum of opinion. It is by far the best single source on contemporary Nicaragua. I should note that since 2006 *Envío*, though a non-partisan publication, has generally been critical of the Ortega administration. While initially to the left of the Sandinista government on many issues, over the years it has become more moderate.

2 Guevara Jerez 2007.

3 Debussman 2005.

4 Diederich 2007, p. 25.

Criticised for nepotism for allowing his wife to exercise these governmental functions, Ortega replied: 'They don't love Rosario. They say terrible things about her every day. And I say to them: don't forget, we said we'd put 50% men and 50% women in government ... And now in the presidency I'm complying: 50% Rosario and 50% Daniel'. His critics, he said, were *machista* and had no respect for women.[5] In truth, though, Murillo's governmental role was unconstitutional. She had not stood for public office and no one had elected her, and yet she functioned as a co-president – some said she was more powerful than Daniel – and would continue in that role for two presidential terms. The first FSLN government of 1979 had been led by a National Directorate made up of revolutionary leaders; now the party was led by the president and his wife and a small circle of trusted advisors.

Who was this woman who came to exercise such power in Nicaragua? Murillo was born in Managua on 22 June 1951 to a prosperous family. Her parents sent her for her primary education to Switzerland and then to high school in England. When she returned at the age of 15 to spend the vacation with her family, she became pregnant with the child of her sweetheart Jorge Naváez. Though she told her parents that she was not in love with him, they forced the pair to marry, and she gave birth to her daughter Zoilamérica in 1967. Murillo soon fled the husband, the daughter, and the marriage and went again to Switzerland to study art for a year and then returned to Managua where she studied languages. In the early 1970s, she became the secretary of Pedro Joaquín Chamorro, the Conservative Party leader and publisher of *La Prensa* until his assassination in 1978. Later she also worked with Pablo Antonio Cuadra, another important conservative political leader. During this period, she began to write and publish poetry and to consider herself a poet.[6]

Already in 1969 she had joined the Sandinistas and carried on clandestine work until 1977 when, fearing arrest, she went to Costa Rica to continue her political work from there. She had met Daniel Ortega in Managua shortly after he had been released from prison, but it was while on a trip to Venezuela for the FSLN in 1978 that she once again saw Ortega, they established their relationship and began to live together. Married in a secret civil ceremony in Costa Rica in 1979, together they had six children. Daniel Ortega also adopted his wife's daughter Zoilamérica, the step-daughter who later accused him of having sexually molested her throughout her adolescence.[7] Throughout her

---

5   Nitlápan Envío Team 2007a.
6   'Rosario Murillo: La mujer más poderosa de Nicaragua' 2008.
7   Laguna 2007.

marriage to Ortega, Murillo proved to be his equal in political ambition and leadership, and many thought she was a more competent administrator.

The Ortega-Murillo children also came to be important figures in the party, in government, and in the Ortega's private businesses. The press frequently criticised Ortega, Murrillo, and their offspring because of the children's inappropriate and extra-legal role in government affairs. In April of 2007, their son Rafael Ortega, for example, who held no post in the Nicaraguan foreign service, was dispatched to Libya to meet President Muammar Gaddafi in preparation for Daniel Ortega's visit in June.[8] In 2009, Daniel Ortega took his wife and children Rafael, Camila, and Luciana along to the Summit of Latin American and Caribbean States where they quite irregularly attended official sessions.[9] In addition to their extra-legal governmental roles, the Ortega children also took charge of the television channels and radio stations acquired by Ortega with the Venezuela-financed Albanisa funds.[10] Throughout Ortega's presidency (and on into his second term), Rafael and other Ortega children took on more responsibility and power in the administration and in the Albanisa businesses. This was not merely nepotism; these were steps in the construction of a dynasty.

Ortega's official cabinet reflected the complexity of the twenty-first century Sandinistas: a hodgepodge of former revolutionaries who considered themselves socialists, leaders of the labour unions, and up-and-coming businesspeople from the private sector operating in the world of capitalism, as well as professionals and technicians with no apparent politics or ideals. The fingerprints of Ortega and Murillo's special economic advisor, veteran Sandinista and businessman Bayardo Arce, were all over the appointments.

The cabinet's character was determined by the combination of FSLN loyalists and up-and-coming members of the business class. Long-time FSLN leader Lenin Cerna, a diehard Ortega man, became head of the Ministry of Security. Samuel Santos López, entrepreneur, head of the Nicaraguan Democratic Movement, and a business partner of Bayardo Arce, became Foreign Secretary. His under-secretary was Manuel Coronel Kautz, one of the negotiators of the Pact of 1999 with the PLC, and a founder of the FSLN Businesspeople's Bloc. Fernando Martínez Espinoza, a long-time Sandinista, an engineer and a businessman, backed by the Nicaraguan Chamber of Construction and the Association of Architects and Engineers, was named Minister of Transport and Infrastructure. Retired Colonel Antenor Rosales, a lawyer and professor of law

---

8   'Rafael Ortega: El nuevo poder en la familia' 2007.

9   Picón Duarte 2009.

10   Pantoja 2001.

at the Central American University, who represented Bayardo Arce's business interests and had served as FSLN representative to the Socialist International, was appointed to head the Central Bank. Emilio Rappaccioli Baltodano, head of the FSLN Businesspeople's Bloc and former Secretary of Energy from 1979 to 1997 in both the Sandinista and Chamorro administrations, was reappointed to the post of Secretary of Energy. Orlando Núñez Soto, a former anarchist and head of an NGO promoting agricultural cooperatives, became head of the Food Security and Sovereignty Council and leader of the Zero Hunger initiative. Ariel Bucardo Rocha, a former peasant who was one of the founders of the National Farmers and Ranchers Union (UNAG), the Rural Workers Association (ATC) and the National Cooperatives Federation (FENACOOP) became Minister of Agriculture and Forestry.

Ortega's and Murillo's appointments of women would be particularly disturbing to the independent women's movement. Amanda Lorío Arana, a sociologist who had been involved in agrarian reform and who later went to Europe and studied the New Age therapy called 'reflexology' – with Daniel Ortega and Rosarillo Murillo becoming her patients – became head of the Ministry of Environment and Natural Resources. Two former National Assembly representatives, Emilia Torres and Rita Fletes, were appointed to the leadership of the Nicaraguan Women's Institute. Both had voted to criminalise therapeutic abortion in October 2006 and neither considered herself a feminist. Another Bayardo Arce associate, Glenda Ramírez Noguera, a business administrator for the National Assembly with little political experience, became Minister of the Family. The one surprise in the female appointments was Ruth Selma Herrera, appointed president of the National Water and Sewage Company (ENACAL). She was a renowned defender of the people's right to water, and an advocate of the renationalisation of all public services, as well as an opponent of Bayardo Arce.[11] None of the women appointees could be considered feminists and some had demonstrated their hostility toward feminist policies.

The cabinet revealed just how inextricably linked politics and business had become in the FSLN and the government. While many of the cabinet appointees had expertise and experience in their fields, the overriding consideration in their appointment, of course, was their relation to the Ortega-Murillo inner circle and their political reliability. Ortega and Murillo would be the ultimate arbiters of this congeries of personalities and interests.

While constructing the cabinet, Ortega and Murillo also undertook to reinforce the relationships that had brought them into power, most importantly

11   Guevara Jerez 2007.

with the Constitutionalist Liberal Party and the Catholic Church. On 16 March 2007, the courts allowed Arnoldo Alemán to go free under a novel formula called 'country arrest', granted as a personal concession by President Ortega who controlled the judges. Alemán, though a convicted criminal supposedly still serving his sentence, was allowed to travel anywhere in the country and even to continue to be involved in politics. His conviction, however, was not lifted, so, though he had appeals still before the courts, he remained for the time being entirely dependent upon Ortega.

To solidify his alliance with Cardinal Miguel Obando y Bravo, Ortega asked the prelate to become the head of the Commission of Verification, Peace, Reconciliation and Justice. When criticised by Nicaraguan bishops for allying himself with Ortega and thus with the corrupt Alemán, Obando y Bravo flew to Rome to meet with the Pope, who neither forbade nor approved of the Cardinal heading the commission. Nevertheless, upon returning to Managua, Obando y Bravo accepted the post, lending the authority of his position to legitimise the Ortega administration.

While securing his position domestically, Ortega also reached out for assistance from President Hugo Chávez, the leftist leader of Venezuela. Chávez, awash in oil, was attempting to extend his influence through his largesse. On 1 May 2007, International Labour Day, Ortega, who had just returned from the Latin American Bolivarian Alliance (ALBA) meeting in Barquisimeto, Venezuela, told a mass rally of workers in Managua that his alliance with Hugo Chávez of Venezuela would make it possible for the Nicaraguan government to lift the country out of poverty. While ALBA did not do everything that Ortega promised, it did have a very large impact on Nicaraguan economy and politics. Over the next five years, the Venezuela funds – amounting to $2.2 billion in loans and concessionary oil credits – were deposited in a private company called Albanisa that invested in Nicaraguan enterprises, electricity, credit cooperatives, agriculture, transport, construction, hotels, mining, and petroleum, among other industries. Venezuela became one of the largest foreign investors in Nicaragua. Albanisa also supported such programmes as Zero Hunger, aimed at improving the nutrition of the poorest Nicaraguans, and provided zinc roofing materials to improve poor housing, micro-credit loans to very small businesses, assistance to needy farmers, and scholarships for low-income students.

The Venezuelan assistance to Nicaragua administered through Albanisa did not go to the Nicaraguan government's treasury, but directly to accounts that were personally controlled by Daniel Ortega. In effect, he controlled a slush fund of $200 million a year, unaudited and unsupervised by the FSLN or the state, that he could use to deal with social issues, economic matters, or to solve political problems. He could bribe or buy party leaders and legislators (many were for sale), make donations to influence the NGOs and church officials, or suborn anyone else who was willing to take money in exchange for political loyalty. The most important example of Ortega's largesse was the monthly 'Christian, Socialist and Solidarity' bonus of US$30 per month paid to tens of thousands of public employees, a 'gift of thanks from *comandante* Ortega'.[12]

Though he had joined ALBA and aligned himself with the leftist, socialist, and Communist governments of Latin America, Ortega was not opposed to dealing with the United States and the capitalist international financial institutions. Even before he took office in 2006, Ortega had met with the International Monetary Fund (IMF), the financial disciplinarian of the capitalist world, and worked out a continued Poverty Reduction and Growth Facility arrangement for Nicaragua. Anoop Singh, Director of the IMF's Western Hemisphere Department, reported that 'President-elect Ortega has emphasised to me his commitment to prudent macroeconomic policies and intensifying poverty reduction. In particular, the President-elect expressed his intention to work with the Fund towards an early new economic programme that would entrench stability in Nicaragua, and move ahead with reforms critical for raising investment and sustainable growth, and accelerating employment creation and poverty reduction'.[13] Over the next several months, the Ortega government and the IMF came to an agreement that, while accepting the IMF's neoliberal framework, recognised that the Nicaraguan government would focus internally on the issues of food, health, education, and water.[14] And over the following years, Ortega would work out other agreements with the IMF that, in exchange for his promise to operate within neoliberal parameters, led to the cancellation of an IMF debt of US$200 million and a World Bank debt of US$1.5 billion.[15]

Nicaragua under Ortega, though he railed against the Colossus of the North, continued to receive aid directly from the United States government. In September 2007, for example, Ortega denounced the United States before the United Nations as 'the imperialist world empire', but such speeches were simply rhetorical. Ortega was deeply committed to cooperation with the United States. The United States' Millennium Challenge Account was a development pro-

---

12   Rogers 2012c; Riley 2010.

13   An account of all IMF dealings with Nicaragua can be found in International Monetary Fund 2014. For a critique of IMF policies in Nicaragua by Adolfo Acevedo, based on a Kepa Finland report, see Acevedo 2008.

14   The Letter of Intent and Memorandum of Understanding of 24 August 2007 can be found in International Monetary Fund 2007.

15   Ribando Seelke 2008.

gramme involving $175 million in economic aid to eradicate poverty in León and Chinandega that began in 2005 and was scheduled to continue until 2011. Ortega also collaborated with the US Drug Enforcement Agency, accepting military equipment, though he then criticised the agency for giving him 'old junk'. He used leftist rhetoric and his alliance with Chávez to promote his international reputation as a radical, but continued to seek foreign aid from the United States, the European nations, the IMF and the World Bank, which required the country to establish and maintain neoliberal, free market norms that tended to increase capitalist wealth on the basis of low wage workers. Altogether the United States provided Nicaragua with US$50 million in foreign aid in FY2006, US$36.9 million in FY2007, and US$28.6 million in FY2008.[16] Much as in his domestic alliances with the Alemán Liberals and the Church, so too in international economic affairs Ortega dealt pragmatically with both ALBA and the IMF, with Venezuela and the United States.

Rebuilding the FSLN

Once they had reinforced their ties to Alemán and the Church and insured economic support from Venezuela, the United States, and the IMF, Ortega and Murillo turned to what they saw as their most important task, the strengthening of the FSLN as it faced the coming municipal and national elections. From the presidency they carried out a thorough reconstruction of the Sandinista Front for National Liberation, finishing the process of transforming it from a party of leftist political cadres into a party of electoral operatives and precinct workers. The party had already changed significantly from the revolutionary organisation of the 1980s. *Comandante* Mónica Baltodano told *Envío*:

> Already by 1996 the relative 'party life' that had existed in the eighties had disappeared, further diluting the scant organisational structure and institutional norms that had existed up until then. Debate stopped happening and the project was limited to Ortega's determination to get back into government. All party efforts were reserved for elections, for guaranteeing the 'hard-core vote'. That's how it went in 1996 and 2001, until in 2006, with barely 38% of the vote, Daniel Ortega finally got what he wanted.[17]

---

16   Ibid.
17   Nitlápan-Envío Team 2009f.

FSLN membership, once exclusive, now became virtually open to all. Baltodano stated: 'Organisation within the FSLN decreased dramatically and the
party ended up as nothing more than ... some 30,000 election monitors, voting
table members, and other guarantors of the party's votes ... subordinated to the
FSLN secretary, former intelligence chief Lenín Cerna'. She also asserted:

> Today the FSLN gives out memberships as if they were candy at a chil-
> dren's party. In a total state-party symbiosis, all public employees have
> for some months been urged to 'voluntarily' request membership in the
> party, and even those who don't apply for it get it anyway. Memberships
> are also given out in the barrios to anyone who asks for one. It's enough
> to fill out a simple sheet with basic data, supply a photo and, of course,
> pay dues. One no longer needs to show a history of commitment or refer-
> ences.[18]

By 2009, there was an enormous expansion of party membership. The FSLN
presented membership cards to 1.1 million 'voluntary members' among public
employees and community members.[19] Few of these new members had any
sort of Marxist education or understanding of the concept of socialism; they
did not play an active role in the internal life of the party, for it had none;
they were not active in social movements which had atrophied and largely
disappeared; they were motivated principally by a desire to keep their jobs,
advance their careers, and receive gifts from the party. As *Envío* wrote: 'The
advantage of the party membership card is similar to that of *"la magnífica"*,
the card showing affiliation to Somoza's now extinct National Liberal Party: it
protected its bearer, opened doors and guaranteed benefits'.[20]

While the membership had been reduced to mostly passive followers, the
leaders were being exalted, almost deified. The July 2007 celebration of the
Nicaraguan Revolution of 1979 saw the beginning of the construction of a
cult of personality around Ortega. Huge billboards were erected throughout
Managua and other cities showing an enormous Ortega standing with the sil-
houette of Sandino behind him against a pink background with the words
'Arise ye wretched of the earth', a line from the socialist hymn, the 'Interna-
tionale'. All of this would only increase during election periods. Throughout
both terms of his presidency, and especially during elections, these billboards

18   Ibid.
19   Nitlápan-Envío Team 2009e.
20   Nitlápan-Envío Team 2009f.

and other manifestations of 'Danielismo' would form an important part of the propaganda organised by his wife.

Yet, at the same time, Daniel Ortega became increasingly reclusive, carrying out his political and financial business in private hours, attending only the most important state functions and almost never leaving the house in daylight hours. Ortega had reportedly suffered a heart attack in 1994 and travelled every year to Cuba for a check-up, though it was rumoured that he actually went there for chemotherapy treatments for an unknown disease that also accounted for his nocturnal schedule. It was speculated that he suffered from lupus, an autoimmune disease that leads to sun sensitivity. Once Marxist-Leninists, Ortega and Murillo had become practising and very public Catholics, though they also consulted with spiritual advisors and fortune-tellers, leading people to ask: what were their real religious beliefs? Ortega and Murillo, one writer said, lived in separate and clearly divided spaces in their common home, suggesting that they did not enjoy a normal marital relationship. All of these popular speculations created an aura of mystery about Ortega, the great revolutionary leader of the past who today as the sickly president lived in a solitary, nocturnal world protected by his wife.[21]

Rosario Murillo herself adopted an increasingly mystical rhetoric when talking about Ortega, the FSLN, and the Nicaraguan government. Speaking in 2007, Murillo told the press:

> We are going to work with a new style, a new language, a new image. And we will do so because we have a new proposal. A new content. Essential. Spiritual. Evolutionary. It is all about the Evolution of the Revolution. We will continue making a Revolution, now in Peace; and the Revolution is incarnated in a consciousness that acquires new vigor and grows in the heart and the imagination of Nicaraguans like trees after they have been pruned. We are before a consciousness that is growing and building a new Political Culture. In essence and in form. In conviction and in historic commitment. In ideals and in practice. In Life and in Miracles, as corresponds to the revolutionary essence.[22]

Rhetoric without content, it nonetheless enveloped all discussions of Ortega and the FSLN with an aura of spirituality. Her spiritualist rhetoric and mys-

---

21   One gets a sense of the curiosity surrounding Ortega in a newspaper story such as this: Brenes 2010. I heard many such stories and speculations about Daniel Ortega while living in Managua in 2013.

22   Nitlápan-Envío Team 2007a.

tical incantations led many Nicaraguans to refer to her as *la bruja*, the witch, not necessarily a derogatory term, but suggesting that she called upon the spirits to aid her husband, the Sandinistas, and the state. In a highly religious and superstitious country filled with millions of desperately poor people, her mystical language and style played upon the public's sense of fear and hope.

Between Ortega, Murillo, and their clique at the top on the one hand, and the hundreds of thousands of followers at the bottom of the FSLN on the other, was a middle management layer of several thousand loyal cadres, many originally educated in Marxism-Leninism, some of whom had been in the party since 1979 and many of whom had been members through the 1980s and 1990s. Trained for decades to take orders from the National Directorate – which Ortega had headed – and to carry out those orders in military fashion, many of these cadres continued to do so, believing that in the long-run their leader Daniel would fulfil his revolutionary promises to them and the Nicaraguan people. *Envío* observed in 2009:

> In the end, today's party stalwarts embody the concept that the end justifies the means: the fact that the FSLN is back in control is more important than how it got there. And so they support it, believing, hoping, clinging to Daniel Ortega's promise that he will bring twenty-first century socialism to Nicaragua, even if right now it looks suspiciously like twentieth century neoliberal capitalism.[23]

There was also the fact that the FSLN had been a 'revolutionary military organisation', as it called itself, before it became a political party. It also had then led the nation through a civil war. Dionisio Marenco wrote in 2008:

> ... the military nature of the Sandinista organisation explains a lot of what we're seeing even today. We spent ten years with the slogan, 'National Directorate, order us!' During the revolutionary government, the National Directorate members walked onto the stage of any public act in a given order, and we had to stand up when they came in. That was automatic, like in an army, and it creates a special organisational culture, very different from that of an environmentalist youth club or a club of musicians or philosophers. It creates a military organisation. Moreover, 200,000 people fought [in the Contra War during the revolutionary government period].

---

23   Nitlápan-Envío Team 2009f.

They carried weapons, were trained by the army and acquired military customs that they then brought with them into the party structure.[24]

The combination of the Marxist-Leninist commitments of the cadres and the military training of much of the older rank-and-file created an exceptionally efficient political machine capable of taking commands from Daniel and Rosario on high and turning them into marching orders for the rank-and-file.

Rebuilding the FSLN Mass Organisations

Ortega and Murillo, strengthening their hold over the FSLN, also wanted to expand the party's mass organisations. The FSLN in the 1980s had dominated society through mass organisations of workers, peasants and women. The most important mass organisation in terms of numbers was the Sandinista Defence Committees (CDSs) – part state security apparatus and part popular community organisation – with its 500,000 members. Anxious to recoup the social space lost by the FSLN to civil society, other political parties, the NGOs and independent movements, Murillo promoted the establishment of a new mass organisation, the Citizens' Power Councils (CPC) – a new version of the CDSs – calling them a 'unique and unprecedented' form of direct democracy and suggesting at times that they might become an alternative to the National Assembly. FSLN cadres were ordered to create the CPCs in urban neighbourhoods and rural communities and by the time of the July celebration of the anniversary of the revolution, Murillo announced that 6,334 CPCs had been organised throughout the entire country, with 500,288 members in all, and that by 14 September the entire structure of this 'direct democracy' would be in place, a total of 16,957 CPCs with 938,523 members, not counting those in the northern Caribbean region. The local committees of 100 formed part of a hierarchy of committee structures that at its pinnacle was controlled by the presidential couple.[25] The CPCs were officially established on 30 November 2007 with a network that was national in scope. Run from above, there was nothing democratic about them.

Some thought that Murillo's membership claims were inflated and the CPCs significance exaggerated. Dionisio Marenco, Mayor of Nicaragua from 2004 to 2009, complained that 'the CPCs in the barrios are the same FSLN people and

---

24 Marenco 2008.
25 Nitlápan-Envío Team 2007c.

nobody else joins'.[26] Still, they could wield power. The FSLN's CPCs were given some of the Venezuelan oil money and government funds used for urban and rural projects, such as building houses and paving roads. According to *Envío*, 'Newspaper articles, comments on the many call-in radio opinion shows and the direct information we receive all suggest that the Councils of Citizens' Power will be used to channel aid, scholarships, projects, urea, surgical operations and other vote-buying goodies'.[27] The CPC's ostensible role was social welfare, but they also worked to increase the vote for the FSLN in future elections. 'There are those in the FSLN who see the political project of the CPCs as converting that loyal electoral base into a politically unconditional and economically captive one, inflating it up to at least 50%', reported *Envío*.[28] That goal would prove to be too high, but the CPCs helped the FSLN to keep control of a crucial third of the vote.

The Attack on the Women's Movement

While shoring up their own organisations, Ortega and Murillo launched an attack on the most important – practically the only – independent social movement in the country: the feminist movement. During the 2000s, the FSLN, the PCL, and the Catholic Church fused into a strong conservative bloc and launched an attack on women's reproductive rights. The most significant developments occurred during 2006 and 2007 when the legislature first abolished women's right to therapeutic abortion and then passed a new code that criminalised abortion. In 2007, a Catholic organisation tested the law by filing criminal charges against nine women leaders, accusing them of accessories after the fact in an illegal abortion in the case of 'Rosita', a nine-year-old rape victim. The Network of Women Against Violence, working with the Attorney General's Office and other governmental agencies and NGOs had in fact arranged an abortion for the girl.[29] Almost one year later, in October 2008, the Attorney General's officers raided the offices of the Autonomous Women's Movement (MAM) and threatened to do the same with other women's organisations, accusing them of laundering money and promoting abortion.[30]

---

26   Marenco 2008.
27   Nitlápan-Envío Team 2007b. Also McKinely 2008.
28   Nitlápan-Envío Team 2007d.
29   Garvin 2008.
30   Cuadra Lira and Jiménez Martinez 2009, p. 207.

Murillo produced a three-and-a-half page tract titled 'Feminism and Low Intensity Warfare' in which she accused Nicaragua's feminists of being upper-class intellectuals out of touch with ordinary women. The feminists, she argued, were women who served the interests of the country's oligarchs and of the 'Empire'. Murillo wrote:

> Evil designs its low intensity wars, which are today fundamentally political media ones, and those of fabricated street images, given the lack of resonance with or welcome from the peoples victimised by their ominous campaigns. Their executors are the wealthy and egocentric oligarchic strata, who thus aim to defend their economic interests and their malignant political model. They organise their sects, or 'peaceful' arms and call them 'civil societies'; they create 'clear', 'politically correct' movements, manipulating causes of justice; they march against prefabricated 'authoritarianisms' and 'tyrannies' cut in series from the same pattern with the same scissors. Evil usurps banners, brings together castes, adds the resentful and the perverted, and tries to split us, to then kill us, wherever a Project of genuine Social Justice is being raised.

She concluded her attack by describing the feminists as 'counter-revolutionaries' who 'dress in women's clothing, but have never known the sensibility of a woman's heart'.[31]

Challenging the women's movement, Murillo created overnight her own women's organisation, the Blanca Arauz Movement for the Dignity of Women's Rights, named after Sandino's last wife, an organisation staffed by loyal FSLN cadres. Her organisation pledged its support for the Ortega government and offered its solidarity to Daniel Ortega and Rosario Murillo against what it called 'the cruel international campaign' being orchestrated against them.[32] In response to the feminists, Murillo argued the importance of women's roles as wives and mothers in terms very much in line with the Catholic Church hierarchy and conservative traditions.

Zoilamérica Nerváez's charges that Daniel Ortega had sexually abused her, which were still before the Inter-American Court of Justice, as well as Ortega's and Murillo's attack on women's reproductive rights, on their organisations, and on the whole concept of feminism had international repercussions. Gloria

---

31   Nitlápan-Envío Team 2008c.
32   'Nace movimiento de mujeres Blanca Aráuz' 2008. A manifesto of the organisation can be found at 'Movimiento por la Dignidad y Derechos de las Mujeres', Blanca Arauz 2008.

Rubin, the minister of women's affairs in Paraguay's left-wing government, charged Ortega with being 'a rapist', leading him to decline an invitation to the inauguration of President Fernando Lugo. Selma Estrada, minister of the National Institute of Women of Honduras, resigned her position in protest over her government's official invitation of Ortega to Tegucigalpa. European Social Democratic parties expressed shock and indignation at the Nicaraguan government's position on women's rights. Latin American women's organisations issued a joint statement denouncing Ortega's government for 'institutionalised misogyny' and a 'campaign to criminalise feminists'.[33] Ortega and Murillo defended themselves from attacks on their government's attitude toward women – and from other criticisms – emphasising his alignment with the governments of Chávez and Castro and the struggle for 'twenty-first century socialism'.

The Taxi, Bus, and Truck Drivers' Rebellion

While Ortega was rebuilding his organisation and preparing for the coming municipal elections in the spring of 2008, he suddenly faced a working-class rebellion led by two independent unions. The Federation of Taxi Drivers-National Transportation Coordinator and the Interurban Transportation Directorate initiated a strike on 5 May to demand that gasoline fuel, then at about us$4.70 per gallon, be reduced by more than us$2.00 per gallon and frozen at the lower price. The unions did not call for any increase in fares or rates, knowing that working people could not afford to pay any more. The unions demanded that Ortega get the Venezuelan government to help with fuel costs. Managua Mayor Dioniso Marenco suggested Ortega go to Venezuela to see if Chávez could give Nicaragua a preferential price. The Minister of Transportation offered to reduce the price by us$0.30 per gallon, but said that any greater reduction would be impossible.

Parking their busses, trucks and taxis at strategic locations blocking streets and highway, the drivers waited with their vehicles for a better resolution. In a rare development, they were joined by drivers on the Atlantic Coast.[34] While bus and truck drivers were not always popular, on this occasion the public supported the drivers, some bringing food and drink to the men who had stayed with their equipment. In some areas, such as León and Masaya,

33   Rogers 2008.
34   Gellman and Danoff 2008.

the people also came out to defend the drivers from the police. Daniel Ortega was said to have personally ordered the police to break the strike, sending the police in León to tow the strikers' vehicles from the streets. As they did, the police purposefully broke the trucks' windows. When after a week the Minister of Transportation met with trucking company owners, many of whom were owner-operators, proposing a fuel reduction of mere cents, he was booed. Ortega proposed that Cardinal Obando y Bravo mediate, but the drivers – many of whom described themselves as Sandinistas – refused to deal with anyone but Ortega himself.[35]

The police made a violent assault on the drivers' roadblocks on 13 May and the battles between them spread into neighbourhoods involving local residents. In Las Maderas, a human rights organisation reported that the police had gone on a rampage through the community leaving dozens injured. The next day, Police Commissioner Aminta Granera, one of the most popular figures in the country, went to Las Maderas and personally apologised and ordered the release of jailed drivers and residents. That night Ortega '... appealed to the people's "conscience" and "Christian spirit" to halt the strike'. He offered to lower fuel prices by fifty cents. His offer was not acceptable. Two days later, Ortega gave in to the workers' demands, promising inter-urban bus and taxi workers a $1.30 discount in diesel and gas prices at government-designated stations, without specifying where this subsidy would come from. National and international trucking companies were excluded from the agreement. With that offer the strike ended, though owners and drivers later complained that many of the problems persisted.[36] The truck and bus drivers' 12-day strike represented a very significant struggle, but it did not lead to any further development in the unions, nor did it find expression in any political party. One strike, even a major one, could not change the country's political direction. As the elections approached, the strike was forgotten and the struggle for political power and privilege was renewed.

Municipal Elections of 2008

Ortega and Murillo had their first real test of strength in the November 2008 municipal elections, which proved to be a harbinger of the future of democracy in Nicaragua. Some 3.8 million registered voters were entitled to cast votes for

---

35   Nitlápan-Envío Team 2008a.
36   Ibid.

mayors, deputy mayors, and municipal council members in 146 of the country's 153 municipalities. The Supreme Electoral Council (CSE), controlled by Roberto Rivas, a key figure in the Nicaraguan political system, nominally politically neutral but in reality loyal to the FSLN, had the power to keep parties off the ballot.[37] In 2008, Rivas excluded from the election both the Sandinista Renovation Movement (MRS) and the Conservative Party, the two parties that stood outside the FSLN-Liberal alliance, on the grounds that they had not run candidates in 80 percent of the previous municipal races, which in the case of the Conservatives was not true. The exclusion of the MRS was clearly intended to prevent disappointed Sandinista voters and independents from breaking to the left. MRS leader Dora María Téllez refused to accept the CSE decision without making a political statement.

Téllez, a former FSLN *comandante*, a hero of the revolution, and one of the principal leaders of the MRS, decided to protest against her party's exclusion through a hunger strike. On 4 June, she began her fast in the middle of Managua, not only protesting against the exclusion of her party, but also excoriating the Pact of 1999 between Ortega and Alemán and the corruption that had come in its wake, as well as the unconstitutionality of the government. Throughout her hunger strike, which lasted until 16 June when doctors advised her to end it for health reasons, she was visited by leaders of civil society and joined by members of her own party and other parties. Thousands rallied round her, waving red flags and the Nicaraguan flag with signs reading 'Basta Ya' ('We've had enough') and 'Stop the Ortega-Murillo Dictatorship, Democracy Now'.[38]

On 20 June, having recuperated from her fast, Téllez was back again, speaking at a rally to 15,000 MRS and Conservative Party members carrying signs against the pact, the Ortega-Murillo dictatorship, and hunger, and calling for democracy. A week later, on 27 June, there was a dissident protest march, but this time involving not only the MRS and the Conservatives, but also Alemán's Liberals and Montealegre's Liberals – a development that did not sit well with the left opposition. Many on the left were not willing to join in a united opposition that included *somocistas* like Alemán and US-backed neoliberals like Montealegre.[39]

---

37   Rivas, originally appointed to the electoral council by Violeta Chamorro, was rumoured to be the son of Cardinal Obando y Bravo as well as his political protégé, an accusation that Rivas denied. 'No soy protegido del Cardenal Obando' 2000.

38   Nitlápan-Envío 2008b. There are many YouTube videos of the hunger strike online. See Téllez 2008, where Dora María Téllez explains her motivation for the hunger strike.

39   Nitlápan-Envío Team 2008b.

Despite the protests, the election was not going to be fair. In November 2008, the CSE, under Rivas's direction, also excluded Nicaragua's non-governmental election watchdog organisation Ethics and Transparency (E&T), which had observed in several previous elections, though E&T went ahead and did so unofficially from outside the polling places. Other requests and proposals for election observers from European governments, from the Supreme Council of Entrepreneurs (COSEP), and from Cardinal Obando y Bravo were all ignored, though at the last moment a few Latin American observer organisations, including one from Ortega's ally Venezuela, were permitted to be present. What they would witness would be a charade.

The Supreme Electoral Council reported five days after the election that the FSLN won more than 90 mayoral seats, including the capital city Managua, while the PLC, running in alliance with the We're Going with Eduardo [Montealegre] (VCE) movement, had won 50 races for mayor. The elections were a stunning victory for Ortega and the FSLN – but they were rigged.

Ethics and Transparency, with approximately 10,000 volunteer unofficial observers, reported that the elections were highly irregular: opposition party observers had been excluded from polling places, there had been a fraudulent annulment of votes as well as substitution of votes and of tallies by local boards, there were also many cases of the fraudulent invalidation of votes during the closed-door counting process, some 20 percent of polling places had been closed while voters were still waiting to vote, and many voters had experienced an intimidating and 'threatening atmosphere'. In 50 municipalities it was reported that the ruling party and the election authorities had irregularly processed and distributed voter IDs to their supporters. Some 30 percent of the vote simply seemed to have disappeared. Everywhere in the cities and towns the CPCs had gone from house to house, supposedly doing a survey on social conditions, but in reality working to get out the FSLN vote.[40]

The Institute for Development and Democracy (IPADE), headed by former *comandante* and FSLN National Directorate Jaime Wheelock, published a report on the November 2008 municipal elections that found fraud in 46 of the 146 municipalities, but found no single pattern. 'A sum of acts altered the popular will', said IPADE director Mauricio Zúñiga. The report explained that Alemán's PLC had acted in complicity with the FSLN to help the latter 'win' races in which the real winners were mainly candidates from the Montealegre's VCE, which, ironically, had run on the PLC ticket in a 'supposed alliance'.[41]

---

40   Nitlápan-Envío Team 2008e. See also Cerda 2008.
41   Nitlápan-Envío Team 2009d.

How was such election fraud perpetrated? Not long after the election, *El Diario* as well as several television and radio stations made public a letter written to Daniel Ortega and Rosario Murillo by an FSLN election worker who called herself Manuelita. *Envío* summarised the letter's contents:

> Manipulating all the electoral materials behind closed doors for 28 hours, this woman allegedly transferred ballots from one polling place to another, introduced challenges in polling places where it served her party's interests, and pulled out and burned original vote tallies from dozens of polling places in which the Liberals had won. She kept robbing Peter to pay Paul until she had whittled the 11,031 votes with which the Liberals had defeated the FSLN down to 7,132, more than enough to give the FSLN victory with a revised figure for it of 8,850 votes.

> Manuelita claims she spoke up to free herself of death threats from some Liberals who knew what she had done, and because she never received the house and thousands of córdobas she says she was promised by Ortega and Murillo. Her story suggests similar operations with similar operators in other municipalities.[42]

While not verifiable, the story had a ring of truth and it fit accounts of ballots and election materials found in garbage dumps shortly after the election.

Following the election, FSLN supporters took up positions in Managua's many large rotundas or turnabouts, wearing t-shirts reading 'Love, Peace, and Reconciliation', and threw stones at the caravans of PLI leader Eduardo Montealegre's protesting supporters, some of them on their way to the Organisation of American States to file papers alleging election fraud.[43] There was general agreement – excepting from the FSLN and the CSE – that the fraud had been massive and outrageous. The Nicaraguan Bishops Conference, from which Obando y Bravo had retired, issued a statement criticising the electoral process and calling for a recount.[44] José Miguel Insulza, secretary general of the Organisation of American States, expressed his concern over the alleged irregularities in the election.[45]

Donor countries, appalled not only by the election irregularities but also by the tendency toward authoritarianism that they represented, began either to

---

42   Nitlápan-Envío Team 2009b.
43   'Orteguistas sigen lanzando 'amor' en las calles' 2008.
44   Nitlápan-Envío Team 2008b.
45   'Insulza expresa preocupación por recuento de votos' 2008.

withdraw from Nicaragua or to cut their donations. In this period, Sweden, Norway, Austria, and Denmark all discontinued aid to Nicaragua, while the Netherlands reduced its assistance.[46] A study by German Technical Cooperation (GTZ), published in April of 2009, concluded that the FSLN only won 69 mayoral seats, while the results of investigation in another 37 locations remained inconclusive. The Germans decided to support projects only in municipalities where the mayor had won the election legitimately.[47] The US government froze its Millennium Challenge Account until the government of Nicaragua did something about the 'credible charges of fraud during municipal elections'.[48]

Protest – Repression – Protest

While Ortega and Murillo built their machine, the opposition also continued to protest. In August of 2008, in the city of León, members of an opposition group arriving for a protest march had been so violently assaulted by Sandinista supporters – young men, some masked and armed with rocks, clubs and mortars – that the dissidents were forced to abandon their march altogether. This tactic, which the Sandinistas called 'preventive war', had been used frequently to prevent and suppress protests since Ortega returned to power. The government took the position that 'the streets belong to the people' – meaning the FSLN – and the police ignored the attacks.

Determined to take a stand against suppression of the right to assemble and protest, civil society organisations and the broad political opposition, reaching from the MRS to Conservatives and Liberals, planned a protest march to be held in Managua on Saturday 21 November. Government officials and FSLN leaders issued statements intended to intimidate and dissuade the marchers, letting them know that they should be prepared for violence. Finally, the FSLN called for its own march on the same day and along the same route. The National Police issued permits for both, well aware that this could lead to a riot. In the end, the opposition held its march in the morning and the FSLN rallied in the evening. The opposition march was 50,000 strong with all the flags of the opposition – the Liberal's red, the Conservative's green, the MRS's orange, and the feminists violet, and most numerous the blue and white national flag –

46   Castán 2011.
47   Nitlápan-Envío Team 2009b.
48   Ibid.

along a four-kilometre route through midtown Managua. The organisers issued a manifesto proclaiming that the country was living under 'a new model of government that is nothing more than a triangle of abuse of power, corruption and the manipulation of poverty'. While the FSLN rally was more than twice as large, swelled with public employees bussed in from around the country, the opposition had made its point.[49]

Discontent over the electoral fraud and the repression of the opposition simmered through the Christmas holiday season and the New Year, finally manifesting itself in street demonstrations by the opposition held in eight cities on 28 February 2009. Three thousand marched in Managua, a thousand in Masaya, and a few hundred in the other cities, where threats and violence led many to stay home. In Jinotega, Chinandega, and León FSLN youth gangs stoned the protestors and threatened them with homemade mortars, leaving more than 50 injured, some seriously. The Managua march also led to violence, though the incidents there were not very serious. In the other cities – Teustepe, Ometepe and Juigalpa – protestors marched without incident, but in small numbers. In Masaya, a thousand marched without provocation.[50] The 2008 municipal elections made it clear that Ortega and the FSLN would use fraud and violence to win every election, with the goal of becoming the country's permanent hegemonic political power. The protest demonstrations also indicated that the opposition was too weak to have any great effect on the course of events.

Ortega – Overcoming Obstacles to a Second Term

Ortega's central preoccupation was to insure that he would be able to run for president in the next presidential election. Article 147 of the Nicaraguan Constitution stated that a sitting president could not be re-elected to a consecutive term or to more than two terms. Ortega, having served as president from 1985 to 1990 and then for two terms 2006 to 2012, was doubly prohibited from seeking re-election. In 2008, Ortega attempted to put together the 56 votes in the National Assembly needed to reform the article, but failed. In 2009, the FSLN had 38 votes and could have bought – literally bought – most of the 18 independent representatives but would still have needed a couple of Alemán's PLC votes, which were unobtainable.

---

49   Nitlápan-Envío Team 2008d.
50   Nitlápan-Envío Team 2009a.

Blocked in the legislature, Ortega decided to turn to the Supreme Court, but first some changes would have to be made to insure his victory there. He pushed through the National Assembly a law that decreased the Supreme Court quorum necessary to issue a ruling. Unlike a Constitutional reform, the quorum bill could be passed by the simple majority, which he had. Then, joined by 149 FSLN mayors who were also prohibited from standing for re-election – the mayors who had been installed in office through the 2008 election fraud – Ortega petitioned the Supreme Court to have Article 147's restrictions lifted for himself and the mayors. Ortega's eight handpicked justices ruled on 19 October that Constitutional Article 147 was 'inapplicable', making Ortega eligible for re-election to the presidency.[51]

Shocked – if not surprised – at the Supreme Court's decision, all of the opposition parties, civil society, and business organisations held a conclave on 9 November at the Metrocenter II shopping mall at which they adopted a resolution promising that their representatives would not vote for any sitting members of the Supreme Electoral Council, would only vote for new CSE members sworn to uphold the people's will, and would not vote for any individual who was not capable, honest and impartial. The Metrocenter II Agreement, however, had little weight since the opposition did not have the 56 of 90 votes needed to approve new appointments, not as long as the rock-hard Sandinista delegation had 40 votes.

Still, fearing that the opposition in the National Assembly might somehow cobble together the votes necessary to block his appointments, President Ortega himself usurped the legislative branch's responsibilities, and on 3 January issued Degree 03–2010 which declared that the 25 officials – CSE members and Supreme Court justices – whose terms were variously due to end in January, April, or June, would remain in office until the National Assembly either re-elected them or elected their replacements. Ortega defended this extraordinary unconstitutional and illegal measure, arguing that he had a responsibility to avoid the 'chaos' that would occur if these posts were not filled and functioning.[52]

Furious at this unconstitutional usurpation of legislative power by the president, the opposition refused to accept Ortega's decree. With his opponents refusing to budge, Ortega turned to another subterfuge. Parliamentary president René Núñez – a long-time FSLN legislator – announced on 7 April that he had 'discovered' that Paragraph 2 of Article 201 of an early edition of the

---

51   Nitlápan-Envío Team 2009c.

52   Nitlápan-Envío Team 2010b.

1987 Constitution – modified several times since – provided that legislatively-appointed officials would remain in their posts until their replacements were named.[53]

When the Supreme Court justices' terms ended on 11 April, the liberal justices left office, but citing Ortega's decree and the obscure constitutional justification of the 1987 Constitution, the two FSLN justices, Rafael Solís and Armengol Cuadra, remained at their posts. Ortega's opponents railed against the government, while his supporters rallied to the FSLN justices. Sandinista judges closed courts around the country in solidarity. These events united and increased the size of the parliamentary opposition. When 47 opposition representatives, a clear simple majority, announced that they would vote to annul Decree 03–2010, the Sandinista government sent state employees and armed youth gangs – led by the FSLN's Supreme Court Justices Solís and Cuadra – to surround the National Assembly in order to prevent the legislators from entering the building and voting.

Unable to convene in the National Assembly building, the opposition legislators met in the Managua Holiday Inn Hotel to begin drafting the annulment legislation. Solis and Cuadra then led government employees and the paramilitary gangs to the hotel where they fired dozens of homemade mortar shells at the building, causing damage and pandemonium, as hotel guests fled for safety. Throughout these events, the police stood by, permitting the FSLN supporters to stone and bombard the hotel and to terrorise its guests. The next day, the crowds again surrounded the National Assembly, bombarding it too with mortars and showering it with rocks. On another street, the crowd trapped 18 Liberals and one MRS member in an office, holding them prisoner, while outside they burned their cars.

When the violence subsided, both groups held to their positions: Ortega supporters claimed that his decree and the clause of the 1987 Constitution were valid, while the opposition – delighted at finally having created a majority in the National Assembly – argued for the legitimacy of the Holiday Inn legislative session.

Ortega moved quickly and cleverly against the united opposition. First, he revived three criminal charges for corruption that had been hanging over Alemán's head for several years. Then the Prosecutor General called for stripping Montealegre of immunity so he could stand trial for alleged corruption in the issuance of government bonds during the bank scandals of a decade

---

53   Ibid.

before.[54] To protect their party leaders, the Liberals in the National Assembly immediately introduced an amnesty bill for Alemán and Montealgre, an act that scandalised the MRS as well as religious and social movement opponents of Ortega who were unwilling to countenance corruption and impunity. The opposition's brief moment of unity was shattered, while Ortega moved on toward his goal.[55] As Eduardo Enríquez, editor of *La Prensa*, says: 'Orteguismo has one objective: to perpetuate itself in power, and to take advantage of power to enrich itself'.[56]

Meanwhile – The Economic Crisis

While Ortega and Murillo focused on building the electoral machine that could win the 2012 election, Nicaragua's people were experiencing an economic crisis. When elected in 2006, Ortega took over a country already mired in economic and social problems. Chamorro, Alemán, and Bolaños had done little for the country's working people and the poor. The electric power generation and distribution system was unreliable and there were constant problems of blackouts in Managua and other cities. While there had been some highway construction, the country's highways and roads were still inadequate and many in poor condition. Housing for the country's urban working class and rural farm labourers was miserable, often little more than shacks. Outside of Managua, there was no potable running water and sewage systems were lacking throughout rural Nicaragua.

Nicaragua's economy grew at a rate of 3.5 percent in 2007, but that was the lowest in Central America, while inflation rose to 17 percent, the highest in the region. Then, in 2008, the housing bubble burst in the United States, detonating a world economic crisis, the most severe since the Crash of 1929 that led to the Great Depression of the 1930s. The United States was Nicaragua's largest trading partner at the time and the principal market for Nicaragua's exports, and by 2009 the depression in the north had hit home. For example, that year there were five million pounds of lobster in Nicaraguan freezers with no buyers in the United States. The price for Nicaraguan beef dropped from 52 *córdobas* a kilo before the great recession to 36 in February 2009. Exports fell between

---

54 On this scandal over the Central Bank's issuance of paper known as CENIS (Certificados Negociables de Inversión), and of Montealegre's role in these matters, see Mayorga 2007, Appendix, pp. 162–84.

55 Nitlápan-Envío Team 2010a.

56 Enríquez 2012, p. 101.

2008 and 2009 by 26 percent. Remittances from Nicaraguan workers in Costa Rica and the United States also declined since they had become unemployed or underemployed in those countries as a result of the recession.

The international financial crisis also caused a credit crunch and it became hard for Nicaragua to procure loans. The government therefore did not have the funds to continue to make micro-credit loans to businesses that supported 350,000 families. Foreign direct investment came to a standstill, while foreign-owned maquiladoras laid off 22,000 workers. The crisis left Nicaragua with an enormous fiscal deficit of over 16 percent of GDP compared to the World Bank's recommended 3 percent, a deficit covered by international donors who were themselves in trouble. With all of this, unemployment rose to 8.2 percent, purchasing power of real wages fell by 17 percent, and 70 percent of the population lived below the poverty line in 2009.[57] By late 2009, the worst of the crisis had passed, and in 2010 the GDP grew by 3 to 4 percent, though that was hardly sufficient to recoup the losses of the recession, much less to carry the nation forward and out of poverty.

Unlike the previous post-revolutionary governments, Ortega had both a lingering ideological and rhetorical commitment to the working class, the peasantry, and the urban poor, and a very real need to improve their situations, at least minimally, since they formed his political base, making up the largest bloc of FSLN voters. Recognising his genuine if pragmatic commitment to maintain and enhance social programmes, Japan, Taiwan, and some European countries continued to offer support to such programmes, as did the International Development Bank and the technical missions of the IMF. Venezuelan aid provided millions of dollars for the Zero Hunger food programmes and the Zero Usury micro-credit programmes.[58] Nevertheless, social spending for 2009–11 still had to be reduced by 8.6 percent because of the withdrawal of support by international donors in response to the 2008 electoral fraud.[59] While Ortega was not constructing socialism, or even a European social-democratic welfare state, it must be recognised that, far more than the three previous administrations, he did attempt to protect and improve the lives of the poor, who nevertheless remained terribly impoverished, even by Central American or any other standards. There is little doubt that as the country began to prepare for the 2011 presidential elections, the working class and the poor believed that they would do better with Ortega and the FSLN than they would with the Liberals.

---

57   Grigsby 2009.
58   Nitlápan-Envío Team 2009a.
59   Nitlápan-Envío Team 2010c.

The 2011 Election

Having used the Supreme Court to remove legal obstacles to his re-election, Ortega had begun his sixth presidential campaign arguing that the economy was improving, that the country was addressing its educational deficits, and that his government would finally bring prosperity to the people.[60] During the 2011 campaign, just as in 2006, Ortega appeared in civilian clothing, accompanied by his wife and children, with 'Give Peace a Chance' playing in the background, and once again his speeches were a combination of religious rhetoric and populism. The FSLN constructed an electoral political alliance that demonstrated just how opportunistic both the Sandinistas and their former opponents had become. The FSLN bloc included YATAMA, the Miskito indigenous party, the Nicaraguan Resistance Party (PRN), the party of the former Contras, the Christian Alternative (AC), which had run Edén Pastora for president in 2006, and Somoza's former organisation, the National Liberal Party.[61]

Nicaragua's electorate was far different from what it had been when Ortega had been elected in 1984. The population had grown from less than three million to just under six million. About half of the population had been born since the 1979 revolution and most had come of age under the neoliberal governments of Chamorro, Alemán, Bolaños, and Ortega. While the wealthy lived in gated communities, shopped at the malls, and travelled abroad, and some in the small and struggling middle class owned cars and cell phones, the working classes remained poor. Half the population still lived beneath the poverty line, official unemployment was above seven percent, and nearly half the population was underemployed. While the country was generally secure, gangs had become a problem in poorer neighbourhoods such as Barrio Jorge Dimitrov in Managua.

Ortega would have to win the votes of the majority of Nicaragua's working class, farmers and the poor in order to win the election. Most important would be the hundreds of old FSLN cadres trained in democratic centralism who would turn orders from above into action below, motivating the one million FSLN members, and they in turn the CPCs' hundreds of thousands of households, all of them motivated by a desire to share in the jobs, building materials, and scholarships that the Ortega campaign would be

---

60   Ortega had been the FSLN presidential candidate in 1984, 1990, 1996, 2001, 2006 and 2012. He won the 1984, 2006 and 2012 elections.

61   Nitlápan-Envío Team 2009e.

promising, or even just to get one of the t-shirts or hats handed out to party faithful at the rallies.

The mass media would be key to Ortega's election campaign. Between his election in 2006 and the 2011 campaign, the president, his family, his party, and Albanisa had bought up most of the television stations. In 2005, Ortega and the FSLN only controlled Channel 4, but by June of 2011 they controlled six of the country's eight TV channels.[62] It was a family affair:

> Not long after the FSLN bought Channel 8, allegedly with ALBA money, a new TV channel (Channel 13), also in the hands of the presidential family, went on the air, adding to the media empire of the Ortega-Murillo family … Son Rafael Ortega Murillo, who heads the firm called Nueva Imagen, negotiated the family's entrance into the Nicaraguan TV spectrum with powerful Mexican businessman Ángel González in 2007. Carlos Enrique and Daniel Edmundo Ortega Murillo now direct Channel 4; Juan Carlos Ortega Murillo directs Canal 8; Maurice Ortega Murillo directs the TV production company RGB Media and, together with sisters Camila and Luciana, also directs the new Channel 13, which is on 24 hours a day. Channel 91 also belongs to the family …[63]

Most disturbing to many Nicaraguans was the FSLN purchase of the independent Channel 8, the home of Carlos Fernando Chamorro, the opposition journalist. Chamorro, anchorman of *Esta Noche* and *Esta Semana*, said that Albanisa had paid $10 million for the channel which it jointly managed with the Institute of Telecommunications (TELCOR). With Ortega now in charge, Chamorro left the station but could find no other station willing to broadcast his shows.[64] Ortega's control of the media represented a pillar of his political operation.

The Liberals were, as in the previous elections, not only divided, but now split into nearly a dozen parties united around three rival coalitions – but it would turn out that a surprise candidate appeared at the last moment who offered them a chance at victory. The Liberals 2011 began like this:

– Alemán created a political coalition made up of his PLC and three others, the Neoliberal Party (PALI), the Central American Unity Party (PUCA), and the Multiethnic Indigenous Party (PIM) of the Caribbean Coast.

---

62   'Nicaragua: Los Ortega acaparan una sexta televisión' 2001.

63   Envío Team 2011a.

64   'Albanisa pagó y Telcor amarró la compra del Canal 8' n.d.; Martínez n.d.

- Eduardo Montealegre's coalition included the Nicaraguan Liberal Alliance (ALN), the Independent Liberal Party (PLI), and the Multiethnic Party for the Unity of the Coast (PAMUC).
- Finally, the Alliance for the Republic (APRE), which Bolaños had created as an alternative to the PLC, established an alliance with the Conservative Party (PC), the Citizens Action Party (PAC), and a PLI splinter led by Vigilio Godoy.[65]

With the election approaching, the Liberals could not agree on a method to choose a common candidate, it looked as if they might fail completely. Then in August of 2009, Fabio Gadea Mantilla threw his hat in the ring.

At the age of 79, Gadea was an unlikely candidate, but a very popular personality. Born in Ocotal, Nueva Segovia, in 1931, at the age of 17 he began working in the radio business. He was a pioneer of radio journalism who in 1962 founded the Radio Corporation, the country's most popular radio station, with a large following in rural Nicaragua. Beginning in 1959, he created a radio personality, 'Pancho Madrigal', for which he wrote thousands of stories, one broadcast each morning and another one each night. His stories' leading character Pancho Madrigal became a beloved figure among generations of Nicaraguans who treasured Gadea's homespun homilies.

During the 1960s, Gadea spoke his mind on all issues, and because he criticised the Somoza dictatorship, his station was censored, fined, and nearly ruined. He was, however, equally opposed to the Sandinistas throughout the revolutionary decade of the 1980s and did not hesitate to speak out against them either. Again, his station was repressed and nearly put out of business. In 1982, he joined the Nicaraguan Democratic Movement (MDN), founded by Alfonso Robelo, but eventually went into exile and supported the Contras. When he returned to Nicaragua in 1990, he went back into the radio business and also became involved in Alemán's PLC. The two men were quite close for a while and during that period one of Gadea's sons married a daughter of Alemán.[66] Gadea had a regular column in *La Prensa* in which he wrote regularly his 'Love Letters to Nicaragua', writes Andrés Pérez Baltodano. 'In them he expressed in an explicit way: a profound anti-sandinismo; an elitist vision of society, and a profound social conservatism with regard to abortion and homosexuality.'[67]

---

65   Nitlápan-Envío team 2009e.
66   Nitlápan-Envío Team 2010d.
67   Pérez-Baltodano 2012, p. 216.

It had been expected that Arnoldo Alemán or Eduardo Montealegre would lead the Liberals – or running separately that they might lead the Liberals to defeat – but with the various coalitions unable to come to an agreement, Gadea's announcement of his interest in running for the presidency found favour and he became the Liberals' consensus candidate. In December of 2009, Gadea brought together nine different political groups in the coalition called Nicaraguan Unity for Hope or UNE, an acronym spelling 'join' in Spanish. The two principal backers of Gadea were the right-wing Liberal Montealegre's We're Going with Eduardo Movement (MVE) and the now rightward drifting Sandinista Renovation Movement (MRS), both of which were forbidden by the CSE in 2008 from running candidates for office on their own tickets in the municipal elections that year, a prohibition still in force. Of all the Liberal groups, only Alemán's party refused to join the UNE coalition, saying that the presence of the MRS showed that Gadea's group had been infiltrated by the Sandinistas.[68] The participation of the MRS in the Gadea coalition did not represent the left infiltration of the Liberals, though it did spell the end of the MRS's reputation as an honourable independent party. And by running a separate Liberal campaign, Alemán was of course aiding the FSLN.

During the campaign, Gadea declined to discuss the many issues that divided those in his broad alliance, saying they would have to be worked out in the future. On the question of overturning the law banning therapeutic abortions, Gadea would only say that he was pro-life, but that such questions would have to be decided in the legislature. Arguing that the election was 'a struggle between dictatorship and democracy', Gadea's rallies drew as many as 40,000 people just two weeks before the election.[69] Polls showed him leading by 30 percent. As popular as he was, however, there was no way he could overcome the division in the liberal camp between his coalition and Alemán's or the Ortega machine.

On 6 November 2011, the CSE, headed by FSLN loyalist Roberto Rivas, announced that Ortega had won a landslide victory with 62.46 percent of the vote to Gadea's 31 percent and Arnoldo Alemán's 5.9 percent, with less than 1.0 percent going to two other parties. Ortega's vote – more than twice Gadea's – was a smashing if dubious victory. The FSLN also won 62 of the National Assembly seats, while the Independent Liberal Party won 26, and the Liberal Constitutionalist Party of Alemán won only 2. With 62 votes in the Assembly, Ortega would be able not only to pass legislation but also to amend the Constitution. Though the Constitution still said that no one could be re-elected to the presidency on a second separate occasion or succeed himself, Ortega had done both. He now controlled all four branches of the Nicaraguan government: the executive, the National Assembly, the Supreme Court, and the Supreme Electoral Council.

Claiming that he had beaten Ortega by two to one, Gadea organised a protest demonstration, claiming that 100,000 would come into the streets to protest against the election, but only 10,000 showed up. Some, such as María López Vigil, editor of *Envío*, a woman who calls herself a Sandinista (though not an Ortega supporter or FSLN member), thought that Gadea might well have won the election – even if not by the extraordinary margin he claimed – though no one would ever know for sure.[70] The European Union's report on the election suggested, in very diplomatic language, that it had been rigged and possibly stolen. The report found:

> Throughout the process the CSE, a CSE that was virtually monocolor [that is, everyone of the same party] at each of its levels, demonstrated scant independence from the ruling party and created unequal conditions for competition as well as outright obstructions to the opposition, who were prevented from having any effective representation within the election administration. Some experienced national election observation organisations were not accredited and auditing of the process by the opposition was impeded by the Supreme Electoral council.[71]

And on election day, 'an absolute lack of transparency characterised the aggregation and publication of the results, marking a serious deterioration in the quality of the electoral process'.[72] All of that hardly mattered. Ortega was president with control of all of the state institutions, connections to all of the business interests, and the acquiescence of the Catholic Church. Increasingly people called him a 'dictator' and compared him to Somoza, and though the charge was unjust – Ortega did not murder and torture his opponents – many saw a good deal of truth in the accusation.

---

70   Lemoine 2012.

71   EU Election Observation Mission 2011.

72   EU Election Observation Mission 2011.

Ortega's Foreign Policy

While consolidating power at home, Ortega also sought allies abroad. Like his domestic policy, Ortega's foreign policy was pragmatic and unaffected by principles; though in general he aligned himself with former Communist regimes, with the Latin American left, and with Third World dictators. Since 1959, the Sandinistas' principal allies in the 1970s and 1980s had been Fidel Castro's Communist Cuba, and, until it collapsed in 1991, the Soviet Union and the Eastern Bloc. When he returned to power in 2007, Ortega allied himself with Cuba, now ruled by Fidel's brother Raúl Castro, and, as we have seen, with Hugo Chávez of Venezuela and Evo Morales of Bolivia. Ortega situated Nicaragua as part of the far left of the leftward-moving Latin American nations in the 2000s.[73] Nicaragua even maintained relations with North Korea's notorious dictator Kim Jong-Il. Kim, who had been congratulated by Ortega on his re-election, was later mourned by Ortega and Murillo who offered their 'profound condolences for death of dear leader Kim Jong-Il' when he died in December 2011.[74] To many supporters within Nicaragua and abroad, it seemed that Ortega remained the same sort of pro-Communist revolutionary that he had been back in the 1980s.

In Latin America, Ortega identified with the leftist governments. As we have already seen, Ortega maintained close relations with both Raúl Castro in Cuba, Hugo Chávez in Venezuela, and Evo Morales in Bolivia. Most important to him was Chávez of Venezuela, who provided oil money for the Albanisa funds controlled by Ortega. Similarly, Ortega established friendly relationships with the dictator Muammar Gaddafi of Libya and with the head of the authoritarian Iranian government President Mahmoud Ahmadinejad. In the case of these political relationships, a previous history of solidarity among former colonial Third World nations coincided with the political evolution of those nations into dictatorships, as well as with Ortega's desire to find political and economic allies as a counterweight to the United States. Both Libya and Iran had lots of oil.

While presenting the image of being part of an anti-imperialist alliance, Ortega, as is explained below, opened up Nicaragua to foreign investors with apparently little concern for the country's sovereignty. What is clear is that in the area of foreign policy, Ortega and his administration identified with the authoritarian and repressive governments of Cuba and Korea, Libya and Iran, and not with the democratic and labour movements within them that were

---

73   La Botz 2007a and La Botz 2007b.
74   'Ortega laments death of "dear leader"' 2011.

fighting for democracy and in some cases for socialism. Even as he projected abroad a policy that identified Nicaragua with the Latin American left and other Third World governments, at home Ortega constructed a government that served the rich, principally Nicaragua's historic oligarchy which, under his government, attained new levels of wealth and economic power.

A Government for the Rich

Since his first post-revolutionary election in 2006, Ortega had made it clear that unlike the FSLN of the 1980s, his government wanted a partnership with capital both domestic and foreign. He told business that he was committed to working with the International Monetary Fund, to remaining a member of the Central American Free Trade Agreement (CAFTA-DR), to guaranteeing property rights, and to insuring that businessmen could succeed. 'We want to establish an open channel of communication between our government and the private sector', Ortega told businessmen in 2006.[75] 'An elaborate series of private-public working groups and senior-level meetings between Nicaragua's top capitalists and government ministers maintain fluid relations', wrote *Foreign Policy*.[76]

Ortega's government, through its control of the Venezuelan funds flowing into Albanisa, was itself a major investor in the Nicaraguan economy. Albanisa invested in agriculture, industry, utilities and many other areas of the economy in amounts of hundreds of millions of dollars. Albanisa-owned companies, since they were not owned and controlled by the Nicaraguan government, did not form part of the state sector but rather formed part of the private sector. While Albanisa has little transparency, most of its funds seem to have gone to enterprises directed by Ortega or his family members; and if not directly owned by them, the businesses were frequently controlled by them. Albanisa also played the role of partner in enterprises with other Nicaraguans from both the old oligarchy and the new bourgeoisie.

The Ortega administration also worked closely with FLSN veteran leaders, the winners of *la piñata* of 1979, who had become businesspeople themselves. Bayardo Arce, Ortega's principal economic advisor, had turned the FSLN properties that he came to control into a profitable complex of businesses, most important among them Agricorp, in which he was a partner, which had a vir-

---

75   'Carlos Pellas, el más rico entre los ricos de Nicaragua, dice que empresarios acordaron "buena comunicación" con Ortega' 2006.

76   Feinberg 2011.

tual monopoly on staples of the Nicaraguan diet such as rice, beans, and eggs.[77] Most capitalists, however, the richest and most powerful, were holdovers from the oligarchy of the old regime.

Ortega worked closely with Nicaragua's old bourgeoisie whose wealth and economic power were far greater than that of the Sandinista *nouveau riche*. Ortega was particularly solicitous of Carlos Pellas, a billionaire and the country's richest man. Pellas was the grandson of Francisco Alfredo Pellas, who emigrated to Nicaragua from Italy and in 1875 established the Nicaraguan Steamship Navigation Company. Unlike other members of the old bourgeoisie, when the revolution came in 1979, Carlos Pellas stayed in Nicaragua despite the nationalisation of some of his property. He survived both the revolutionary and post-revolutionary years, and by the 2000s his Grupo Pellas was the country's most important conglomerate and involved in nearly every aspect of the Nicaraguan economy. When Ortega returned to the presidency in 2006, his government supported Pellas in the development of his businesses, including new luxury hotels with spas and golf courses.

Foreign capital also played a major and growing role in Nicaragua under Ortega. In 2012, foreign direct investment in Nicaragua reached $1.28 billion, a 33 percent increase over the previous year which had seen an astounding 91 percent increase. The leading foreign investor nations were Venezuela, Panama, and the United States, in that order, but there were also others, such as Spain and Mexico in the communications industry. Investors put their money in industry, energy, and mining, in trade and services, and in the free trade zones' maquiladoras.[78] Venezuelan investment had a tremendous impact, as journalist Tim Rogers wrote:

> The influx of petrodollars into Nicaragua has created a new group of Sandinista economic elite, the 'ALBAgarchs', as it were. The Sandinistas have used their newfound riches to corner the country's petroleum market and invest heavily in media, tourism, agriculture, timber, and renewable energy. New car sales are at an all-time high, construction is up and the banks have more money than ever.[79]

The Venezuelan money and the private sector and the free market were not enough to keep the government and the society afloat. Nicaragua also remained

---

77   The company is self-described at Agricorp 2014.

78   Rogers 2013.

79   Rogers 2012c.

dependent upon foreign cooperation, that is, loans and donations principally from the governments of the United States and the European Union, as well as from foreign political parties and NGOs. In 2012, such cooperation amounted to US$670 million, 64 percent to the private sector and 36 percent to the public sector. Much of this went to the construction of infrastructure and to public administration. Some 73 percent came in the form of loans, and the rest came as donations.[80] Still, notwithstanding the importance of foreign direct investment and international cooperation, it was native capitalists who controlled most of the economy. Their position had improved significantly.

Nicaragua's New Bourgeoisie and New Economic Model

During the post-revolutionary government and continuing under Ortega, the bourgeoisie had strengthened its control over the economy. In 2007, Francisco Mayorga, an economist and former banker, published a book titled *Megacapitales de Nicaragua*, in which he demonstrated that a dozen families, almost all of them from the old, pre-revolutionary bourgeoisie, each with more than $100 million in wealth, controlled the Nicaraguan economy. Each of these families exercised a hegemonic or even monopoly control over one or more sectors of the economy: Pellas Chamorro, Chamorro Chamorro, Lacayo Lacayo, Baltodano Cabrera, Ortiz Gurdián, Zamora Llanes, Coen Montealegre, Lacayo Gil, and the overseas group Ernesto Fernández Holmann, René Morales Carazo, José Ignacio González Holmann and Jaime Montealegre Lacayo. Mayorga argued that, controlled by these families, three bank groups dominated finances in the country: Grupo Uno (Banco Uno), Grupo Proamérica (Banpro), and Grupo Lafise (Bancentro). Below these dozen families and their banks was another layer of less wealthy multimillionaires, among whom were the richest Sandinistas such as the Ortega brothers, Bayardo Arce, and a few others.[81]

Mayorga argued that 'a new social class is rapidly taking shape, an elite which appears to be different from those that previously existed: capitalists on a Latin American scale'. The members of this new capitalist class owned banks and corporations capable of earnings on the order of one billion dollars. Unlike the traditional capitalist class of the late nineteenth and twentieth centuries, the new bourgeoisie had liquid capital that permitted them to engage in the

---

80   Japan International Cooperation Agency 2012.

81   Mayorga 2007, *passim*.

development of regional projects, something their predecessors had never been able to accomplish.[82]

Beyond this description of Nicaragua's rich, Mayorga offered a class analysis of contemporary Nicaragua that bears citing at length:

> Nicaragua no longer had an oligarchy, a middle class, and a proletariat and became a country with five social classes. At the top are twelve families with mega-capital of more than 100 million dollars ... then some 1,500 millionaires, then a stunted middle class – professionals, merchants, those dependent on remittances – then a low-income class, the poor such as the peasants who migrate to the city, and then the fifth class, the expatriates, the hundreds of thousands of Nicaraguans who live in California, Florida, San José and Costa Rica.[83]

Mayorga's scheme provides a useful view of Nicaragua's post-revolutionary social pyramid, though he somehow omits the significant numbers of the industrial working class, agricultural workers, and public employees, that is, he omits the working class. His class bias may account for this important oversight.

His emphasis on the central role of migrants, however, is particularly important. More than ten percent of Nicaraguans, some 800,000, migrated legally to live and work abroad either permanently or temporarily in 2012, driven by their own country's 50 percent sub-employment level. There were also thousands of others who migrated without documents. The total number of migrants can be estimated to be over one million, more than a sixth of the country's population. Most migrants were young, and some studies estimated that 25 percent were under the age of 18, some migrating with their families and others to work themselves. Most Nicaraguans migrated to work in Costa Rica or the United States, though some also went to El Salvador, Panama and Spain, while Nicaragua's English-speaking Caribbean migrants often went to work in Jamaica, Gran Cayman or Belize.

Men generally went abroad to work in construction, agriculture, fishing, and the lumber industry, while women worked in services. Some of the Caribbean Coast migrants worked on cruise ships under a variety of flags sailing mostly in the Caribbean. Few migrant workers had labour unions to fight to improve their wages, benefits and conditions. Undocumented workers were often subject to

---

82   Mayorga 2007, p. 125.

83   Marenco 2007.

special exploitation because of their lack of papers, including poor housing, low pay, and especially difficult and sometimes dangerous working conditions. The Nicaraguan migrants' remittances, which reached US\$1 billion in 2012, represented 12.5 percent of the country's GDP, that is, one of the country's principal sources of income.[84] They were, as Mayorga suggested, the Nicaraguan underclass, though they often earned more than the country's resident poor.

Workers' Rights and Labour Unions

Workers who stayed at home found that their work lives were circumscribed by the government, the employers, and the official unions. Nicaragua had never had a strong, independent labour movement. When labour unions first appeared in the early twentieth century, they were small, marginal and easily manipulated and controlled by the Somoza dictatorship. With the Triumph of 1979, the Sandinistas had encouraged labour union organisation, and unions grew rapidly, but they were entirely subordinated to the FSLN and had little independence. During the 1980s, the labour movement was deeply fragmented, and those divisions continued for years after. For the last 40 years Nicaragua has had several labour federations, many linked to rival political parties, though the Sandinistas and their unions were the largest. The various leftist groups, such as the Communists and the Maoists, organised their own small unions and federations, and conservative Nicaraguan groups working with the CIA did the same.

The FSLN created the National Workers Front (FNT) as the umbrella organisation covering all of its federations and unions under the leadership of Dr. Gustavo Porras, who was also a FSLN representative in the National Assembly. A long-time union leader, Onofre Guevara, a former PSN leader, FSLN member and ex-editor of its newspaper *Barricada*, coined the term 'porrismo' to refer to the FSLN's control of the unions for political and particularly electoral purposes. 'According to Guevara, *porrismo* is characterised by the party's manipulation of workers with the threat of being fired – which has enormous clout in a country with such high unemployment – and the neutralisation of their social and labour demands to prioritise party activities and objectives'.[85] Resentful of this political control, the increasingly independent Sandinista Workers Centre (CST) tended to move away from Porras and the FSLN.

---

84   González Briones 2012. Also Rocha 2010.

85   Nitlápan-Envío Team 2010b.

The Nicaraguan government, through its participation in CAFTA, had been successful in attracting greater foreign investment in industry, particularly in its free trade zones. These zones located in Managua, Masaya, Granada and on the Pacific coast had textile factories built by North American, Nicaraguan, Mexican, Korean and Taiwanese capital. Other factories produced shrimp, cigars, and automobile harnesses. By 2012, there were 161 companies in the free trade zones, exporting $2 billion worth of products and employing nearly 100,000 Nicaraguans or one-sixth of the country's entire formal-sector workforce. Among those were 57 apparel firms employing 66,000 workers, 53 percent of whom were women. The apparel industry represented the most important part of the free trade zones, with US$1,348.2 million in exports, almost all of it shipped to the US market. Workers in Nicaragua earned on average $1.05 per hour, less than half the hourly wages in Mexico.[86]

During the 1990s and early 2000s, when they were first developed under the governments of Chamorro, Alemán and Bolaños, these industrial parks and light manufacturing plants predicated upon cheap labour were the site of continuous labour-management tensions and numerous conflicts over wages and conditions. Both the Ortega government and the employers wanted to bring these labour conflicts under control, the latter because they wanted to maintain uninterrupted production and the former because he wished to attract more domestic and foreign investment. Since the 1980s, Nicaragua had willy-nilly arrived at a system of labour relations more or less like that of Mexico, based in large part on tripartite agreements between the government, the employers and the unions, an arrangement that was especially dominant in the free trade zones with their maquiladoras.

In an attempt to reduce class conflict in the free trade zones, in 2012 the Ortega administration worked out through tripartite negotiations an agreement to provide a graduated minimum wage increase of 9 percent over three years and a voluntary programme of outside monitoring of workers' rights and conditions. Anxious to maintain good relations with foreign manufacturers in the textile industry and with the brand names behind them such as Gap, Levi's, Target, Walmart and J C Penney, Ortega welcomed the US Department of Labor's suggestion of bringing Better Work, a partnership between the International Labour Organisation and the International Finance Corporation, working with the National Free Trade Zone Commission to oversee and report on conditions in the plants.

As one reporter wrote:

---

86   Rogers 2012b.

From a business owners' viewpoint, the tripartite agreement has minimised tire-burning labour protests and increased the accuracy of labour-cost projections. That allows factory owners to focus more on production orders and less on negotiating with recalcitrant union bosses shouting hackneyed revolutionary slogans through bullhorns. The agreement also allows the Sandinistas to feel less guilty about promoting a free-market capitalist model because they can now point to their efforts to 'socialise' labour conditions for the good of the working poor. In that sense, the Ortega government claims it has humanised the frigid framework of CAFTA.[87]

Even the FSLN unions were not happy with the results of this programme. Pedro Ortega, secretary general of the Federation of Textile Unions, filed formal complaints with the National Free Trade Zone Commission on 1 May, International Labour Day, accusing free-zone factory owners of noncompliance. He claimed that dozens of factories were not, for example, providing the subsidised food baskets promised to workers. Other companies denied workers access to health programmes because it would mean that they would miss work. Some factory owners said the agreement only applied to the biggest corporations producing for name brands, but not to them. When Better Work issued its first report in August 2013, it found that in fact a large minority of employers were not compliant with labour union contracts, while 60 percent failed to pay the contractual severance pay, 75 percent would not let workers take leave, 45 percent did not pay overtime, and 95 percent ignored health and safety issues.[88]

As Josefa Rivera, a former garment worker and organiser with the 'María Elena Cuadra' Working and Unemployed, said: 'Nicaragua has lots of pretty laws; they are precious. But in the end it's us, the workers, who have to follow up and pressure companies to obey them'.[89] And workers were not very successful in doing so.

Workers in the public sector had challenges of their own, despite a 120 percent increase in the minimum wage between 2008 and 2012. While they had the relative security and stability of a government job, wages still remained inadequate. In 2012, a typical Nicaraguan teacher earned between $185 to $226 a month, a wage lower than that of construction workers, factory workers, and many market vendors. Their wage could pay for only half of the list of

---

87   Ibid.
88   Better Work Nicaragua 2013.
89   Rogers 2012b.

56 basic food and household items in the government's basic market basket of goods necessary for subsistence. With their low wages, workers were more than ready to line up for their Christian, Socialist and Solidarity Bonus of 30 dollars doled out each month to 160,000 state workers as a special gift of thanks from President Ortega and financed by ALBA. They understood without being told that in exchange for the bonus, they were expected to give their votes to Ortega and the FSLN.

Public employees who worked for Ortega's government were expected to support his party and its labour unions, and those who did not often faced problems. 'The situation is particularly bad for public employees, who have a very unstable labour environment where there is no respect for independent unions or collective bargaining', said Alvaro Leiva, secretary of labour affairs for the Democratic Federation of Public Sector Workers (FEDETRASEP), in the spring of 2012. Between President Ortega's return to power in 2007 and May Day 2012, FEDETRASEP documented more than 23,000 cases of public workers who were 'arbitrarily fired without due process'. According to Leiva, in most of those cases, workers were laid-off for not being Sandinista party members. The government has also refused to give severance pay to fired workers, Leavid said, and became $28.6 million in arrears to 19,000 former state employees. In 2010, FEDETRASEP filed complaints against the Government of Nicaragua before the Central American Court of Justice and the Inter-American Commission on Human Rights. Leiva told the press: 'The Ortega administration has also gone after non-Sandinista workers' unions, firing 150 of them in the past five years. In total the Sandinista government has violated 15 out of 70 international labour conventions related to collective bargaining, freedom to form independent unions, work inspections, and child labour'.[90]

Ortega and Murillo could no longer really control workers through their labour unions, but they could control them through the tripartite government-employer-union negotiations. Even in its heroic period, the FSLN had not been a workers' government. By 2012, it was clearly a government over and against the workers, making sure they were paid just well enough and remained intimidated enough that they would not rebel in strikes and threaten foreign investment.

---

90   Rogers 2012a.

Poverty Remains

The United Nations World Food Program, as it began a new programme in Nicaragua, reported:

> Nicaragua is one of the poorest countries in Latin America, with gross national income per capita at US$1,080; 42 percent of the population lives below the poverty line, and 15 percent live in extreme poverty. Poverty levels are highest in rural areas, particularly the North Atlantic Autonomous Region, home to most indigenous communities, where 37 percent of the population lives in extreme poverty. In indigenous areas, 40 percent of children do not attend primary school, and the average length of schooling is only three years. Chronic malnutrition affects 22 percent of children under 5; stunting is highest in the dry corridor, reaching 35 percent in Madriz and 28 percent in Nueva Segovia. Nicaragua is also vulnerable to recurrent natural disasters that impede progress in addressing poverty and food insecurity.[91]

The Nicaraguan Revolution of 1979 had initially made important attempts and had some successes in dealing with illiteracy and healthcare which so disproportionately affect the poor. The United States' backing for the Contra War had frustrated the forward motion of the Sandinista government in those areas while also devastating the economy. The subsequent governments, all neoliberal, had other priorities, particularly the encouragement of capitalism, private enterprise, and the making of profit. While the later Sandinista government, with the support of foreign aid, did create poverty programmes, they could not address the fundamental mechanism that created poverty, namely the capitalist system. The U.N. Food Program report suggested that it was 'natural disasters that impede progress', but history suggests that it has been the decisions of the leaders of the Chamorro administrations, and the Liberal governments of Alemán, Bolaños, and the Sandinistas that were largely responsible for the continuing poverty and hunger of the country.

---

91   United Nations World Food Program 2013.

Results and Prospects

In January 2014, the Nicaraguan National Assembly, dominated by the Sandinista Front for National Liberation, passed a reform of the Constitution permitting a sitting president to run for re-election. Thus Daniel Ortega, now in his third term as president (his second consecutive term), will be eligible to run for office in 2016 and indefinitely in elections thereafter. The FSLN claims that this only ratifies the Supreme Court decision that permitted Ortega to run for office in 2011, though the opposition argued convincingly that the earlier decision itself violated the Constitution. In any case, Ortega seems well positioned to be re-elected for another term or two, and then there is a good possibility that he may be succeeded by his wife or one of their children. It seems likely that we are at the beginning of the Ortega-Murillo dynasty.

The other 38 proposed constitutional reforms put forward at the same time in the Nicaraguan Assembly appear to be intended to create a corporate or corporativist regime, giving a constitutional status to community, labour, and business organisations, affiliating them directly to the government in a way that could diminish the power of the National Assembly.[1] These reforms would weaken the system of checks and balances and overturn many of the 1995 constitutional amendments that restrained presidential and governmental power.[2] As the Jesuit newsletter *Envío* wrote in December 2013: 'The constitutional reforms will institutionalize Ortega's total control'.[3]

In October 2013, shortly before the reforms were introduced, *Envío* explained why this was so:

> The 'model' Ortega is proposing to institutionalize at the constitutional level is the alliance between the government, the business elite, and union structures linked to the governing party as the only and exclusionary representation of the interests of the other national sectors. This corporative government model is what the Institutional Revolutionary Party organ-

---

1 The Fascist Mussolini created the first corporate regime in Italy in the 1920s, though since then the term has been used to describe both leftist and rightist governments such as those of Cárdenas in Mexico, Perón in Argentina, Vargas in Brazil, and others such as Suharto in Indonesia after the coup of 1965.

2 'Power Grab in Nicaragua: The Comandante's Comandments' 2013.

3 Eliseo Núñez Morales 2013.

ised and headed in Mexico for decades. It is an authoritarian plutocracy because the power is concentrated in the hands of those who unlawfully hold the national wealth and administer it in an authoritarian manner, either going over the heads of institutions and laws, or adjusting them to suit their own interests while the unions receive perks and privileges derived from the alliance ... In the Nicaraguan 'model', that alliance is made up of the traditional oligarchy grouped within COSEP, the FSLN's own business bloc, and the FSLN-linked Albanisa economic group.[4]

Increasing numbers of observers draw the parallel between the Somoza dictatorship and the Ortega regime, though few speak with as much authority as retired Brigadier General Hugo Torres, a veteran FSLN member and the organiser of the taking of Chema Castillo's house in 1974 and of the National Palace in 1978. He wrote in January 2010:

> It is chilling how many similarities exist between the current government of Daniel Ortega and that fabric the Somoza dictatorship managed to weave. Ortega has taken over the Sandinista National Liberation Front (FSLN), the party responsible for the revolution, perverting it and turning it into his own family-based party. He has now organised and trained shock troops, which made their public debut in the context of the November 2008 electoral fraud ... His public policies are also based on patronage and seek social control. He's been unable to control the Catholic Church hierarchy as a whole, but his blackmail efforts in that direction did attract Cardinal Obando, who [became] an accomplice of his misdeeds. He has also been maintaining the best of relations with big capital, under the same slogan as *somocismo*: 'You dedicate yourselves to business and leave politics to me'. Big capital has been perfectly happy to do that. And if that isn't enough, Ortega is feeding a scandalous messianic personality cult that's even more exaggerated than the one practiced by the Somozas.

> Ortega has done the same with the whole of the State that he did with the FSLN: privatizing it and turning it into an instrument of his particular interests. All state institutions – the judicial branch, the electoral branch, the Public Prosecutor's Office, the Office of Human Rights Ombudsperson – are politically subordinated to his will. Daniel Ortega has achieved greater subordination of the state institutions than the Somozas did,

---

4   Envío Team 2013.

because in Somoza's time there was a certain degree of independence in the judicial branch with judges who stood up to Somoza and acted in accordance with the law.[5]

Whether or not Ortega is another Somoza, his is now a fundamentally reactionary government.

Since being elected president in 2006, Daniel Ortega and his wife Rosario Murillo have constructed not simply a government, but an authoritarian regime that is the foundation of a dynasty – with Rafael Ortega as the likely heir. The ruling couple's power derives from several different sources: their political control of the state above all, but also their investment in and management of the Venezuelan Albanisa industries, and their personal wealth in the ownership of hotels and other businesses. Their hold on political power is based on a coterie of political loyalists, many of whom have also become business partners, and who form the dominant group within the country's political class. Many members of this coterie are both part of the political elite and of the country's capitalist class, a new ruling class created during the post-revolutionary period out of the fusion with those who formed the landlord and merchant class during the Somoza years and the new capitalists created by the *piñata* of 1979, which bestowed real estate, homes, and businesses on the Sandinistas, and by the opportunities opened up since 2006 by control of the Venezuelan Alba money. Ortega and Murillo sit at the centre of a web of political and economic power that gives them and their associates control over all of the major decisions made in the country. Nicaragua today has nothing in common with the Christian or socialist ideals it proclaims; it is simply an ordinary capitalist country of an authoritarian cast and Ortega, Murillo, the FSLN leaders, and their wealthy business associates together form the executive committee of the ruling class.

Ortega and Murillo rule largely through the FSLN, but, of course, this is not the FSLN of 1962, 1979, 1985, or even of the 1990s. The National Directorate no longer leads the FSLN, which is completely in the hands of Ortega and Murillo, while mid-level cadres function to hand down orders to the largely apolitical rank-and-file below. Once a revolutionary military organisation whose members were hardened cadres, during the 1980s and 1990s the FSLN transformed itself into a political party whose primary function was to win elections. By the 2000s, the membership had been increased to a million members in a nation of six million, most of them people with no particular political ideology or

---

5   Torres 2010.

experience, but a willingness to work as election workers in exchange for government favours. The most enduring characteristics of the FSLN were its veneer of Marxist-Leninist ideology, a remnant from the years when it was founded under the influence of the Soviet Union and Cuba, and the 'democratic centralism', which had never been democratic and has become ever more centralist. While 'democratic centralism' once functioned as the method by which the revolutionary leadership handed down military orders to its scattered handfuls of guerrillas, today it is the system by which Ortega and Murillo direct their army of dependent and therefore loyal followers.

Ortega and Murillo gained and have retained their power principally through a combination of political pacts, the effectiveness of the FSLN's electoral machine, and the domination of the media, though they have not been above using the state's judicial and police power to harass their political enemies on the left and the right. State repression has seldom been used against political enemies since the 1980s, though physical violence by the Sandinista Youth's paramilitary thugs – while the police stand idly by – has become increasingly common. Yet the Ortega government cannot be characterised as a totalitarian government or a police state; and while it is authoritarian, it has not used the prison system and the police against its opponents and critics. Amnesty International, Human Rights Watch, the Washington Office on Latin America, and the US State Department occasionally issue statements concerning human rights violations in Nicaragua – this happened particularly during 2008 – but not one of them would characterise Nicaragua as a police state or gross violator of human rights.

The Ortega regime's authoritarianism is a variant of political bossism of the sort often found in Mexico and common in the United States in the late nineteenth and early twentieth centuries. For all the admiration he once had for Fidel Castro, Daniel Ortega ended up looking a lot more like Chicago Mayor Richard J. Daley of the 1950s and 60s. The FSLN government maintains its control primarily through patronage and the establishment of clientelistic relationships between political bosses and citizens at all levels. The combination of fear and favours, the fear of losing and the hope of gaining access to some government programme, usually suffices to establish control over the majority of middle-class, working-class, and poor people. The FSLN is a political patronage machine. If the people are moved by Ortega's populist oratory and Murillo's mystical incantations, they are also motivated to support the Sandinista government because it offers them material goods in exchange for their votes.

Ortega and his wife have built a cult of personality around 'Daniel', whose portrait graces the giant billboards throughout Managua and other cities picturing him as a heroic leader, through rallies where thousands chant 'Daniel!

Daniel! Daniel!', and through the creation of a certain mystique surrounding his increasingly reclusive presence. His stature has been enhanced over the years through photographs showing him with Fidel Castro, Raúl Castro, Hugo Chávez, and Evo Morales. Ortega is a *caudillo*, or better, Ortega and Murrillo together are a bicephalic *caudillo*. María López Vigil, a Cuban-Nicaraguan theologian, writer, and editor of *Envío*, commented on Ortega and Murillo:

> The *caudillo* believes himself to be indispensable, the caudillo thinks that he is the only one who knows, who can, and consequently, he respects neither laws, nor institutions, nor persons. That is to say, 'I am the state', and only an absolutist says that. The *caudillo* and Rosario Murillo say the same thing, 'The Sandinista Front is Daniel Ortega', and she says, 'We are two'. What does that mean to say 'We are two'? It means they are the two who give the orders in this country. These are ideas very typical of the political concept of *caudillismo*, which is a political concept, and of messianic leadership, which is a religious concept ... [T]hey are convinced that they have a divine mission, to lead this country to justice, to be what in religious language is called the messiah. The word messiah is the equivalent of the political word *caudillo*.[6]

Their sense of 'divine mission' represents a combination of self-delusion and political propaganda that proves very effective in creating around the Ortegas an aura of exalted spiritual and social destiny. Ortega and Murillo are not mere politicians; they are God's chosen instruments, leading Nicaraguans to the Promised Land, an appealing idea in a religious and superstitious country where three-quarters of the population is poor and many are once again illiterate.

How had the Sandinista Front for National Liberation, a revolutionary organisation supposedly fighting for socialism, ended up as nothing more than a political machine in a typical liberal-democratic state working to preserve capitalism? How did a party, originally inspired by the idea of serving the majority and bringing social equality to the nation, become the political arm of the economic elite, of the minority, pursuing policies that increased social inequality? As the story told here has demonstrated, the roots of the Sandinistas' transformation into an authoritarian and corrupt capitalist political party are to be found in its origins. The FSLN's founders, educated and convinced of Stalinist and Castroite politics and the authoritarian doctrine of Marxism-Leninism,

---

6   Álvarez 2011.

with its revolutionary vanguard and caricature of democratic centralism, never had any conception of democracy in any meaningful sense, that is, the right of the members of a working-class party to discuss and debate issues, to choose their leaders, and to do so through genuinely democratic processes where the majority decides while minority rights are protected.

Neither did the FSLN ever have any conception of genuine political pluralism in a socialist society where working-class parties and other parties might offer up their programmes to people who would democratically decide and collectively implement their future. The Sandinistas' desire and goal from their founding in 1962 until 1990 – a goal they could not achieve – was to establish a state, an economy, and a society like that in Cuba. They saw themselves as becoming part of the Communist bloc, until Communism collapsed and the bloc disintegrated. Their model was the Communist one-party state where the economy is nationalised and the bureaucracy makes all of the political and economic decisions. While sometimes paying lip service to democratic ideals, the FSLN, like the Communists, but different from various other socialist traditions, had no conception of the relationship between representative democracy and participatory democracy, no conception of the role of independent labour unions, no commitment to workers' control.

Like the Cuban and Soviet Communists who provided their model, the Sandinistas were hostile to any group's independent self-organisation and to any sort of organisational and political autonomy. They opposed and sometimes used the military and the police to suppress the self-organisation of workers, women, the indigenous, the Afro-Caribbean population and anyone else. Hostile to capitalism, they were equally hostile to the self-organisation of workers and other oppressed and exploited groups, which is the only possible basis for building a socialist movement. When the FSLN's plans for creating a Communist state failed, given their hostility to independent working-class organisation and antipathy towards democracy, they could not conceive of turning to the working class and relying on its initiative and creativity in order to continue the struggle for social equality. Their would-be bureaucratic ruling class project defeated, and forced by their underlying principle to reject a democratic socialist project, Ortega and the FSLN leadership turned to an alliance with the capitalist class. The Sandinista leadership recognised that their incipient bureaucratic ruling class – even if fundamentally hostile to capitalism – had more in common with the capitalists than it did with the working class. Once allied with the capitalist class and forced to accept the overarching neoliberal project, their desire to enhance the lives of working people diminished to little more than a tepid and ineffective project of social welfare. While they had begun navigating toward Cuba, they ended up arriving in Mexico. That is, they failed to create a bureaucratic collectivist and totalitarian regime that they aimed for, and instead created an authoritarian capitalism with a veneer of social welfare.

Why No Left Opposition?

Why, one must ask, has no opposition movement been capable of challenging Ortega? The right opposition, the Liberal Party, as we saw, succumbed to corruption and to the pacts. The Conservative Party, without a clear and coherent ideology, with little organisation, and hardly any social base, had little chance. The left's problems were somewhat more complicated. Ortega claimed the mantel of the FSLN which had embodied the modern Nicaraguan left and which, because of its heroic role in leading the revolution, had a tremendous hold on the Nicaraguan people's imagination, a grip that proved impossible to break for two generations. Small Maoist and Trotskyist groups, some with a working-class following, often held ambiguous attitudes toward the FSLN, attitudes that made it difficult for them to be a genuinely independent opposition, while at the same time they proved incapable of growth because of the dominant position of the FSLN as well as the repression that they suffered.

When the Sandinista Renovation Movement (MRS) developed in 1994, led by Sergio Ramírez and Dora María Téllez, it represented an alternative left leadership. The MRS was a group with a broad spectrum of left opinion from social democrats to revolutionaries, but without a significant social base among the working class, the urban poor, and the peasantry. The MRS was an impressive general staff with few lieutenants and no army. In the end, it proved incapable of developing a clear ideological and political position, even aligning itself at times with parties on the right.

During the early years of the Ortega regime, it seemed for a brief historical moment that a constellation of forces existed – the MRS, the Movement for the Rescue of Sandinismo (MPRS), the independent feminist movement, and pockets of working-class resistance – which, had they been able to coalesce, might have begun to create a new left in Nicaragua. But the strength of the Ortega regime, its strong ideological and organisational hold over working-class and urban poor communities, as well as its use of harassment and low-level physical violence against its opponents in that period, blew away the flimsy opposition. While there continue to exist intellectual critics of the regime, at this point there are no organised political forces or social movements capable of challenging it. Ortega is thus able not only to remain in power, but also to continue to lay claim to the FSLN's revolutionary legacy. Social struggle, however, may be on the horizon.

What Alternative was There?

One may well ask: What alternative was there to the Sandinista organisational model based on their Stalinist Communist origins, the Castro-Guevara
example of guerrilla warfare, and their own military hierarchy? Some may
argue that only such a centralised, disciplined, and authoritarian organisation
could have undertaken the struggle against the brutal Somoza dictatorship.
Yet, as we have seen, that model, which failed to build a dynamic interrelation
between the revolutionary organisation and the working class and people at
large, led to problems which ultimately distorted any struggle for a democratic
socialist society. Among the problems: the Sandinistas' initial failure to build
a broader party than the small Communist-trained nucleus with which they
began; their failure (with a couple of important exceptions) to build an underground industrial labour union and peasant union movement; their failure to
listen to the peasantry and to turn land over to the peasants themselves, a key
failing which led to the growth of the Contras; their initial failure to work out
an autonomy agreement with the indigenous people, which also contributed
to the growth of the Contras; and, finally, the failure even after the victory of
the revolution to call a convention and create a democratic organisation, the
result of which was the concentration of power in a handful of leaders accompanied by personal self-aggrandisement and self-enrichment. If these failings
had their roots in the Sandinistas' early Stalinist indoctrination, they were all
exacerbated by the Castro-Guevara notion of the *foco*, the small band of dedicated revolutionaries who could spark a revolution and seize power. The Cuban
model was the greatest problem.

What then were the alternatives? To begin with, the Sandinistas might have
continued with their early attempts to unify the small bands of radicals in
the early 1960s, a process which would have led to a larger and less homogen-
eous organisation, one where democratic debate would have been necessary.
Secondly, instead of recruiting the most dedicated working-class and peasant
activists to join the guerrillas in the mountains (where many died in vain), the
Sandinistas might have worked with those activists to build an underground
labour and peasant movement. Had they built a clandestine labour movement
among workers and peasants, they might have avoided their later conflicts with
the peasants who demanded title to the lands for which they had fought. They
might have joined with other left groups in a united front against the Somoza
dictatorship. If they had such models of democratic functioning, they might
also have approached the indigenous groups on the Atlantic coast more openly
and flexibly in an attempt to work with them, rather than trying to impose
a political system on them through military occupation. Finally, if upon seiz-

ing power the Sandinistas had called a convention to create a democratically organised political party, they might have had a healthier relationship to the mass movements of the country, rather than running them as party front groups. That would have been especially true had they permitted genuine discussion, debate, and competition among all of the left parties and other parties that accepted the revolution, avoiding the FSLN's fusion with the state. All of this would have reduced the attractiveness of the Contras and might possibly have avoided the civil war, even if it could not have stopped the United States from its depredations.

While in this book we have not dealt with the geopolitical situation at any length, one can speculate that a democratic revolutionary organisation in Nicaragua might have had a salutary effect on other revolutionary groups in Central America. And a democratic socialist organisation in Nicaragua might even have had some impact on the Cubans with whom they interacted, even if it is unlikely to have had any impact on Castro's bureaucratic Communist one-party-state. The existence of a democratic socialist alternative in Nicaragua – such as many radicals believed existed there in the first few years after the revolution – in the long-run would have had a beneficial effect on the left in Latin America and around the world. As an alternative to the Commun-ist and Guevarist models, there would have been a revolutionary, democratic socialist, and internationalist alternative. All of this is based on the conviction that democracy is central to the construction of any socialist society, and that socialism is the only basis for genuinely democratic society. Such a revolution-ary, democratic, socialist revolution might also have failed, but it would have done so while fighting for humanistic ideals, not by succumbing to power and avarice.

Forward into the Past: The Canal

In what seems almost like a re-enactment of an earlier government's deal with Cornelius Vanderbilt in the 1850s, Daniel Ortega decided in 2013 that Nicaragua's future lay in the development of a trans-oceanic canal to be built by the world's rising economic power: China. Wang Jing, a Chinese businessman who made his fortune in telecommunications, proposed to build a 180-mile, cross-country canal from Bluefield on the Caribbean, passing through Lake Nicaragua, to Brito on the Pacific – a waterway with twice the draught of the Panama Canal and three times as long – at a cost of $40 billion. Wang and his Honk Kong-based HKND Group promised to raise all the money in exchange for a 50-year concession, renewable up to 100 years; in return, Nicaragua would receive $10 million per year and 10 percent ownership each year, so that in 100 years it will become the sole owner of the canal.[7]

When Ortega first proposed to build the canal, critics pointed out that the Panama Canal was undergoing improvements that would make it capable of accommodating what are called supermax cargo ships and so it was unlikely that a new, competing canal would prove profitable. Other critics, horrified at the thought of the damage that would be caused by both the construction as well as the pollution that would result from the passage of ocean-going ships through Lake Nicaragua, predicted that the canal would be an environmental disaster. There were also objections that much of the construction work would be done by Chinese, not Nicaraguans. Yet others pointed out that in granting Wang complete control over vast tracts of land, while at the same time allowing his company to operate tax free, Nicaragua would be losing its national sovereignty to a foreign country. The contract states that the canal will not revert to Nicaragua for 100 years. Finally, critics found it hard to believe that in the long-run the United States would permit China to gain control over a canal in the Western Hemisphere.

Ortega, nevertheless, pushed the legislation through the National Assembly with little public discussion and debate. As was to be expected, in July 2013 the Assembly, dominated by the FSLN, passed the inter-oceanic canal law granting the concession to Wang's company. Immediately, Wang's subcontractors went to work. British Environmental Resources Management was hired to conduct an environmental impact study. The China Railway Construction Company had been brought in to determine how to meet international technical standards. Australian engineers were employed to figure out how to move and where to put millions of tons of earth. And McKinsey & Company, the American business consulting firm that has played such a historic role in the construction of global capitalism, has been brought in to advise HKND. Thousands are now at work in China, in offices around the world, and in Nicaragua laying the groundwork for the canal.

The Nicaraguan opponents of the canal brought 30 different appeals before the Nicaraguan Supreme Court, arguing that the construction of the canal would violate the country's constitution. But the court, also controlled by the FSLN, rejected all of them at the end of 2013.[8] Environmental organisations in Nicaragua issued statements warning that the canal would have a devastating effect upon the country's ecosystems. There were protests in Managua over

---

7   Cave 2013; Moore 2013; 'A man, a plan – and little else' 2013.
8   'Nicaragua's top court rejects challenges to canal' 2013.

environmental, sovereignty, and employment issues related to the canal. As construction work on the canal began in December 2014, peasants concerned about their land and water in the towns of El Tule in the province of Río San Juan in the south of the country and in Tola in Rivas province on the Pacific Coast, protested and set up roadblocks. By early 2015, demonstrations against the canal by the indigenous, peasants, environmentalists and others had grown to involve tens of thousands, and the protesters continued to face harassment and repression by the government. The Ortega government came down on the protests with a heavy hand, with newspapers reporting that as many as 50 had been injured and more than 80 arrested.[9] Ortega's government with its plans for the trans-oceanic canal appeared to have put class struggle back on the agenda in Nicaragua, only now it was the peasants and workers against his capitalist government.

In March of 2016 there were credible reports that an anti-government guerrilla organization, a new contra group sometimes referred to as the *rearmados* (the rearmed) was operating in the mountains. Catholic Bishop Abelardo Mata suggested that with no foreign backing these guerrillas were financed by drug dealers. Half a century later, Nicaragua's authoritarian government faces a guerrilla *foco* in the *sierra*.[10]

Postscript

In late July 2016 President Daniel Ortega, running for his third consecutive term as president – his fourth term altogether – succeeded in having sixteen members of the opposition expelled from the Congress.[11] Also removed were their 12 alternates, 28 legislators altogether.[12] Those who were removed belonged to both the conservative Independent Liberal Party (PLI) led by banker Eduardo Montealegre and to the Movement for Sandinista Renovation (MRS), originally a leftist breakaway from Ortega's own FSLN. The legislators' removal ended any semblance of political pluralism and gave Ortega absolute control over the parliament, making Nicaragua effectively a one-party state on the eve of the election.

---

9   Salinas 2014; EFE and AP 2014; Staff 2014; EFE 2014.

10   Frances Robles, 'Ortega vs. the Contras: Nicaragua Endures an '80s Revival', *New York Times*, March 7, 2016.

11   Associated Press, 2016.

12   'Nicaragua: Tibunal Electoral Destituye at 28 legisladores', *El Periódico*, http://elperiodico .com.gt/2016/07/30/internacional/nicaragua-tribunal-electoral-destituye-a-28-diputados -opositores/.

Then at the beginning of August, Ortega announced that his running mate for vice-president would be his wife Rosario Murrillo, now the Minister of Communications and in practice already the country's co-president. The Nicaraguan Constitution once forbid anyone from holding the office of president for two consecutive terms or from holding more than two non-consecutive terms as president, as well as forbidding a spouse from being a candidate.[13] Ortega's control of the Supreme Court, the Congress, and the Supreme Electoral Council made it possible for him to create a new constitution in 2014 that allowed him to run for president for a third term. To make sure that there is no questioning of the election procedure, Ortega has forbidden any international election observers. Ortega and his wife, who have placed their children in positions in government, appear to have insured that, like the Somozas before them, they will establish a dynastic dictatorship.

These developments – Ortega's suppression of the political opposition and the choice of his wife to be his vice-presidential candidate – confirm the analysis of the FSLN put forth in this book. Ortega, like other Sandinistas an admirer of the Soviet Union, the Eastern Bloc, and especially of the Cuban government, always desired a one-party state. If at one time he hoped to create a bureaucratic Communist (bureaucratic collectivist) regime, Ortega, Murrillo, and their associates are now happy to rule over a state-capitalist partnership. Ortega's dictatorship has become a virtual monarchy.

Nicaragua's National Coalition for Democracy called the coming elections carried out under these conditions 'a farce', while the Bishops of the Catholic Church condemned Ortega's attempt to impose a one-party regime. Faced with the closing off of democratic options, important figures on both the right and the left have suggested that a revolt may be the only alternative. On the right, Carlos Fernando Chamorro, the last son of former president Violeta Chamorro, told the Nicaraguans that the situation had 'legitimized the right to rebel'. Vilma Núñez, a longtime FSLN activist who had challenged Ortega for the FSLN presidential nomination in 1996 and who today heads the Nicaraguan Human Rights Center (CENIDH), went even further, calling upon the Nicaraguan people to exercise their 'right to rebellion'.[14] Creating a new dictatorship, Ortega may also be creating the conditions for a future revolution.

Lamentably, much of the Latin American and U.S. left continues to support Ortega and the Sandinista government, largely because of its alliance with the Cuban Communist regime and Venezuelan Bolivarian government. The Foro

---

13   Nicaraguan Constitution of 1987, 2005, see Article 147, pp. 37–8.
14   Envío Team 2016.

de São Paulo, the conference of Latin America's left parties, continues to treat Nicaragua as if it were a genuine left party, despite its rightward movement since the 1990s. Some on the left in the United States brush off any criticism of Ortega and the FSLN, with the suggestion that such criticism aids the Nicaraguan rightwing and the U.S. State Department.[15] While it is undeniable that U.S. imperialism, the U.S. support for the Somoza regime, the U.S.-backed Contra War, and U.S. backing of conservative candidates have all played a reactionary and destructive role in Nicaragua, at the same time the fact is that the Sandinistas' undemocratic theory and practice also contributed to bringing the country to its current situation: the rule of a conservative, dictatorial, capitalist government.

Failure to frankly criticise the Ortega government and to show solidarity with its opponents in the social movements and the left political opposition – such as the environmentalists and peasants fighting the transoceanic canal – contributes to maintaining the Ortega dictatorship in power. Those of us who fight for the labour movement, for social justice, for democracy, and for socialism must speak truth to power in all societies, no matter what their ideology.

We know from world history, and from the history of Nicaragua itself, that a new opposition to the existing system – an opposition from below – will inevitably develop, and perhaps, drawing on the previous history of their own country, will create a new revolutionary movement that places at the centre of its political ideals the understanding that socialism is only possible with democracy, and democracy is only possible with socialism. If it does, perhaps it can fulfil the dreams of those who in the 1960s and 1970s fought to overthrow Somoza and create a better society and who in the 1980s found themselves frustrated in the process not only by their external enemies, but also by the ambitions of their own leaders and the authoritarian party they had built. Today, around the world new forces are developing and their slogan everywhere has been 'Another World is Possible'. We might also say: 'Another Nicaragua is Possible' – socialist and democratic – and a new movement will arise one day to fight for it.

Economic development with social justice, that is, with social equality, can only come through a mass democratic, socialist, and revolutionary movement in Nicaragua and throughout Central America. A working-class movement fighting for democratic control of the state and society, that is, for democratic socialism, remains the alternative to global capitalism. The sardines of the world must turn on the sharks.

---

15   Kaufman 2016.

Bibliography

'A man, a plan – and little else' 2013, *The Economist*, 5 October, available at: http://www
.economist.com/news/americas/21587218-yet-again-nicaraguans-are-letting-their-
longing-trans-oceanic-canal-get-better.

Acevedo, Adolfo 2008, 'Sixteen Years Lost in Five Agreements with the IMF', *Envío*, 321
(April), available at: http://www.envio.org.ni/articulo/3748.

Agricorp home page 2014, available at: http://agricorp.com.ni/.

'Albanisa pagó y Telcor amarró la compra del Canal 8' n.d., *La Prensa*.

Alexander, Robert J. 1991, *International Trotskyism, 1929–1985*, Durham, NC: Duke University Press.

Álvarez, Leonor 2011, 'Ortega y Murillo "están convencidos de su deidad"', *El Nuevo
Diario*, 24 June, available at: http://www.elnuevodiario.com.ni/politica/108647.

AP 2013, 'Nicaragua's top court rejects challenges to canal', *Huffington Post*, 18 December, available at: http://www.huffingtonpost.com/huff-wires/20131218/lt-nicaragua
-canal/.

Arévalo, Juan José 1961, *The Shark and the Sardines*, translated by June Cobb and Raúl
Osegueda, New York: Lyle Stuart.

Associated Press 1987, 'Taiwan Says It Did Provide Aid to Contras', *Los Angeles Times*,
16 May.

———— 2016, 'Nicaragua Electoral Authority Unseats Opposition Lawmakers', *New York
Times* 29 July 2016, http://www.nytimes.com/aponline/2016/07/29/world/
americas/ap-lt-nicaragua-ommoisition.html.

Azul, Rafael and Patrick Martin 2006, 'Nicaraguan election: Ortega's victory and the
dead-end of Sandinismo', *World Socialist Web Site*, 30 November, available at: http://
www.wsws.org/en/articles/2006/11/nica-n30.html.

Babb, Florence 2011, *After Revolution: Mapping Gender and Cultural Politics in Neoliberal
Nicaragua*, Austin, TX: University of Texas Press.

———— 2012 [2011], *Después de la revolución: género y cultura política en Nicaragua
neoliberal*, Managua: UCA-INCHA.

Baltodano, Mónica 2010, *Memorias de la lucha Sandinista*, Vols. 1–3, Managua: IHNCA.

Baracco, Luciano 2005, *Nicaragua: The Imagining of a Nation: From Nineteenth Century
Liberals to Twentieth-Century Sandinistas*, New York: Algora Publishing.

Barcelona Centre for International Affairs 2011a, 'Daniel Ortega Saavedra', at: http://
www.cidob.org/es/documentacio/biografias_lideres_politicos/america_central_y_
caribe/nicaragua/daniel_ortega_saavedra.

———— 2011b, 'Enrique Bolaños Geyer', at: http://www.cidob.org/en/documentacio/
biografias_lideres_politicos/america_central_y_caribe/nicaragua/enrique_bolanos
_geyer.

———— 2011c, 'Jose Arnoldo Alemán Lacayo', available at: http://www.cidob.org/es/ documentacio/biografias_lideres_politicos/america_central_y_caribe/nicaragua/ arnoldo_aleman_lacayo.

Beals, Carleton 1932, *Banana Gold*, Philadelphia: J.B. Lippincott Company.

Belausteguigoitia, Román 1981 [1933], *Con Sandino en Nicaragua: La hora de paz*, Managua: Editorial Nueva Nicaragua.

Bell, Susan Groag and Karen M. Offen (eds.) 1983, *Women, the Family, and Freedom: The Debate in Documents, Volume One, 1750–1880*, translated by Karen M. Offen, Palo Alto, CA: Stanford University Press.

Belli, Giaconda 2002, *The Country Under My Skin: A Memoir of Love and War*, New York: Alfred A. Knopf.

Bensaïd, Daniel 2004, *Une lente impatience*, Paris: Editions Stock.

Better Work Nicaragua 2013, 'Better Work Nicaragua: Garment Industry 1st Compliance Synthesis Report, August 22, 2013', available at: http://betterwork.org/global/wp -content/uploads/Better-Work-Nicaragua-First-Compliance-Synthesis-Report.pdf.

Bickham Méndez, Jennifer 2005, *From the Revolution to the Maquiladoras: Gender, Labor and Globalization in Nicaragua*, Durham, NC: Duke University Press.

Biderman, Jaime 1983, 'The Development of Capitalism in Nicaragua: A Political Economic History', *Latin American Perspectives*, 10, 1(Winter): 7–32.

Black, George 1981, *The Triumph of the People: The Sandinista Revolution in Nicaragua*, London: Zed.

Bolaños Geyer, Alejandro 1976, *El filibuster: Clinton Rollins*, Masaya: n.p.

Bolshevik Tendency 1977, 'Declaration of the Bolshevik Tendency', January, available at: http://www.marxists.org/history/etol/document/fi/1963-1985/usfi/bolshevik/ bolshevik01.htm.

Borge, Tomás 1992 [1989], *The Patient Impatience: From Boyhood to Guerilla: A Personal Narrative of Nicargua's Struggle for Liberation*, Willimantic, CT: Curbstone Press.

Brenes, María Haydeé n.d., 'Las 10 incógnitas sobre Ortega', *La Prensa*.

Brooks, Ray et al. 1998, *External Debt Histories of Ten Low-Income Developing Countries: Lessons from Their Experience*, International Monetary Fund, May, available at: http://www.imf.org/external/pubs/ft/wp/wp9872.pdf.

Brown, Charles H. 1980, *Agents of Manifest Destiny: The Lives and Times of the Filibusters*, Chapel Hill, NC: University of North Carolina Press.

Burbach, Roger 2009, 'Et tu Daniel? The Betrayal of the Sandinista Revolution', *Counter-Punch*, 1–3 March, avialable at: http://www.counterpunch.org/2009/03/01/the-betrayal-of-the-sandinista-revolution/

Cabezas, Omar 2007 [1982], *La Montaña es algo más que una inmensa estepa verde*, Managua: Anamá Ediciones.

Calero Portocarrero, Adolfo 2010, *Crónicas de un contra*, Managua: La Prensa.

Canin, Eric 1997, '"Work, a Roof, and Bread for the Poor": Managua's Christian Base Communities in the Nicaraguan "Revolution from Below"', *Latin American Perspectives*, Issue 93, Vol. 24, 2(March): 88–100.

Cardenal, Ernest 2001 [1998], *Vida perdida* (Memorias Tomo I), Tercera Edición. Managua: Ediciones Anamá.

Cardenal, Fernando S.J. 2008, *Sacerdote en la revolución*, 2 Vols., Managua: Anamá Ediciones.

'Carlos Pellas, el más rico entre los ricos de Nicaragua, dice que empresarios acordaron "buena comunicación" con Ortega' 2006, Radio Primerísima, 10 November, available at: http://www.radiolaprimerisima.com/noticias/6097/carlos-pellas-el-mas-rico-entre-los-ricos-de-nicaragua-dice-que-empresarios-acordaron-buena-comunicacion-con-ortega.

Castán, José María 2011, 'Concerns about the New Course of International Cooperation', *Envío*, 354(January), available at: http://www.envio.org.ni/articulo/4298.

Castañeda, Jorge G. 1993, *Utopia Unarmed: The Latin American Left After the Cold War*, New York: Alfred A. Knopf.

Cave, Damien 2013, 'Nicaragua Approves Building Its Own Canal', *The New York Times*, 13 June, available at: http://www.nytimes.com/2013/06/14/world/americas/nicaragua-approves-building-its-own-canal.html?_r=0.

Cerda, Arlen 2008, 'Obispos piden recuento de votos', *La Prensa*, 13 November, available at: http://archivo.laprensa.com.ni/archivo/2008/noviembre/13/elecciones/noticias/294613.shtml.

Chaffin, Tom 1996, *Fatal Glory: Narciso López and the First Clandestine US War against Cuba*, Charlottesville, VA: University of Virginia Press.

Chamorro Cardenal, Pedro Joaquín 2001 [1957], *Estirpe sangrienta: los Somoza*, (Quinta edición por La Prensa), Managua: Fundación Violeta B. de Chamorro.

Christian, Shirley 1986 [1985], *Nicaragua: Revolution in the Family*, New York: Vintage Books.

Clayton-Bulwer Treaty 1850, available at: http://www.cubahistory.org/en/british-occupation-and-us-independence/us-independence.html.

Close, David 1998, *Politics, Economics and Society*, New York: Pinter Publishers.

——— 2005 [1999], *Los años de Doña Violeta*, Managua: Lea Grupo Editorial.

Close, David and Kalowatie Deonandan 2004, *Undoing Democracy: The Politics of Electoral Caudillismo*, Boulder, CO: Lexington Books.

'A Country Study: Nicaragua' n.d., Country Studies, Library of Congress, available at: http://lcweb2.loc.gov/frd/cs/nitoc.html.

Cuadra Lira, Elvira and Juana Jiménez Martinez 2009, 'The Women's Movement and the Struggle for their Rights in Nicaragua', (November), Managua.

Cuba History n.d., available at: http://www.cubahistory.org/en/british-occupation-and-us-independence/us-independence.html.

Debray, Regis 1967, *Revolution in the Revolution? Armed Struggle and Political Struggle in Latin America*, New York: Monthly Review.

———— 1974, *La critique des armes*, Paris: Éditions du Seuil.

Debusmann, Bernd 2005, 'Reportaje de la agencia Reuters sobre Rosario Murillo', 8 January, Radio Primerísima, available at: http://www.radiolaprimerisima.com/noticias/9064/reportaje-de-la-agencia-reuters-sobre-rosario-murillo.

Decree Number 59 1979, *La Gaceta*, 13, 13 September.

Diederich, Bernard 2007 [1981], *Somoza and the Legacy of US Involvement in Central America*, Princeton, NJ: Markus Wiener Publishers.

Dore, Elizabeth 2003, 'Debt Peonage in Granada, Nicaragua, 1870–1930: Labor in a Non-Capitalist Transition', *Hispanic American Historical Review*, 83, 3(August): 521–59.

Doyle, Kate and Peter Kornbluh n.d., 'CIA and Assassinations: The Guatemala 1954 Documents', The National Security Archives, The George Washington University, available at: http://www2.gwu.edu/~nsarchiv/NSAEBB/NSAEBB4/.

Draper, Hal 1966, 'The Two Souls of Socialism', *New Politics*, 5, 1(Winter): 57–84.

———— 1977, *Karl Marx's Theory of Revolution: State and Bureaucracy*, New York: Monthly Review Press.

Dunbar-Ortiz, Roxanne 2005, *Blood on the Border: A Memoir of the Contra War*, Cambridge, MA: South End Press.

EFE 2014, 'Exigen la libertad de campesinos presos por protestar contra el canal de Nicaragua', *La Prensa*, 27 December, available at: http://www.laprensa.hn/mundo/780032-410/exigen-la-libertad-de-campesinos-presos-por-protestar-contra-el-canal-de.

EFE and AP 2014, 'Unos 87 detenidos en las protestas contra el canal de Nicaragua', *Semana*, 25 December, available at: http://www.semana.com/mundo/articulo/unos-87-detenidos-en-las-protestas-contra-el-canal-de-nicaragua/413318-3.

Ellsberg, M.C. et al. 1999, 'Wife abuse among women of childbearing age in Nicaragua', *American Journal of Public Health*, 89, 2(February): 241–4.

Enríquez, Eduardo 2012, *Muerte de una República*, Managua: Editorial La Prensa.

Enríquez, Laura n.d., 'The Varying Impact of Structural Adjustment on Nicaragua's Small Farmers', available at: http://publicsociology.berkeley.edu/publications/producing/enriquez.pdf.

Enríquez, Octavio 2011, 'Fundador del FSLN millonario', *La Prensa*, available at: http://www.laprensa.com.ni/especial/la-revolucion-del-exministro-del/45.

Envío Team 1981a, 'The Case Regarding COSEP and caus members' *Envío*, 6(November), available at: http://www.envio.org.ni/articulo/23.

———— 1981b, 'Political Parties in Nicaragua Today in Relation to Proposed Legislation', *Envío*, 7(December), available at: http://www.envio.org.ni/articulo/3131.

———— 1982a, 'Nicaragua: Three Years of Achievements', 13(July), available at: http://www.envio.org.ni/articulo/3368.

———— 1982b, 'Sandinista Defense Committees (CDSS): Impressions After Four Years of Existence', *Envío*, 16(October), available at: http://www.envio.org.ni/articulo/3378.

———— 1983a, 'Other Events and Conclusions', 21(March), available at: http://www.envio.org.ni/articulo/3475.

———— 1983b, 'The Health Situation in Revolutionary Nicaragua', 23(May), available at: http://www.envio.org.ni/articulo/3481.

———— 1984, 'Nicaragua's Labor Unions in the Face of Aggression', *Envío*, 35(May), available at: http://www.envio.org.ni/articulo/3915.

———— 1988a, 'Revolutionizing Health – A Study in Complexity', 80(February), available at: http://www.envio.org.ni/articulo/3166.

———— 1988b, 'Economic Reform: Taking it to the Streets', *Envío*, 82(April), available at: http://www.envio.org.ni/portada.en/82.

———— 1989, 'CDS: Revolution in the Barrio', *Envío*, 98(September), available at: http://www.envio.org.ni/articulo/2738.

———— 1990, 'FSLN Discussion Papers', *Envío*, 105(July), available at: http://www.envio.org.ni/articulo/2632.

———— 1991a, 'Cuatro discursos escuchados en el Primer Congreso del FSLN', *Envío*, 118(August), available at: http://www.envio.org.ni/articulo/680.

———— 1991b, 'The Labor Code: Workers' Rights vs. Economic Recovery?' *Envío*, 134(September), available at: http://www.envio.org.ni/articulo/2546.

———— 1992, 'The Social Tidal Wave', 136(November), available at: http://www.envio.org.ni/articulo/2553.

———— 2001, 'The Road to the Elections Was Paved with Fraud', *Envío*, 244(November), http://www.envio.org.ni/articulo/1548.

———— 2011a, 'Mysteries, times, fears, and challenges', *Envío*, 360(July), available at: http://www.envio.org.ni/articulo/4372.

———— 2013, 'The Corporative Government's "Miracle"', *Envío*, 387(October), available at: http://www.envio.org.ni/articulo/4760.

———— 2016, 'No Bridge Over These Troubled Waters', *Envío*, 412(July), http://www.envio.org.ni/articulo/5204.

EU Election Observation Mission 2011, 'Nicaragua: Final Report on the General Elections and Parlacen Elections', available at: http://www.eueom.eu/files/dmfile/moeue-nicaragua-final-report-22022012_en.pdf.

Farber, Samuel 1976, *Revolution and Reaction in Cuba, 1933–1960: A Political Sociology from Machado to Castro*, Middletown, CT: Wesleyan University Press.

———— 2006, *Origins of the Cuban Revolution Reconsidered*, Chapel Hill, NC: University of North Carolina Press.

———— 2011, *Cuba Since the Revolution of 1959: A Critical Assessment*, Chicago, IL: Haymarket Books.

Feijto, François 1971, *A History of the People's Democracies*, London: Pall Mall Press.

Feinberg, Richard 2011, 'Daniel Ortega and Nicaragua's Soft Authoritarianism', *Foreign Policy*, 2 November, available at: http://www.foreignaffairs.com/features/letters -from/daniel-ortega-and-nicaraguas-soft-authoritarianism.

Fonseca, Carlos 1985 [1981], *Obras*, Managua: Nueva Editorial Nicaragua.

Fonseca L., Roberto 2001, 'Ingenio "Victoria de Julio" se desploma y agoniza', *La Prensa*, 3 October, available at: http://archivo.laprensa.com.ni/archivo/2001/octubre/03/ nacionales/nacionales-20011003-15.html.

Fonseca Terán, Carlos 2005, *El poder, la propiedad, nosotros: La Revolución Sandinista y el problema del poder en la transformación revolucionaria de la sociedad nicaragüense*, Managua: Editorial Hispamer.

Fontaine, André 1968–9, *History of the Cold War*, 2 Vols., New York, Pantheon Books.

Frente Sandinista de Liberación Nacional 1969, 'Programa Histórico', available at: http:// www.cedema.org/ver.php?id=3399.

FSLN 1999, 'Programa Histórico del FSLN', Cedema, available at: http://www.cedema .org/ver.php?id=3399.

Funes, José Antonio 2010, 'Froylán Turcios y la campaña a favor de Sandino en la revista Ariel (1925–1928)', *Cuadernos Americanos*, 181–208, available at: http://www .cialc.unam.mx/cuadamer/textos/ca133-181.pdf.

Garvin, Penn 2008, 'Information on the case against the Network of Women against Violence', *CAWN: Promoting Women's Rights and Gender Equality*, available at: http:// www.cawn.org/news/genderviolence.htm.

Gellman, Mneesha and Josh Danoff 2008, 'Rising Fuel Costs Provoke Transportation Strike in Nicaragua', 12 May, available at: http://upsidedownworld.org/main/ nicaragua-archives-62/1279-rising-fuel-costs-provoke-transportation-strike-in-nicaragua.

Gerson, Noel B. 1976, *Sad Swashbuckler: The Life of William Walker*, Nashville, TN: Thomas Nelson Inc.

Gilly, Adolfo 2005 [1971], *The Mexican Revolution*, New York: The New Press.

González Briones, Heydi José et al. 2012, *Perfil migratorio de Nicaragua 2012*, International Organization for Migration, available at: http://migracionesnicaragua.files .wordpress.com/2011/05/perfil_migratorio_de_nicaragua.pdf.

González, Javier 2013, 'A Mayoral Hopeful Now, de Blasio Was Once a Young Leftist', *The New York Times*, 22 September, available at: http://www.nytimes.com/2013/09/ 23/nyregion/a-mayoral-hopeful-now-de-blasio-was-once-a-young-leftist.html.

González, Mike 1985, *Nicaragua: Revolution under Siege*, London: Bookmarks.

———— 1990, *Nicaragua: What Went Wrong?*, London: Bookmarks.

Gooren, Henri 2010, 'Ortega for President: The Religious Rebirth of Sandinismo in Nicaragua', *European Review of Latin American and Caribbean Studies*, 89(October): 47–63.

Gould, Jeffry, L. 1973, '"¡Vaya Illusion!" The Highlands Indians and the Myth of Nicaragua Meztiza, 1880–1925', *Hispanic American Historical Review*, 73, 3: 400–1.

Greene, Lawrence 1937, *The Filibuster: The Career of William Walker*, New York: The Bobbs-Merrill Company.

Grigsby, Arturo 2009, 'Blow by Blow, Step by Step, the Global Crisis is Hitting us Hard', *Envío*, 332(March), available at: http://www.envio.org.ni/articulo/3951.

Guardian Staff 2014, 'Protests erupt in Nicaragua over interoceanic canal', *Guardian*, 24 December, available at: http://www.theguardian.com/world/2014/dec/24/nicaragua-protests-interoceanic-canal-rivas.

Guevara, Ernesto 'Che' 2003 [1965], 'Socialism and Man in Cuba', in *The Che Reader*, New York: Ocean Press, available at: http://www.marxists.org/archive/guevara/1965/03/man-socialism.htm.

Guevara Jerez, Francisco A. 2007, 'Who's Who in the New Cabinet', *Envío*, 307(February), available at: http://www.envio.org.ni/articulo/3460.

Guevara López, Onofre n.d., *Cien años de movimiento social en Nicaragua: Relato cronológico*, Managua: IHNCA-UCA.

Gwertzman, Bernard 1983, 'Steps to the Invasion: No More "Paper Tiger"', *New York Times*, 30 October, available at: http://www.nytimes.com/1983/10/30/world/steps-to-the-invasion-no-more-paper-tiger.html?pagewanted=1.

Hale, Charles R. 1994, *Resistance and Contradiction: Miskitu Indians and the Nicaraguan State, 1894–1987*, Stanford, CA: Stanford University Press.

Harris, Nigel 1978, *The Mandate of Heaven: Marx and Mao in Modern China*, New York: Quartet Books.

Hassan Morales, Moïses 2009, *La maldición del Güegüense*, Managua: Pavsa.

Hodges, Donald C. 1986, *Intellectual Foundations of the Nicaraguan Revolution*, Austin, TX: University of Texas Press.

Horton, Lynn 1998, *Peasants in Arms: War and Peace in the Mountains of Nicaragua, 1979–1994*, Athens: Ohio University Center for International Studies.

'Insulza expresa preocupación por recuento de votos' 2008, *La Prensa*, 13 November, available at: http://archivo.laprensa.com.ni/archivo/2008/noviembre/13/elecciones/noticias/294504.shtml.

International Labor Rights Forum 2004, 'Study of labor laws and obstacles to compliance in Nicaragua', 1 March, available at: http://www.laborrights.org/creating-a-sweatfree-world/changing-global-trade-rules/resources/10764.

International Monetary Fund 1997, 'International Monetary Fund Nicaragua: Enhanced Structural Adjustment Facility Policy Framework Paper', 1994–7.

———— 2001, 'Nicaragua: Enhanced Structural Adjustment Facility, Economic Policy Framework Paper for 1999–2001', available at: http://www.imf.org/external/np/pfp/1999/nicarag/.

———— 2006, 'Statement by Anoop Singh,' available at: http://www.imf.org/external/np/sec/pr/2006/pro6292.htm.

———— 2007, 'Letter of Intent and Memorandum of Understanding', 24 August, available at: http://www.imf.org/external/np/loi/2007/nic/082407.pdf.

———— 2014, 'Nicaragua and the IMF', available at: http://www.imf.org/external/country/nic/index.htm?pn=0.

'Intervention and Exploitation: US and UK Government International Actions Since 1945' n.d., available at: http://www.us-uk-interventions.org/Nicaragua.html.

Japan International Cooperation Agency 2012, 'Monthly Report: Macroeconomic Indicators of Nicaragua', July, available at: http://www.jica.go.jp/nicaragua/english/office/others/c8hovmoo0068sumh-att/report_201207.pdf.

Kaufman, Chuck 2016, 'Political Turmoil on the Right Gives a Pretext for the US to Question Upcoming Election', *Nicanotes, Alliance for Global Justice*, email to subscribers, August 3, 2016.

Kinzer, Stephen 2007 [1991], *Blood of Brothers: Life and War in Nicaragua*, Cambridge, MA: Harvard University Press.

Knight, Alan 1986, *The Mexican Revolution*, 2 vols., Lincoln, NE: University of Nebraska Press.

Knox, Philander C. 1909, 'Knox Note', available at: http://archive.org/stream/jstor-2212542/2212542_djvu.txt.

———— 1910, 'Secretary Knox's Note to the Nicaraguan Charge D' Affaires, 1 December 1909', *The American Journal of International Law*, 4, 3, Supplement: Official Documents (July 1910).

Kornblush, Peter n.d., 'Top Secret CIA "Official History" of the Bay of Pigs: Revelations', The National Security Archives, The George Washington University, available at: http://www2.gwu.edu/~nsarchiv/NSAEBB/NSAEBB355/index.htm.

Kurin, K.N. 2010, 'Nicaraguan Socialist Party', in *The Great Soviet Encyclopedia*, 3rd Edition (1970–1979), The Gale Group, Inc.

La Botz, Dan 1988, *The Crisis of Mexican Labor*, New York: Praeger.

———— 1997, Review of Donald C. Hodges's *Mexican Anarchism After the Revolution*, H-Net Review, available at: http://www.h-net.org/reviews/showpdf.php?id=780.

———— 2006, 'American "Slackers" in the Mexican Revolution: International Proletarian Politics in the Midst of a National Revolution', *The Americas*, 62, 4(April).

———— 2007a, 'Latin America Leans Left: Labor and the Politics of Anti-Imperialism', *New Labor Forum*, May.

———— 2007b, 'The Role of Labor in Latin America's "Left Turn"', *NACLA*, 11 September, available at: http://nacla.org/news/role-labor-latin-america%E2%80%99s-%E2%80%98left-turn%E2%80%99.

———— 2012, 'China: From Bureaucratic Communism to Bureaucratic Capitalism', *New Politics Blog*, 20 November, available at: http://newpol.org/content/china-bureaucratic-communism-bureaucratic-capitalism.

La Feber, Walter 1993, *Inevitable Revolutions: The United States in Central America*, Second Edition, New York: W.W. Norton.

———— 1994, *The American Age: US Foreign Policy at Home and Abroad, 1750 to Present*, 2nd edition, New York: W.W. Norton.

Lacayo, Antonio 2006, *La difícil transición nicaragüense*, Managua: Fundación UNO.

Laguna, Xiomara 2007, 'Etapas más importantes de Rosario Murillo', TV Channel 2, Nicaragua, 'Noticias', 20 March.

Lemoine, Maurice 2012, 'Why Nicaragua Chose Ortega', *Le Monde Diplomatique*, available at: http://mondediplo.com/2012/06/11nicaragua.

LeoGrande, William M. 1996, 'Making the Economy Scream: US Economic Sanctions against Sandinista Nicaragua', *Third World Quarterly*, 17, 2(June): 329–48.

———— 1998, *Our Own Backyard: The United States in Central America, 1977–1992*, Chapel Hill, NC: University of North Carolina Press.

Leviné-Meyer, Rosa 1973, *Leviné: The Life of a Revolutionary*, Introduction by E.J. Hobsbawm, Farnborough: Saxon House.

Library of Congress Country Studies n.d., *Nicaragua*, available at: http://lcweb2.loc.gov/frd/cs/cshome.html.

'Lillian Somoza Debayle' n.d., Wikipedia (Spanish Language Edition), available at: http://es.wikipedia.org/wiki/Lillian_Somoza_Debayle.

López Castellanos, Nayar 2013, *Nicaragua, los avatares de una democracia pactada*, Managua: UCA.

López Maltez, Nicolás n.d., 'Biografía Anastasio Somoza Debayle', video available at: http://www.ovguide.com/anastasio-somoza-garcia-9202a8c04000641f800000000021b486.

López Vigil, María 2000, 'The Silence About Incest Needs to be Broken', *Envío*, 230(September), available at: http://www.envio.org.ni/articulo/1445.

Löwy, Michael 1982 [1980], *El marxismo en América Latina*, Mexico: Ediciones Era.

Luján Muñoz, Jorge 2002, *Historia de Guatemala*, Segunda Edición, Mexico: Fondo de la Cultura Económica.

Macaulay, Neill 1985 [1967], *The Sandino Affair*, Durham, NC: Duke University Press.

MacLeod, Murdo J. 2008 [1973], *Spanish Central America: A Socioeconomic History, 1520–1720*, Austin, TX: University of Texas Press.

Marenco, Dionisio 2008, 'I Know the FSLN's History Well, But I Can't Envision Its Future', *Envío*, 326(September), available at: http://www.envio.org.ni/articulo/3878.

Marenco, Eduardo 2007, 'Los dueños de Nicaragua', *El Nuevo Diario*, 3 December, available at: http://impreso.elnuevodiario.com.ni/2007/03/12/nacionales/43534.

Martí I Puig, Salvador 2010, 'The Adaptation of the FSLN: Daniel Ortega's Leadership and Democracy in Nicaragua', *Latin American Politics and Society*, 52, 4(Winter): 79–106.

Martínez, Moïses n.d., 'La limpia fiscal de Canal 8', *La Prensa*

May, Robert E. 1973, *The Southern Dream of a Caribbean Empire, 1854–1861*, Baton Rouge, LA: Louisiana State University Press.

———— 2002, *Manifest Destiny's Underworld*, Chapel Hill, NC: University of North Carolina Press.

Mayorga, Francisco J. 2007, *Megacapitales de Nicaragua*, Second Edition, Managua: Ediciones Albertus.

McKinely, James C. Jr. 2008, 'Nicaraguan Councils Stir Fear of Dictatorship', *The New York Times*, 4 May, available at: http://www.nytimes.com/2008/05/04/world/americas/04nicaragua.html?pagewanted=all&_r=0.

Medal Mendieta, Luis Adolfo 2010, *Apuntes de la economía y de la formación social nicaragüense: una perspectiva histórica, 1523–2010*, Managua: Amerrisque.

Millett, Richard 1977, *Guardians of the Dynasty*, Maryknoll, NY: Orbis Books.

Moncada, José María 1942, *Estados Unidos en Nicaragua*, Managua: Tipografía Atenas.

Moore, Malcolm 2013, 'Chinese entrepreneur reveals route for Nicaraguan canal', *Telegraph*, 30 July, available at: http://www.telegraph.co.uk/news/worldnews/asia/china/10212169/Chinese-entrepreneur-reveals-route-for-Nicaraguan-canal.html.

Morris, Kenneth E. 2010, *The Unfinished Revolution: Daniel Ortega and Nicaragua's Struggle for Liberation*, Chicago, IL: Lawrence Hill Books.

Morrison, Elting E. 1966, *Turmoil and Tradition: A Study of the Life and Times of Henry L. Stimson*, New York: Atheneum.

Movimiento por la Dignidad y Derechos de las Mujeres 'Blanca Arauz' 2008, 'Pronunciamiento de Constitución'.

Mulligan, Joseph E. 1991, *The Nicaraguan Church and the Revolution*, Kansas City, MO: Sheed & Ward.

'Nace movimiento de mujeres Blanca Aráuz' 2008, *Radio la Primerísima*, Managua, Informe Pastrán, 22 September, available at: http://www.radiolaprimerisima.com/noticias/38185/nace-movimiento-de-mujeres-blanca-arauz.

Navarro-Génie, Marco Aurelio 2002, *Augusto 'Cesar' Sandino: Messiah of Light and Truth*, Syracuse, NY: Syracuse University Press.

Newson, Linda 1982, 'The Depopulation of Nicaragua in the Sixteenth Century', *Journal of Latin American Studies*, 14, 2(November).

———— 1987, *Indian Survival in Colonial Nicaragua*, Norman, OK: University of Oklahoma Press.

'Nicaragua: Tribunal Electoral Destituye a 28 legisladores', 2016 *El Periódico*, 7 July, http://elperiodico.com.gt/2016/07/30/internacional/nicaragua-tribunal-electoral-destituye-a-28-diputados-opositores/.

'Nicaragua: Los Ortega acaparan una sexta televisión' 2011, Radio Netherlands Latin America, 21 June.

'Nicaragua's top court rejects challenges to canal' 2013, AP, *Huffington Post*, 18 December, at: http://www.huffingtonpost.com/huff-wires/20131218/lt-nicaragua-canal/.

Nicaraguan Constitution of 1987, in English 2005, https://222.constituteproject.org/constitution/Nicaragua2005.pdf.

Nitlápan-Envío Team 2000, 'The Interbank Bankruptcy Opens a Pandora's Box', *Envío*, 230(September), available at: http://www.envio.org.ni/articulo/1444.

───── 2007a, 'Sixty Days On: Signals, Seals and Superficiality', *Envío*, 308(March), available at: http://www.envio.org.ni/articulo/3517.

───── 2007b, 'The Ortega-Murillo Project: Personal, Family, National or International?', *Envío*, 312(July), available at: http://www.envio.org.ni/articulo/3602.

───── 2007c, 'The Cards are on the Table,' *Envío*, 313(August), available at: http://www.envio.org.ni/articulo/3627.

───── 2007d, 'How Many Conflicts Will the New 'Direct Democracy' Trigger?' *Envío*, 317(December), available at: http://www.envio.org.ni/articulo/3699.

───── 2008a, 'Nicaraguans Squeezed on All Sides', 323(June), available at: http://www.envio.org.ni/articulo/3819.

───── 2008b, 'Where Are We After 29 Years, And After 290 Hours?' *Envío*, 324(July), available at: http://www.envio.org.ni/articulo/3834.

───── 2008c, 'Criticism Isn't Synonymous with Hatred', *Envío*, 326(September), available at: http://www.envio.org.ni/articulo/3876.

───── 2008d, 'The Rules of the Game', 327(October), available at: http://www.envio.org.ni/articulo/3884.

───── 2008e, 'Nicaragua Is the Municipal Elections' Big Loser', *Envío*, 328(November), available at: http://www.envio.org.ni/articulo/3907.

───── 2009a, 'Before the Night Gets Much Darker ...', *Envío*, 332(March), available at: http://www.envio.org.ni/articulo/3949.

───── 2009b, 'Vulnerable to the Bottom-feeding Suckermouth', *Envío*, 333(April), available at: http://www.envio.org.ni/articulo/3979.

───── 2009c, 'Riding the Wind with the Sails Full', *Envío*, 340(November), available at: http://www.envio.org.ni/articulo/4094.

───── 2009d, 'Major Signs of Crisis, Minor Signs of Flexibility', *Envío*, 337(August), available at: http://www.envio.org.ni/articulo/4042.

───── 2009e, 'What Surprises will the End of this Third Year Bring?', *Envío*, 339(October), available at: http://www.envio.org.ni/articulo/4075.

───── 2009f, 'Thirty Years Seen Through the Time Tunnel', *Envío*, 336(November), available at http://www.envio.org.ni/articulo/4026.

───── 2010a, 'Chaos All Around', *Envío*, 344(March), available at: http://www.envio.org.ni/articulo/4146.

───── 2010b, 'Broad Brushstrokes and Fine Touches', *Envío*, 346(May), available at: http://www.envio.org.ni/articulo/4180.

───── 2010c, 'Living with Ghosts', *Envío*, 349(August), available at: http://www.envio.org.ni/articulo/4224.

───── 2010d, 'The Sacarrín Effect', *Envío*, 350(September), available at: http://www.envio.org.ni/articulo/4238.

Nixon, Edgar B. (ed.) 1969, *Franklin Delano Roosevelt and Foreign Affairs*, Cambridge, MA: Belknap Press.

'No soy protegido del Cardenal Obando' 2000, *El Nuevo Diario*, 11 February, available at: http://archivo.elnuevodiario.com.ni/2000/febrero/11-febrero-2000/nacional/nacional10.html.

Nolan, David 1984, *The Ideology of the Sandinistas and the Nicaraguan Revolution*, Coral Gables, FL: Institute of Interamerican Studies, Graduate School of International Studies.

Nuñez, Carol et al. 2010, 'Reconstructing the Population History of Nicaragua by Means of mtDNA, Y-Chromosome STRs, and Autosomal STR Markers', *American Journal of Physical Anthropology*, 143, 4: 591–600.

Nuñez, Leon 2005, 'Alemán Still Controls the PLC and Will Hand Ortega the Victory', *Envío*, 194(November), available at: http://www.envio.org.ni/articulo/3111.

Núñez Morales, Eliseo 2013, 'The constitutional reforms will institutionalize Ortega's total control', *Envío*, 389(December), available at: http://www.envio.org.ni/articulo/4789.

Orozco, Manuel 2008, 'The Nicaraguan diaspora: trends and opportunities for diaspora engagement in skills transfers and development', paper commissioned by OECD, available at: http://www.folade.org/new/Coloquio/PRESENTACIONES/the%20nicaragun%20diaspora.pdf.

Ortega, Humberto 2010, *Epopeya de la Insurrección / Nicaragua siglo XX: Pensamiento y acción, análisis histórico, narración inédita*. Segunda edición, Managua: Lea Grupo editorial.

———— 2013, *La odisea por Nicaragua*, Managua: Lea Grupo Editorial.

'Ortega laments death of "dear leader"' 2011, *Nicaragua Dispatch*, 19 December, available at: http://www.nicaraguadispatch.com/news/2011/12/ortega-laments-death-of-%E2%80%98dear-leader%E2%80%99/1685.

'Orteguistas sigen lanzando "amor" en las calles' 2008, *La Prensa*, 13 November, available at: http://archivo.laprensa.com.ni/archivo/2008/noviembre/13/elecciones/noticias/294631.shtml.

Palmer, Steven 1988, 'Carlos Fonseca and the Construction of Sandinismo in Nicaragua', *Latin American Research Review*, 23, 1: 91–109.

Pantoja, Ary 2001, 'Los 'Hijos del Pode'', *Nuevo Diario*, 16 September, available at: http://www.elnuevodiario.com.ni/politica/113965.

Paszyn, Danuta 2000, *The Soviet Attitude to Political and Social Change in Central America, 1979–1990*, New York: St. Martin's Press.

Payne, Anthony, Paul Sutton and Tony Thorndike 1984, *Grenada: Revolution and Invasion*, New York: St. Martin's Press.

Pérez-Baltodano, Andrés 2008 [2003], *Entre el Estado Conquistador y El Estado Nación: Providencialismo, pensamiento político y estructuras de poder en el desarrollo histórico*, Managua: IHNCA-UCA.

———— 2009, *La subversión ética e nuestra realidad: Crisis y renovación del pensamiento crítico latinoamericano*, Managua: UCA-IHNCA.

———— 2012, 'Nicaragua: Democracia electoral sin consenso social', *Revista de Ciencia Política*, 32, 1: 211–28.

Picón Duarte, Gloria 2009, 'Hijos de Ortega viajan como "funcionarios"', *La Prensa*.

Pope Paul VI 1967, *Populorum Progressio*, available at: http://www.vatican.va/holy_father/paul_vi/encyclicals/documents/hf_p-vi_enc_26031967_populorum_en.html.

'Power Grab in Nicaragua: The Comandante's Comandments' 2013, *The Economist*, 9 November, available at: http://www.economist.com/news/americas/21589473-sandinistas-propose-re-election-without-end-daniel-ortega-comandantes-commandments.

'Qué pasa en Nicaragua?' 1993, *Semana*, 23 August, available at: http://www.semana.com/mundo/articulo/que-pasa-nicaragua/20473-3.

'Rafael Ortega: El nuevo poder en la familia' 2007, *Nicaragua Hoy*, 28 May, available at: http://www.nicaraguahoy.info/dir_cgi/topics.cgi?op=view_topic;cat=NoticiasGenerales;id=5117.

Ramírez, Sergio 1984, 'Sandino: Clase e ideología', *Augusto C. Sandino, El pensamiento vivo*, Managua: Editorial Nueva Nicaragua.

———— 1991, *Confesión de Amor*, Managua: Nicarao.

———— 1999, *Adiós muchachos: una memoria de la revolución Sandinista*, San José, Costa Rica: Aguilar.

———— 2008 [2007], *Tambor Olvidado*, San Jose, Costa Rica: Aguilar.

Randall, Margaret 1981, *Sandino's Daughters: Testimonies of Nicaraguan Women in Struggle*, London: Zed.

Ribando Seelke, Clare 2008, 'Congressional Research Service Report RS22836, Nicaragua: Political Situation and US Relations', released by WikiLeaks, available at: http://archives.1wise.es/crs/RS22836.txt.

Riding, Alan 1980, 'Somoza, Long a US Ally, Was Bitter Over "Betrayal"', *The New York Times*, 18 September.

Riley, Brendan 2010, 'Nicaragua & Albanisa: The Privatization of Venezuelan Aid', *Council on Hemispheric Affairs*, 13 August, available at: http://www.coha.org/nicaragua-albanisa-the-privatization-of-venezuelan-aid/.

Rocha, José Luis 2009, 'The Lessons of Mitch', 300(January), available at: http://www.envio.org.ni/articulo/3938.

———— 2010, 'When the Youngest Emigrate', *Envío*, 351(October), available at: http://www.envio.org.ni/articulo/4262.

———— 2011, 'The Second Horseman of Neoliberalism: Nongovernmental Organizations', *Envío*, 363(October), available at: http://www.envio.org.ni/articulo/4439.

Rogers, Tim 2008, 'President Ortega vs. the Feminists', *Time*, 16 October, available at: http://content.time.com/time/world/article/0,8599,1850451,00.html.

——— 2011a, 'Will MRS Split vote on the right?', *Nicaragua Dispatch*, 16 October, available at: http://www.nicaraguadispatch.com/news/2011/10/could-mrs-split-the-vote-on-the-right/503.

——— 2011b, 'Gadea: "This is a battle between democracy and dictatorship"', *Nicaragua Dispatch*, 24 October, available at: http://www.nicaraguadispatch.com/news/2011/10/gadea-%E2%80%98this-is-a-battle-between-democracy-and-dictatorship%E2%80%99/965.

——— 2011c, 'Ortega laments death of "dear leader"', *Nicaragua Dispatch*, 19 December, available at: http://www.nicaraguadispatch.com/news/2011/12/ortega-laments-death-of-%E2%80%98dear-leader%E2%80%99/1685.

——— 2012a, 'May Day divides Nicaraguan workers', *Nicaraguan Dispatch*, 1 May, available at: http://www.nicaraguadispatch.com/news/2012/05/may-day-divides-nicaraguan-workers/3686/3686.

——— 2012b, 'Nicaragua's Marxist government gets religion on free trade zones', *Global Post*, 4 May, available at: http://www.globalpost.com/dispatch/news/regions/americas/120503/nicaragua-s-marxist-government-gets-religion-free-trade-zones?page=0,1.

——— 2012c, 'Could Nicaragua's president survive without Venezuela's Chavez?', *Global Post*, 6 October, available at: http://www.globalpost.com/dispatch/news/regions/americas/121005/nicaragua-impact-venezuela-election-chavez-ortega-alba?page=0,1.

——— 2013 'Nicaragua notches record investments in '12', *Nicaragua Dispatch*, 9 July, available at: http://www.nicaraguadispatch.com/news/2013/07/nicaragua-notches-record-investments-in-12/8148.

Román, José 1983, *Maldito país*, Edición definitive, Managua: Nicaragua.

'Rosario Murillo: La mujer más poderosa de Nicaragua' 2008, *Terra* (Chile), 30 July, available at: http://www.terra.cl/zonamujer/index.cfm?id_cat=2007&id_reg=1008096.

Rosengarten Jr., Frederick 1978, *Freebooters Must Die!*, Wayne, PA: Haverford House Publishers.

Sabia, Debra 1997, *Contradiction and Conflict: The Popular Church in Nicaragua*, Tuscaloosa, AL: University of Alabama Press.

Salinas, Carlos 2014, 'Hasta 50 heridos en Nicaragua en las protestas contral el canal oceánico', *El País* (Spain), available at: http://internacional.elpais.com/internacional/2014/12/24/actualidad/1419444251_610241.html.

Sandford, Gregory and Richard Vigilante 1984, *Grenada: The Untold Story*, New York: Madison Books.

Sandino, Augusto C. 1990, *Sandino: The Testimony of a Nicaraguan Patriot, 1921–1934*, compiled and edited by Sergio Ramírez, edited and translated with an introduction and additional selections by Robert Edgar Conrad, Princeton, NJ: Princeton University Press.

———— 2010, *Augusto C. Sandino: Entrevistas-reportajes*, Managua: Aldilà y Cía Ltda.

Santamaría, Gema n.d., 'Alianza y autonomía: las estrategias políticas del movimiento de mujeres en Nicaragua'.

Schroeder, Michael J., n.d-a., 'La Guardia Nacional Homepage', available at: http://www .sandinorebellion.com/HomePages/guardia.html.

———— n.d.-b, 'Marine Corps Casualties', available at: http://www.sandinorebellion .com/USMC-Docs/USMC-docs-Casualties.html.

Searle, Chris 1983, *Grenada: The Struggle Against Destabilization*, London: Writers and Readers Publishing Cooperative.

Selser, Gregorio 1960, *Sandino: General de Hombres Libres*, available at: http:// historiadeamericalatina.files.wordpress.com/2011/02/selser-gregorio-sandino -general-de-hombres-libres.pdf.

———— 1981, *Sandino*, translated by Cedric Belfrage, New York: Monthly Review Press.

Shachtman, Max 1962, *The Bureaucratic Revolution: The Rise of the Stalinist State*, New York: Donald Press.

Slater, R. Giuseppi 1989, 'Reflections on Curative Health Care in Nicaragua', *American Journal of Public Health*, 79, 5(May): 646–51.

Smith, Christian 1996, *Resisting Reagan: The US Central American Peace Movement*, Chicago, IL: University of Chicago Press.

Smith, Peter H. 2000, *Talons of the Eagle: Dynamics of US-Latin American Relations*, Second Edition, New York: Oxford.

Solà i Montserrat, Roser 2008, *Estructura económica de Nicaragua y su contexto centro-americano y mundial*, Managua: Hispamer.

Somoza García, Anastasio 1936, *El verdadero Sandino; O, el Calvario de las Segovias* Managua: Tip Robelo.

Spalding, Rose J. 1994, *Capitalists and Revolution in Nicaragua: Opposition and Accom-modation, 1979–1993*, Chapel Hill, NC: University of North Carolina Press.

Stalin, Joseph 1939, *The Foundations of Leninism*, New York: International Publishers.

Stanisfer, Charles L. 1974, 'Una nueva interpretación de José Santos Zelaya, Dictador de Nicaragua, 1893–1909', *Anuario de Estudios Centroamericanos*, 1: 47–59.

Stiles, T.J. 2009, *The First Tycoon: The Epic Life of Cornelius Vanderbilt*, New York: Alfred A. Knopf.

Stout Jr., Joseph Allen 1973, *The Liberators: Filbustering Expeditions into Mexico, 1848–1862 and the Last Thrust of Manifest Destiny*, Los Angeles, CA: Westernlore Press.

Strange, Hannah 2010, 'Nicaragua Accused of Helping Colombian Drug Lords to Estab-lish Trafficking Routes', *Times*, 1 May, available at: http://www.thetimes.co.uk/tto/ news/world/americas/article2498234.ece.

Tannenbaum, Frank 1968 [1933], *Peace by Revolution*, New York: Colombia University Press.

Téllez, Dora María 2005, 'The Alliance Around Herty Lewites Is a Unique Opportunity

We Mustn't Waste', *Envío*, 293(December), available at: http://www.envio.org.ni/ articulo/3152.

———— 2008, 'Nicaragua's Drastic Situation Obliged Me to Go on a Hunger Strike' *Envío*, 324(July), available at: http://www.envio.org.ni/articulo/3836.

———— 2013, 'The FSLN is now one family's political machinery', *Envío*, 378(January), available at: http://www.envio.org.ni/articulo/4646.

Tinoco, Victor Hugo 2005, 'This Crisis Began in the FSLN, With an Unethical Pact', *Envío*, 288(July), available at: http://www.envio.org.ni/articulo/2987.

Torres, Hugo 2010, 'Chilling Similarities Between Ortega and the Somozas', *Envío*, 342(January), available at: http://www.envio.org.ni/articulo/4140.

Trivelli, Paul A. 2005, 'Confidential communication to the Secretary of State', 22 June, Cable 06MANAGUA1370, released by WikiLeaks, available at: https://wikileaks.org/ plusd/cables/06MANAGUA1370_a.html.

Trotsky, Leon 1937, *The Revolution Betrayed*, London: Faber & Faber.

———— 1938, 'Nationalized Industry and Workers' Management', translated by Duncan Ferguson, May or June, *Fourth International* [New York], 7, 8, 239–42, available at: http://www.marxists.org/archive/trotsky/1938/xx/mexico03.htm.

Tunnerman, Carlos 1979, 'Orígenes de la dictadura dinástica de los Somoza', *Anuario de Estudios Centroamericanos*, 5: 65–79.

United Nations World Food Program 2013, 'Nicaragua 2013–18', available at: http://one .wfp.org/operations/current_operations/project_docs/200434.pdf.

USAID June 2006, *Nicaragua Economic Performance Assessment*, (Washington, D.C.: USAID), available at: http://pdf.usaid.gov/pdf_docs/PNADG309.pdf.

US State Department 1987, 'The 72-hour document': The Sandinista Blueprint for Constructing Communism in Nicaragua*, Washington, D.C.

US Trade Representative 2005, 'Labor Rights Report: Costa Rica, Dominican Republic, El Salvador, Guatemala, Honduras and Nicaragua', June, 120–36.

Vargas Llosa, Álvaro 2006, 'Viva el Capitalismo!', *New York Times*, 13 November, available at: http://www.nytimes.com/2006/11/13/opinion/13llosa.html?_r=1&oref=slogin.

Vigil, María López 2000, 'The Silence about incest needs to be broken', *Envío*, 230(September), available at: http://www.envio.org.ni/articulo/1445.

Vilas, Carlos M. 1984, *Nicaragua una transición diferente*, Tamiami Trail, Miami, FL: Latin American and Caribbean Center of Florida International University.

———— 1986, *The Sandinista Revolution: National Liberation and Social Transformation in Central America*, New York: Monthly Review Press.

———— 1990 'What Went Wrong?', in *NACLA: Report on the Americas*.

Villas, Claudio 2008, 'Nicaragua: Lessons of a country that did not finish its revolution', *In Defense of Marxism*, available in two parts at: http://www.marxist.com/lessons -nicaragua-part-one.htm and http://www.marxist.com/lessons-nicaragua-part-two .htm.

Vukelich, Donna 1994, 'Welcome to the Free Trade Zone', *Envío*, 150(January), available at: http://www.envio.org.ni/articulo/1741.

'Waiting for the fat man to sing' 2002, *The Economist*, 22 August.

Walker, Thomas W. 1982, *Nicaragua in Revolution*, New York: Praeger.

———— (ed.) 1987, *Reagan versus the Sandinistas*, Boulder, CO: Westview.

———— (ed.) 1991, *Revolution and Counterrevolution in Nicaragua*, Boulder, CO: Westview Press.

———— (ed.) 1997, *Nicaragua without Illusions: Regime Transition and Structural Adjustments in the 1990s*, Wilmington, DE: Scholarly Resources.

Walker, Thomas W. and Christine Wade 2011, *Nicaragua: Living in the Shadow of the Eagle*, Fifth Edition, Boulder, CO: Westview Press.

Walker, William 1860, *War in Nicaragua*, Mobile, AL: S.H. Goetzel & Co.

Walter, Knut 1993, *The Regime of Anastasio Somoza: 1936–1956*, Chapel Hill, NC: University of North Carolina Press.

Warren, Ambassador Fletcher 1945, 'Letter to Secretary of State James F. Byrnes, 21 November 1945', *Foreign Relations, 1945*, IX: 1212, available at: http://images.library.wisc.edu/FRUS/EFacs/1945v09/reference/frus.frus1945v09.i0020.pdf.

Weber, Henri 1981, *Nicaragua: The Sandinista Revolution*, London: Verso.

Webster, Sidney 1893, 'Mr. Marcy, the Cuban Question and the Ostend Manifesto', *Political Science Quarterly*, 8, 1(March).

West, Gordon W. 1992, 'The Sandinista Record on Human Rights in Nicaragua', *Droit et Société*, 22: 393–408.

Wheelock, Jaime 1980, *Raíces indígenas de la lucha anticolonista en Nicaragua: de Gil González a Joaquín Zavala, 1523–1881*, México, D.F.: Siglo Veintiuno Editores.

Williams, Philip 1994, 'Dual Transition from Authoritarian Rule: Popular and Electoral Democracy in Nicaragua', *Comparative Politics*, 26, 2(January).

Wolfe, Justin 2004, 'Those That Live by the Work of Their Hands; Labour, Ethnicity, and Nation-State Formation in Nicaragua, 1850–1900', *Journal of Latin American Studies*, 36, 1(February).

Wilson, S. Brian 2006, 'How the US Purchased the 1990 Nicaragua Elections', 1 July 1990, available at: http://www.brianwillson.com/how-the-u-s-purchased-the-1990-nicaragua-elections/.

'Women's Social Movements in Nicaragua' n.d., *New Social Movements: Latin American Social Movements and Neoliberalism*, available at: http://latinamericansocialmovements.wikidot.com/women-s-social-movements-in-nicaragua.

Woodward, Bob and David B. Ottaway 1987, 'President, Saudis Met Twice; Funds Flowed to Contras After Talks', *Washington Post*, 12 May, front page.

Yu, Au Loong 2012, *China's Rise: Strength and Fragility*, Pontypool: Resistance Books.

Zaballos, Hernán 2012, 'El Lado obscuro', *El Diario*, 14 June, available at: http://www.eldiario.net/noticias/2012/2012_06/nt120614/opinion.php?n=35.

Zelaya, José Santos 1910, *The Revolution of Nicaragua and the United States*, Madrid: Bernardo Rodríguez, available at: http://www.ebooksread.com/authors-eng/jos -santos-zelaya/the-revolution-of-nicaragua-and-the-united-states-hci.shtml.

Zimmerman, Matilde 2000, *Sandinista: Carlos Fonseca and the Nicaraguan Revolution*, Durham, NC: Duke University Press.

Index